D0879000

DISCARDED

Black Families
at the Crossroads

Leanor Boulin Johnson
Robert Staples

Foreword by Robert B. Hill

Black Families at the Crossroads

Challenges and Prospects

Revised Edition

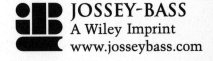

JOSSEY-BASS
A Wiley Imprint
www.josseybass.com

Published by Jossey-Bass
A Wiley Imprint
989 Market Street, San Francisco, CA 94103-1741   www.josseybass.com

Jossey-Bass books and products are available through most bookstores. To contact Jossey-Bass directly, call our Customer Care Department within the U.S. at 800-956-7739 or outside the U.S. at 317-572-3986, or fax to 317-572-4002.

Jossey-Bass also publishes its books in a variety of electronic formats. Some content that appears in print may not be available in electronic books.

Library of Congress Cataloging-in-Publication Data
Johnson, Leanor Boulin, date
   Black families at the crossroads : Challenges and prospects / Leanor Boulin Johnson, Robert Staples.—Rev. ed.
       p. cm.
   Rev. ed. of: Black families at the crossroads / Robert Staples, Leanor Boulin Johnson. 1st ed. c1993.
   Includes bibliographical references and index.
   ISBN 0-7879-7222-3 (alk. paper)
   1. African American families. I. Staples, Robert.
II. Staples, Robert.
Black families at the crossroads. III. Title.
   E185.86.S698 2004
   306.85'089'96073—dc22   2004010951

Printed in the United States of America
SECOND EDITION
PB Printing 10 9 8 7 6 5 4 3 2 1

Contents

Foreword

Once again, Leanor Johnson and Robert Staples, who combine more than sixty years of writing and research as family sociologists, have produced a work that greatly enhances the understanding of the complexity and diversity in the functioning of Black families today. This revised edition provides rare insights regarding how the cultural values, attitudes, and aspirations of African American families interact with structural conditions and social policies to produce a wide range of positive and negative outcomes. Thus, this work makes many important contributions to our knowledge about external and internal forces that affect African American families.

First and foremost, this is a book about the institution of the Black family. There is a widespread tendency to misrepresent many works that concentrate on problems, such as unemployment, poverty, and adolescent pregnancy, as studies of Black families when actually the individual or community is the focus of study. It is for this reason that research in which Black families are the primary unit of analysis, as in this book, continues to comprise only a tiny fraction of the studies of African Americans.

Second, a historical perspective is incorporated throughout this work. A major deficiency in most other studies of Black families is their ahistorical approach. Over a century ago, W.E.B. Du Bois argued that researchers could not adequately study Black people without placing their work within a historical and cultural context.

Thus, Johnson and Staples begin not with slavery in America but with family life on the continent of Africa. They make a strong case for understanding how African cultural continuities or adaptations contribute to the structure and functioning of contemporary African American families. This discussion is enriched by the inclusion of recent historical reinterpretations on the nature of North American slavery.

Third, this book applies a framework for studying Black families that integrates conceptual models from various perspectives. Another major shortcoming of most Black family studies is their ad hoc nature and the lack of a unifying theoretical or conceptual approach. The authors adopt as a primary perspective the Afrocentric model, which concentrates on the impact of African cultural continuities on contemporary African Americans. But they also incorporate propositions from internal colonialism, historical materialism, assimilation theory, exchange theory, and Black feminist theory to support their explanations.

Fourth, unlike most other Black family studies, this work places its primary focus on the internal processes that affect all class strata among African American families. Many researchers think that they understand "the" Black family after studying only the "lower-class" or "underclass" subgroups. The Black working class, middle class, and upper class have been largely ignored in the mainstream family literature. It is also unfortunate that because of the undue concentration on single-parent families, there continue to be very few studies of two-parent families among Blacks. Moreover, while there is an obsession with families that break up, there have been few studies of the processes that can lead to marriage (such as dating or courtship) or factors that help to sustain marriages among African Americans. Johnson and Staples have contributed disproportionately to such progressive research. Since this book is replete with important insights about African American families, it is important to underscore some of them.

Their discussion of the Atlantic Creoles (persons of African and European lineage), who came to North America as indentured servants prior to the development of the American slave trade, is enlightening. The Dutch West India Company transported these Creoles, who served as multilingual traders between Africa, North and South America, and Europe to the New World. Most of them obtained their freedom at the end of their period of indenture after paying off any debts. Their role provides a basis for understanding how Blacks who remained free throughout the antebellum period were able to own property and businesses and establish self-help institutions (such as churches, schools, hospitals, credit unions, insurance companies, banks, orphanages, and homes for the elderly) that contributed to the growth of the Black middle class.

According to conventional wisdom, house slaves were an elite group who had easier work than field slaves. Yet the authors inform us that this romanticized view of household work is not accurate. On the contrary, many studies reveal that most house slaves had to juggle multiple tasks and laborious work responsibilities (such as cleaning, laundering, and cooking) from sunup to long after sundown. For these reasons, many slaves preferred field work to household duties.

This book also reminds us of how immigration policies historically had adverse effects on the economic well-being of Black families. Few Americans realize that Northern firms aggressively recruited immigrants from European countries to prevent those jobs from going to large numbers of newly freed blacks whom they feared would soon flood their cities. Poor economic conditions in Europe at the time (such as the potato famines) helped to accelerate the exodus of many immigrants. Thus, it was only during World Wars I and II, when immigration from Europe was curtailed, that Black men and women made their strongest employment and occupational gains. In addition to the impact of European immigration, the authors shed light on Caribbean Black migrants' quest for economic stability in America and its implications for native Black Americans.

Like other scholars, Johnson and Staples find working wives to be more important to the economic viability of Black than White families, since they contribute more to the total income of their families. But contrary to conventional wisdom, Black husbands have more positive attitudes than White husbands do toward wife employment. And the sense of job competence is greater among Black husbands with working wives than among White husbands with working wives. In addition, there is more role flexibility and shared decision making in Black families with dual earners than among White families with dual earners.

Black youth are more likely to engage in premarital sexual activity at earlier ages than White youth. But the authors offer social and economic explanations for such early sexuality in the place of allegations of unbridled biological impulses. One factor is the more prominent role of sexual socialization from same-sex peer groups among Black than White youth, especially in low-income families. Overcrowded living conditions are also more likely to expose lower-income young people than youth in middle-income families at earlier ages to sexual behavior among adults.

It is often asserted that because of the greater prevalence of female-headed families, Black males reared in those families are likely to have a higher incidence of homosexuality than White males. Yet the authors find no credible research that supports such beliefs. On the contrary, they cite studies that found that Black males are more comfortable around homosexuals than White males are and do not perceive them as a threat to their manhood. Moreover, they find no empirical support for the claim that Black women are more prone to lesbianism than White women due to the disproportionate shortage of Black men.

This work also strongly challenges the widespread belief that boys reared in female-headed families are not socialized into male roles. In fact, Black boys have numerous male role models to choose from inside and outside their families. They develop masculine identities from male relatives (such as nonresident fathers, grandfathers, uncles, and older brothers) and male nonrelatives (including neighbors, coaches, ministers, teachers, and tutors). Even in two-parent families, boys may emulate their fathers in some areas and other men in other aspects. More important, Johnson and Staples also cite studies that reveal that mothers can communicate appropriate male roles to their sons. They identify successful men (such as Dr. Ben Carson and Ralph Bunche) who were reared in families headed by Black women.

The authors reject the narrow definitions of Black fatherhood that minimize their expressive contributions to children and of Black motherhood that marginalize their provider role. They conclude, "Given that Black fathers and mothers deem it appropriate to interchange or share the provider and expressive roles, the father-daughter and mother-son relationships are just as important for understanding child development and aspirations as are the mother-daughter and father-son relationships." Thus, they underscore the need for more studies of the impact of Black fathers on the development of their daughters and how Black mothers influence the development of their sons.

Some feminists contend that singlehood is a viable alternative to marriage for African Americans. Yet Johnson and Staples argue that most Blacks perceive their singleness not as a preferred option but as a status forced on them by certain conditions in American life. They contend that many Blacks have found alternative lifestyles characterized as family substitutes, such as open marriage, communal living, and heterosexual cohabitation, to be less desirable than formal marriage. However, they readily acknowledge that the unavailability of sufficient numbers of marriageable males, due to the institutional decimation of Black men, continues to be a major obstacle for many Blacks to achieve their desired goal of marriage.

Regarding mate selection, Black men are reported to give preference to light-skinned women, while light-skinned Black women find dark-skinned men more desirable, especially since the 1960s. Moreover, cross-racial dating on college campuses is inversely related to the number of Blacks in the student body. Interracial mating decreases as the number of Black students increases. But while Black male–White female relationships continue to comprise the majority of Black interracial marriages, marriages involving White males and Black females are sharply increasing.

Although noncustodial Black fathers typically are portrayed as uncaring and uninvolved, many studies have shown that they have regular contact with their children and make many contributions to their well-being. Moreover, Black fathers are more likely to raise their children as single parents than White fathers are. Thus, many nonresident Black fathers perform important expressive functions and provide a broad range of support to their children and families.

Although the Black extended family has lost some of its influence, the authors note that it continues to play an important role in the survival and upward mobility of African American families. It is responsible for transmitting the family's cultural traditions and history, reducing child abuse, providing long-term support to teen mothers, assisting adult single parents during crises, and rearing kin children when their biological parents are not able to care for them. While most grandmothers and aunts care for their kin without government intervention, there has been a surge of Black children in the foster care system who are reared by kin due to the onset of HIV/AIDS, drug abuse, and incarceration of fathers and mothers. Unfortunately, kinship care providers receive lower stipends and fewer social services than nonrelated caregivers.

This book has important implications for many family policies. Since the Bush administration has placed a high priority on promoting marriage among low-income couples, this work should be carefully reviewed to understand the social, economic, and cultural dynamics of male-female relationships before implementing these programs. For example, while most low-income Black women prefer marriage, they nevertheless apply a cost-benefit analysis: Do the costs of marriage outweigh its benefits? Moreover, since many of these women have experienced or observed unsatisfying and volatile marriages, culturally insensitive programs may have little success in convincing them to get into another relationship.

The future prospects for strengthening African American families will be greatly enhanced only when individual and institutional barriers to the development of children and families of color are removed; policies and programs are developed that are specifically targeted to families rather than individuals; and African American national organizations, churches, community-based groups, historically Black colleges and universities, and scholars play major roles in the planning, development, implementation, and evaluation of these policies and programs.

This outstanding work by Staples and Johnson should be read by professionals and laypeople in all fields who seek to enhance the well-being of Black families.

Robert B. Hill
Washington, D.C.

*To my mother, Anna Staples, for her love
and devotion to the end of her life.
—Robert Staples*

*To the memory of my parents,
Herbert Fitzgerald Constantine Boulin
and Linda Louise Rashford Boulin,
who for forty years demonstrated
the glory and warmth of love.
And to my only grandchild,
Asia Denise Mims Johnson, who
never knew her maternal grandparents
but will always feel their love.
—Leanor Boulin Johnson*

Preface to the Revised Edition

In the twelve years since the first edition of this book was published, there was an economic boom during the 1990s that brought about a marked improvement in the lives of Black families. The effects of those improvements are likely to erode in the economic recession of the first decade of the twenty-first century. Our revised chapters cover mostly the improvements, not the declines, since they are too recent to be reflected as a pattern in current census data and empirical studies. Approximately one-fourth of the book has been revised, mostly to take into account newer research studies and more recent census and economic data. Our basic conceptualization of Black family structure and dynamics remains the same, although the intervening twelve years gave us time to reflect on enhancements to the original book.

Among the major changes to the first edition are different historical interpretations of the nature of North American slavery and its impact on the family life of the bondsmen. In our inclusion of Black immigrant families, we describe the neoassimilation model and how, unlike the classic assimilation model, it is applicable to families that face both racial barriers and adjustment to different cultures. The largest group of Black immigrants comes from the Caribbean region, and their voluntary migration informs our understanding of the quest for economic stability among native-born Black American families whose ancestors came to North America in chains.

Included in the significant changes of the past decade are cultural patterns and their impact on aspects of the family. Hip-hop music, after withstanding two decades of predictions of its imminent demise, has now become the dominant music of American youth, with important implications for gender relations and equity. We examine its form for the tendency to be misogynist and profane. Some might attribute its stylistic traits as contributing to an increase in liberalized sexual attitudes and behavior. To provide a better understanding of America's sexual liberation in the past decade, we look at some of the most recent research on Black sexuality and develop an expanded discussion of the AIDS crisis in lower-income Black communities.

Finally, we have considerably revised our final chapter on the problems and prospects for Black families in the twenty-first century. Despite the progress of the 1990s, significant changes in Black families await more positive improvements in the situation of Black males. Large numbers of Black men cannot enact the conventional roles of husband and father due to the problems of substance abuse, imprisonment, unemployment, and low skills. Black women continue to make progress on the educational, employment, and income fronts, only to discover that what awaits them is out-of-wedlock births, single parenthood, and an unmarried life because there are few eligible males willing and able to take on the responsibility of forming and maintaining a family. This chapter examines those economic trends.

Also in the final chapter, we examine the welfare reform policy passed during the boom years of the 1990s and the flaws of a policy that deprives women and children of a safety net during economic decline. The lack of universal health care, available in most other developed nations, will be one of the greatest challenges for Black families in the years ahead, as will be the quest for affordable housing in America's largest and most expensive cities. Those who entered the labor market during the 1980s and 1990s, Generation X, are projected to be the first cohort who will have a lower standard of living than their parents. For Blacks who are part of Generation X, this projection is far more likely to be realized. In an era when the American government is running a large deficit, increasing the amount spent on war and prisons while assigning secondary funding to social and educational programs, the challenges are formidable.

August 2004   Leonor Boulin Johnson
                                                 Scottsdale, Arizona
                                                 Robert Staples
                                                 San Francisco, California

Preface to the First Edition

This collaboration grew out of our awareness that there is no central source of information on the Afro-American family. Anthologies on Black families lack the systematic analysis and consistency of an authored book. Other books are too specialized in the topics discussed or neglect the institutional role of Afro-American families. We both have the advantage of having been specifically trained in the sociology of the family and have taught a variety of classes on the family at different universities. Together, we combine more than fifty years of teaching about and studying Black American families, our primary specialization being in family sociology. Because we had collaborated on a number of projects over the years, belonged to the same professional organizations, and shared a similar perspective on the Afro-American family, our collaboration on this project seemed natural.

No other institution in American life has been subjected to the intense scrutiny that the Black family has. From its beginning on the American continent, where its structure and function have been shaped by the institution of slavery, to the current era—in which cultural, political, and economic changes have left an indelible mark on its structure—the Black family has had to confront the vicissitudes of life in the United States. Given the remarkable changes the Black family has undergone, it is surprising that no macrosociological analysis has been conducted to depict its dynamics in relation to the social forces against which it has struggled. Not since the pioneering work of E. Franklin Frazier, whose book *The Negro Family in the United States* (1939) traced the evolution of Black families, has there been a work that viewed this institution in all its dimensions.

Whereas there has been a proliferation of books and articles on aspects of Black family life, that literature has generally focused on limited segments of the Black population and has therefore sponsored a rather narrow perspective of the family as an institution. Few of the books, for instance, have systematically covered such topics as sexuality, marital patterns and interaction, singlehood, the female-headed household, and family life among the aged. Although those topics have been addressed separately, no attempt has been made to discuss them as part of a unified treatment of the Black family.

In particular, there is a need to describe and interpret the Black family form as it is unfolding in contemporary America. Due to social and cultural changes, the salient aspects of Black family life that require examination are dating and sexuality, marriage and divorce, singlehood, the female-headed household, and the extended family. The statistical data tell us that the majority of Black children are born out of wedlock, many of them to teenage mothers. Yet there are few data on patterns of dating and sexual norms that could help to explain the prevalence of such behavior. Census data inform us that a majority of adult Black women are not married. We need to know the particular set of sociocultural forces that are responsible for these unprecedented marital patterns among the majority of Black Americans, including the developments occurring in Black marriages that cause two out of three to end in divorce.

A significant trend has been the rise of Black female-headed households. Single-parent families constitute a majority of Black families. Most Black children live in such households. Consequently, the nuclear family model, especially for the lower-income groups, is no longer the dominant family type among Afro-Americans. Hence, we have examined the extended family system to ascertain its role in the rearing of children, economic assistance, emotional nurturance of family members, and so on.

The primary purpose of this book is to serve as a basic text on the Black family as an institution. To facilitate an understanding of the Black American family, the book presents an analysis of the various sociocultural forces that shape both the structure and the functions of the family as well as the way the family has experienced changes. We also analyze the larger forces outside the Black community, such as assimilation and acculturation, unemployment and underemployment, the role of government and public policy, and the imbalance in the gender ratio. Since Blacks do not comprise a monolithic group, we have attempted to consider class and gender variations in family life-styles. Moreover, this book places these various themes and orientations within Black family life in a theoretical perspective that facilitates a better understanding of the family itself. That theoretical perspective is a political economy model that assumes that the contemporary Black family structure is a function of political and economic forces that have shaped its existence for several centuries.

A primary method in writing this book has been the interpretation and synthesis of existing research on Black family life. Since 1970, more than 1,000 articles and 100 books have been published on some aspect of the Black family experience. To provide a foundation for investigating Black families in more recent periods, we have examined literature prior to 1970. We have also relied on census and survey data, integrating them into our portrait of Black families. Finally, in areas where the literature is sparse or nonexistent, we have used our own research and writings over the past twenty years selectively.

Audience

While the book holds to the highest standards of scholarship in terms of the interpretation of data and research, it is written in a style accessible to a wide readership. Its target audience is made up of faculty, students, policy makers, and anyone who works with Black families. We have tried to meet the needs both of people who have no knowledge of the Black family and of professionals working with Black families who require a reference source on the special issues and perspectives of this group. Most important, we hope that this book can be used as a teaching tool in colleges and universities throughout the world.

Presently, there is no book available that presents a view of the Black family as an institution and that surveys the significant changes that have affected it. The primary importance of such a study is the fact that it incorporates in one work the most significant information about America's largest racial minority. Because changes in the Black family are often a barometer of future trends in the larger society, a study of the Black family has implications for the direction of the American family. The book will be a valuable resource for scholars of the family and social institutions, can be used as a basic text in courses on the Black family, and will be adoptable as a supplementary text in courses on the family as well as for courses in the helping professions, sociology, anthropology, human development, psychology, ethnic studies, and home economics.

Overview of the Contents

Chapter One is an examination of classic historical theories that claim that the institution of slavery destroyed the basis of Black family life and of neohistorical theories that assert that the family structure of the African slaves was largely untouched by the slave owners. The chapter also looks at the postslavery existence of Black families; for example, it discusses the formation of values related to family life in the antebellum South.

In Chapter Two, we review the theories concerning the nature of Afro-American family life-styles, beginning with the groundbreaking study of W.E.B. Du Bois, continuing with the classic work of E. Franklin Frazier, and including the theories of Daniel Patrick Moynihan, Jessie Bernard, Lee Rainwater, and others. Each theory is placed in a historical context and evaluated for its strengths and weaknesses in enhancing our understanding of the Black family.

Chapter Three explores the impact of economic forces on the structure and stability of the Black family. It delineates the lack of fit between the skills of Blacks and the high-technology economy, as well as the role of gender in the economics of Black family life. Some statistical data are used to depict marital strain, stress, and stability as a function of the occupational and income levels of husbands and wives. We show the contribution of economic success to marital happiness and discuss the stratification of the Black community that has arisen over the last thirty years.

Chapter Four is an analysis of the bonding process among young Black men and women. We first provide historical background, focusing on the impact of slavery. Then we examine how dating evolves into sexual behavior at very young ages and the factors that facilitate young people's entry into or avoidance of premarital sexual behavior. We discuss how sex is defined by males and females, and the convergence and divergence of attitudes toward sexuality along gender and class lines. Finally, we review current research on Black sexual values, customs, and practices, within and outside marriage.

In Chapter Five, we examine how Blacks enter the world of singles and the life-styles they lead as unmarrieds in a society that places a strong emphasis on marriage and the family. A typology of singles is developed as they exist in the Black community. The coping styles of singles are examined as they confront the need to develop social supports. This chapter contains a demographic review of singles, their marriage chances, and the norms of mate selection.

Chapter Six provides an assessment of gender roles, with particular attention to male dominance in the Black family and community. We describe how male and female roles evolved in Afro-American culture in relation to its unique history and circumstances. We also review trend data, to assess the gender gap in education, income, and occupational levels. Finally, we offer an analysis of the interaction between race and gender, focusing on the problem of sexism in the Black community.

Chapter Seven examines the unique problems encountered in the conjugal relationships of Black Americans. We focus on the definition of husband and wife roles, power relationships, and the sources of stress in Black marriages. The chapter contains a review of the reasons for marital dissolution and covers the demography of divorced Blacks and the stable marrieds. Also, we discuss the relationship of class and gender to marriage, divorce, and remarriage rates.

An assessment of how children are born and reared in the Black community is the focus of Chapter Eight. We discuss how the decision, if consciously done, is made to bear children and the limits imposed on the size of families. We ask who constitutes the primary socializing agent for Black children and what the role of Black fathers is. We discuss the consequences, for childrearing, of childbirth to teenage mothers and the mother's multiple roles as mother, wife, and worker. We also explore how children fare in households with only a single parent.

In Chapter Nine, we analyze the roles older generations and members of the extended kinship network play in the family. The question of how these family members supplement the primary roles of father and mother is addressed. We explore how they represent a positive force in the family constellation. We examine the role of the Black church as a source of family support.

Our final chapter is a summary of the sociocultural variables affecting the Black family, such as racism, government policies, political factors, and economic forces. The problems and prospects are examined, and best- and worst-case scenarios are offered for the future of the Black family.

September 1992

Robert Staples
San Francisco, California
Leanor Boulin Johnson
Phoenix, Arizona

Acknowledgments

Within my professional world, I am indebted to numerous mentors, including Harold Christensen, Harriette P. McAdoo, and Robert E. Staples, who provided avenues for my creative scholarship during my early professional development. Collecting relevant documentation for this revised edition was greatly assisted by the support of the African and African American Studies Department at Arizona State University and its interim director, Patricia M. Neff, and the graduate assistance of Yanyun Yang. A special thanks to Tammy L. Henderson for her professional commitment and integrity in assisting in the completion of this revised edition. Finally, special thanks to the editorial staff at Jossey-Bass for their patience and constructive comments.

Within my family, I thank the significant individuals who have touched my life. In my tender years, I was endowed with an abundance of love, support, and spirituality. For this rich inheritance, I give thanks to my circle of childhood family: Linda and Herbert Boulin (my parents), Yvonne Maudlin Washington and Homer Linton Boulin (my siblings), uncles, aunts, cousins, adopted kin, and my Black church community. Anyone who has tried to balance family life with obtaining an academic degree or employment knows the value of a supportive spouse. Thank you, Bill, for your steadfast confidence in my ability and the sacrifices you made to support my professional goals. Your own achievements and dedication as a physician and parent continue to inspire me to maintain the highest professional and family integrity. Even spouses supporting each other cannot always meet the demands of work and family. Thus, I am deeply grateful to my mother-in-law, Margaret B. Duncan, who on countless occasions stepped in so that my sons could attend high school band practice or football games, religious services, and club meetings and who, while I was working on the revised edition, gave me strength by providing home-cooked meals. Finally, I thank our three sons, Linton Eugene, Donovan Omari, and Mark Louis; our granddaughter, Asia Denise; and my nephews and nieces, Khari, Jabari, Hakeem, Shomari, Wesley, Xavier, Vallamar, Michelle, and Sonia who continue to do all the wonderful things they do to enrich my life and who provide me with challenging pragmatic experiences in family studies.

—L.B.J.

Professionally, I am indebted to Patricia Bell-Scott of the University of Georgia, Robert Hall of Northeastern University, Erma Lawson of the University of Kentucky, and Patricia Wilson of Arizona State University, who read and critiqued the first draft of our manuscript. Also, I am grateful to Paul Glick of Arizona State University and anonymous reviewers, who provided feedback on some of the chapters. For the first edition, I thank the support staff in our departments—Kathleen McClung, Sally Maeth, and Elizabeth Sherman—for typing, editing, and bibliographical services. I also wish to acknowledge the support of the Department of Family Studies and African and African American Studies at Arizona State University and the Graduate Program in Sociology at the University of California, San Francisco, which approved phone calls, faxing, and express mail during a period of severe fiscal cutbacks. For the revised edition, I give special thanks to Sharon Solorio, who consistently provided electronic file transfers between the authors. Also, appreciation is given to Tammy Henderson, who against many odds assisted in bringing this second edition to completion. Without these basic services, a joint effort would have moved at a much slower pace.

In our collaborative effort, Leanor Boulin Johnson and I thank each other for mutual support and trust throughout the challenging process of putting a book together. While we are grateful to the people just mentioned for their help, the final responsibility for the book rests with us.

—R. S.

Black Families
at the Crossroads

History as Fact and Fiction

As an institution, the Black family continues to be a subject of intense and controversial public concern. This interest is generated in part by the lack of consensus on what its form and function should be. The controversy is heightened by the way scholars have depicted the Black family in the past and by an ongoing debate over how the family history of Blacks relates to their current situation. Before examining developments in earlier periods, it is necessary to place some parameters around this historical review. The areas of interest are the precolonial era in sub-Saharan Africa, slavery in general, and the various views on the impact of slavery on Black family life.

The Preslavery Period

There are several historical periods of interest in tracing the background of Black family life in the United States. One era is the precolonial period on the African continent, where the Black American population originated. The basis of African family life was the kinship group, which was bound together by blood ties and the common interest of corporate functions. Within each village, there were elaborate legal codes and court systems that regulated the marital and family behavior of individual members. The philosophical basis of the family was one of humanitarianism, mutual aid, and community participation. Although no two tribes in Africa were the same, the continent was generally humane in its treatment of the individual and the creation of meaningful roles for each person (Kayongo-Male and Onyango, 1984).

In African communities, marriage was not just a matter between individuals but the concern of all family members. A woman, for instance, was not just a man's wife but "the wife of the family." As a result of this community control of marriages, the dissolution of a marriage was a drastic action and used only as a last resort. Most marriages involved the payment of a bride-price by the husband's family to compensate her family for the loss of her services and to guarantee her good treatment. This was not the purchase of a woman who became her husband's property. After marriage, a woman remained a member of her own family, since they retained a sincere interest in her well-being (Sudarkasa, 1981).

Regardless of the meaningful role of women in precolonial Africa, the authority pattern in the family was patriarchal. This male control in the family was based not so much on benign dominance as on the reverence attached to his role as the protector and provider for the family. His role was to perform the heavy manual labor and to make decisions for the family. Only if he successfully carried out these roles would respect and admiration be accorded him. On certain days, the wife and children would bestow as much respect on him as subjects would a king. If it was a fête day, his sons-in-law and daughters would be there to present him with some small gifts. They would pay him reverence, bring him a pipe, and then go into another room, where they all ate together with their mother (Frazier, 1939).

Children in African societies were considered symbols of the continuity of life. During their formative years, they enjoyed a carefree life. Until they reached the age of nine or ten, they had no responsibilities. Afterward, they began to learn their role requirements and responsibilities to the tribe. The boys would build small huts and hunt fierce game. Girls played house and cared for their "babies" (often a younger sister). When they reached the age of fifteen, they were considered adults and would soon begin families of their own (Sudarkasa, 1981). The structure and function of the Black family was to change radically under the system of slavery. What did not change, however, was the importance of the family to African peoples in the New World. While the nature of marriage and family patterns was eventually taken from the control of the kinship group, the family nevertheless managed to sustain individuals in the face of the many destructive forces they encountered in American society.

The Causes and Nature of North American Slavery

The first two hundred years of slavery differed significantly from the final century. In the early centuries, few slaves grew cotton, resided in the Deep South, and embraced Christianity. Among the early arrivals were the Atlantic Creoles, people of African and European lineage who were transported to the new world by the Dutch West India Company. Middlemen in trade between Africa, North and South America, and Europe, they spoke not only numerous European and African languages but the common language of trade: Creole. Their previous interactions with Europeans meant that they understood their religion, complex patron-client relations, and general way of life. Thus, rather than the transatlantic journey eroding their skills as cultural negotiators, merchants, sailors, and trappers, it merely transported them to a somewhat familiar new world (Berlin, 2003).

With few exceptions, these Blacks entered the New World as unfree indentured servants, a status that many Whites shared. Indentured servants were people who had their passage paid to this continent and were contractually obligated to work for a specified period of time, usually three to seven years, for the people who paid for their passage. Once their debts were paid, the indentured servants were free to pursue their own interests. According to historians of this period, race played a significant but not central role in the social relations between White and Black indentured servants.

They worked together as equals and at times formed coalitions to resist the policies and cruel practices of wealthy landowners (Berlin, 2003; Hine, Hine, and Harrold, 2004; J. H. Franklin, 1987).

In the absence of both a well-defined racial order and a high-profit staple crop with its demand for mass human labor, seventeenth-century free and bonded Creoles in Dutch New Netherland, English Chesapeake, and Spanish Florida traded their knowledge and labor for favors unknown to nineteenth-century slaves. Caring only for short-term profits, companies such as the Dutch West India allowed its slaves to live and work independently in return for a stipulated amount of labor and annual tribute. Slaves used this marginal freedom to master the Dutch cultural ways, trade freely, accumulate property, convert to Dutch Reformed Christianity, and, most important, establish families. In New Amsterdam (present-day New York), twenty-five Black couples took their vows in the Dutch Reformed Church, and later their children received baptism in the church. Although by the mid-seventeenth century a fifth of Blacks in New Amsterdam, St. Augustine, and Virginia's Eastern Shore gained their freedom, escaping servitude was difficult. The Dutch company was willing to liberate the elderly, considered a liability, but not their children. Both Blacks and Whites protested this half-free status with partial success. By the middle of the seventeenth century, Blacks in New Netherland participated, however unequally, in nearly all aspects of life. In addition to marrying and baptizing in the established church, they created institutional family patterns that served their unique need; foremost among them were legal adoption agencies for orphaned Black children (Berlin, 2003).

In Florida, the Creole society acquired freedom for their families by joining the Spanish militia. Threatened by expansion of English settlement in the Carolinas, the Spanish created alliances with their own slaves. Black militia then raided their former Carolina plantations, freeing family members and friends. The Spanish Crown provided freedom to all slave fugitives who converted to Catholicism and rewarded those Creoles who showed exemplary valor resisting the English. Membership in both the church and militia provided the catalyst for connecting Floridian Black people to each other and to the larger community. Pulling the lever of patronage, they skillfully afforded privileges for themselves and their families. Through the church, they sanctified their marriages, baptized their children, and selected Black and White godparents from the congregation. Their imbalanced gender ratio resulted in marriages with American Indians and newly arriving slaves from Mexico, Cuba, and Spain. After nearly one hundred years, the first generation of Floridian Blacks and their children (the Charter generation) was far more incorporated into the life of mainland society than were the Northern colonies (Berlin, 2003).

The Atlantic Creoles, Black indentured servants, and mulatto offspring of slaveholders numbered about half a million in the 1860s. Because they had opportunities for education, owning property, and skilled occupations, their family life was quite stable. They represent the early development of a Black middle class (Berry and Blassingame, 1982).

Atlantic Creoles' ability to trade freely, secure freedom, acquire modest prosperity, gain access to courts, and serve in organized militia was eroded with the discovery of products that could be sold internationally for high profits—sugar, rice, tobacco, and later cotton. This economic shift triggered the massive influx of slaves, strict slave codes, and dehumanizing racial ideologies to justify slave status. (Berlin, 1998, 2003; Graves, 2001). Taken from the deep interiors of Africa, the later generations of transported slaves were linguistically isolated and deskilled by the process of enslavement, and they suffered enormous psychological and physical degradation. The depth of their dehumanization is best understood in the light of the flourishing civilization they left behind—societies with mores and folkways for regulating the behavior of their members, communication systems, and an extensive network of trade relations throughout the African continent. This human tragedy was inconsequential to slave magnates, whose insatiable appetite for greater profit could be quenched only with a large-scale, inexpensive human labor force.

Slavery, despite the problems it posed in terms of regulating human labor in a coercive relationship, was the most profitable source of labor available. There was little concern, in the beginning of the slave system, for the racial composition of the enslaved group. Subordination and control was valued more than race. In the West Indies, Atlantic Creoles, for example, were rejected as too savvy in European ways to be trusted working among the mass number of slaves needed to cultivate the profitable sugar plantations. Whereas North America had not yet developed a competitive slave economy, would-be slaveholders snapped up these Creoles to work alongside Whites and American Indians in building forts, hunting, trapping, tending animals and fields, and transporting merchandise.

However, there were certain difficulties surrounding the use of the non-Creole groups. Whites, being part of the same racial group, easily escaped and avoided detection by assimilating into the non-slave society. They also disappeared into the frontiers of the virgin western territory, where their recovery was improbable. Enslaved Native Americans, decimated by European diseases and overwork, were soon found unsuitable. Despite the thousands captured, American Indians put up enough formidable resistance and could retreat when necessary into familiar territory (Berlin, 1998, 2003; Patterson, 1982). In the end, Black labor was ideal. Blacks were easily identifiable and unfamiliar with the terrain. An unregulated transatlantic slave trade provided an endless source of labor, which allowed masters to replace slaves who became useless from overwork. Moreover, enslaved Africans brought with them the essential skills and knowledge needed in growing tobacco and rice.

In Africa, rice was largely a women's crop. In disregarding this West African gender role tradition, planters reduced their profit margin. In slavery, male slaves with lesser knowledge of the process were assigned to milling rice. A task that took less than an hour when performed by African women prior to the transatlantic enslavement demanded as many as six hours of arduous labor by slave men. This ignorance of female knowledge systems also resulted in slaves' having to adjust to new symbols of male-female propriety and role relations (Morgan, 2001).

Although slavery was not new to humankind or a North American invention, the enslavement of Africans and their brutal transportation to this country marked a new chapter in the history of man's inhumanity to man. Previous slave systems were not characterized by distinctions of race (Graves, 2001; Snowden, 1970). As Brown (1949, p. 34) says of the slave system in Greece, "The slave populations were enormous, but the slave and the master in Greece were commonly of the same race and there was no occasion to associate any given physical type with the slave status." Similarly, in Rome, slaves were not differentiated from free men in their external appearance. Authorities on the subject have noted that any citizen might conceivably become a slave, and almost any slave might become a citizen. In Europe and Africa, losing in battle often resulted in those defeated becoming enslaved (Graves, 2001; Snowden, 1970).

Basing slavery status on race made American slavery distinct. A racial ideology categorizing Africans as a subhuman race provided the justification for exploiting this ideal source of human labor. The blocked mobility of the nineteenth-century slaves was also peculiar to the United States. To illustrate this point, slavery in the United States is frequently compared to the same institution in South America. According to this view, the Spanish slave code and the Catholic church in Latin America provided safeguards for the slaves and their families and emphasized their worth as human beings. These two forces supposedly led to the encouragement of manumission and stable marriage among free and slave Blacks (Patterson, 1982). Slaves lost their freedom but retained the right to regain it. In the United States, Blacks were consigned to a slave status from birth to grave (Elkins, 1968). The American slave system abrogated all rights the Africans had as human beings. Slaveholders could not be punished for the way they treated their slaves; families were broken up by the sale of one of their members; there was no legal marriage for slaves; the children of a slave mother were automatically slaves; and the status of a slave was a position from which no mobility was permitted (Patterson, 1982).

But this polarity of the two slave systems in North and South America does not consistently hold up under close examination. There was considerable variation among the Latin American societies in their use and treatment of slaves. In some areas of Latin America, there was very humane treatment of slaves, and in others, brutal treatment. As for the Spanish slave code, it was not only unenforced, but it was never promulgated in any of the Spanish Caribbean colonies. Moreover, some of the measures encouraging marriage among the slaves in South America were designed to hold the slaves to the plantation estates with family ties (Hall, 1970). Likewise, in North America, the slave-master relationship took on different forms and meanings over time and from place to place, depending on the centrality of slave labor to the economic goals of the slaveholder, pressures from competitors, the heightened anxiety generated by domestic and foreign slave revolts, and the effect of democratic and religious revolutions (Berlin, 1998). If not consistent in practice, there was one undeniable stark contrast: South America had humane secular and sacred codes, which North America lacked. Regardless of system, slavery was restrictive, and the slaves' welfare was secondary to economic gain. Yet with their modicum of freedom, slaves nevertheless managed to build a community and family life (Berlin, 2003).

The Slave Family

Slavery had its greatest impact on the family life of the Africans brought to the United States. Most of the slaves who came in the beginning were males. The Black female population was not equal to the number of males until 1830. As a result, the frequency of sexual relations between Black slaves and indentured White women was fairly high. Some of these interracial relationships were more than casual contacts and ended in marriage. The intermarriage rate between male slaves and free White women increased to the extent that laws against them were passed as a prohibitive measure. Before the alarm over the rate of intermarriages, male slaves were encouraged to marry White women, since the children from such unions were also slaves, thereby increasing the property of the slave master (Stember, 1976).

In attempting to get an accurate description of the family life of slaves, one has to sift through a conflicting array of opinions on the subject. Scholarly contradictions partially stemmed from historians' using their findings from a particular region as typical of slavery across time and place. Recent findings reveal that at any point in slave history, family life varied as a function of gender composition, region, mode of production, the nature of the planter's business interest, size and location of the master's properties, and the slaveholder's commitment to family stability (Berlin, 1998; Schwartz, 2000; Stevenson, 1996). Yet certain aspects of the slaves' family life during the last hundred years are undisputed. Unlike the earlier periods, African slaves had no civil court of last resort and were not allowed to enter into binding contractual relationships (Berlin, 2003). Since marriage is basically a legal relationship that imposes obligations on both parties and exacts penalties for their violation, there was no legal basis to any marriage between two individuals in bondage. Slave marriages were regulated at the discretion of the slave master. As a result, some marriages were initiated by slave owners and just as easily dissolved (J. H. Franklin, 1988).

Hence, there were numerous cases where the slave owner ordered slave women to marry men of his own choosing after they reached puberty. The slave owners preferred a marriage between slaves on the same plantation, since the primary reason for slave unions was the breeding of children who would become future slaves. Children born to a slave woman on a different plantation were looked on by the slaveholder as wasting his man's seed. Sometimes when two slaves desired to be together and it was advantageous to the master, the matter was resolved by the sale of one of the parties to the other owner. Yet many slaves who were allowed to get married preferred women from a neighboring plantation. This allowed them to avoid witnessing the many assaults on slave women that occurred (Blassingame, 1972).

Historians are divided on the question of how many slave families were involuntarily separated from each other by their owners. Recent historical work documents greater structural diversity than previously understood. In general, a slave master's business decisions created a variety of slave marital and familial relationships and structures. For those wealthy planters with hundreds or thousands of acres scattered throughout the colonies and the West Indies, production priorities, not slave marriages or families, determined slave residence. Any concern for imbalanced gender ratio or slave reproduction could be resolved through buying additional slaves on location. Smaller slaveholders had more reason for uniting slave couples, because a coresidential slave couple could substantially increase their human property through consistent childbearing.

Most vulnerable to being sold or rented out away from their families were children between the ages of ten and fifteen, when they showed the greatest mastery of adult work tasks and work potential. State legislatures supported the sale of all children capable of fieldwork. While slave owners viewed the maturation of enslaved children as positive, slaves considered adolescence a time of deep sorrow as a result of losing their children. Sales in the interregional slave trade increased for preteens though the twenties and began to decline as slaves moved into their thirties. The older the child, the more likely it was that family ties were discounted (Schwartz, 2000).

Despite some slaveholders' commitment to holding slave families together, the intervening events of a slaveholder's death, bankruptcy, or lack of capital made the forcible sale or renting of some spouses or children inevitable (Berlin, 2003; Schwartz, 2000; Stevenson, 1996). In instances where the slave master was indifferent to the fate of slave families, he would still strive to keep them together simply to enforce plantation discipline. A married slave who was concerned about his wife and children, it was believed, was less inclined to rebel or escape than a "single" slave. Schwartz notes that in "trying to prevent their sale, some slave youths 'fout an' kick lak crazy folks' when placed on the auction block" (2000, p. 171). Some slaves went further. When faced with possible separation from her infant child, one slave mother "took the baby by its feet. . . . And with the baby's head swinging downward, she vowed to smash its brains out before she'd leave it" (Berlin, 2003, p. 216). Sometimes their threats and supplications convinced the owners or potential buyers that the cost of family separation was not worth completing the transaction. Whatever their reasoning or circumstances, the few available records show that slave owners did not separate a majority of slave couples (Blassingame, 1972; Fogel and Engerman, 1974). Although there are examples of some slave families' living together for forty years or more, the majority of slave unions did not last long. They were dissolved by death from overwork and poor nutrition, the sale of one partner by the master, or personal choice.

Although individual families may not have remained together for long periods of time, the institution of the family was an important asset in the perilous era of slavery. Despite the prevalent theories about the destruction of the family under slavery, it was one of the most important survival mechanisms for African people held in bondage (Blassingame, 1972). In their state of involuntary servitude, the slaves began to form a new sense of family. Whereas in African society, the family was based on the system of kinship within the tribe, under slavery it was in the community of slaves that individuals found their identity. The community consisted of abroad marriages (where spouses were not physically present from day to day), matrifocality, patrifocality, all-male households, and sibling households. Sibling households represented the most common form of nonnuclear households among Louisiana slaves. The most common form of extended family households in this region was that of families having a brother or sister of one of the spouses in their households. All of these diverse forms found stability through the extended kin network. Both blood and fictive kin provided the glue holding together simple and nuclear families and singles of all types—young, old, widowed, or never married (Stevenson, 1996; Malone, 1992). At the broadest level of community identity, former tribal affiliation was reorganized to encompass those individuals bound together by the commonality of their race and their enslavement. In this context, many of the traditional functions of the family were carried out, and the philosophical principle of survival of the tribe held fast (Nobles and Goddard, 1986).

In the slave quarters, Black families existed as functioning institutions and as models for others. The slave narratives provide some indication of the importance of family relations under slavery. In the family, slaves received affection, companionship, love, and empathy with their suffering under this brutal system. Through the family, they learned how to cooperate with their fellow slaves and to retain some semblance of self-esteem. Some parents taught them submission as a way of avoiding suffering and death. However, they were not taught categorical obedience. Rather, they were frequently instructed to fight the master when their relatives were in danger. One example was W. H. Robinson's father, who told him, "I want you to die in defense of your mother" (Blassingame, 1972, p. 99).

When children stayed near their parents, they vicariously learned how to work at a pace that would not tax them to exhaustion while pretending to satisfy the unreasonable faster work pace of their overseers. Some parents taught their children pride in their African heritage. One father often boasted to his child that he had a pure strain of Black blood in his veins and could trace his ancestors back to the very heart of Africa (Frazier, 1939). Yet parents found their authority undermined by owners' using gifts and coddling to solicit the allegiance of young children. Masters attempted to get these children to spy on the social life in slave quarters, prompting parents to instruct children to monitor their conversations carefully outside their quarters. The master's attention meant better treatment of their children.

However, too much attention curtailed the ability of slave families to create a cultural space where children could be critical of servitude and learn standards of behavior that differed from those of their owners. Differential practices included the slaves' taboos against blood-cousin marriages, which were accepted among the elite planters. To the frustration of owners, slave parents shared with their children interpretations of the Bible favorable to slaves.

The struggle over the children's allegiance was ongoing. In order to minimize parental control without taking on child-rearing responsibilities themselves, owners sought opportunities to release parenting responsibilities from slaves. "Ungroomed or neglected" children provided owners with an excuse to turn the children over to others. A Sunday morning ritual enacted on plantations throughout the South was for masters and mistresses to call all slaves to the big house for inspection. White mistresses joined their husbands in blaming child neglect on the ignorance or laziness of Black women rather than the mothers' overworked schedules and poor clothing provisions (Gutman, 1976; Hine, Hine, and Harrold, 2004; J. H. Franklin, 1988; Schwartz, 2000).

A planter's success in reassigning child care duties from parents to others depended on the number of children, their ages, available nonparent adults who could be trusted, the planter's wealth, and the cycle of cultivation associated with the market crop grown. On rice plantations, masters were aided by the high prevalence of disease. Malaria was poorly understood, but planters knew that mortality rates rose for children who remained in swampy areas during the warmer months. Consequently, for weeks or months wealthy rice planters rented young children out to other slave masters located in distant camps. Unlike owners, slave parents did not accompany their children. Younger slave children experienced anxiety with these lengthy separations (Schwartz, 2000).

Parents of infants experienced other obstacles to their parenting. Breastfeeding competed with work production. Observing that infant and toddler care reduced the productivity of new mothers, owners with sizable slave holdings shifted child care to unrelated slaves in nurseries, thus freeing mothers for tending the fields. Supervision in nurseries tended to be minimal. While caring for the children, owners expected adult slaves to spin, sew, cook, and care for the ill and elderly. Children as young as two or three years old were expected to rock babies or keep them from wandering off. Although women withdrew from the fields during the day to nurse their infants, work was given priority during the busiest times of year. And some infants fed regularly at the breast of their White mistresses when the slave mother's labor was indispensable. The rarity of this practice is clearly reflected in the cyclical infant mortality. Cotton plantation records show infant mortality highest at the peak of the cotton-picking season and lowest at harvest end, in November and December. The highest death toll occurred on rice plantations where the unhealthiest conditions existed and production called for year-round labor (Schwartz, 2000).

Much has been written about the elimination of the male's traditional functions under the slave system. It is true that he was often relegated to working in the fields and siring children rather than providing economic maintenance or physical protection for his family. Yet the father's role was not as insignificant as presumed. Ex-slaves often spoke of their affection for their fathers and the pain of separation. Young courting couples were often chaperoned by the father. "He sit . . . de boy in one corner an' de girl she sit in dis corner" (Malone, 1992, p. 234). This practice may have had African origins. Although they could not perform many of the functions traditionally assigned to fathers, there were other ways they could acquire respect from their families. They could gain the approval of their families and fellow bondsmen by making furniture for the cabin or building partitions between cabins that contained more than one family. Men worked together to construct houses for their families and in so doing strengthened their sense of community. Where possible, fathers could add to the family's meager rations of food by hunting, fishing, and raising domestic livestock. While mothers taught girls domestic tasks, fathers taught boys how to trap animals, carve wood, and make baskets. Even if fathers lived on nearby plantations, they would come with animal game during their weekly visits and spend considerable time chopping and hauling wood for heating and cooking. Fathers used money earned from extra work to purchase blankets or cloth for keeping their children warm. In attempting to keep their families intact, fathers were more inclined than mothers to bargain with their labor (Blassingame, 1972; Lockley, 2001; Schwartz, 2000).

Until recently, the independent economic activities of slaves attracted little scholarly attention. Yet these informal economics had political and psychological meaning for both the slaves and their owners. Most plantations provided slaves with their own gardens as a means of making slaves responsible for their own diet and saving money for the owner. Tended primarily by bondswomen, these gardens were used not only to improve family diet, but provided the basis of an informal economy. Surplus produce could be sold to local shopkeepers, tavern keepers, and boatmen for cash, which could be used to purchase other goods. Bondsmen accompanied their wives to urban markets, and the wives sold produce while the husbands hired themselves out for unskilled labor or artisan work. Bondsmen had more occupational opportunities than their wives; hence their unskilled, semiskilled, and skilled labor enhanced the possibility of a better life for their families. In Georgia and other slave states, the growth of this informal economy gradually led to legislation protecting the interest of the slave master and imposing larger fines on those whites, often of the lower class, who hired slaves illegally. Although the slave code of 1755 limited slaves to trading only garden produce, fruit, and fish, loopholes provided slaves and White traders opportunities to trade much more (Berlin, 2003; Lockley, 2001).

Yet the modicum of independence etched from the informal economy could not compensate for the bondsman's limited ability to protect his family. And it was his inability to protect his wife from the physical and sexual abuse of the master that most pained him.

Yet few tried, since the consequences were often fatal. Nevertheless, it is significant that tales of their intervention occur frequently in the slave narratives. There is one story of a slave who could no longer tolerate the humiliation of his wife's sexual abuse by the master before his eyes. He choked him to death with the knowledge that it meant his own death (Absug, 1971).

The importance of the family is underlined by the numerous cases of fugitive slaves who ran away to find mates who had been sold away from them. In most cases, these couples were bound together by affection, not morality or a contractual agreement. These bonds were often very strong even when there was no legal marriage. As Nobles and Goddard (1986) have noted, the valid African marriage does not need any kind of ceremonial sanction—a bride-price or a sacred or secular ceremony—apart from the domestic consent. Yet slaves had a reverence for legal marriage and the protection the law afforded. Bibb states that "there are no class of people in the United States who so highly appreciate the legality of marriage as those persons who have been held and treated as property" (Bibb, 1849, p. 152).

After Emancipation

An indication of the importance attached to the family is provided by the numerous cases of freed slaves searching out family members from whom they had been separated during slavery. Sometimes they had been apart for as long as thirty years. The means used to reunite families ranged from placing ads in Black newspapers to the trek of one ex-slave who walked six hundred miles during a two-month stretch. Those Black men serving as Civil War soldiers pleaded with the secretary of war to provide their families protection in their absence. Many of the slaves who had cohabited made plans for a legal marriage with the knowledge that they no longer faced the possibility of exploitation and separation (Berlin and Rowland, 1997; J. H. Franklin, 1988).

There has been a prevailing notion that the experience of slavery weakened the value of marriage as an institution among Black Americans. Yet ex-slaves married in record numbers when they obtained this right by governmental decree. A legal marriage was a status symbol, and weddings were events of great gaiety. In a careful examination of census data and marriage licenses for the period after 1850, Gutman (1976) found that the typical household in New York and in Southern rural and urban areas was a double-headed kin-related household. Further evidence that Black people were successful in forming a biparental family structure are the data that show that 90 percent of all Black children were born in wedlock by the year 1917 (Bernard, 1966).

Many students of the Reconstruction era observed the strong family orientation of the ex-slaves. One newspaper reported a Black group's petition to the state of North Carolina asking for the right "to work with the assurance of good faith and fair treatment, to educate their children, to sanctify the family relation, to reunite scattered families, and to provide for the orphan and infirm" (Absug, 1971, p. 34). Children were of special value to the freed slaves, whose memories were fresh with the history of their offspring being sold away. After slavery, the slave-born generation of freed slaves cherished their children all the more and devoted their lives to providing them with land and an education.

During the late nineteenth century, the strong role of women emerged. Males preferred their wives to remain at home, since a working woman was considered a mark of slavery. But during a period considered the most racist of American history, Black men found it very difficult to obtain jobs and in some instances found work only as strikebreakers. Thus, the official organ of the African Methodist Episcopal church exhorted Black families to teach their daughters not to avoid work, since many of them would marry men who would not make, on the average, more than seventy-five cents a day (Absug, 1971). By 1880, approximately three times as many

Black women as White women were in the labor force (Goldin, 1983). What was important, then, was not whether the husband or wife worked, but the family's will to survive in an era when Blacks were systematically deprived of educational and work opportunities. Despite these obstacles, Black families achieved a level of stability based on role integration. Males shared equally in the rearing of children; women participated in the defense of the family. A system where the family disintegrates due to the loss of one member would be in opposition to the traditional principles of unity that defined the African family (Krech, 1982).

This principle was to be tested during the period of the great Black migration from the rural areas of the South to the cities of the North. The rise of Black out-of-wedlock birthrates and female-headed households is a feature of twentieth-century urban ghettos. The condition of many lower-class Black families is a function of the economic contingencies of industrial America (Litwack, 1979). Unlike the European immigrants before them, Blacks were disadvantaged by the oppressiveness of Northern segregation along racial lines. Furthermore, families in cities are more vulnerable to disruptions due to the traumatizing experiences of urbanization, the reduction of family functions, and the loss of extended family supports. Because of the higher level of racial discrimination facing Blacks in the South, they were less likely to retreat from the more vulnerable conditions of urban poverty in the North than White migrants from the South (Lemann, 1991).

In many cases, slavery was replaced by sharecropping and debt peonage for landless Blacks. Their status changed from slaves to sharecroppers; the slave barracks near the big house became dispersed wooden shacks, and money lending charged against the value of the sharecropper's share of the crop became an economic surrogate for slavery. Through constant indebtedness, the ex-slaves were as tied to the land and the landlord as they had been under slavery. The planters saw to it that there was always a debt and therefore an obligation to remain. And, if necessary, they did not hesitate to use force to discourage their tenants from escaping (J. H. Franklin, 1988). Still, sharecropping was an improvement over slavery, and there was considerably more freedom for Blacks to marry, assume custody of children, discipline them, spend more time with their spouses, and engage in family relations without the constant threat of family separation (Jones, 1985). However, J. H. Franklin (1988) claims that sharecropping and the great migration of Blacks to the urban North during World War I did not adversely affect the stability of the Black family to any significant degree. Until 1925, most Black families were intact, although extended and augmented households increased in importance.

In the transition from Africa to the American continent, there can be no doubt that African culture was not retained in any pure form. Blacks lacked the autonomy to maintain their cultural traditions under the severe pressures to take on American standards of behavior. Yet Africanisms survive in agricultural techniques, Black speech patterns, aesthetics, folklore, and religion (Herskovits, 1941; Morgan, 2001). These were combined with aspects of American culture. And out of the common experiences Blacks have shared, a new culture has been forged that is uniquely Black American. The elements of that culture are still to be found in their family life (Foster, 1983).

The Historical Role of Black Women

Anthropologists and historians tell us that most African societies were (and still are) male dominated. One should not assume from this fact that the role of women was unimportant. The historical deeds of Black women in the preslavery period of Africa are recorded on tombs of ancient Egypt, are enumerated by Semitic writers, and are part of Greek mythology. Women formed the economic bulwark of Nigerian society. In the Balonda tribe of southern Africa, women held a position economically superior to that of men (Sudarkasa, 1981). They played an important role in the political organization of various tribal societies in Africa, as reported in local chronicles and in the records of early travelers there. In West Africa, the ancestral home of most Black Americans, the women of the Ashanti tribe were reputed to have founded small states such as Mampong, Wenchi, and Juaban. Among the peoples of Niger and Chad, women reputedly founded cities, led migrations, and conquered kingdoms. There are also accounts of the courage of the female legions who fought in the armies of Monomotapa (an empire located at the southern tip of Africa, later named the Republic of South Africa) and of the privileges they enjoyed (Steady, 1981).

Some cultural continuity exists between the roles of African and Black American women. But while African women had the opportunity to play a central role in their society, Black American women had their role fashioned out of the racial subjugation they endured and the need to assume the task of Black survival.

Until the middle of the nineteenth century, most Black slaves were male. Originally, the slave master's preference was for males who could perform the heavy duties required of bondsmen. Black men were encouraged to "marry" White women in order to augment the human capital of the slave-owning class. The intermarriage rate, however, became so high that unions between Black men and White women were prohibited. After that time, there was a marked increase in the number of Black women. The end of the slave trade also led to an increased emphasis on the domestic breeding of slaves, a task for which Black women bore primary responsibility (White, 1985). In addition, black women had the responsibilities of laboring in the fields and in the slave master's house. This was the beginning of their dual oppression as breeding instruments and captive labor force. Although the Black man was formally stripped of virtually all paternal functions except the biological one, Black women hardly fared better.

The slave woman was first a full-time worker for her owner and only incidentally a wife, mother, and homemaker. She was allowed to spend only a small fraction of her time in her quarters, she often did no cooking or sewing, and she was not allowed to nurse her children during their illnesses. If she was a field slave, she performed hard labor daily in the fields even when she was pregnant and shortly after childbirth. Since the children were the master's property and did not belong to the parents, slave women frequently were breeding instruments for children who were later sold. During this period of slavery, the Black woman's body was forcibly subjected to the carnal desires of any male who took a fancy to her, including slave masters, overseers, their sons, or any male slave. If she was permitted a husband, he was not allowed to protect her. Essentially she was left defenseless against sexual onslaught by other males on the plantation. This was especially true of her relations with the White slave master. Children born from such unions were often denied knowledge of their paternity in the hope of protecting themselves and their children from reprisals by angry mistresses, who often took out their frustration on the slave women, thereby victimizing them twice (Schwartz, 2000; White, 1985). In her autobiography, Harriet Jacobs wrote, "I cannot tell how much I suffered in the presence of these wrongs, nor how I am still pained by the retrospect" (Hine, Hine, and Harrold, 2004, p. 91; Schwartz, 2000).

White Southerners justified violations of Black women's bodies in several ways. They maintained that Black women were genetically promiscuous and seduced White men. Others argued that exploitation of Black women by White men reduced prostitution and promoted purity among White women. Angela Davis (1971) has suggested that the sexual subjugation of the slave woman was the slave master's symbolic attempt to break her will to resist. According to Davis (1971, p. 13), "In confronting the Black woman as adversary in a sexual contest, the master would be subjecting her to the most elemental form of terrorism distinctively suited for the female: rape. Given the already terroristic texture of plantation life, it would be as a potential victim of rape that the slave woman would be most unguarded. Further, she might be most conveniently manipulable if the master contrived a ransom system of sorts, forcing her to pay with her body for food, diminished severity in treatment, the safety of her children, etc."

The sexual exploitation of the slave woman did not derive simply from carnal desire but from the slave master's design to intimidate the entire slave population. He wanted to assert his control over the entirety of the slave's being—over that of the male as well as the female slave. The rape of the slave woman brought home to the slave man his inability to protect his woman. Once his masculine role was undermined in this and other respects, he would begin to experience profound doubts about his power to break the chains of bondage (Davis, 1983).

Historically, fathers are expected to be the protector of their children and wives. Yet the slaveholder continuously challenged the male slave's protector role. Slave mothers played the traditional role of bearing and rearing children, and if only one parent was present, it was most likely the mother. It is this fact that led to the emergence of the notorious Black matriarchy hypothesis. A matriarchy is formally defined as a system of government ruled by women. This concept implies great advantages for women in the society. Instead of having any particular privileges under the slave system, Black women were, in reality, burdened with the dual role of laborer and mother. Hence, this is the origin of her two-pronged burden, which has been mislabeled a matriarchy (Collins, 1990; White, 1985). In reality, both male and female slaves' dependent status limited the amount of protection that they could provide. Nevertheless, within the restraints of their dependency, they defended their family as best they could, often at enormous risk to themselves (Malone, 1992).

The Historical Debate

Among other topics, the growing literature on Black families has focused on the impact of slavery on Black families. Historical studies have both developed and corrected many misconceptions about the nature of family life among the Black slave population. As was true of other investigations of Black family life, early historians constructed their view of slave family life from preconceived assumptions and faulty methodology. A popularly held theory was that slavery destroyed the family traditions and values brought to the North American continent by Africans (Elkins, 1968; Frazier, 1939). There was much validity to the old historical research that found no legal basis for a marriage between slaves, that slave families could be and were disrupted by the sale of their members, and that the exercise of normative sex and parental roles was constrained. These findings were partly built on theories of history, which were supplemented by the use of plantation records and slave owners' diaries. But the new historical research employs a more extensive and reliable analysis of slave narratives and census records as well as the traditional sources.

African survival is a controversial theory that states that Blacks in the diaspora have retained many of the cultural traits they brought over from the African continent. Primarily associated with the late anthropologist Melville Herskovits (1941), it begs the question of how these traits have been maintained and in what form. The Herskovits answer was that some Africanisms, including practices such as voodoo, were retained by New World Blacks because they were practiced in secret. As to the form they took, he claims they were often disguised as a combination of cultural elements that had been integrated to form one cultural complex. This process of syncretism is expressed in Black American music, language, customs, food, and religion. In the case of Black American social organization and production skills, many characteristics regarded as European were actually African in origin. Respect for elders was central to African family life. The sophisticated soil and water management techniques used in low country South Carolina derived not from Europe but from the Upper Guinea Coast of Africa (Morgan, 2001; Foster, 1983).

However, no matter how convenient it might be to believe that Black Americans are an African people in their cultural behavior, there is not sufficient evidence to reach such a conclusion. The retention of African features has a stronger case in some Caribbean and South American societies, for reasons that are peculiar to them. Yet a group rarely is totally stripped of all its cultural heritage, especially when they live the kind of segregated existence of American Blacks. Blassingame (1972, p. 18) provides a good evaluative yardstick for assessing Africanisms in Black American culture: "Whenever the elements of Black culture are more closely similar to African than European traits, we can be reasonably certain that we have identified African survivals."

For years, work by Frazier (1939) and Elkins (1968) was accepted as the definitive history of Black families and posited as a causal explanation of their contemporary condition. Applying traditional historical methods and using plantation records and the testimony of slave owners, both men reached the conclusion that the culture of the slaves was decimated and, in particular, that the family was destroyed under slavery. The first historian to challenge that thesis was Blassingame (1972), whose use of slave narratives indicated that in the slave quarters, Black families did exist as functioning institutions and role models for others. Moreover, strong family ties persisted in face of the frequent breakups deriving from the slave trade. To further counter the Frazier-Elkins thesis, Fogel and Engerman (1974) used elaborate quantitative methods to document that slave owners did not separate a majority of the slave families. Their contention, also controversial, was that the capitalistic efficiency of the slave system meant it was more practical to keep slave families intact.

Continuing in the vein of revisionist historical research, Genovese (1974) used a mix of slaveholders' papers and slave testimony. He concluded that Black culture, through compromise and negotiation between slaves and slave owners, did flourish during slavery. Within that cultural framework existed a variety of socially approved and sanctioned relationships between slave men and women. The alleged female matriarchy that was extant during that era is described by Genovese as a closer approximation to a healthy gender equality than was possible for Whites.

Historical demographers have also made contributions to our understanding of Black family history. Furstenberg, Hershberg, and Modell (1975) investigated the origin of the female-headed Black family and its relationship to the urban experience. Basing their analysis on samples from the decennial federal population manuscript schedules for the period from 1850 to 1880, they found that Blacks were only slightly less likely to reside in nuclear households than native Whites and immigrants to Philadelphia.

It was the landmark study by Gutman (1976) that put to rest one of the most common and enduring myths about Black families. Using census data for a number of cities between 1880 and 1925, he found that the majority of Blacks of all social classes were lodged in nuclear families. Through the use of plantation birth records and marriage applications, he concluded that the biparental household was the dominant form during slavery. More important than Gutman's compelling evidence that slavery did not destroy the Black family was his contention that this family form evolved from family and kinship patterns that emerged under slavery, thus giving credence to the notion of Black culture surviving slavery.

Between 1990 and 2003, several slavery scholars stressed the developmental and ever-changing structure of Black family. Their studies built on the pioneering work of John Hope Franklin, John Blassingame, Eugene Genovese, and Herbert Gutman. From an array of diverse qualitative and quantitative sources, Berlin (2003, 1998), Lockley (2001), Stevenson (1996), Malone (1992), and others showed how the structure and function of slave families, as well as cross-racial interactions, varied with the mode of productions, interregional and foreign competition, and geographical region. Also, by giving attention to the informal slave economy and issues of class and gender within the societies of both Whites and Blacks, these later works teased out a complex cultural and economic context within which slaves sculptured their family life. Across these studies, far stronger support emerged for the presence of various forms of nuclear and extended family arrangements than for an all present and pervasive female-headed slave family system.

While these historical works have successfully challenged the Moynihan (1965) view that slavery created the conditions for Black family disorganization, the prevalence of marital breakups at the hands of slave owners means that many marriages were not stable. And even the use of slave accounts does not eliminate bias in slave history. Many of the slave narratives were edited by Northern abolitionists, and they constitute the reports of highly literate slaves. This raises questions about ideology and its role in the conceptualization of Black family organization. The role of ideology is not unique to the field of family history. Under the rubric of the sociology of knowledge, it has been asserted that the social location of individuals within a given society will influence the knowledge they possess (Mannheim, 1936). Since the study of Black families has been dominated by White middle-class males, a debate centering around the insider-outsider thesis has arisen (Merton, 1972; Staples and Mirande, 1980). One side contends that Blacks possess a special capacity to understand the behavior of their group, while the other side contends that the use of objective scientific methods nullifies the racial membership of the investigator as a significant factor. Those holding the latter view often choose to conceptualize this whole issue as a conflict between ideology and science (Zollar, 1986).

Other questions concern the division of historical researchers according to methodology. Many of the Black researchers have used the slave narratives as their main tool in understanding slave families. In part, this is due to a need for a broader understanding of the behavioral processes that constitute the historical background of American Blacks. Since White males have dominated the historical studies of slave families, they have often dismissed their Black counterparts with the charge of being polemicists who substituted speculation and ideology for objective data. This question of objectivity versus ideology would be beyond cavil were it not for the fact that Black families were treated pejoratively in the historical literature for the longest time.

As of the 1990s, there ceased to be a clear-cut racial division in the study of some aspects of Black history. Many of the corrective historical studies were undertaken by White historians such as Berlin

(1998, 2003), Gutman (1976), and Genovese (1974). However, with the exception of the work of the White anthropologist Herskovits (1941), their research did not change until America's racial climate changed. This fact led novelist and author-historian Chancellor Williams (quoted in Toure, 1991) to assert, "There are two widely different schools of scholarship. Members of the orthodox majority develop their work faithfully in line with the authorities in the field, relying on them as sources of final truth. . . . The other school dares to challenge much of this authoritarian scholarship by subjecting the masters to critical analysis, raising all kinds of questions . . . and even inquiring about some fundamental presuppositions which underlie and color so much of their work" (p. E-l).

The fact must be accepted that the Black family cannot be explained by the use of normative historical methods. For the most part, history has been a traditionalist science operating with the acceptance of the status quo models. What this means is that the traditional approach to the study of Black family life has been to define the history of Black American family behavior on the basis of standards set by the White community—not by the White community in general, but by White middle-class people in particular. Rather than using a more objective approach and accepting the fact that Black families are different and that one must understand the way they function and their values and standards—other values and standards—White norms have been imposed on the historical study of Black family life. The result has been that the Black family continues to be defined as a pathological unit whose unique way of functioning sustains the conditions of its oppression.

However, there is no definitive evidence of a racial polarization of historical research on the Black family. The purveyors of the pathology view have belonged to both racial groups, just as the defenders of the Black family have. The difference most likely arises from adherence to a class ideology and values rather than a value-free approach to the study of Black family history. A problem remains that much of what we know is an oversimplification of popular stereotypes about Black family life, which serve to inculcate in the public mind a host of useless and invalidated generalizations—and there is much that we need to know that has not yet been explored.

Summary

Sorting out the validity of different historical theories and research on the evolution of Black American families is a daunting task. Just as historians are challenged by the task of determining the nature of historical events, it is difficult for us to evaluate the validity of their interpretation. What has been learned is that slavery, particularly in the nineteenth century, radically altered the family system known to Africans before their forced transplantation to the Americas. However much they may have attempted to maintain their family organization under slavery, the vicissitudes of bondage made an indelible mark on the type of family life they were allowed to have. That slavery made its mark on Black American families is unquestionable. Whether the experience of maintaining family life over a period of three hundred years in bondage left much of a legacy continues to be debated.

The classic historical theories that slavery created the basis for a deinstitutionalization of marriage and an inversion of gender roles in the family seem to have been successfully challenged by the neo-historical theories of Blassingame (1972), Genovese (1974), and Gutman (1976) and confirmed by general consensus of historians in the 1990s. Their research has the advantage of letting slaves speak in their own voices and of using census data and government records that more effectively document marriage and out-of-wedlock birthrates. The fact that 75 percent of Black families were intact up to 1925 serves as a strong antidote to the historical generalization that the institutional role of marriage was destroyed under slavery. If one accepts the hypothesis that slavery created the conditions for a Black matriarchy, more current research on power relationships within Black American families provides strong evidence to the contrary.

Finally, we must examine how history illuminates the role of class and race in influencing Black family patterns. Traditionally, historians have posited race as the dominant variable, because certain historical experiences (slavery, Jim Crow) were unique to Black Americans and were thought to have created a pathological culture and personality in Black communities. Yet slavery was first and foremost an economic system. Black slavery occurred in the Americas because it was the cheapest and "best" economic system from a certain standpoint (Patterson, 1982). It acquired its racial characteristic in its latter stages to serve economic ends (Berlin, 2003). Given the social class traits that differentiate intact and broken Black American families, it seems apparent that current economic conditions supersede historical events as the main factor in Black family disorganization.

2

Studying Black Families

For many years, the Black family has been the focus of research studies by sociologists, psychologists, and educators. Yet there is no comprehensive theory that fully explains its nature and structure. In a limited sense, various disciplines have attempted to relate their theoretical framework to the study of this institution. But at this point, no family sociologist has integrated the separate theories into a general theory of the Black family (Engram, 1982). One reason for the paucity of theories specifically concerning the Black family has been the lack of theories on the family in general. According to some scholars, no such theory is needed; the family can be studied by the theories already available. Goode (1959) has observed that "there remains a widespread feeling among younger theorists that the structure and workings of the family do not explain the rest of the social structure. The family is said to be made up of dependent, not independent, variables—i.e., it is thought possible to explain the family by other institutions but not other institutions by the family." He further asserts that "no theorists have been able to state, let alone prove, any set of systematic propositions about the relations between the family and other institutions, no matter which is independent" (p. 180).

One of the most important concerns of family sociologists has been theory building in the area of marriage and the family (Booth, 1991). The general consensus is that systematic theory building is a major need in family study. Hill and Hansen (1960) note that most past research was sophisticated in method but needed to grow in theoretical relevance. Empirical studies should be theory oriented to help structure the research design and avoid erroneous ex post facto interpretations of research findings. In an important article on the development of family theory, Reuben Hill (1966) cites three goals for developing a theory of the family: (1) establishing an all-purpose family framework that can be used by the members of the various disciplines working in family study; (2) building interpretive bridges linking each of the conceptual frameworks and enabling theories developed in one framework to be translated into the concepts and language of other frameworks; and (3) creating a way of moving from descriptive taxonomic frameworks to explanatory models for the mutual enrichment of each.

Looking through the sociological literature, it is difficult to find a consensus on the definition of theory. It is sometimes viewed in terms of the classic works of the famous sociologists of the past or as a commentary on sociological writing from a historical perspective (Zetterberg, 1965). As the discipline of sociology becomes more oriented toward theory, more precise definitions must be used. In a theory, one should be able to develop more abstract propositions from which empirical generalizations can be derived. To test a theory, propositions—or interrelationships of individual concepts—should conform to data, and several propositions in conjunction with each other should account for the outcome of a given situation. In other words, observed events will conform to known propositions as an indirect test of the theory (Zetterberg, 1965).

Probably none of the frameworks used to study families can meet the most stringent definitions of a theory. Several decades ago, Hill and Hansen (1960) referred to the main approaches in the family field as conceptual models. They are not systematic theories of the family but contain concepts that alert family researchers to what is important for them to pay attention to when studying family relationships. Hill and Hansen identified five conceptual models as particularly appropriate to the study of the family: institutional, interactional, structural-functional, situational, and family development. Two additional models emerged in the 1970s as major approaches to the family: the exchange and conflict models (Nye and Berardo, 1981).

Reviewing the studies of Black families over a hundred-year time span reveals that most have been atheoretical. While the frameworks just mentioned have occasionally been used in research on Black American families, other conceptual models not normally associated with mainstream family research have more frequently been applied. While we will critique the Black family frameworks, it should be noted that we are in agreement with Engram (1982), who notes that "most of the frameworks so examined were conceptualized in response to the empirical stimuli of western and mainstream families. Often the analysis of ethnic and lower-class families within the context of these frameworks has, therefore, required truncation or stretching of data to fit the theoretical realities posed by them" (p. 7).

Conceptual Models for Studying Black Family Life

In this section, we review some of the most relevant conceptual models that contain elements useful for understanding the structure and dynamics of Black family life. Some of these models may not have found wide application in Black family research, but we believe that they are relevant to the understanding of Black families in the United States. While we realize that these are conceptual models, not theories, we will use the two terms interchangeably, as they are used in much of the family literature (Dilworth-Anderson, Johnson, and Burton, 1992; Davis, 1990).

The Afrocentric Model

If we applied this model to the study of Black life in America, our focus would be on the continuities in African cultural strands among the Black American population. Afrocentricity sees all people of African descent as having a common history, experience, and culture. Hence, Black Americans are considered dislocated Africans.

The structure of African culture remains the same, although the form may have changed through the adaptations imposed on Black Americans. A basic assumption is that a culture group never completely loses its cultural heritage; it simply evolves into another form (Asante, 1987; Nobles, 1988). A virtue of this model is its focus on the comparative study of African and Black American cultures. It provides an important link to the past and serves as the foundation for any analysis of Black cultural values and patterns. Some significant work has already been done in the areas of music, speech, and family patterns. However, much historical research is needed to determine the origin of African cultural traits, the means of transmitting them among Africans in another country, and the forms they exist in among contemporary Black Americans (Sudarkasa, 1988).

Cultural variations can be determined by studying the different forms of family behavior found among peoples of African descent. This refers not only to the variations that exist within the African continent (for example, matrilineal and patrilineal systems), but the different types of African family forms in other parts of the world. For instance, in the United States, one might compare Muslim and Christian families, working- and middle-class families, rural and urban families, and so on (Nobles and Goddard, 1986). The significance of the Afrocentric approach is that it liberates the study of Black American families from the domination of White referents in the study of Black life. A comparison of Blacks and Whites in America is useful for illustrating the effects of racial inequality. But others believe that if a meaningful analysis of Black cultural forms is what we are about, the focus must be on those cultural traditions that are maintained in the nature and function of institutions such as the family (Harvey, 1985).

Although the Afrocentric perspective is valuable for understanding the family traditions that remained intact or were modified in the diaspora, the political and economic forces that the Black American family encountered that influenced its character also need to be understood. Afrocentricity as a conceptual model has concentrated more on cultural forms than on the effect of a society's political economy. Moreover, historical and anthropological methodologies have to be refined and strengthened so that contemporary Black American families can be understood in the light of historical and cross-cultural facts (Staples and Mirande, 1980). Proponents of this school of thought acknowledge that they have to develop a literature and data base (Coughlin, 1987).

Black Feminist Theory

The burgeoning of the women's movement gave rise to a number of books on Black women. In earlier years, they tended to be non-empirical works that focused on the role of Black women in their community and the larger society (Cade, 1970; Rodgers-Rose, 1980; Staples, 1973; Noble, 1978). Among the better books was Ladner's study (1971) of Black teenage females growing up in a low-income community. Through the use of systematic open-ended interviews, participatory observation, and her own experiences, she explored how these young women coped with the forces of poverty and maintained a sense of positive identity. Many of the early books on Black women emphasized that they were strong because of the need to face adverse forces in the society but were not overbearing matriarchs. At the end of the 1970s, a young Black feminist broke ranks with her more conciliatory sisters and issued a broadside attack on male chauvinism in the Black community (Wallace, 1979). Her book was a harbinger of the 1990s. This book, along with later literature on Black gender roles, has reflected a feminist ideology.

Feminist theory in the Black community arose later than it did in the White community; moreover, it has different concerns and has dealt with separate issues or given them a different priority. While White feminists have protested White male domination of society's values, Black women have found themselves the victims of Black men's powerlessness. Many White feminists reject conventional family structures and roles, whereas Black women have rarely had access to those structures and roles. Some White feminists advocate singlehood, careerism, alternative lifestyles, and childlessness (Komarovsky, 1988; Thorne and Yalom, 1982). Most Black feminists have wanted to promote the goals of racial equality, the care and nurturing of children, and the strengthening of the Black family system (Joseph and Lewis, 1981). A major impetus for Black feminism was Black women's feeling of exclusion from Black movements and institutions because of male chauvinism, as well as alienation from the mainstream women's movements because of the problems caused by racial tensions (Collins, 1990).

For the Black community, the 1980s might be termed the decade of women. In that decade, most of the few Black gains in the areas of education, occupations, income, health, and literature were achieved by women, while Black men lost ground (Staples, 1991a). Still, despite narrowing the gap between themselves and Black men, Black American women continue to occupy the bottom of the socioeconomic ladder in comparison to other gender-race groupings. Not only are they the poorest of all gender-race groups, but they are increasingly forced to fend for themselves, since only one-third of Black females age 15 and over were married and living with a spouse in 2002, compared to 55 percent of non-Hispanic white females (U.S. Census Bureau, 2002a). One consequence of the decline in Black marriage rates has been a more strident attack on sexism in the Black community (hooks, 1981).

The volume of work on and by Black women has contributed to our understanding of Black family life. As more and more Black women have explored their gender identity, a rich literature has evolved (Bell-Scott, 1991; Hull, Scott, and Smith, 1982). However, it is limited as a holistic theoretical framework for understanding Black American families. While the family is often the center of gender domination, violence, and sexual problems, that is not all it is about. By focusing on women's roles, including child rearing, Black feminists neglect an entire half of the family formation. Even when men are absent as husbands and fathers, they have an involvement with women as boyfriends, sons, and brothers. And everything about the roles they play in the family is not necessarily negative. Thus, Black feminist studies need to be supplemented by Black family studies.

The Culture of Poverty

A slight variant of the cultural deprivation theory, this theory assumes that Black culture is a pathological version of the general American culture. Black culture is characterized as a response to poverty that results in specific traits, such as female dominance, desire for immediate gratification, fatalism, and disorganization (Demos, 1990). This theoretical approach often focuses on Black family organization and the values springing from the family environment as the major source of these negative traits. The studies by Rainwater (1970) and Moynihan (1965) in particular charge the Black family with being a major cause of racial inequality in American society.

The basis of the model is that poverty breeds poverty, that is, that the conditions imposed on the poor account for the pathological cultural forms that keep them in impoverished circumstances. Poverty, then, becomes something transmitted from generation to generation, because the daily focus on their impoverished state or addressing their basic needs may be an deterrent to achieving upward mobility. Among the criticisms of this approach are that many of the features associated with the culture of poverty—unemployment, substandard incomes, congested living conditions—are merely definitions of poverty itself, not of a distinct culture. In essence, this theory is an attempt to shift the responsibility for the conditions of racial and class inequality onto the victims themselves. It is an effort to rationalize why some Americans fail to achieve the culturally prescribed goals of the society (Valentine, 1968).

Assimilation Model

The classic assimilation model assumes a direct link between upward socioeconomic mobility and adoption of American values, practices, and identity. Early-twentieth-century European immigrants provided support for this theory. Each consecutive European ethnic generation showed increasing upward status as they and their children internalized American culture. During the 1930s, E. Franklin Frazier used this model in challenging scholars who linked Black family disorganization to genetic disposition. Viewing the city of Chicago as concentric zones, he demonstrated that as the Southern Black migrants moved from the poverty-stricken central city to the periphery, where the more acculturated Blacks resided, there occurred a decrease in the rate of female-headed households, out-of-wedlock births, delinquency, and other "social pathologies." Hence, Frazier's study created a paradigm shift from racial-biological determinism to social determinism (Johnson, 1978a). Nevertheless, he depicts Blacks as no different from European peasants arriving in Northern cities; institutionalized inequality is seen as inevitably surmountable. Moreover, this biracial model ignores ethnic differences among Blacks (Ostine, 1998).

Challenging this model are the experiences of post-1965 Black immigrants from the West Indies, Africa, and Latin America. For these recent immigrants, Americanization does not necessarily lead to upward mobility. Some immigrants and their children become Americanized and do poorly, while others who retain strong ethnic identity achieve high socioeconomic status.

A neoassimilation model decouples Americanization from social mobility. It recognizes two realities. First, race remains a powerful determinant of lifestyles. Immigrants from Africa, for instance, are one of the most educated groups in America, with an average of 14.5 years of education, compared to 13.9 years for Asians and 13.5 years for whites. Yet based on the 2000 census statistics of annual salaries by ethnicity, African immigrants earn $40,300, compared to $52,000 for whites. The race factor cannot be dismissed. Second, America has had an economic restructuring, which shapes the economic well-being of immigrants and marginalized groups. Service and skilled jobs have replaced manufactory jobs that gave opportunities to the immigrants in the early twentieth century (Rodriquez, 2003; Hill, 1999; Waters, 1999).

In contrast to the classic model, neoassimilationism does not assume a monolithic American culture, which is middle class, individualistic, and upwardly mobile. Nor does it assume that "American" culture and identity are of higher social status than the immigrants' culture. Black immigrants may be multilingual, arrive with a broad range of skills, and face more options for assimilation and identification than available to those Southern Blacks migrating to Northern American cities at the turn of the twentieth century. From the perspective of the dominant group, Black immigrants' "exotic" characteristics may afford them less harsh treatment. In turn, these immigrants may not even perceive the same level of racism as native Blacks, providing them with more optimism to pursue opportunities.

This model does assume that racial privilege and cultural domination bind individuals of African descent together. However, commonality in oppression represents a partial understanding of group experiences and outcome. For instance, postcolonial experiences weigh heavily on feelings of efficacy and power. West Indian families witness in their home country Blacks moving from poverty to the highest ranks of leadership and authority, providing hope for their children. In contrast, American Blacks have yet to see a Black president. The virtue of the neoassimilation model is that it not only recognizes that a common oppressor can unite Black people, but assumes that postcolonial cultural experiences can also divide Black families in ways that present differential outcomes for their children and upward mobility. This is discussed further in Chapters Three and Eight.

Exchange Theory

This theory focuses on the reinforcement patterns and the idea of rewards and costs that prompt people to behave in a particular manner or engage in a certain pattern of interaction (Blau, 1964; Homans, 1961). Essentially, the theory argues that people will continue to do what they have found rewarding in the past. We believe that this perspective, plus the individual's history of rewards and costs, assists in understanding contemporary marriage and family patterns. Our basic premise is that there is a relationship between family structures and ideas of reinforcement, rewards, and costs as these relate to exchange values among those engaged in family interaction.

When we speak of family life, we should note that the general pattern consists of a one-to-one relationship between a man and a woman. This male-female bond is very important to the majority of Blacks, especially women. The fact that a majority of Black Americans are not married and living in traditional nuclear family units does not necessarily imply a devaluation of marriage as an institution; it is often a function of limited opportunities to find acceptable individuals in an increasingly restricted and small pool of potential partners who can successfully fulfill the normatively prescribed familial roles. While many Blacks fail to marry, the history of those who do marry indicates that only a minority survive a lifetime with the same spouse. Exchange theory suggests that a person will not want to remain in a relationship where the rewards provided seem relatively meager compared to what the person knows or perceives about other relationships.

Based on that assumption, we might surmise that many Blacks may prefer to remain single because the perceived outcome, based on their own experience or on the experience of friends and relatives, might suggest that the costs and risks far outweigh the rewards (Thibaut and Kelley, 1959). This cost-benefit analysis is mediated by the sociocultural and economic conditions that adversely affect the Black male population and thus helps to give rise to dissonance between Black family ideology and actual family arrangement (Jewell, 1988).

While exchange theory indicates that individuals use a cost-benefit analysis to determine their actions and relationships, the idea of exchange is actually a system of mutual expectations in a relationship (Hatfield and Walster, 1981). Men and women like to think they get what they deserve in a relationship. The most common exchange in patriarchal societies is that of female sexual access for a male's socioeconomic status. This sort of transaction has been undermined by the sexual revolution and female economic independence. Exchange theory seems most applicable to dating situations and bad marriages, since it is unlikely that most family relationships are ordered in such a calculated and rational manner. Although exchange theory has been used by students of Black families (Jewell, 1988; Staples, 1981), it is limited in its application to this institution. Unless they are members of the middle class, Black men and women do not have extensive resources to exchange.

Historical Materialism

This school of thought, which views the family as a product of economic forces, is primarily attributed to the socialist theoretician Karl Marx (1936). According to Marx, the functions of the family are determined by class relationships. In capitalist societies, women and children are mere appendages of machines, to be used as a reserve labor supply during periods of economic expansion. Marx believed that the capitalist economic order makes family life almost impossible for the working class, since women are forced to work and their employment destroys the family. His collaborator, Engels (1950), asserted that the working man is dependent on the family and that the result is a succession of family troubles. These include domestic quarrels, neglect of domestic duties, and increases in juvenile delinquency and child mortality.

Historical materialism's emphasis on political and economic influences in shaping family life has considerable significance for understanding variations among Black families of the diaspora. There are indications, for instance, that the female-centered family is primarily related to wage-labor systems that require a mobile male labor force, which produces an imbalance in the gender ratio (Davis, 1989). In North America, the political system may have produced the same results (Davis and Davis, 1986; Staples, 1985). This model also is useful for understanding the oppression of women, family conflict, and other forces that act on the family. A good combination of Afrocentric elements and insights from historical materialism would be a syncretic model that illustrates how economic forces act on family relations and how these forces are counteracted by cultural adaptations to each event. Moreover, one might analyze families of the diaspora by examining the economic forces that characterized various eras and the modification of family forms in response to those vagaries. However, the economic base is not the only causal factor in the historical movement and transformation of Black families. Other elements of a given society also influence the quality of a group's family life. Using only economic factors does not sufficiently distinguish the Black family from poor White families. Racial factors must be integrated into any study of Black families (Robinson, 1983).

Internal Colonialism

This conceptual model contains some of the essential elements of historical materialism but focuses on the use of racism for the purposes of political and economic exploitation. A colonial system is typified by the differentiation of racial groups into superordinate and subordinate categories, with the racially subordinate group being denied equal participation in society and the dominant group accorded special privileges at its expense (Blauner, 1972). Central to the understanding of Black American family life are the concepts of racial privilege and cultural domination. As Blauner (1972) has noted, internal colonialism is distinguished from capitalism by its use of culture as an instrument of domination. In the case of Black American families, the Anglo-Saxon family pattern was imposed on them while attempts were made to destroy the African family system. A good example is the vitiation of the parents' rights in their children under the system of slavery. The husband's domestic rights in his wife were also eliminated, since they were abrogated by the slave master. The continuation of White cultural domination is seen in the negative labeling of Black families who do not conform to Anglo-Saxon family norms. Furthermore, the conditions necessary for approximating the middle-class family model are denied many Black Americans, since the economic needs of the higher classes take precedence over Black family requisites.

Among the special privileges historically accorded White American males was sexual access to Black females, while Black males were denied similar contact with White females. Black females were used sexually to maintain the sexual "purity" of White females while existing themselves beyond the pale of consideration for marriage. The barriers to interracial marriage maintained the special privileges of the dominant racial group. As King (1973, p. 17) has observed, "Marriage between members of the ruling class and those whom they oppress inevitably undermines the rationale for the basis of oppression." The social taboos on interracial marriage prevent challenge to the superior position assigned to Whites in other ways. A low frequency of racial intermarriage makes Black accumulation of wealth through inheritance from a White improbable. It also prohibits Blacks from obtaining jobs through social contacts and kin connections and prevents them from obtaining a familiarity with the social world of Whites, which is necessary for obtaining certain jobs and otherwise advancing in a White-dominated society (Spickard, 1989). Even when interracial marriages are permitted on a limited basis, they reflect the colonial relationships extant in the United States. Since the dominant culture assigns positive values to beauty and personality traits possessed primarily by White females, they become more desirable marriage partners to some Black males. Because of the differences in the social status of Black males (low) and White females (high), a large proportion of interracial marriages involve Black males in fairly high economic brackets. The theory is that the woman is exchanging her higher social status for the man's higher economic status (Murstein, Merighi, and Malloy, 1989; Tucker and Mitchell-Kernan, 1990).

The internal colonialism model may explain other aspects of Black family behavior not adequately captured by the pathological approach to studying Black American family patterns. By employing this framework, we might better understand Black family violence, the middle-class Black family's contradictions, and how the strengths of Black families have been defined by the nature of racism. This approach, however, needs to become more theoretically sophisticated, lest it be applied mechanically to the American experience and specifically to Black American family life (Staples, 1987).

A further limitation of this model is its emphasis on the negative and oppressive aspects of Black American life. It needs to be combined with the Afrocentric perspective to shed light on the continuity of cultural strands as well as the imposition of Anglo-Saxon cultural forms that threaten to destroy the African cultural heritage.

Stages of Black Family Studies

For a hundred years, the Black family has been the subject of scientific investigation. This study has had a variety of purposes, methodologies, and conclusions (Davis, 1990; Demos, 1990). Concomitant with these have been the prevailing state of race relations and other circumstances of the Black population. This observation is congruent with Mannheim's thesis (1936) that ideas are a function of environment, that the nature of a society influences the kind of knowledge that individuals are exposed to depending on their location in a certain niche within the social structure. This obviously raises the question of what type of Black family really exists in the United States. Probably there is no monolithic Black family grouping that we can use as a model, since there are numerous differences in family organization and functioning within the Black community. These variations exist by class, along religious, ethnic, and regional lines, and so on. However, there are similar conditions that all Black families encounter, and adaptations to those circumstances will produce similarities in their family lifestyles.

Another problem is that the study of Black American families has always used the White middle-class family as a referent. Black

families will always be perceived negatively according to this yardstick, among other reasons because the White middle-class family
is only an analytical construct, an ideal type that no longer fits the
majority of White families in this country. About 110.6 million (56
percent) of American households consisted of a married couple with
children under age eighteen in 1998 (Lugalia, 1998).

Poverty Acculturation

The original studies of Black family life (Du Bois, 1908; Frazier, 1932a,
1932b, 1939) focused on the economic conditions of the Black population that allegedly brought about their family "disorganization." It
is important to note that these studies were undertaken at a time when
urbanization was having its most devastating effect on the Black community. In particular, Du Bois (1908) wrote his classic work, *The Negro
American Family*, at a time when the massive migration of Black folk
from an agrarian setting to the city was taking place. Hence, it is not
surprising that he found much higher rates of out-of-wedlock births
and female-headed households than in the past century, when free
Black families lived in the rural South. He was not studying a stable
group of Blacks but one that was being uprooted from its folk culture
and forced to the cities, where it became part of the landless urban
proletariat.

But much of Black family organization reflected a continuation of
African values relating to family life. Because Du Bois, Frazier, and
others believed that the solution to Black poverty was the integration
of Blacks into the White world, they stressed that Black family norms
must come into conformity with White middle-class family behavior.
At the same time, they gave recognition to the African past, although
in different ways, and noted the variety of Black family types. Moreover, they believed that the disorganization of Black families was a result of slavery, racism, and poverty. Family disorganization was not
cited as a major cause of Black poverty and oppression by Black scholars during that period (Engram, 1982; Davis, 1990).

The Pathologists

The pathologists' approach is primarily identified with Daniel Patrick Moynihan's report (1965) on the Negro family, which contained the thesis that weaknesses in the Black family are at the heart of the deterioration of the Black community. While using many of the same indexes of family disorganization as the poverty-acculturation approach, Moynihan's approach is distinguished by at least three other factors: (1) it occurred in a different era and had significant import for the formulation of public policy; (2) most scholars using this model were White; and (3) in effect, it placed the blame for racial inequality on the Black family, specifically on Black women.

Moynihan and his followers (Aldous, 1969; Bernard, 1966; Rainwater, 1970) initiated the study of the Black family as a pathological form of social organization at precisely the time when Blacks were beginning to indict institutional racism as the cause of their lower status. The civil rights movement was entering a militant phase when the government-subsidized Moynihan study made public the assertion that weaknesses in the Black family, such as out-of-wedlock births, female-headed households, and welfare dependency, were responsible for poverty, educational failures, and lack of employment in the Black population. Moynihan's efforts put Blacks on the defensive and diverted their energy into responding to his charges (Rainwater and Yancey, 1967). In the mid-1960s, the Moynihan thesis was taken up by a number of behavioral scientists who found it very easy to get funds for studies concentrating on the identification of Black family dysfunctions. During this period, one found the strange situation of the majority of White family research being based on middle-class families and almost all studies of Black families dealing with the lower 25 percent of the Black class strata (Allen, 1995; Demos, 1990).

The Reactive Period

Lasting roughly from 1966 to 1971, the behavioral scientists during the reactive period included both Blacks and Whites. Basically, this group argued that Black families were much like White families except for their impoverished status and history of slavery. Although there were exceptions, most agreed that permissive sex, out-of-wedlock children, and female-headed households were undesirable and that improved economic conditions would reduce the prevalence of these phenomena among Black families. In some cases, investigators denied any significant distinctions between Black and White families. If one considered social class differences, Black families were much the same as White families. Even upper lower-class Black families were found to have the same value system as White families (Liebow, 1966; Scanzoni, 1978; Willie, 1970).

While the research and theory during this period portrayed the Black family as victim rather than criminal, it still gave no positive value to the unique traits of Black family structure. For the most part, it apologized for the political economic system that had imposed these "undesirable" family characteristics on Black Americans. It was rare for any members of this group to call into question the value of the dominant group's form of family organization. To have done so would have undermined the dominance of the Anglo-Saxon values, which had prevailed since the first White settlement on these shores. However, as White youth of America began to reject traditional family lifestyles, their emerging forms of marriage and the family approximated those of Black families. Hence, what had been negatively labeled when associated with Blacks had to be validated when it became part of the White cultural system.

What was known as the notorious matriarchy among Blacks is now regarded as female-centered families in the White community. The common law marriages (or living together) that existed among Blacks have been redefined and reevaluated as heterosexual cohabitation for Whites. In the past, Black involvement in premarital sexual relations was seen as immoral and licentious. Today, it is interpreted as part of the sexual freedom movement and has become an annual $10 billion industry. All of these changes may be perceived as part of a social system that denies any value to a racial minority's value system unless or until it becomes a part of the dominant group's cultural context (Skolnick, 1992).

Black Nationalist Family Studies

Research from a Black nationalist perspective not only considers Black families nonpathological but delineates their strengths as well. The first significant work was that of Andrew Billingsley (1968) in the era of Black Power movements. Billingsley's work was a combination of the reactive and nationalist orientations. He challenged the Moynihan report for its depiction of the Black family as pathological but continued to accept many normative values of White middle-class family life. Billingsley was, however, one of the first scholars to perceive the Black family as viable and to indict the political and economic system for its neglect of Black families. His initial study has been elaborated on and extended by a number of other Black scholars. In the post-Billingsley period, the more significant works on Black families were produced by young Black scholars. A large number of articles and books were devoted to the strengths of Black women (Cade, 1970; Ladner, 1971; Staples, 1973). In general, these studies focused on the severe conditions that Black women encountered and their courage and strength in overcoming those obstacles. Another landmark study was by Robert Hill (1972), the first scholar to systematically define and examine the strengths of the Black family. Furthermore, he used quantitative data to support his propositions about the positive values in the Black American family life.

At the end of the 1960s, controversy was still raging over the Moynihan report (1965). Moynihan's assertion that "at the root of the deterioration of Black society was the deterioration of the Black family" (p. 5.) stimulated extensive theory formation and research on the Black family. Over one hundred books and one thousand articles related to the Black family were published between 1970 and 1990. That twenty-year period produced ten times more Black family literature than the entire hundred years before. Moreover, this work was of a qualitatively different genre. In the early stages, it was primarily a response to the triumvirate of Frazier (1939), Moynihan (1965), and Rainwater (1970), who had uniformly depicted the lower-class Black family as pathological. Subsequently, researchers began to produce studies of the Black family as an autonomous unit.

The Neoconservative Era

Two decades after the Moynihan report, there was a basic transformation in ideology and research on the Black family. Prior to the 1970s, the common wisdom was that Black families, in comparison to White middle-class families, were dysfunctional units that could not carry out the normative functions ascribed to that institution. In the following decades, the research emphasis shifted to the investigation of stable Black families and their conformity to middle-class family norms. However, it was in those same decades that the economic losses of Blacks were translated into greater family instability for many of them, again raising the question of the relationship between Black family stability and changes in the larger society. Based on the latest census data (U.S. Census Bureau, 1990), there was a dramatic increase in teenage pregnancies, out-of-wedlock births, single-parent households, and marital dissolution among Blacks of all social classes. While these trends parallel developments in White families during the same period, they inspired a change in theory and research on the Black family.

The neoconservative mood of the 1980s gave rise to a greater visibility of books on the Black family that could be embraced by political conservatives. Among those books were work by Jewell (1988) and Wilson (1987). Although both authors appear to disclaim the label of neoconservatives for themselves, their theories of Black family problems lend themselves to the conservative side of the political spectrum. For example, Wilson simply repeats the Moynihan line about the social pathology of inner-city Black families. His call for the deemphasis of race-specific policies would be used to undercut support for affirmative action and a host of social welfare measures. Jewell's book (1988) advances the thesis that liberal social programs played a major role in the decline of two-parent Black families over a twenty-year period. Her alternatives to these welfare measures are a combination of self-help measures through the use of kinship networks and institutions in the Black community.

Along with the expansion of Black family research came the development of new theoretical constructs. Allen (1978) identified three ideological perspectives or value orientations in Black family studies: cultural deviant, cultural equivalent, and cultural variant. The cultural deviant approach views Black families as pathological. The cultural equivalent perspective confers a legitimacy on Black families as long as their family lifestyle conforms to middle-class family norms. The cultural variant orientation depicts Black families as different but functional family forms. In an analysis of the treatment of Black families in the research literature between 1965 and 1978, Johnson (1988) discovered that the literature shifted dramatically from a cultural deviant to a cultural equivalent perspective in the 1970s. The cultural variant perspective, which views the Black family as a culturally unique, legitimate unit, continues to be underrepresented in mainstream journals. In fact, predominantly Black journals and a special issue of the *Journal of Marriage and the Family* on Black families (Peters, 1978) accounted for 74 percent of the articles published using a cultural variant perspective in the 1970s.

Major Scholars of the Black Family

It is generally accepted that the precursor of sociological research and theories on the Black family was the late Black sociologist E. Franklin Frazier. He began investigating the Black family in the 1920s, and his works are still considered the classic studies of Black family life in America (Frazier, 1932a, 1932b, 1939). As a sociologist, Frazier was primarily interested in race relations as a social process, and he sought to explain that process through the study of the Black family.

Through his training in the University of Chicago's social ecology school, Frazier came to believe that race relations proceeded through different stages of development, with the final stage being assimilation. Since it is through the family that the culture of a group is transmitted, Frazier chose this group as the object of his sociological study. Using the natural history approach to the study of Black family life, he explained the condition of this group as the culmination of an evolutionary process, its structure strongly affected by the vestiges of slavery, racism, and economic exploitation. Slavery virtually destroyed the cultural moorings of Blacks and prevented any perpetuation of African kinship and family relations. Consequently, the Black family developed variegated forms according to the different situations it encountered (Frazier, 1939).

Variations in sex and marital practices, according to Frazier, grew out of the social heritage of slavery, and what slavery began, the pattern of racism and economic deprivation continued to impose on the family life of Black Americans. The variations that he spoke of included the following: (1) the matriarchal character of the Black family, whereby Black males became marginal and ineffective figures in the family constellation; (2) the instability of marital life, because the lack of a legal basis for marriage during the period of slavery meant that marriage never acquired the position of a strong institution in Black life and casual sex relations were the norm; and (3) the destruction, through the process of urbanization, of the stability of family life that had existed among Black peasant folk in an agrarian society (Frazier, 1939). Most of Frazier's studies were limited to pre–World War II Black family life. His research method was the use of case studies and documents whose content he analyzed and from which he attempted to deduce a pattern of Black family life.

The next large-scale "theory" of the Black family was developed by Moynihan (1965) and pertained to Black family life in the 1960s; it was based largely on census data. Moynihan developed the thesis that "at the heart of the deterioration of the fabric of Negro society is the deterioration of the Negro family" (p. 5). He attempted to document his major proposition by citing statistics on the diminishing rate of Black marriages, the higher rate of Black out-of-wedlock births, the prevalence of female-headed households in the Black community, and the shocking increase in welfare dependency caused by the deterioration of the Black family.

This study of Black families, commonly referred to as the Moynihan report, generated a largely critical response. In effect, Moynihan had made a generalized indictment of all Black families. And although he cited the antecedents of slavery and high unemployment as important variables historically, he shifted the burden of Black deprivation onto the Black family rather than indicting the American social structure (Rainwater and Yancey, 1967). The Moynihan report assumed a greater importance than other studies on the Black family for several reasons. As an official government publication, it implied a shift in the government's position on dealing with the effects of racism and economic deprivation on the Black community. The conclusion drawn by most people was that whatever his solution, it would focus on strengthening the Black family rather than dealing with the more relevant problems of racial segregation and discrimination.

It is reasonable to assume that if Frazier had written in a later period, he would probably have taken Black nationalist tendencies and their impact on Black family structure into account. Unlike Moynihan, he would undoubtedly not have placed the blame for the Black condition on family structure. But Frazier's and Moynihan's studies share certain commonalities. Both deal with the Black family in a structural manner. That is, they examine its form and the arrangement of roles within the family constellation rather than the behavior that transpires within the structure (Platt, 1987). Only in the post-Moynihan study by Lee Rainwater (1970) are the dynamic processes that take place critically examined.

Just as Moynihan attempts to quantify Frazier's suppositions about the Black family, Rainwater tries to expand on, and analyze in depth, the Black family's role in the "tangle of pathology" that pervades the Black community. The Rainwater thesis is essentially the same as Moynihan's: Black family disorganization evolved out of a history of enslavement and racial discrimination, and as a result, Black family life itself has become a major factor in sustaining and perpetuating the poor conditions under which Black Americans are forced to live. As Rainwater (1966, p. 258) states the problem, "The victimization process as it operates in families prepares and toughens its members to function in the ghetto world, at the same time that it seriously interferes with their ability to operate in any other world." There are some, albeit minor, distinctions between the Moynihan and Rainwater investigations of Black family life. Unlike Moynihan, Rainwater confines his analysis to lower-income Black families and does not generalize his findings of massive family disorganization to the entire Black population. But he does note that other literature on Black family life suggests that his findings are applicable beyond his sample of ten thousand people in the Pruitt-Igoe housing projects in St. Louis.

The work of Jessie Bernard (1966) reflects a typical middle-class bias in studying Black family life. Bernard ignores income levels as determinant variables in the explanation of Black family life and formulates the concept of two "cultural strands" to shed light on Black family patterns. These relate to the degree of acculturation—that is, the extent to which individuals have internalized the moral norms of Western society as these exist in the United States. One strand is labeled the acculturated; in this case, Western norms become an intrinsic part of people's personality. This is generally considered the "respectable" strand. The other strand is known as the externally adapted. Among this group, the norms relating to marriage and the family are only superficially adhered to; they are not a matter of internal conviction. This group learns to use and manipulate White culture rather than take over its norms (Bernard, 1966).

A somewhat similar middle-class bias occurs in Billingsley's work (1968), but unlike Bernard, he concentrates heavily on economic forces influencing the pattern of Black family life. Billingsley views many manifestations of the Black family as a result of the overrepresentation of Black families in the poverty category. The Billingsley position differs from that of Moynihan and Rainwater in that he sees the Black family as a strong and resilient institution in both a historical and a contemporary sense. However, Billingsley uses middle-class models and norms to support his position. Instead of stressing the fact that Black marital and family behaviors represent positive functions and values in the social organization of the Black community, he accepts the negative view of the Black family and responds that this negative situation is a predictable response to repressive forces in American society. For example, he devotes an entire chapter to successful upper-class Black families rather than outlining the positive values in much of working-class family life (Billingsley, 1968).

Billingsley's middle-class bias is strongly reflected in his structural study of Black families. Like previous authors, he confines himself to describing the family structure and the arrangement of roles in the family constellation. He does not explore the interior of the Black family and examine some of the sociodynamic processes that contribute to its character. His view is mostly that of a middle-class sociologist who accepts middle-class norms, concludes that most Black families share middle-class value orientations, and prescribes action to eliminate poverty to bring disadvantaged Black families into conformity with the model middle-class family.

But despite its weaknesses, Billingsley's work represents an advance over previous research and theory on the Black family. At least he recognizes that the Black family constitutes a unit of considerable variety and complexity, that many of its constituent features are a misunderstood source of strength in the Black community, and that some of its characteristics have been given invidious labels by those whose motives are politically suspect.

On this foundation, others have tried to develop a sociology of the Black family. In the post-Billingsley era, most of the theorists have responded to the Moynihan thesis about the instability of Black families. In addition, they have attempted to delineate the structure and function of Black families. The goals may have been similar, but the perspectives have fallen into one of Allen's typologies (1978). Studies by Heiss (1975), Scanzoni (1978), and Willie (1988) would belong in the cultural equivalent category. Both Heiss and Scanzoni use quantitative analysis to illustrate that Black families are stable, egalitarian, and functional units. They make this judgment on the basis of how well these families meet the Anglo-Saxon middle-class ideal. Willie uses qualitative analysis and examines a variety of Black families. Poor Black families are still depicted as less-than-healthy units. Hill's study (1972) of the strengths of Black families occupies a middle ground. Through the use of census data, he demonstrates that Black families, like White families, adhere to such sacrosanct American values as strong work, achievement, and religious orientations. He also stresses the traits of strong kinship bonds and role flexibility in the Black family, although he does not link them to an autonomous cultural system.

Reflecting the conservative political ideology of the period, many books and articles appearing in the 1980s argued that liberal welfare and social policies had created a welfare-dependent class that was destroying the Black family. One of those books was by K. Sue Jewell (1988). She contends that these social policies not only failed to bring about the significant Black progress expected in the civil rights era, but they destroyed the mutual aid and support networks of Black American families. Her methodology consists mostly of examining the literature on Black families and social policies and drawing her own conclusions about the status of Black families and the effectiveness of social policies. Although she claims a nonpartisan approach, most of her criticism is reserved for the liberal social policies of the 1960s and 1970s. This thesis has several serious flaws that render it less than useful to policymakers and students of the Black American family.

One is her central assumption that social welfare policies played a major role in the decline of two-parent families among Black Americans. Her main support for this thesis is that the decline of biparental black families happened during the twenty-year period when these social policies were created or were in effect. Other students of Black family destabilization have been more inclined to attribute those changes in family structure—for both Blacks and Whites—largely to the shift of American jobs overseas, the change from industrial jobs to service and high-technology occupations, and the redistribution of wealth from the poor to the wealthy in the 1980s.

The work of Wilson (1987) has assumed the dominant position in Black family studies once occupied by the Moynihan report (1965) and is almost as controversial in some circles. Wilson's book *The Truly Disadvantaged: The Inner City, the Underclass, and Public Policy* is not a study of the Black family but of the lower-income Black population in general. Only one chapter in the book directly concerns Black families, and it discusses solely the impact of economic changes on its structure. While Wilson acknowledges that the cause of Black family destabilization is the high rate of unemployment among Black males, he sees only economic forces as a contributing factor; he fails to emphasize the combination of racial and economic forces that have placed Blacks in such a high-risk position in the American economy from the outset. When he deals with noneconomic variables, it is to depict the culture of inner-city Blacks as dysfunctional in meeting the requirements of American industry. This work is a logical continuation of his earlier book *The Declining Significance of Race: Blacks and Changing American Institutions* (1980), in which he argues that class factors have become more important than racial forces. The appeal of that earlier work seemed to be the deemphasis on racial discrimination as a significant variable and the attendant implication that race-specific remedies were no longer necessary.

Melvin Oliver and Thomas Shapiro's book *Black Wealth/White Wealth* (1995) represents one of the most significant scholarly works of the 1990s to challenge the centrality of class in Black families' marginalized status. While it is not a book on Black families per se, it provides insights into the roots of the struggle that Black families endure. The rise of Black middle-class families is heralded by some as evidence that Blacks can succeed if they possess an upward mobility orientation and acquire the necessary education. In contrast, Oliver and Shapiro argue that racial comparisons by income are misleading. If wealth is the unit of analysis, most Black families, middle class included, are truly disadvantaged. The racial gap in wealth—including home ownership and other assets—supersedes income gaps. Most Blacks do not have "transformative assets": gifts from parents and significant others that work to minimize debt and move succeeding generations economically and socially beyond the achievements of their predecessors.

The authors assert that in order for Black families to meet the challenges of a shifting economy Blacks must not only receive adequate training, they must also begin on a level playing field. Government policies of suburbanization, redlining, and federal taxation work to the disadvantage of Blacks: three times as many Whites as Blacks grow up in households with three months of financial reserves. And 61 percent of Black households have no financial assets—twice as many as White households.

By focusing on wealth—including total assets and debts—rather than income alone, the authors uncover deep and persistent racial inequality in the United States that reveals a qualitative difference in lifestyle between Black and White families with similar income. Oliver and Shapiro challenge the assertions that the failure of Black entrepreneurship and upward mobility is rooted in a poor work ethic. Their study provides not a rebuttal of the importance of class but rather an insight into how class is racialized. They thus provide a counterpoint to the class-based social inequality thesis and challenge beliefs of economic parity between Black and White middle-class families.

Summary

In this review of perspectives on Black family life, it is clear that few studies have had the explanatory power to enrich our understanding of this institution. This theoretical deficit exists partly because there is no theory of the family in general and also because the theories applied to this unique institution have been designed to explain nonfamily phenomena. All explanations of Black family functioning were developed in some kind of political context, either positive or negative. Politics enters the study of the Black family because this social unit has been perceived not as an institution but as a social problem. The research has focused disproportionately on lower-class Black families to address poverty, welfare dependency, and crime. These problems might best be understood by other theories regarding social structure, not by studying their consequences in the family life of Black Americans.

In summary, it can be said that in trying to understand Black family life, there remain questions to be answered and answers to be questioned. What we know from past research is that the Black family has evolved a unique structure and style to cope with the circumstances it has confronted. To build a theory of the Black family, we must ascertain the norms and values that animate the process of family interaction and determine how that process is related to the forces that have shaped it and its various expressions in American life. This is the task before us; how we can fulfill it is not clear. In this summary and analysis of theory on the Black family in the past century, one fact seems certain: we cannot develop a viable theory of the Black family based on the myths and stereotypes that have pervaded past research.

3

Work and Money

The Struggle

Money derived from work is a basic determinant of the way families survive, maintain self-esteem, and acquire social prestige within their communities. While work has always been a part of the Black experience, it has not always generated monetary and self-gratifying rewards. Underemployment, pay inequity, job layoffs, and the lack of wealth (through inheritance, savings, and earnings) have resulted in dehumanizing experiences for far too many throughout history. Among Blacks in precolonial Africa, work took place within two distinct arenas: their home and their own communities. There, work and money were equally yoked: one reaped what one sowed. After colonization, a third arena was added: the unpaid and paid workforce of the White world. It is in this last arena that the equity between work and money broke. Within these three arenas, we chronicle the work and money nexus and its impact on Black family life.

Transition Economy: Africa, Slavery, Freedom

Since antiquity, the family has been an economic unit that most often divides its labor along gender lines. This is not to imply that "men's work" and "women's work" are biological imperatives, noninterchangeable, or never shared. Cross-cultural studies clearly show that task assignments (apart from childbearing) are primarily a function of cultural, political, and economic forces, not biology. Among the

African Nambikwara, for example, infants are cared for by the fathers, and the chiefs' concubines prefer to engage in hunting rather than domestic work (Strong and DeVault, 1995). Among the Ibo tribe of the Niger Delta region, women and men toil together in planting, weeding, and harvesting, whereas the Yoruba women only help with harvest. While caution must be taken in generalizing from the diverse traditions of various African peoples, studies of contemporary West African women reveal a fairly common feature of economic independence, a pattern rooted in their early history.

In precolonial West African societies, for example, women had entrepreneurial relationships with domestic and foreign traders. As producers, processors, traders, craftswomen, distributors, and manufacturers, they parlayed their profits into larger and more profitable enterprises. Not only were women cherished as daughters, but they were an economic asset as wives and a cornerstone of the economy; thus, they accrued high self-esteem and enormous influence in their communities. African wives enjoyed complete control over their goods and profits. While family authority rested with the husbands, the wives' ownership of goods remained completely separate from their husbands'. Their earnings enabled them to buy clothes and jewelry, improve the family menu, provide gifts for relatives, and in effect contribute to the family's wealth. In patrilineal societies, wives' economic independence was facilitated by the fact that children belonged to the fathers. A wife had no primary responsibility for either the rearing or economic support of the children, thus allowing her greater liberty in using her earnings to satisfy her own desires (Griffin, 1982).

With the advent of slavery in the United States, the ruthless exploitation of Black labor began: the linkage between money, work, wealth, and self-worth was broken. The division of labor that existed prior to enslavement was replaced with a work structure of the master's choosing. Without a legal right to acquire property and other assets or to acquire literacy skills, slaves had no relationship to the means of production that could bring them status in the slave or nonslave communities and gained few tangible physical benefits from their work. Self-esteem and worth primarily derived from the slaves' contribution to their own families and communities. Grannies' folk medicine usurped the White physician, who rarely took calls from the slave quarters. Despite inordinate hours of slave work, fathers and grandfathers found energy to make animal traps for catching game and tend gardens in order to supplement their families' limited diet. They also made furniture and shoes to enhance their families' comfort and health. Ironically, even their efforts to care for themselves and their families helped maintain their masters' workforce and increase their profits (Jones, 1985; Blassingame, 1972).

Men and women were equal in the sense that neither gender wielded economic power over the other. Slaveholders did not support sentimental platitudes about the delicate constitution of female slaves. Both genders worked at a forced pace under close supervision of White men and women. Because slave masters frequently suspected slave women of faking illness or "playing the lady" at their expense, many were brutal in forcing women into the field during pregnancy and soon after childbirth. Women at times were mandated to labor in areas generally reserved for men, such as in the muscle power work of clearing land of trees, rolling logs, and chopping and hauling wood. However, only male slaves labored as skilled artisans or mechanics. The cost of training women for these trades was considered too high, since their work lives were frequently interrupted by childbearing and nursing.

While many historians often make distinctions between the workload intensity of the house and field slave, there is little evidence supporting the advantages of housework. From late July to December, every man, woman, and child engaged in picking cotton. As few as 5 percent of all antebellum adult slaves served in their master's house. Of these, most lived in the slave cabin at night and rose early in the morning to perform duties in the master's house before heading for the fields. Furthermore, housework was laborious, and juggling the demands of each member of the master's family was frustrating. Meals had to be cooked and served three times a day, "flies minded" with peacock-feather brushes, and dishes washed (Jones, 1982, 1985; Griffin, 1982). An account of a son's memory of his mother's work illustrates how writers have exaggerated the elite position of the house slave. She served as personal maid to the master's daughter, cooked for all hands on the plantation, carded cotton, spun a daily quota of thread, and wove and dyed cloth. Every Wednesday she carried the White family's laundry three-quarters of a mile to a creek, where she beat each garment with a wooden paddle. Ironing consumed the rest of her day. Like the lowliest field hand, she felt the lash if any tasks went undone (Jones, 1982). Because of the watchful eyes of multiple masters within the house, many slaves preferred the open field. Regardless of work location, unremitting toil without pay was the dominant characteristic of enslaved Africans.

Their chains loosened by the distractions of the Civil War, nearly 400,000 slaves voluntarily or involuntarily joined the Union Army in hopes of freedom for themselves and their families. For most, it was their first promise of a cash incentive for their labors as well as the beginning of their experience with unpredictable and unequal wages. Throughout the war and into the early 1900s, Blacks resisted the Northern work ethic of yielding to employers all authority over their individual working conditions. They also resisted the Southern system, which expected the entire family—husband, wife, and children—to work in the fields (Pinderhughes, 1991; Malveaux, 1988; Jones, 1985). In an effort to control both their labor and family life, former slaves turned to sharecropping.

As sharecroppers, they cultivated and harvested all the crops on a White person's land in exchange for shelter and a share of the profits or produce. This voluntary system, however, was not benevolent. Blacks were disenfranchised and constantly struggled with the unscrupulous financial dealings of their White employers. The constant pressure of poverty meant that sharecroppers in the rural South experienced many of the situations common in contemporary inner cities. For example, female-headed households increased as men migrated from rural areas in search of temporary work in the burgeoning industrialized Southern towns. Men's mobility and the labor-intensive agrarian economy meant that there was little social condemnation of out-of-wedlock childbearing. Under these conditions, children were a genuine labor asset. Nevertheless, most families were headed by two adults who (like single parents) were often embedded in a supportive extended family (Lemann, 1991; Williams, 1990; Jones, 1985; Harris, 1976; Johnson, 1934).

Exercising the limited control they had over how family labor would be organized, sharecroppers chose to sharpen the sexual division of labor; the major obligation of wives was domestic, and husbands' responsibility was fieldwork. This was not an effort to model the White nuclear family, for, as seen in Chapter Nine, the extended family was a viable structure. Rather, all efforts were being made to keep wives and daughters away from the exploitation of White supervisors.

Low and unpredictable wages meant that most families relied less on wages and more on family farming, fishing, and trapping to keep body and soul together. Few wives could remain home tending children. Some wives tried to turn special talents and skills into a secure living, but the poor Black community could not support such professions as seamstresses, midwives, and schoolteachers. Furthermore, Whites as employers were too resentful and unreliable. Whites believed that any able-bodied Black should be confined to the soil or serving as a domestic worker. To the liking of Whites, low wages paid to Black men forced most Black working women into one of the few available occupations: domestic work with White families. According to the 1890 census, almost 40 percent of all Black women were employed outside the home, the overwhelming majority in farming and the legendary domestic and washerwomen occupations. Household employment not only paid poorly, but it was irregular, part time, and seasonal, a pattern that remains even today. In some areas, domestics waited on designated streets as potential employers drove by to choose their employee for the day. The low pay and unpredictability of such work forced Black women into holding multiple jobs (Harrison, 1989; Jones, 1985; Malveaux, 1988).

Pushed out of the South by agricultural mechanization as well as by boll weevil infestation and storms that destroyed cotton in the early 1900s, Blacks began moving north in what is referred to as the Great Migration. On arrival, Black domestic workers found themselves in head-on competition with White immigrants, who organized to keep Black men and women out of the most menial jobs. Consequently, the majority of Black workers remained in agriculture. When European immigration was stopped during World War I, Black workers replaced White immigrants in domestic work. As the demands of the war economy increased and the national manpower crises intensified, Blacks were overtly recruited from the South to the North to work in the steel mills, auto and railroad companies, and cotton industries. Some entered factory work over the resistance of lower-class Whites, who wanted these higher-paying jobs for themselves. These jobs doubled the salaries of many Blacks. From 1910 to 1920, more than fifty thousand Blacks arrived in Chicago, increasing the Black population by 117.1 percent. Similar influxes were reported in Pittsburgh, New York, Philadelphia, and St. Louis (Lemann, 1991; Harrison, 1989; Wilson, 1980).

It was shortly after this period that Frazier (1939) wrote about the disorganizing effect that slavery and urbanization had on Black families. Occasionally the men came first, with the idea of sending for their wives and children later. Some families that were reunited later experienced the husband-father deserting when jobs were not forthcoming, while others were never reunited. Thus, female-headed households rose in number. Frazier further notes that marriages were kept together in the South by the social control exercised by the church, the Negro Masonic lodges, and the opinions of socially close neighbors; these controls were lost in the Northern cities. The social upheaval that resulted in loss of community support for family stability was compounded when the White soldiers returned from each of the world wars and took over their old jobs, leaving many Black heads of households unemployed or underemployed and struggling to capture the most menial work.

The Great Depression placed hardships on all Americans, but Blacks were hit the hardest. Black and White wives, who were more likely to get a job than their male partners, pitched in to weather the economic storm. This is not to say that women had economic superiority during this time. When men worked, regardless of race, they were more likely to work more hours per week and earn substantially more than their wives; thus, as an aggregate, they did better than the women. For those who could not find work, the New Deal programs developed under the Roosevelt administration helped to create jobs, reducing unemployment from 17 to 7 million (Darity and Myers, 1984; Bullock and Stallybrass, 1977; Harwood and Hodge, 1971). But even here, legislation was designed in such a way that it discriminated against some of the occupations—agricultural and domestic—in which Blacks were concentrated (Jones, 1985). Moreover, the states' standard for Aid to Dependent Children (ADC) eligibility was based on adherence to traditional marital and family arrangements. Indigent unmarried, divorced, or separated Black mothers were thus disqualified to receive ADC benefits. In 1931, 96 percent of ADC recipients were White, while 3 percent were Black (Yao, 1999). In fact, Black workers fell through the cracks of many social programs.

Until recently, this trend of economic hardships was said to have created a fragile Black family. Some have argued from the perspective of exchange theory (see Chapter Two) that no woman wants to marry or stay married to a man who lacks a job. Conversely, men without jobs and money lose not only status in the eyes of women, but faith in their ability to perform the culturally prescribed roles of husband and father. Thus, a Black man is less likely to ask for a woman's hand in marriage or stay in a marriage. Lack of job or money is the most frequently emphasized explanation for marital instability. However, the contemporary indictment of unemployment and poverty for hindering marital formation and stability is not historically justified.

Historical revisionists note that Black families have survived periods of severe hardship. Despite Frazier's concern about female-headed households emerging from slavery and the Great Migration, the overwhelming number of Black marriages was intact during these periods as well as up until the late 1960s. The question that begs an answer is why poverty and unemployment create family disorganization in contemporary society but built family strength in an earlier era. A response to this question is needed to fully understand the socioeconomic dynamics of marital relationships today without placing primary blame on Black families.

Some argue that under slavery, Blacks were exploited but fully employed. Because they were valued as property, the White masters ensured them a minimum subsistence: meals, lodging, and clothing. For the sake of worker morale, families were generally preserved (Frederickson, 1976). Fogel and Engerman (1974) extend the nonexploitation argument by claiming that slaves were willing collaborators in a capitalist enterprise. They worked for real incentives, which included upward mobility within the slave system and protection of their families. Yet emancipation brought massive unemployment and meager wages, and the marital union remained intact. This is attributed to the fact that postslavery families were often able to make ends meet by combined efforts of family members working at multiple jobs. Moreover, the farming experience of Blacks matched the demands of an agrarian workforce. When the economy moved toward industrialism, Blacks found jobs as reserve labor during the two world wars and as strikebreakers during labor disputes (Johnson, 1989b).

Contemporary Challenges

Today, competition for the most menial jobs is keen. This situation is due to several factors: job relocation, immigration, trade policies, and other legislation. When the current information-based and tech-nological-driven economy replaced the agricultural and industrial economies, Blacks lacked the skills required to compete. This was especially true of Blacks residing in the inner cities. For the general public, this crisis intensified when manufacturing jobs were elimi-nated and replaced by service sector jobs, which are characterized by low pay, few or no benefits, and poor opportunities for career ad-vancement (Cooper, 1998; Mishel, Berstein, and Schmitt, 1997).

For Blacks in the inner city, this crisis intensified when jobs moved from the inner city to the suburbs. A lack of efficient trans-portation from city to suburbs meant that suburbanites and those most affluent captured these jobs. Moreover, within the urban Black ghetto a substantial number of the mom-and-pop stores that pro-vided employment for local residents closed not only as a result of the urban riots of the 1960s, but also because of the changing na-ture of the Black family residential patterns. As Black consumers have become less segregated, they no longer provide the captive sta-ble consumer market on which Black retail merchants depend.

Furthermore, Black merchants must compete against two major groups: large regional or national corporations with outlets in the ghetto and merchants of other ethnic and racial descent. Finding few job opportunities outside the Black community, Asian, His-panic, and Middle Eastern immigrants have replaced Black family stores, filling the new stores with their own family members as em-ployees. As a result, these merchants have been targeted with anger, protest, and riots from Black residents, who claim that they take from the community without giving back jobs. These groups, along with White women, have also displaced Blacks in menial service and domestic jobs in restaurants, airports, and department stores (Brock, 1991; Gibbs, 1988b).

Mom-and-pop stores proved to be a mixed blessing for Black American urban dwellers. These stores served as a stepping-stone for many families, who used the stores' proceeds to educate their children in colleges desegregated by the civil rights movement.

Rather than use their education, management, and technical experience to expand the family business, these children chose less risky occupations with higher and more predictable pay. Of those who pursued entrepreneurship, the majority developed service firms (for example, law, accounting, and automobile sales). Given the reluctance of banks to lend money to businesses located in the ghetto, most of the firms are outside the reach of ghetto residents. Unfortunately, for those remaining in lower-income urban neighborhoods, the family store stepping-stone has vanished (Brock, 1991; Jeffries and Brock, 1991; Hill, 1990; White, 1992).

Adding to this situation is the loss of jobs due to imports and downsizing. Black men are disproportionately affected by imports in the auto, steel, and rubber industries and Black women by imports in the apparel industry. During the 1970s, the American economy began to globalize. Japanese and Western European electronics producers and automakers, among other foreign firms, began importing to the United States. The foreign competition forced many American factories to close. In 1970, for example, Blacks gained 229,000 jobs through exports but lost 287,000 jobs because of imports, for a net loss of 58,000 jobs. Once unemployed, Blacks are twice as likely as White displaced workers to remain without work (Jeffries and Brock, 1991; Hill, 1990).

Whether public assistance undermines the institution of marriage is an ongoing debate, spurred by the fact that among welfare families, marital dissolution is almost twice as high as the chances of marital formation. However, it is a mistake to assume that welfare itself increases marital dissolution, deters marriage formation, and increases the number of children born out of wedlock. There is no convincing evidence that length of time on welfare, changes in welfare benefits, or number of programs from which benefits are received have any significant effects on the likelihood of marital formation or divorce (Washington, 1989; Furstenberg, Brooks-Gunn, and Morgan, 1987; Rank, 1987; Darity and Myers, 1984; Karger and Stoesz, 2002). The culprit is not welfare but the economic difficulties that Black families face. High male unemployment and the declining pool of eligible men to head families also contribute to declines in marital formation.

The lack of fit between the skills of Blacks and the information- and technological-based economy, coupled with unintended negative consequences of trade and immigration policies, has created an unprecedented job crisis for Black families. This crisis occurred during a period when American firms were engaged in large-scale mass production of consumer goods. The capacity of American families to consume these goods emerged as and gave definition to the American dream. Of course, the ability to consume depends on adequate incomes from jobs. Because most Whites had jobs, they were able to consume these goods without seriously straining the household budget; thus, they achieved a new and higher standard of family living. The high unemployment and heavy concentration of Blacks in blue-collar and low-paying occupations mean that many Blacks cannot hope to create this new lifestyle for themselves or their families. Thus, many are discouraged from marrying. For example, among both Black and non-Black men, the proportion with intact marriages rises as income increases (U.S. Census Bureau, 2000). Not surprisingly, this income–marital status relationship is stronger for Blacks than for Whites (Brien, 1997; Jeffries and Brock, 1991; Myers, 1990; Taylor, Chatters, Tucker, and Lewis, 1990; U.S. Census Bureau, 1983).

Given this economic context, it is not surprising that most recent studies focusing on Black-White differences in divorce find that Blacks have higher marital separation and dissolution rates than whites (U.S. Census Bureau, 2002a; McLoyd, Cauce, Takeuchi, and Wilson, 2001). In fact, if divorce and separation rates are combined, the Black-White differences are even greater. The justification for combining the two is that desertion and separation are "the poor person's divorce," reflecting the difficulty those in the low-income brackets have in paying for divorce. Despite this difficulty, Blacks are more likely to separate and divorce regardless of income (or the presence of children), although the differences rapidly narrow as income increases (Bumpass, Sweet, and Martin, 1990; Glenn and Supancic, 1984; Hampton, 1982;

Leslie and Grady, 1985; McLoyd, Cauce, Takeuchi, and Wilson, 2001; U.S. Census Bureau, 1999). Once divorced, Blacks relative to Whites have lower remarriage rates (one-fourth that of Whites), a faster declining remarriage rate, and a longer period between divorce and remarriage. For example, between 1990 and 1998 (McLoyd, Cauce, Takeuchi, and Wilson, 2001), Black men had lower remarriage rates (36.6) than White men (40.7), and they spent longer periods between first divorce and second marriages (U.S. Census Bureau, 2002a).

Some scholars remain undaunted by strong structural arguments that link Black family success and functions to broad societal forces. These scholars prefer cultural models that imply that values and responses learned from previous generations determine the success of individuals and groups (see Chapter Two). Moynihan clearly took a cultural perspective when he concluded that slavery created a value for an "inferior" family structure—female-headed households. For him, the Black family plight results not from racism or the lack of job opportunities, but the inability of Black women to socialize their sons into male-achieving behavior: self-discipline, decisiveness, and a command presence. He and other scholars find support in examples of the "high achievement" of Blacks from the West Indies in the United States.

These notions of foreign-born Blacks' superior economic, occupational, educational, and labor force participation relative to native Blacks can be traced to the early work of Ira Reid, a Black sociologist who conducted a study of West Indian immigrants in the 1930s. Reid (1939) contended that in New York, where most West Indians settled, as many as one-third of Negro professionals—physicians, dentists, lawyers—were foreign born. Some stereotypically labeled them "Black Jews" in recognition of their fine business acumen. Reid's work provides support for those who argue that native Blacks attain lower occupational status because they lack the West Indians' ethos of hard work, saving, investing, and educational pursuit. Although Reid's work provided initial insights, it suffered from limited available data on West Indians. However, his seminal work stimulated Glazer and Moynihan in the 1960s and Thomas Sowell in the 1970s to continuing arguing his point.

Based on the 1970 census, Sowell (1978) found that relative to native Blacks, first- and second-generation West Indians had the highest family income (nearly equal to Whites), educational attainment, labor force participation, business ownership, and family stability. Since employers of second-generation Caribbeans often could not identify them by their accent, he concluded that their relative success undermines White discrimination as a cause of Black poverty. A later study by Reynolds Farley and Walter Allen (1987) refuted most of Sowell's findings. Based on the 1980 census, they found that while West Indians had higher educational attainment, their family income, stability, and labor force participation was similar to native Blacks. Similarly, Robert Hill (1983) found higher educational attainment among West Indian Blacks who responded to the 1979–1980 Black Pulse Survey, a nationally representative survey of three thousand Black households. However, West Indians had similar or only slight advantages in professional attainment and middle-class family income. Given that many foreign born have patterns of segmented immigration—leaving members of their family behind until they get settled—it is not surprising that higher rates of female-headed households emerged among West Indians.

These contrasting findings can be explained by shifting immigration policies. When Reid wrote, immigrants entered the United States under strict immigration laws. This first wave (1910–1920) contained eighty-five thousand immigrants selected on literacy. College-bound students or those with professional degrees received priority. Their arrival coincided with the Great Migration of Blacks from the South to those Northern cities that had experienced labor shortages resulting from World War I. Joining the Blacks already residing in the area, the Black population swelled. Many in this group rose to intellectual, political, and economic prominence during the Harlem Renaissance of the 1930s. By the 1950s, immigration fell to one hundred per year due to restrictive quotas that made Britain more accessible and gave

preference to family reunification, professional occupations, labor certification, and middle-class students. After the 1965 Hart-Celler Act
lifted racial and country quotas, a mass influx of Black immigrants from
every social stratum landed on U.S. soil. By 1975, West Indian immigration exceeded that of the previous seventy years. And by the 1980s,
each year the United States received fifty thousand legal Anglo-
Caribbeans and six thousand to ten thousand Haitians, and half of
them settled in New York. Today, approximately 2.5 million foreign-
born and Caribbean-descent people strive and thrive in America
(Waters, 1999; Billingsley, 1992).

Clearly selective migration has played a major role in the perceived
success of West Indians. But apart from shifts in immigration policies,
consideration must be given to the reality that immigrants are those
with the ambition and drive to move to a place they think provides
better opportunities. It may be that these personalities add up to create a collective profile of highly successful immigrants. The debate now
centers around whether the post-1965 immigrant families and their
children exceed native Blacks in upward mobility or socioeconomic
status. The evidence remains mixed (Hill, 1999; Waters, 1999).

There does tend to be a consensus on labor force participation.
West Indians would rather work than be on welfare; this is particularly true of West Indian women, whose employment rate is higher
than any other major demographic group in New York. Even those
in female-headed households showed higher labor force participation. In 1990, a comparison between native and foreign-born Blacks
showed West Indian men's labor force rate to be 12.3 percent higher
and West Indian women's 13.8 percent higher (89.1 versus 76.8 and
83.0 versus 69.2). Many work two or more jobs. Their work orientation prompted the popular 1990s TV show *In Living Color* to create a Jamaican character who satirically worked twenty-eight jobs
(Waters, 1999). The hilarious skits eclipsed serious issues, such as
child care crises for those parents chasing the American dream (see
Chapter Eight).

Waters (1999) argues that these immigrants are more likely to
accept low-wage, low-status jobs because immigrants' sense of self

is not as bound up with the job. They judge jobs based on comparisons with opportunities available to them back home. They do not perceive the same stigma attached to low-status jobs as do natives. Jobs merely provide a means to save, invest, and acquire tools for family upward mobility. Furthermore, because of their attitudes and their optimistic assessment of American race relations, employers are more likely to hire them than native Blacks. Other scholars find that relative to native Blacks, they perceive more racial discrimination in employment, housing, and transportation (Billingsley, 1992). Perhaps coming from a country where Blacks rule at all levels of government, they may be more sensitive to signs of discrimination, less tolerant of it, and more optimistic about their ability to overcome discrimination.

Unfortunately, too many in the first generation, particularly those arriving without social or economic capital, are not able to pass on their optimism to their children. Inferior public schools and dangerous neighborhoods undermine their hopes for their children's future. Their children who use American, not Caribbean, standards to measure paths to success find jobs with low wages and poor working conditions unacceptable. Furthermore, on the streets and in the schools, these children experience racism firsthand or live it vicariously through the life of their native-born Black peer group. Hence, unlike their parents, racism weighs heavily on their attitudes and behavior toward the dominant culture.

Contrary to classic assimilation theory (see Chapter Two), which assumes upward mobility through integration and adaptation to American culture, second-generation children who hold onto their ethnic background have higher rates of success. Ethnic retention is particularly important for those arriving with few economic resources. Resisting Americanization by actively participating in Caribbean social networks within ethnically rooted churches and voluntary Caribbean organizations provides them with the social resources for job networking and educational subsidies, as well as the context for the community of older Caribbean adults to reinforce the strategies and values that gave their parents an upward-bound advantage.

As Black immigrants strive to succeed, a clearer understanding of the distinction between race and ethnicity emerges. Unlike European immigrants, who struggle to minimize their ethnicity by shedding their Irish, Polish, German, or Slavic identity in favor of becoming White Americans, Black immigrants often lose status if they deny their cultural distinctiveness. Black immigrants seeking acceptance face a no-win situation: in an anti-immigrant environment, race adds a further handicap to their foreign status. Yet shedding their immigrant identity to become a Black American does not preclude stigmatization; they merely become a member of a low-status group. In general, for Black immigrants, the more socially mobile they are, the more that ethnic identity serves as a hedge against their racial identity (Waters, 1999; Ostine, 1998).

No theory can explain all the intricate aspects of human interaction within the varied cultural context. Without question, family structure and functions continuously adapt to the pressures and opportunities presented by society. The question remains as to whether the family or society exerts more pressure. It certainly may be the case, as Andrew Billingsley (1992) notes: "Subcultural differences, as important as they are, are no match for the forces of powerful social systems" (p. 274). Yet the human will to overcome odds cannot be denied. An eclectic perspective seems reasonable in that varying degrees of cultural and structural factors operate to provide differential outcomes for native Blacks and those of Caribbean descent. As we have seen with the 1966 Moynihan report, taking a strong structural or cultural position is not merely an academic pursuit; emphasis given to one or the other has strong implications for policy (Waters, 1999).

Gender Economics

Apart from the purely economic issues, there is an important interplay between social norms and economics that weighs heavily on Black families. In American tradition, the role of wage carrier is prescribed to the male, leaving housekeeping and child rearing to the female. The economic stability of the White patriarchal family is based on this division of labor—most important, on the economic dependency and general subordination of the wives. Inadequacy in these prescribed roles is likely to create individual and marital tension. In attempting to fulfill these roles, Black American marriages have faced obstacles not encountered by most other Americans. Black men generally are assumed to be in a humiliating double bind: they must prove their manhood by being the primary—or, ideally, the sole—wage earner, but they are denied access to legitimate ways in which to fulfill this role (Cazenave, 1981). They are the last to be hired and the first to be fired. Young Black men on average earned three-quarters of the income of Whites in 1995 (Mishel, Bernstein, and Schmitt, 1997). Once unemployed, they are about twice as likely as White displaced workers to remain unemployed (Hill, 1990). While it is true that during the 1970 and 1980 periods of economic recession and recovery, unemployed Black women found jobs more slowly than Black men, White men, and White women, society holds men responsible for being the primary family breadwinner; a woman's unemployment is viewed less harshly. A sizable majority of young Black people, particularly females, believe that regardless of who is the better wage earner, the primary responsibility of the man is to provide financially for his family (Harrison, 1989; Heiss, 1988; Johnson, 1980). This preference for male financial leadership is perhaps even stronger in American West Indian families, who represent a growing minority within the Black community. For them, any departure from male authority directly attacks manhood and is totally intolerable (Millette, 1990).

The double bind tightens in the face of flashy mass media messages that stimulate in American families an insatiable appetite for material goods. Black more than White wives play the role of "chief consumptionist." Regardless of their own financial contribution, many Black women, particularly middle-class women, expect marriage to double their material wealth (Heiss, 1988; Osmond, 1977; Scanzoni, 1978). A honeymoon on a luxury cruise ship and yearly vacations thereafter, a home, fine clothing, the latest home technology, cars, campers, and so on are all part of their American dream. In trying to fulfill this dream, credit buying is used to compensate for lower income. Almost twice as many Black as White middle-class people owe on their credit accounts. The higher the social class, the more likely Black families will be to be in debt with a new car. In contrast, the White upper and lower middle classes have new cars in the same proportions.

Moreover, there is no evidence that Blacks have given up their fetish for "fine threads," or what Frazier in 1957 labeled the "clothing cult." Even when their income is lower and their families smaller, Black upper- and lower-middle-class families spend more on clothes than their White counterparts (Landry, 1987). In the wake of low income, pay disparities, desires for increased consumption, and mounting debts, the American dream is a nightmare for many Black males. This nightmare is intensified by four back-to-back recessions and record-level inflations of the 1970s and 1980s, which reduced the real income of Blacks to a greater extent than Whites. Hence, the median income of Black families in 1994 was 40 percent of that of White families with a mere increase of $1,132 from 1989 to 1995 (Mishel, Bernstein, and Schmitt, 1997).

Not surprisingly, Blacks are half as likely as Whites to express satisfaction with their salary and more likely to complain about the cost of living (Bowman, 1991; Firebaugh and Harley, 1995; Riley, 2000). They cannot even expect to live up to the standards of the particular class in which they find themselves. Even among the upper-middle class Black families, Whites not only exceed the income of Blacks but they have twelve times the median wealth of Blacks (Oliver and Shapiro, 1995).

Tragically, the Black male's best efforts in preparing for the job market do not necessarily ensure him equal employment opportunities or the chance to live out the American dream. One such example is reflected in the relationship between education and unemployment rates of Blacks and Whites (U.S. Census Bureau, 2001b; see Table 3.1). Whites with less than a high school diploma have lower unemploy-

**Table 3.1. Unemployment Rates by Educational
Attainment and Race, 1992–2000.**

Educational Levels	Whites	Blacks	Difference
All educational levels	3.0	5.4	−2.4
Less than a high school diploma	7.5	10.4	−2.9
High school graduate, no degree	3.3	6.3	−3.0
Less than a bachelor's degree	2.7	4.3	−1.6
College graduate	1.4	2.5	−1.1

Source: U.S. Census Bureau (2001b).

ment rates than Blacks at that same level, and at each of the other educational levels, Blacks are twice as likely as Whites to be unemployed. Institutionalized employment discrimination is an inescapable reality (Cooper, 1998; Oliver and Shapiro, 1995). The exclusion of Black youth from the expanding sectors of the economy destroys hope of racial parity in the near or distant future (Myers, 1990; Gardecki, 2001; Harrison, 1989; Malveaux, 1988; Larson, 1988; Smith, 1985; Beckett and Smith, 1981).

Moreover, Blacks learn early that even money does not give them the sense of mastery over their life that is available to Whites. Blacks at the same social status as Whites receive fewer dollars and less respect, prestige, and sense of social worth. Over the past few decades, Blacks have shifted their measurement of family well-being. Rather than using their distance from slavery as their benchmark, they now evaluate how close they are to the American dream relative to Whites. Of particular interest to Blacks is parity in education, income, and job status. Unfortunately, while Blacks have made absolute progress in terms of educational, occupational, and income attainment, the more they strive, the more they become disadvantaged in terms of earnings and wealth relative to Whites (U.S. Census Bureau, 2002d; Oliver and Shapiro, 1995; Scanzoni, 1978). A review of every age and educational group since 1940 provides strong support for the fact that Blacks are disproportionately "learning without earning." The 2000

Table 3.2. Mean Incomes by Years of School Completed, March 2002.

	Years of High School		Years of College		
	Less Than Four	*Four*	*One to Three*	*Four*	*Five or More*
White men	22,773	35,545	38,501	65,046	92,305
Black men	18,682	25,307	31,084	46,511	67,011
Difference	–4,091	–8,508	–7,417	–18,535	–25,294
White women	14,747	20,866	24,387	36,698	51,498
Black women	16,480	18,683	23,511	35,448	48,084
Difference	–1,733	–2,183	–876	–1,250	3,414

Source: U.S. Census Bureau (2002b).

census data (U.S. Census Bureau, 2002b) illustrate this continuing disparity (see Table 3.2).

Blacks represent around 12 percent of the population but own 3 percent of the total wealth in the United States (Malveaux, 1998). The income, net wealth, and financial assets of middle-class Blacks— those individuals holding a college degree, white-collar job, or annual salaries of $25,000 to $50,000 during 1988—was lower than that of similarly situated Whites. Oliver and Shapiro (1995) found that Whites in white-collar professions earned $33,765 annually compared to $23,799 for Blacks. As seen in Table 3.3, the average worth for Blacks was $48,000 less than that of Whites, and they had zero financial assets. In a study on wealth disparities and home ownership using 1994 data, Blacks' net wealth was $43,000 compared to $220,000 for Whites (Charles and Hurst, 2002). Hence, in order to survive and to reach the American dream, many Blacks have taken on alternative lifestyles. Most noteworthy are the dual-worker couples.

Dual Earners

The high proportion of dual earners among Black families reflects their strong work ethic and their determination to survive in a racially hostile society. Although the majority is clustered in low-paying and

Table 3.3. Race, Wealth, and Various Conceptions
          of the Middle Class.

	Income	Net Worth	Net Financial
Whites	$25,000–50,000	$44,069	$6,998
College degree	$38,700	$74,922	$19,823
White-collar job	$33,765	$56,487	$11,952
Blacks	$25,000–50,000	$15,250	$290
College degree	$29,440	$17,437	$290
White-collar job	$23,799	$8,299	$0

Source: Oliver and Shapiro (1995). Copyright © 1995 from *Black Wealth/White Wealth: A New Perspective on Racial Inequality* by Melvin L. Oliver and Thomas M. Shapiro. Reproduced by permission of Routledge/Taylor & Francis Books, Inc.

unskilled jobs without fringe benefits or the protection of a union, they seldom voluntarily leave the workforce. In 1999, 47 percent of the 8.4 million Black families were married-couple families; half of Black married couples had incomes of $50,000 compared to 60 percent of White couples (U.S. Census Bureau, 2001a). Of the 3.5 million married couples in 1984, the majority (64 percent) had working wives (Malveaux, 1988). This dual-earner tradition traces back to 1890, when Black wives were ten times more likely than White wives to be in the labor force. In 1984, when Black families earned 55.7 percent of White family income, income from the wife narrowed this gap to 82 percent. By the mid-1990s, 47 percent of middle-class White families with wives aged twenty-five to forty-four had two full-time spouses. In contrast, 67 percent of similar middle-class Black families had dual full-time earners. Throughout the 1990s, Black wives were more likely than White wives to work full-time and contribute more to their families' income. In 2000, Black families without a working wife made nearly $10,000 less than similar White families ($30,359 versus $40,141). Furthermore, for Blacks, even a working spouse lacked sufficient earnings to close the Black-White family income gap. Among working spouses, White families earned $70,459, versus Black families' average $59,395 per year. When both spouses in White families worked, it took three Black earners to overcome the income disparity: $65,266 for two White workers versus $66,403 for three Black workers (Landry, 2000; Wright, 2003).

Furthermore, Black women contribute more to the total family income than do White working wives (40.6 versus 32.8 percent in 1990), and their relative contribution within the family is projected to increase. The percentage differential between Black male and female employment rates has declined. In 1999, the male-female differential dropped to less than 3 percent (66 percent male to 63.4 percent female).

The Black middle class owes its existence to the working wife. Without wives' income, middle-class Black families fall below their class's standard of living by several thousand dollars, whereas middle-class White families exceed this standard by several thousand dollars. When faced with the hypothetical question of what the impact would be if the wife lost her job, two-thirds of middle-class Blacks said it would make things difficult or create a crisis. Blacks were more likely to anticipate a serious crisis than Whites (Landry, 1987). Yet today we know more about Black female-headed welfare families and absent nonworking husbands and fathers than we know about how the majority of married Black couples negotiate and balance their work and family lives, or how they feel about their work-family experiences.

Because Black women have been more economically independent, many developed attitudes of freedom and equality unknown to most nineteenth-century and even many twentieth-century females—attitudes that predated the modern women's movement. The consequences of this independence for Black marriages are of concern. While African men consider economically independent women an asset, it is unclear whether such women are considered in the same light among Black Americans. Messages received from the mass media strongly indicate that Black males feel threatened by the accomplishments of Black women.

Black working wives tend to increase the perception of their husbands' own sense of job competence and marital happiness, at least among the middle aged. The findings are contradictory at best. Whereas White husbands' perceived job competence rises as wives' employment status drops from white collar to blue collar to unemployed, that of Black husbands is highest when wives hold white-collar jobs and lowest when wives are homemakers (Draughn, 1984). Unlike Whites, both Black males and females expect wives to enact both a family-oriented and a job-oriented role in marriage. Furthermore, Black husbands rate their wives higher than White husbands do on having the knowledge and experience to hold a job. In general, the employment status of wives has a minimal effect or no effect on the likelihood of divorce or feelings of satisfaction with marital affection, companionship, communication, and understanding. Some studies, however, show that husbands' tempers tend to be shorter in dual-job families. And if they have to perform most of the in-home chores without help, they are likely to become dissatisfied with their family life (Broman, 1991; Strong and DeVault, 1995; Taylor, Chatters, Tucker, and Lewis, 1990; Scanzoni, 1978). But these findings appear to be more related to overwork and equity issues than to the gender of the person making the financial contribution.

The weight of the evidence indicates that for Black families, the gender identity of the individual contributing may not be as predictive of satisfaction as overall family lifestyle, prestige, and economic status (Landry, 2000; Strong and DeVault, 1995; Ball and Robbins, 1986; Scanzoni, 1978). Higher occupational status is tantamount to higher income. In the context of traditional gender-role expectations, it is assumed that a family's lifestyle is determined by the male head of household. Thus, when the Black wife works, she creates an illusion that the lifestyle they enjoy can be maintained on his salary alone (Harley, 1994). This illusion may be a fair trade-off for any loss of status experienced by the husband.

In the light of the positive transference of Black wives' employment to their mates' sense of job competency, one would expect Black husbands to have more positive attitudes toward wife employment than White husbands. Recent studies show that both race and class influence the proportion of men who have favorable attitudes toward wives working. Among husbands, more lower-income Black husbands have favorable attitudes than any other class or racial group. Given that higher-income Black husbands are half as likely as lower-income Black husbands to favor their wives working, economic need is clearly shaping the working-class husband's attitude.

Further evidence of the economic factor is reflected in the fact that in the lower-income group, Black wives are more likely to work than their White counterparts when their husbands have a negative attitude toward their employment (Beckett and Smith, 1981). This may be perceived as a potentially serious source of tension. For example, studies find that Black husbands are likely to have low marital satisfaction if there is no substantial financial need for a second income (Orbuch and Eyster, 1997; Orbuch and Custer, 1995). However, while marital quality may suffer, having a wife either gainfully employed or as a homemaker does not create anxiety or depression in Black husbands (Orbuch and Custer, 1995). In contrast, White husbands whose wives work against their wishes become depressed, particularly if their own wages are low (Ulbrich, 1988), or they become anxious if they must complete additional household chores (Orbuch and Custer, 1995).

If the couple's lifestyle is raised, Black men appear to respond positively to the additional income. Furthermore, wives' employment translates into more egalitarian decision making, which in turn increases marital satisfaction (although there is evidence that the highest level of marital quality occurs in husband-dominant couples or couples that hold more traditional roles). Finally, unlike White wives, Black wives who enter the labor force against their husbands' wishes managed to maintain a positive attitude toward their employment. They are more likely to see work as not only a right but part of what it means to be a "good" wife and mother. This attitude no doubt helps defuse any hostility on the husbands' part (Strong and Devault, 1995; Gibbs, 1990; Harrison and Minor, 1978; Osmond, 1977).

Although Black men's psychological well-being does not seem to suffer from an employed wife or the shift to more egalitarian decision making, their own employment is critical to their well-being and their marriage. Social scientists confirm the popular belief that regardless of race, men define their well-being through their work; men who see themselves as successful in the work role will perceive themselves as successful in the husband role (Draughn, 1984; Haynes, 2000; McAdoo and McAdoo, 1995; McLoyd, Cauce, Takeuchi, and Wilson, 2001; Taylor, 2000). Husbands who are satisfied with the rewards of their jobs are the ones who are most likely to express contentment with the amount of companionship, affection, communication, and understanding they receive from their wives (Scanzoni, 1978). An indication of this work-family linkage and its process is evident in a study of Black, predominantly male police officers.

According to this study, quality of marital communication, sex, and emotional support is directly traceable to perceptions of job discrimination. The sources of job strain are many; however, feeling that one's skin color is the reason a deserved assignment or promotion is denied creates a sense of powerlessness that spills over into family life. Black workers who feel powerless become ineffective workers and lovers. In its worst manifestation, those police officers who are discriminated against begin to lose interest in their clients, treating them as impersonal objects. Mates who do not care what happens to their clients at work often bring the same attitude home, creating sufficient detachment and disinterest in the relationship to increase the probability of marital separation and divorce (Johnson, 1989a).

In rural Southern regions, where discrimination is most apparent, Black husbands appear to have the most dissatisfaction with their marriages. A study conducted in this area during the early 1970s showed that regardless of socioeconomic status, young Black married men reported the lowest levels of satisfaction of all marital statuses (Ball and Robbins, 1986). The alarming reality implied is that income does not overcome the sense of powerlessness for rural Southern Black males. The long history of discrimination may have led to low expectations for marriage for even high-income Black men in the South. In the prime of their working years and on the tide of the civil rights movement, they may expect more from their efforts than the racist Southern social order grants. Their deprived economic position relative to Whites may be more obvious in the South, especially in the rural parts, than in other areas of the country, where the legacy of an exploitative past is not as vibrant. Thus, these husbands may perceive their provider role undercut to a greater degree than others of similar status but who live elsewhere.

Perceived relative deprivation may create frustration that leads to still another outcome: hypertension. Black husbands are well aware that their training and efforts will not produce the same rewards as those of White husbands. Although Black men are earning slightly more than Black women (Mishel, Bernstein, and Schmitt, 1997; U.S. Census Bureau, 2002a), Black family incomes and wealth fall far below that of White men, women, and families. The consequences of downsizing, the relocation of manufacturing jobs to developing countries, and property, housing, and tax laws have placed Black husbands at an economic disadvantage. (See Chapter Ten for a more detailed discussion on wealth disparities.) Educational attainment is not closely tied to advancement in unskilled and semiskilled blue-collar jobs, in which many Black husbands find themselves. In contrast, many of their Black wives hold jobs in fields like education, nursing, and social work, where each academic degree or unit of advanced education results in higher pay or prestige. Data from a 1990 study of Black parents where the mother was the senior partner (educationally and economically) suggest that apart from hereditary factors, the combination of racial discrimination and relative deprivation within the marriage could create tension that results in hypertension for Blacks, particularly for men (Myers, 1990).

Women's Multiple Roles

The triple role of wife, mother, and worker that Black women perform is assumed to have negative consequences for family satisfaction. Based on the "scarcity hypothesis," early research assumed that there is a fixed and limited quantity of human energy. Therefore, the more roles a person plays, the greater is the likelihood of stress, overload, and tension from facing incompatible expectations from different people. Women who are saddled with total responsibility for housework and play multiple roles are most likely to experience role strain (Goode, 1960).

In this theoretical context, we observe that compared to White wives, Black wives spend less time on housework and receive more help from their husbands, particularly if they are employed (Landry, 2000; Orbuch and Eyster, 1997; Silver and Goldschneider, 1994; Taylor, 2000). In fact, the more time Black men spend in paid work, the more time they spend doing household chores (John, Shelton, and Luschen, 1995). These findings suggest that the potential for strain as a result of multiple roles is mitigated by husband support. However, employed and unemployed Black wives still perform significantly more child care, cooking, cleaning, and laundry than their husbands (McLoyd, Cauce, Takeuchi, Wilson, 2001; Wilson, Tolson, Hinton, and Kiernan, 1990; Beckett and Smith, 1981). Women who perform home duties as work can become stressed from boredom. The heavy concentration of Black women in domestic work until 1970 emphasizes their historical double duty and the competition between obligations to two households: their own and that of their employer. Yet this redundancy tells only part of the story. As we have seen, domestic workers often hold down multiple jobs, thus increasing the potential for stress from work overload (Malveaux, 1988). As their occupational opportunities broadened, Black women moved from domestic jobs into clerical, service, and low-level white-collar positions (Swinton, 1991; Harrison, 1989; Hesse-Biber and Carter, 2000; Jones, 1985). Although role redundancy may be absent, they may still experience work overload. An example is the blue-collar/white-collar marriages.

The shortage of Black males and their limited opportunities means that many of these nondomestic women workers are married to husbands who are below their social status; that is, their husbands work in semiskilled blue-collar jobs. Whereas white-collar husbands have flexible hours for dealing with work-family conflicts, blue-collar husbands' jobs are characterized by inflexible work schedules that allow little time for family business. Thus, marriages between blue-collar husbands and white-collar wives are more likely than dual-career families to organize family household duties around traditional lines, with women assuming the full-time social roles of wife, mother, and worker. In this situation, wives have few escapes from twenty-four-hour duty and conflictual work-family demands.

Many college-educated Black women also marry Black men who do not have the same educational level. In married-couple families where Black women had a college diploma, only 46 percent of their husbands also had one. In comparison, just over 69 percent of White women with a college degree had husbands at the same degree of education. Moreover, only 12 percent of White women married never-college-educated men ("Special Report: College Degree Awards," 1999). They may experience the same time issues related to the division of household labor. Furthermore, heterogeneous marriages generally have a higher potential for conflict and divorce.

The negative aspects of multiple tasks are reflected in a major study showing those Black women with fewer roles—the unemployed—as having among the highest family life satisfaction regardless of their parental status, while married employed women have among the lowest levels (Broman, 1991). The scarcity hypothesis appears to have firm support. However, scholars are not in agreement on whether multiple roles lead to stress and dissatisfaction. Unfortunately, empirical studies of the 1980s primarily give information on Whites, and the few studies on Blacks provide support for both sides of the argument. Counteracting the findings supporting the scarcity hypothesis is a growing school of thought that extols the virtues of multiple roles for women. Rather than assuming that human energy is fixed, greater role involvement is assumed to enhance or increase resources for ego gratification and development of self-worth. The more roles people perform, the greater is their ability to maintain positive thoughts about some aspects of self, the greater their resources are for trading off negative aspects of each role, and the more legitimate are the excuses they can use for not meeting obligations in a particular role (Linville, 1987; Thoits, 1983).

Consistent with this line of thinking, a study of the social roles of middle-aged and older Black women finds that women who work have higher self-esteem. This is particularly the case for older middle-aged women who have high incomes and are in good health. The role combination of work and marriage appears to especially enhance health for middle-aged Black women. Given their position in the life cycle, few perform all three roles of employment, marriage, and parenting; most perform only two roles—parental and work. Nevertheless, the evidence shows that certain roles, especially the work role, are important for the psychological and physical well-being of middle-aged and older Black women. Given the economic situation of Black Americans and the decreased income and health among older Blacks, being tied to any occupation should enhance self-esteem. Furthermore, in a society of many "manless" and alone Black women, being married must inflate their self-worth (Coleman, Antonucci, Adelmann, and Crohan, 1987).

In a study of Black homemakers and employed women between the ages of twenty-four and fifty-nine, the authors shed additional light on the emotional well-being of Black women holding two different roles: homemakers versus working wives. Compared to working wives, Black homemakers felt greater appreciation, less physical demand, and fewer time pressures (Keith and Riley, 2001). When looking at work conditions and the emotional well-being of women, there was no significant difference in the stress experienced by homemakers and working women, but homemakers showed more depression than working wives did. Those who were married and highly educated had less stress than unmarried and less educated Black women did.

Moreover, self-esteem derives not only from the ego gratification experienced from being among the few married or gainfully employed. The contribution women perceive they are making to their community is also important to their emotional well-being. One study of Black women college students found that those entering nontraditional fields such as law, politics, and medicine did so not for ego needs or competitive urges, but because of their strong drive to serve the needs of Black people. It is reasonable to speculate that for these women, satisfaction derived from contributing to the general welfare of the Black community and financially supporting and nurturing their families outweighed any negatives from performing multiple roles (Harrison, 1989).

In sum, the benefit of multiple roles is controversial. Often the mere existence of multiple roles is assumed to indicate strain or enhancement in Black women's lives. It is possible that those with multiple roles are most likely to be at risk of overload. Thus, it is the overload rather than the number of roles that presents a problem. It is also possible that multiple-role strain seldom becomes an issue. Many Black women create strategies, such as child-rearing support networks, to avoid work-family strain (Malson, 1983). Also, one must question the appropriateness of self-esteem levels as a sufficient measure of the consequences of multiple roles. Self-esteem does not speak to the issue of general strain. Hypertension and high blood pressure, illnesses suffered by many Black women, appear to be more related to lifestyle, such as work overload, than to genetic disposition and personality (Myers, 1990). Even within a hostile environment, Black women and men have managed to feel good about themselves. Harsh conditions often encourage self-reliance, self-confidence, a stronger sense of community, and, for the religious, a test of their steadfast faith (Hamlet, 2004; Harrison, 1989). In sum, self-esteem may rise with increased levels of strain.

We can tentatively conclude that excessive role obligations can impair psychological and physical well-being. However, multiple-role occupancy in and of itself is generally beneficial in a society where "rolelessness" is a social risk factor for Blacks. The paucity of studies and the differences in the study group preclude a definitive conclusion.

Summary

It is often stated that regardless of race, marriage has provided an abundance of rights for husbands and numerous duties (often simultaneous) for wives. The peculiar history of Blacks, however, has distributed the duties somewhat more evenly. Nonetheless, the few relevant studies suggest that Black women are more likely than Black men to feel overworked and dissatisfied with their lot (Strong and DeVault, 1995; Broman, 1988, 1991; Zollar and Williams, 1987). Scanzoni (1978), who studied middle-class Black families, goes so far as to say that the marital union rests strongly on the wife's subjective definition of the family's economic situation. What seems to matter most is her family's consumption potential in comparison to other Blacks. The more positively wives define their economic situation, the more likely they are to be satisfied with the emotional aspects of marriage. Furthermore, since American wives are the emotional housekeepers of their marriages, Black wives are more likely to evaluate these aspects less positively than their husbands, making the husbands' economic success critical.

Although Black husbands express greater satisfaction with marriage than their wives do, economics is also critical to their happiness. Black employed husbands have greater family life satisfaction than unemployed men and employed wives. A report on Black husband-fathers finds that those who experience unemployment or feel discouraged because they are not living up to their image of a "good provider" are at the greatest risk of unhappiness (Bowman, 1989). While provider role failure is bothersome to younger men and unmarried fathers (McLoyd, Cauce, Takeuchi, and Wilson, 2001), it is a more sensitive issue for the middle aged, who have less reason to remain hopeful in face of bleak upward-mobility prospects.

Black husband-fathers who are frustrated by inadequate schooling and labor market barriers are finding it necessary to come to terms with the prospect that their provider role problems may be irreversible. They must face the stark realization of the widening gap between

Black working- and upper-class families and the even greater economic gap between Black and White families. Unfortunately for Black husbands, wives, and children, this inequality has become a permanent part of the American economy (Oliver and Shapiro, 1995; Swinton, 1991; Bowman, 1989; Wilson, 1980).

In his concern for the Black workers who filled the jobs left by White workers during World War II, Marcus Garvey (1967, pp. 36–37) warned that "Negroes are still filling places, and as time goes on and the age grows older our occupations will be gone from us. . . . We will gradually find our places among the millions of permanent unemployed." Although he was anticipating the loss of jobs when the White war veterans returned home to reclaim "their" jobs, his words are prophetic, given the chain of events that has shut a significant number of Blacks out of the shrinking job market in contemporary American society. The hope comes in the realization that gaps may be reduced by Black families committing to education and lifelong learning, as well as striving to continually acquire skills that make them competitive in a global economy. In Chapter Ten, recommendations are made about acquiring wealth to reduce these gaps experienced by Black families.

All in all, it appears that both Black males and females have reasons to venerate or scorn work and marriage. Unfair labor practices have had negative consequences for marital formation and functioning. However, regardless of gender, Blacks who are married are generally happier than the unmarried (Zollar and Williams, 1987). The long historical pattern of role sharing and mutual support continues to serve as an indispensable buffer against the harsh reality of work and income discrimination.

Since money derived from work is the basic determinant of the way families survive, maintain self-esteem, and acquire social prestige within their communities, the contemporary condition of Black families is disturbing. Slavery was demoralizing in its minimum subsistence of individuals and its system of work without pay. But without work in a postslavery society, even minimum subsistence is improbable, presenting numerous Black families with a bleak future. The absence of strengths and adaptive behaviors in the literature, popular media, and textbooks contributes to this image of a bleak future. For example, the examination of unemployment, underemployment, lack of education and economic opportunities, institutional discrimination, and psychological issues faced by Black men has been the focus of the last few years, but the adaptive features of Black men, the contributions of households headed by Black single men, and dimensions that explain successful Black men and husbands fail to find their place in the literature (Gordon, Gordon, and Nembhard, 1994). Where are the voices of Black women and children? Where are the Black-to-Black comparisons that explain successful marriages, marital satisfaction, and roles within dual-earner, traditional, and single-parent families? Is the bleak future constructed by misinformation and negative information?

4

Patterns of Sexual Intimacy

One can speculate that throughout human history, sexual be-havior has been the subject of inordinate interest and that all cultures have attempted to explain its nature. Understanding human sexual behavior, however, has been complicated by the fact that physiological and sociological factors are closely intertwined. Among nonhuman species, inborn tendencies prevail. But in human society, although the basis for sexual motivation is physiological, sexual behavior is never determined solely by physiological factors (Ingoldsby, Smith, and Miller, 2003).

In looking at the painful history of race relations in America, it seems clear that much of the discrimination that Black Americans have encountered is due to the existence of White American stereotypes about their moral character. As a number of polls have revealed, a large number of White Americans see Blacks as a morally loose group. In fact, the sexual stereotypes about Blacks become the ultimate justification for their exclusion from White schools, jobs, and neighborhoods. Many of the ideas held about Black sexuality in particular are exaggerated versions of general attitudes toward the poor. American society was founded on the Protestant ethic, which equated poverty with sinfulness, idleness, vice, and a belief that the poor are sexually indulgent (Yao, 1999; D'Emilio and Freedman, 1988).

The image of Blacks as sexual beings is deeply rooted in American history, culture, and religion. In the early twentieth century, respected scholars imputed a genetic basis to the alleged hotter sexual passions and richer fertility of the Black population (Graves, 2001; Wyatt, 1982; Johnson, 1978b). Subsequent research has done little to invalidate the earlier generalizations about Black sexual drives or to illuminate the sociocultural forces that differentiate between Black and White sexual behavior. Most researchers avoid explicit reference to genetically rooted racial dispositions. Yet they do so implicitly when they give focus to Black sexual behavior without placing it in the context of the meaning sexual behavior has for the individuals involved: emotional connectedness, trust, and romance. Further, when studying ethnic minority adults, researchers recruit largely from low-income populations. But even the poor vary in their sexual expression. Researchers, according to one study, may get very different results from the same neighborhood depending on their recruiting methods. Within an urban northeastern U.S. neighborhood, neighbors were categorized as "decent"—family cohesion, legally sanctioned work, and education—or "street"—illegal work and weak family cohesion. Without expectations of heterogeneity of sexual beliefs, these differences escape researchers who may feel that they have adequately targeted the population. Moreover, "street" people behavior becomes the basis for a broader understanding of Black Americans, middle class and elite alike (Lewis and Kertzner, 2003). The result of this type of research has been limited understanding of subjective experience of sexuality for Blacks and the fostering and reinforcement of stereotypes about Black immorality and hypersexuality. Such false images serve to fuel the fears of those who remain psychologically wedded to America's puritanical view of sexuality and strengthen their resistance to Black demands for equal opportunity in American life.

Historical Background

The diversity of African cultures precludes any generalizations about African sexual behavior. But in the past, African sex life could be understood only in relation to kinship groups, which provided the basis of the mores and folkways that regulated sexual relations. One difference between the African and American concepts of sex is the lack of religious strictures among Africans. Throughout Black Africa, there is a concept of a supreme being and creator, but the supreme being issues no edicts concerning sexual morality. The violation of sexual laws is an offense against individuals, not against God (Diop, 1987). All the available evidence indicates that sexual behavior in Africa before and after marriage was under strict community and family control (Bennett, 1981).

In the experience of slavery, pronounced alterations in Black sexual behavior took place. Whereas community and kinship groups had regulated sexual relations in Africa, most of the control over the Black sexual impulse during the American slave era, particularly in its last century, was exercised by the White slave master. The attitudes of most slave owners toward their slaves was that they were property, a commodity to be bought and sold. During this period, reproduction among the slaves had a certain value to the slave owners, and free sexual activity was tolerated. In some cases, Black females were mated at the onset of puberty in the same way that the livestock of the plantation were mated. Black women were compelled to breed children—to be the breeder of human cattle for the field or auction block (Berlin, 2003; Franklin, 1987).

This practice of human breeding was one factor that encouraged a permissive code of sexual conduct among the slaves. Where there was no coercion, free sex practice was followed as an end in itself. More important, the nexus between sex and marriage was attenuated among America's Black population. Although some slave owners permitted and even encouraged the legal union of their slaves and regarded marriage as a permanent association, many others expected slaves to mate without the formality of a marriage ceremony and did not regard the union as necessarily permanent. With this attitude of the slave masters and the harsh conditions of slave life, a permissive type of sexual behavior developed (duCille, 1990).

The role of organized Black religion was very different from that of the White religions. Although Blacks eventually adopted the religions of their White slave owners, the puritanical traditions that influenced White sexual standards never took hold as strongly among them. The Black church's function related more to tension reduction than the setting of sexual standards (Hamlet, 2004). Premarital and extramarital sexual behavior has never been countenanced by the Black church, but neither has there been any strong attention paid to America's moral code and its violation by their parishioners. Possible exceptions, of course, could be found in certain middle-class and fundamentalist churches in the Black community (Bennett, 1981; Johnson, 1978b, 1989a). After slavery ended, Black Americans probably did have a more permissive sexual code than many European Americans, but that fact has to be placed in the proper historical context. In accordance with Freudian theory (Freud, 1938), we can assume that the sexual drive exists in all individuals and has to be expressed in some form. Historically, males in this culture have been allowed unrestrained libidinal expression. Greater restraints have been placed on women, especially middle-class women. Even among working-class White women, the norm of chastity has been honored more in the breach than in its observance. A major reason for the class difference is the greater use of economic resources by middle-class males to exact sexual chastity from the women in their class. Where there was no exchange value of sex for material reward, the libido thrived in a more liberated way (D'Emilio and Freedman, 1988).

Thus, because the Black masses enjoyed a greater sexual equality than was possible for Whites in the postbellum era, a more permissive sexual code developed. Moreover, some of the controls on European American sexuality did not exist to the same degree among Black Americans. Black males did not classify women into bad and good groups on the basis of their virginal status. White men did make these distinctions, and women were eligible for the respectability of marriage according to their classification in one group or the other. During an epoch in which the majority of White women were economically dependent on men, this was an effective censor of their sexuality. Black women, in the main, were more economically and psychologically independent (Simpson, 1983).

Socialization into Sexual Behavior

While the legacy of slavery and the effect of racial inequality strongly influence the sexual practices of Black Americans, many other social forces impinge on the sexuality of Blacks. Among those forces is socialization into sexual behavior. The process of socialization is designed to condition people to accept the behavioral patterns of their society. This is the way individuals acquire their knowledge of sex and the particular values their society expects them to hold in relation to it. Blacks face a unique situation, in that the sexual values inculcated in them by their parents are counteracted by the conditions under which they live (Wyatt, Peters, and Guthrie, 1988). However, there is little doubt that Black parents want their female children to remain sexually chaste before marriage. When Pietropinto and Simenauer (1977) asked a group of Black adults how important it was that a girl be a virgin when she gets married, almost 30 percent of the men stated that it was very important, compared to 31.5 percent of White males. Among college students, sexual attitudes vary by the liberality of their campus. At the peak of the sexual revolution, during the 1960s and 1970s, religions' break on sexual attitudes and behavior was clearly evident. Whereas only a third of Black students in a nonsecular college approved of premarital coitus, 85 percent of Blacks in a secular college approved. Black Seventh-Day Adventists and White Mormons were far more likely than nondenominational students to express their desire for a virgin mate (69 versus 42 percent). Moreover, when Black women engaged in premarital sex, the majority did so within a committed relationship regardless of religious devotedness (Johnson, 1989a). Without taking religion into consideration, a national 1995 survey found that the majority of Black males and females reported that when they first had sex with their most recent partner the relationship was exclusive and serious—going steady, engaged, or married (Halle, 2002). Their behavior is consistent with both the high value Blacks give to sex within a committed relationship (Wyatt, Myers, Ashing-Giwa, and Durvasula, 1999) and cross-cultural national attitudinal studies showing Blacks expressing more traditionalism as compared to Whites and Hispanics. They express their conservatism by supporting sex within a love relationship and disapproving of teenage premarital sex under all circumstances (Laumann, Gagnon, Michael, and Michaels, 1994). Parents continue to underestimate their influence on teenage children's decisions about sex. Few teens feel they are getting enough information. Eighty-eight percent of teens surveyed in 2003 felt it would be easier to postpone sex or avoid pregnancy if they and their parents could have more open, honest, and accurate sexual conversations. Unwisely, some parents reinforce a chastity standard by using negative sex education techniques for Black children. Sex is made to appear horrible and extremely dangerous. Some females are warned by their parents (usually the mother) that any sexual relations before marriage will automatically result in their contracting a venereal disease. This type of sex education often creates severe anxiety in females about their sexual impulses and responses. They become afraid to have sexual intercourse and are convinced that all sexual behavior is sinful (Fox and Inazu, 1980). In general, teenage surveys during the 2000s show that at least two-thirds of sexually experienced teens wish they had waited longer (National Campaign to Prevent Teen Pregnancy, 2002/2003). In fact, compared to midwestern Whites and Scandinavians, Black females have considerably higher negative feelings after their first premarital coital experience (Christensen and Johnson, 1978; Johnson, 1978b). Rarely do Black females turn to oral sex to protect their virginity. Approximately 30 percent more White women than Black receive or give oral sex. Of those Black women who engage in oral sex, relatively few find it appealing (Quadagno, Sly, Harrison, Eberstein, and Soler, 1998).

In contrast to mothers who induce anxiety in their daughters, which at times carries into marital relationships, some Black mothers encourage their unmarried daughters to use contraceptives (Nathanson and Becker, 1986). Those parents who maintain an awful and complete silence on the subject of sex, yet harshly punish any form of sexual activity, also act unwisely. When the children's interest in sex becomes stronger, they frequently discover that their parents do not wish to discuss sex in a way that is significant to them. Therefore, it is not strange to find that many Black children acquired their knowledge of sex through the folklore and myths of their peers. Most of the Black females in the sexual surveys learned about sex through a source other than their parents (Shah and Zelnick, 1981).

The peer group constitutes an important source of sex information for the Black female. A typical pattern is for most children in urban areas to discover sex for themselves, then discuss their discovery with close friends or relatives. Many Black females choose an older sister for this purpose. Thus, much of the Black female's socialization into sexual behavior takes place among same-sex peer groups (Scott, 1999; Billy and Udry, 1985; Shah and Zelnick, 1981). One reason for the importance of the peer group is the absence of the parents from the home. The prevailing marginal economic status of Black people is an important factor in determining their sexual behavior. A high rate of unemployment and underemployment among Black males forces many Black women into the labor market, leaving the children in many families without parental supervision, as both parents struggle to meet economic needs. Thus, social conditions and economic deprivation under which Black people are compelled to live create a salient difference in the sexual socialization of Black and White women in this society.

The conditions of poverty mean that Black females are often subjected to the many dimensions of sex long before White middle-class females. It is understandable, then, to find that Black females have their first full sexual intercourse some years earlier than the typical White female. According to the Centers for Disease Control (1991), the level of exposure to premarital sexual relations is higher for Black females in their teenage years than for White females. According to the 2001–2002 National Survey of Families and Households (NSFH), more than 75 percent of non-Hispanic Black males had their first coital experience before age eighteen, compared to 60 percent of

Hispanics and 52 percent of White non-Hispanics. Between ages thirteen and fourteen, 25 percent of non-Hispanic Black males reported having sexual intercourse, compared to 16 percent of Hispanics and 10 percent of non-Hispanic Whites. Among females, 63 percent of non-Hispanic Blacks, 57 percent of Hispanics, and 54 percent of non-Hispanic Whites had sex before age eighteen. Black women's greater exposure to a sexualized environment is reflected in the fact that by age eighteen more Black females have experienced sexual intercourse than White males (63 percent versus 52 percent).

Similar to the racial differences between females, White males learn about sexual intercourse at a later age than Black males (Gilmore, DeLamater, and Wagstaff, 1996). Several studies reveal that Black males are more likely to use condoms at a later age than White males (Pleck, 1989), which partially accounts for Black males' slightly lower rate of consistent contraceptive use with a primary partner (41 versus 49). Yet it does not explain why Black and white males have identical contraceptive rates (61) when engaging in virginal sex with a secondary partner. It appears that regardless of race, the risk associated with multiple partners is similarly understood (Laumann, Gagnon, Michael, and Michaels, 1994).

A critical distinction between Black and White males is the tendency of White males to substitute masturbation, fellatio, and fantasy for direct sexual intercourse. Masturbation, for instance, is more likely to be the source of the first ejaculation for the White male, while intercourse is for the Black male (Belcastro, 1985; Laumann, Gagnon, Michael, and Michaels, 1994). A larger percentage of White males reported being sexually aroused by being bitten during sexual activity, seeing a member of the opposite sex in a social situation, seeing themselves nude in the mirror or looking at another man's erect penis, hearing dirty jokes, reading sadomasochistic literature, and viewing sexy pictures. Conversely, Black males tended to engage in premarital intercourse at earlier ages and to have intercourse and reach orgasm more frequently. As Bell (1978) notes in his analysis of these data, the Black male's overabundance of sexuality is a myth. The sexuality of Black and White men just tends to take different forms, and neither group has any more self-control or moral heroism than the other.

The fact that sexual activity among young Black American males begins at an earlier age, is more frequent, and involves more partners than among their White counterparts may partly be a function of differences in social class. Although some studies have focused on college-level males, the studies among Blacks tend to be of individuals who have been shaped by their class of origin's values regarding sexual matters. One racial or cultural factor is the greater involvement of the young Black male with females at a younger age. Apparently White males are more likely to confine their associations in adolescence to other boys. Westney, Jenkins, Butts, and Williams (1991) found that Black male adolescents were likely to be romantically involved with girls as early as age ten. The kind of rigid gender segregation found in White culture is largely absent from Black society. For example, Blacks are less likely to have the extensive number of all-male clubs, organizations, or colleges—although outside the workplace gender segregation in public and private sectors is rapidly declining.

The sexual code of young Black males is a permissive one. They do not, for example, divide Black women into good (suitable for marriage) and bad (unsuitable for marriage) categories. In the lower-income groups, sexual activity is often a measure of masculinity. Thus, there is a greater orientation toward premarital sexual experimentation. In his study of premarital sexual standards among Blacks and Whites, Staples (1978) found that the White male's sexual permissiveness could be affected by a number of social forces, such as religion, but the Black male was influenced by none of them. However, other reports find extremely conservative religions blocking permissive behaviors of Black males (Johnson, 1989a). Hendricks (1982) found that few Black male adolescents were aware of the increased risk of teenage pregnancy, but there was an almost unanimous wish not to impregnate their sexual partner. In another survey, Black male high school students reported that their group believed that a male respects his partner when he uses a condom (Johnson and Staples, 1990; Pleck, 1989). Their behavior reflects their respect: less than a quarter state that they never use contraceptives (Ryan, Manlove, and Franzetta, 2003).

More important than their sexual education are the larger values some young Black men learn. Often this involves buying into a well-defined system for manipulating and controlling women. Early in the life cycle, they realize that money and women are the two most highly valued objects that they can gain in our patriarchal system. Women can supply a male with money or what it can buy and are also a means of satisfying his sexual desires. Hence, a competitive system emerges among men to make as many sexual conquests as possible. It is a system whereby the man with the best rap, clothes, or style wins—with women as the spoils. Lost in this struggle for one-upmanship is a feeling of relatedness toward women and an articulated awareness of women's human qualities (Benjamin, 1983).

A most blatant indicator of the woman-as-property ideology among some Black men is the violence that sometimes accompanies the sexual experience. This can be seen in the legendary practice of "taking sex." By some reports (Anderson, 1989), the strong-arming of Black women into sexual submission is pervasive, and it is not confined to working-class Blacks but is equally represented among the middle class (Anderson, 1989). If it is prevalent, it does not occur in high frequency among teenagers in their first sexual relationship: 12 percent of Blacks report violence, compared with 17 percent for Hispanics and 6 percent for Whites (Ryan, Manlove, and Franzetta, 2003). In contrast, other studies show Black women and their partners agreeing at a higher rate than Whites or Hispanics on the type of sex and when they have sex. Furthermore, among those experiencing forced sex, Blacks as compared to Whites, Hispanics, and Asians report a noticeably lower rate (Laumann, Gagnon, Michael, and Michaels, 1994). These contrasting findings may reflect differences in sampling. The latter reports derived from national probability adult samples with no social class control on the Black sample, whereas the studies of widespread sexual assaults characterize samples of poor Black communities.

This is not to say that forced sex is absent from the affluent class. A number of cases involving sexual assaults by prominent Black males against Black women have made headlines (Williams, 1999; Norment, 1992). And just as White males have traditionally been able to use their privileged economic resources to force sexual submission on White women, there is increasing evidence that a few Black men are not reluctant to use the perquisites of high office or wealth to accomplish the same end. One of the few studies of the attitudes toward rape found no racial differences in these attitudes. However, Blacks anticipated more negative reactions from the police and expressed greater distrust of other institutional agencies than did Whites. Consequently, Black women were more likely to anticipate turning to parents or family members for support (Asbury, 1999; Howard, 1988).

The Influence of Gender

Although we recognize that much of Blacks' sexual behavior is a function of forces beyond their control, there must be some accountability for these individual actions. In every study comparing Black and White sexuality, the greatest conflict exists among gender roles, not racial groups. Black and White men are much more united in the meaning of sex than are Black men and Black women. Men of both races are similar in the very selfish peer-oriented nature of their sexual behavior (Strong, DeVault, and Sayad, 1998; Wyatt and Lyons-Rowe, 1990). Male-female disparities in sexual attitudes and behavior are so obvious, and pervade all strata of the society, that it would be easy to assume that this is the natural order of things. However, any historical or cross-cultural analysis would challenge many notions concerning innate differences among males and females in sexual attitudes, desire, or behavior. From both a historical and a cross-cultural perspective, societies and epochs may vary greatly as to the kinds of behavior approved for different gender-role groupings. These variations reflect the fact that gender has both biological and social components (Ingoldsby, Smith, and Miller, 2004; Christensen and Johnson, 1978; D'Emilio and Freedman, 1988).

Male-female differences in sexual attitudes and behavior are probably influenced by both biological and cultural factors. Females, to a greater degree than males, are oriented toward the responsibilities of parenthood. In patriarchal societies, greater controls are also placed on female than on male sexuality. Women are taught that their self-respect and the respect of others for them are contingent on their use of restraint and discretion in sexual matters. In contrast, patriarchal culture condones, and even encourages, the expression of the male libido. Sexual relations may have various meanings and functions for men. One of those functions is the maintenance of a male virility cult.

What we mean by the male virility cult is that within the male's peer group, status is based on the number of women with whom they have had sex. Thus, the male who has a variety of premarital sexual experiences occupies a prestigious position within his peer group. Sexual conquest of women becomes strongly associated with the definition of masculinity. It is sex as a symbol of manhood that supposedly motivates the male's sexual interest as well as physical desire. The virility cult is supposed to have its strongest adherents among Black males. Because the ordinary manifestations of masculine identity were all but impossible for large numbers of Black men, sex became a major instrument of power and status. Black men are supposed to be emasculated and must resort to emphasizing secondary aspects of masculinity, such as the sexual exploitation of women (Bennett, 2002; Anderson, 1989).

Some Black men do view themselves alternately as lovers and exploiters of women. As Liebow (1966) found in his study of lower-class males, these men are eager to present themselves as exploiters to women as well as to men. Within the lower-class group, men not only see themselves as exploiters of women but expect the same of other men. When the behavior of other men does not meet their expectations, they cannot comprehend their actions. In reality, however, the tendency to use women to gain sexual and economic ends is counteracted by other feelings and goals, especially the male's need to have a meaningful relationship with a woman whom he loves. Despite the self-image of many Black American men as users of women, many Black women find Black men very supportive individuals in both an emotional and an economic sense. Schulz (1991) and Waller (2002) discovered that many of the women in female-headed households were receiving support from boyfriends.

The discrepancy between the rhetoric and the reality can best be explained by the kind of image Black men wish to sustain within the peer group and in their community. Many males do not want to be seen as emotionally dependent on the "weaker" sex. Thus, they counter any suspicions that they are a weakling, sucker, or patsy by projecting an image of being a user of women, a person whose interpersonal involvement is based on only the economic and sexual gain that accrues from such a relationship.

Contrary to prevailing beliefs, Black men are showing increasing concern for the needs of women. The Pietropinto and Simenauer (1977) study reported that only 7.5 percent of Black men found engaging in foreplay an unpleasant aspect of sex. A majority of Black men reported thinking of their current partner during intercourse or masturbation. Approximately a third of Black men said they believe being in love is the most important thing in life, and another third felt if you are in love, sex is better. About a third of Black men felt the sex act ended when they had one or more orgasms, and another third believed it was finished when they both had an orgasm. Almost 71 percent of Black men said they deliberately try to delay their orgasm as long as possible, until their partner has an orgasm or seems satisfied. This effort tends to be reflected in a national study (Laumann,

Gagnon, Michael, and Michaels, 1994) where at least three-quarters of Black males claim that they always have an orgasm with their partners, and a slight majority claimed that their partners always have an orgasm with them. Although an overwhelming majority of females agree that their male partners have consistent orgasms, they report far fewer orgasmic experiences for themselves (38 percent)—a male-female difference consistent across ethnic groups. To the extent that female orgasm is now considered both a right (for women) and a responsibility (for men), this discrepancy undoubtedly constitutes a possible source of male-female tension. And this discrepancy perhaps explains why the majority of Blacks (also Whites), regardless of gender, do not feel extremely satisfied physically or emotionally with their sexual experiences.

Much less research has been done on the sexuality of Black women. Consequently, the cultural beliefs about Black female sexuality run rampant, while the facts remain unexamined. In no other area are there so many stereotypes and myths and much speculation. The image of the Black woman is that she is the most sensual of all female creatures. One Black writer has even described her as "potentially, if not already, the most sexual animal on this planet" (Hernton, 1965, p. 136). Although Hernton's description dates back several decades, contemporary rap music and videos continue to exalt Black women's extraordinary sexuality (Bennett, 2002). While Hernton's description was meant as a compliment, the mainstream view of Black sexuality as demonstrated in rap music culture is rife with negative connotations. The lusty sexuality that White Americans impute to Blacks represents to them the most abnormal, vulgar, and base human instincts. The image of the Black woman as innately sexual is a combination of fact and myth. But that image has been used as a justification of ethnocentric practices, because it suggests unrestrained sexual urges that civilized people do not possess (Douglass, 1999; duCille, 1990).

Cultural beliefs about Black women's sexuality emerged out of the experience of slavery. The sexual availability of slave women allowed

White men to put White women on a pedestal, to be seen as the god-desses of virtue. In a way, this became a self-fulfilling prophecy. For this reason, and also because of general Victorian assumptions about female purity, White women were held aloof from the world of lust and passion and in many cases became inhibited emotionally and sex-ually. But while the White woman's experiences and status inhibited sexual expression, the Black woman's encouraged it.

The Black female's sexual morality was at least partly shaped by the experience of slavery. As the violation of her body became rou-tine, she could not value what was unavailable to her: virginity (Davis, 1983). She sometimes even came to look on herself as the South viewed and treated her. In fact, she often had no other morality by which to shape her womanhood. From a review of the conditions under which Black women lived, it is easy to understand why the rigid sexual regulations so prevalent in the dominant American society failed to emerge in the Black culture.

Considering the different history of Blacks and the different con-ditions under which they now live, mainstream sexual standards may not be applicable to Black females. While Blacks are influenced by the majority culture's moral code, it does not necessarily guide their be-havior, especially in the lower-income group. According to Ladner (1971), premarital sex is not regarded as an immoral act but rather as one of those human functions that one engages in because it is nat-ural. The Ladner study (1971) revealed that working-class Black women basically have two responses to premarital sex: indulgence or nonindulgence. These responses are motivated by pragmatic consid-erations. Those who do not indulge in premarital coitus are concerned with avoiding pregnancy and often do not condemn girls who do not abstain. The abstainers are more likely to be upwardly mobile and are worried lest a premarital pregnancy prevent them from achieving a higher status than their parents. The middle-class element in the Black population has been very conscious of its unique position in relation to the masses of Black folk. In earlier periods, they placed an exagger-ated emphasis on moral conduct and developed a puritanical restraint, in contrast to the free and more liberated sexual behavior of the dominant Black population (Giddings, 1984).

The Class Dimension

Some of the gender role differences concerning sexuality are related to class values. In the lower classes, the expression of masculinity receives a great deal of emphasis. The lower-class male, for example, is distinguished from the middle-class male in that he moves sooner into heterosexual relationships. In lower-class environments, distinctions between masculinity and femininity are sharply drawn. The male frequently sees sexual conquest as a strong sign of his masculinity. In many cases, the sexual act is defined as satisfying only the male, thereby providing him with an activity considered exclusively male. The double standard of sexual conduct is much stronger in the lower-class group. Both sexual rights and sexual pleasure are perceived as male prerogatives. In most cases where a double standard of sexual conduct prevails, it allows males more sexual freedom than females (Hughes, 2003; Strong, DeVault, and Sayad, 1998; Anderson, 1989; Wyatt and Lyons-Rowe, 1990).

Smith and Udry (1985) found, for instance, that Blacks have more knowledge about sex at an earlier age than European Americans do. This is the result of certain elements in Black culture and other variables that are related to their class location. For instance, the greater socialization by peers leads to a heightened awareness of sex at an early age. Also, the fact that Black children become more involved in adult activity affects their sexual socialization. They are more likely to live in overcrowded conditions where they can observe sexual behavior at first hand. This they attempt to imitate, thus making an earlier entrance into heterosexual relations than do Whites. This does not necessarily involve sexual activity, just male-female social interaction. For instance, despite the psychosexual development theories of Freud (1938) and some others that "normal" boys should become interested in girls in early adolescence, in many Black neighborhoods, Black children are socialized at a younger age into heterosexual relationships (Westney, Jenkins, Butts, and Williams, 1991).

There are fewer class differences among females. One difference, however, is very salient to this discussion: the age of first intercourse. In general, the higher the class, the later the age of initial coitus, a relationship that is also true of first marriages. This fact is often attributed to the greater propensity of middle-class females to use substitutes of fantasies and masturbation for intercourse. Among working-class Black females, there is a high probability that the first sexual experience will be a violent one. Wyatt (1985) reports that a Black girl has a good chance of being exposed to rape and violence. Fifty-seven percent of the Black women she interviewed reported at least one incident of sexual abuse prior to age eighteen. National studies do not support such high levels of sex violence among Black teens—12 percent for Blacks, 6 percent for Whites, and 17 percent for Hispanics (Ryan, Manlove, and Franzetta, 2003). After the age of twenty-five, however, race and gender differences disappear. According to a nationwide study by Simenauer and Carroll (1982), only 4 percent of men and 9 percent of women between the ages of twenty and fifty-five have had no sexual partners while single. In the early 1990s, a national study showed that by their senior year of high school, 76 percent of males and 66 percent of females lose their virginity (Laumann, Gagnon, Michael, and Michaels, 1994). With such a large proportion of Americans engaging in nonmarital sexual activity, there is little room for race and gender variations.

One sees the operant effect of class as a differentiator of sexual expression by looking at variations in the Black community itself. While the Black middle class has until recently represented only a small segment of the total Black community, its sexual values and behavior have often been a reflection of the White middle class's. Fairly conservative sexual attitudes have been typical of middle-class Blacks. Many middle-class Black American males prefer that their wives stay at home rather than work. Frazier (1961, p. 771) once observed that "there is much irregularity in this class. The importance of sex to this class is indicated by their extreme sensitivity to any charge that Negroes are more free or more easy in their sexual behavior than whites." In its most extreme manifestation, this sexual conservatism was reflected in the in loco parentis stance of Black colleges in earlier periods. In the 1920s, Fisk University had printed regulations that "it was forbidden for two students of the opposite sex to meet each other without the presence and permission of the Dean of Women or of a teacher." A girl and boy could be sent home for walking together in broad daylight (Walters, 1975).

Until the late 1960s, most Black females adhered to a rather conservative sexual code during their college years. Many of them remained virgins until after graduation or confined their sexual experiences to a man with whom they had a committed relationship. A typical example is a thirty-two-year-old social worker who comments: "My point of comparison would be college—ten years ago. Since then I was a young adult, living in a college dorm, there were some very major changes. Probably sexual expectations are the biggest change; since back then we were still in the 'virgin' syndrome" (Staples, 1981, p. 95). The changes she speaks of have been significant, as attested by a thirty-five-year-old female educator who lost her virginity at the age of twenty-two. She declares that "a sexual relationship is a very normal part of an ongoing dating relationship. It may be an early part of the relationship or may develop over a period of sustained non-sexual contact" (Staples, 1981, p. 96). Consistent with her experience are changing cohort experiences among men. Compared to men raised in the 1980s, men raised in the 1960s and 1970s showed slower progression in courtship when moving from kissing to touching genitals to penile-vaginal intercourse during courtship.

Prolonged singlehood has imposed a more liberal acceptance of nonmarital sexual activity on the overwhelming majority of middle-class Black women. Whether they wanted to be participants in the sexual revolution or not, the conditions of single life have required a significant alteration of their previously conservative sexual values. Only a small number of them could hold to a traditional stance on nonmarital coitus. That small group also exhibits a high degree of religiosity (Wyatt, 1982).

That few middle-class Black women hold a negative attitude toward nonmarital sexual activity is partly due to general societal changes toward that behavior. The women's movement has legitimized the right of women to participate in and enjoy sex on an equal basis with men. Yet the sexual revolution as such was much more in conformity with male than female values. As Hite (1976) notes, "The sexual revolution is a male production, its principles still concentrated on male values (p. 449)." Many Black women are not comfortable with the new sexual morality. They would rather have a relationship develop along other lines than just sexual ones. Being an unattached single woman and wanting to date means having to deal with the sexual expectations of men. Due to their differential socialization, most men view dating as an instrumental (that is, goal-oriented) activity. What they do on the date is not so important as the aftermath. If the outcome is a sexual experience, the evening is a success. For women, the date has more of an expressive goal: to enjoy the activity and the companionship (Wyatt and Lyons-Rowe, 1990). One pensive position is that of a forty-year-old male political scientist: "Your first interest in a woman is sexual, so that you tend to discover what else (some would say everything else) there is to her in the course of the relationship originally stimulated by sexual attraction" (Staples, 1981, p. 96).

Sexual Practices

The 1960s and 1970s gave birth to what is popularly called the sexual revolution, accompanied by greater sexual candor in public discussions, books, film, television, art, and dress. Some sexologists claim that only the attitudes toward sexual behavior and the openness surrounding it were affected, not sexual behavior itself. However, there are indications that Americans now engage in premarital intercourse at an earlier age, with more partners, and in different ways. One thing has definitely changed: people remain single longer, and, at least until the AIDS epidemic emerged, being a mature single adult became synonymous with sexual experimentation (Simenauer and Carroll, 1982). This revolution included growing expectations for not only women's sexual satisfaction but equal responsibility in contraceptive use. This clearly is reflected in Pietropinto and Simenauer's 1977 study. Only 29.6 percent of Black men expressed a belief that women should take responsibility for birth control, whereas 22.9 percent said men should have protection ready and 28.3 percent agreed that both should use some sort of protective method.

One more example of the changing sexual scene is the variety of sexual practices in which Blacks engage. Acts that were once taboo have become commonplace. Probably the greatest change has been in the practice of oral and anal sex. In one study (Pietropinto and Simenauer, 1977), Black men expressed their sexual desires. Their response to the question, "What would you most like to do more often?" indicates that different sexual positions were desired more, along with their second choice of oral sex. The second choice is most interesting, since oral-genital sex was long considered taboo in the Black community. Yet Wyatt and Lyons-Rowe (1990) discovered that 55 percent of Black women have performed fellatio on a man. Those figures, while a dramatic change for Black women, are considerably lower than the percentage of White females who engage in such practices. Pietropinto and Simenauer report that 57 percent of all Black men find cunnilingus acceptable. One way of viewing this change is through cohort differences. Among Black males ages forty-five to forty-nine, only one-quarter find pleasure in performing or receiving oral sex, while among those ages eighteen to forty-four, the majority of Black men find such pleasure in receiving (63 percent) and performing (47 percent) oral sex (Lewis and Kertzner, 2003; Laumann, Gagnon,

Michael, and Michaels, 1994). Thus, it would appear that cunnilingus has become acceptable among Black men in just one generation, a truly remarkable change.

Unlike White females, who often progress into premarital intercourse after extended periods of petting—that is, sexually stimulating behavior—Black females face an all-or-nothing situation. In fact, the word *petting* is almost unknown to Black people. For instance, many White females have allowed sexual intimacies other than intercourse with the male to preserve their virginity. Such women are known as technical virgins (Belcastro, 1985). A technical virgin in the Black population is very rare. One reason is that some of the petting practices, such as oral-genital relations, were unacceptable to many Black women (Lewis and Kertzner, 2003; Smith and Udry, 1985). Another factor is that sexually enticing behavior can provoke the Black male into physical violence against a Black woman who engages in such acts without the intention of sexual consummation (Staples, 1982).

Black lesbians and gays may be more or less prevalent than White lesbians and gays. There are few available data on the subject for Blacks. Some writers have claimed that Blacks have a greater incidence of Black gay men than do White gay men. Earlier reports hypothesize that female-headed households in the Black community have resulted in a lack of male role models for Black male children (Vontress, 1971), increasing the likelihood of Black males' becoming gay. But there is no evidence to support this supposition. Furthermore, few laypeople often think of Black males as being gay (Herek and Capitanio, 1995). As part of their studies of sexual practices, the Kinsey group in 1948 and 1953 investigated Black gays and lesbians. They found that Blacks were more comfortable than Whites around lesbians and gays and did not perceive them as any kind of threat to their manhood. Consequently, Black gays and lesbians were not as isolated from the Black heterosexual population as was the case among Whites. They were not relegated to their own bars or social cliques.

Further, because of actual or perceived racism within the gay community, Black gay men have not relied on social networking through White gay bars, baths, and public places (Cochran and Mays, 1999; Bell and Weinberg, 1978). A more recent study uncovered gendered differences in Black heterosexuals' attitudes: men expressed more negative attitudes toward gay men than they did toward lesbians, and their feelings toward gay men were more negative than were those of Black females. Furthermore, several factors increased favorable attitudes: having personal relationships with gay people; being well educated, a registered voter, or single; believing that homosexuality is not a choice; and infrequent church attendance. The last three were among the most powerful predictors of favorable attitudes (Herek and Capitanio, 1995).

Considering their greater involvement with women, it would be reasonable to conclude that compared to White gay men, Black gay men have lower visibility in their communities. Yet there are no reliable or consistent data on the number of gays. Kinsey, Pomeroy, Martin, and Gebhard (1953) reported that 37 percent of men have had one or more same-sex experiences. Other sexologists have estimated the number of exclusively gay men to be between 1 and 4 percent. The Kinsey associates conducted an extensive study of gays in 1970 that included Blacks. While the Black men made up 11 percent of the gay population surveyed, the study did not use an objective selection process. The Kinsey researchers had difficulty finding Black gay men because they were not as openly engaged in the gay world as were their White counterparts (Bell and Weinberg, 1978). The lack of a visible Black community continues to frustrate health educators attempting to educate Black gays (Cochran and Mays, 1999). Perhaps their relative absence from the gay world stemmed from the fact that they are more likely than Whites to claim bisexuality rather than an exclusively lesbian or gay sexual orientation (Binson, Stall, Coates, Gagnon, and Catania, 1995). For example, in the Pietropinto and Simenauer (1977) study, 9.2

percent of the Black males claimed to be bisexual, compared to 2.6 percent of the White males—and these data are consistent with studies two decades later. While the results of this most extensive post-Kinsey report and pre-1982 study are not directly comparable to Kinsey's, the researchers did ask some of the same questions of the 4,066 men, of whom 240 (5 percent) were Black of the total group studied. These Blacks were unrepresentative in other ways: they had lower incomes and less education than the White men studied. For those claiming to be gay and lesbians, Kinsey and others (1953) discovered that Black gay men have their first same-sex experience earlier than do White gay men, were less likely to hide their sexual orientation from family and friends, and reported more female friends (Bell and Weinberg, 1978).

The Black lesbian, like her White counterpart, is a hidden figure. Some have even suggested that Black lesbianism is on the increase because of the shortage of Black males. However, Black women's response is often to become bisexual (Mays and Cochran, 1991). The most comprehensive examination to date of Black heterosexuals' attitudes show Black communities expressing greater acceptance of lesbians than of gay men (Herek and Capitanio, 1995). However, slightly fewer than a third of Blacks believe that sex between two women is all right, only one-fourth believe lesbianism is a natural expression of sexuality in women, and only 42 percent do not find the practice disgusting (Herek and Capitanio, 1995). These feelings do not necessarily translate into negative interpersonal interactions between heterosexuals, gays, and lesbians. However, some lesbians' experiences with other Blacks do not confirm a disconnect between attitudes and behavior. Lesbian couples complain that their families are not too accepting of their relationship. Some also have to move from their residences because of crank calls and constant threats, indicating that even if their families are accepting, they still face community intolerance (hooks, 1988). When lesbians lose Black community support, the intensity of their triple oppression—Black, female, and lesbian—can be devastating to their self-esteem. They argue that their oppression is based on attributes over which they have no control.

The increasing scientific attention on gays and lesbians stems from the HIV/AIDS crisis. AIDS has become the leading cause of death among men and women twenty-five to forty-four years of age in the United States, particularly those in large urban areas, and it has disproportionately hit minority populations. The death rate from AIDS for Black American women is ten times the rate for White women. More recently, heterosexual transmission has become the most frequent mode of new HIV infections in women, accounting for 37 percent of the new cases but only 4 percent of new cases among men (Lawrence, Eldridge, Reitman, Little, Shelby, and Brasfiled, 1998). Given that a significant number of Black American men report multiple risk factors—multiple partners, drug use, low condom use or all three—we can expect a continuing increase in the heterosexual transmission of HIV to Black American women. Although consistent and correct condom use reduces HIV transmission during vaginal intercourse by approximately 90 percent, condom use among inner-city Black American women remains relatively low. A number of demographic, socioeconomic, situational definitions, and personal barriers interfere with putting a speedy halt to this epidemic.

First, the shortage of men means that particularly among the poor, some women desiring long-term commitments may have to settle for a series of relatively short-term monogamous relationships with men who may concurrently be having sexual relationships with other women and who may also have backgrounds of imprisonment and drug use (Lawrence, Eldridge, Reitman, Little, Shelby, and Brasfiled, 1998; Schneider and Stoller, 1995). However, the shortage of males also may serve as a protective demographic factor. According to one longitudinal study of a heterosexual, multiethnic, randomly selected sample with a median education of some college (Dolcini, Coates, Catania, Kegeles, and Hauck, 1995), White women were more likely than Black American and Hispanic women to have many partners.

Black American men without a primary partner were the most likely to have multiple partners, and Black and Hispanic women with primary partners were less likely than White women to have multiple partners (a Black-White difference replicated in other studies, including Lewis, 1995). In general, condom use was low among those with multiple partners, suggesting high-risk behavior among White women and Black men. As usual, when making racial comparisons, care must be taken not to distort the male-female dynamics within Black communities. It is the consequences of the male shortage within Black communities that have the most relevant meaning for Black women's daily interpersonal interactions. Furthermore, since condom use is under the direct control of men and women perceive that men find condom-protected sex less enjoyable, only those relationships with mutual respect and open sexual communication will experience protective sex.

Second, similar to females in other ethnic groups, Black women, regardless of class, prefer a committed relationship before engaging in sexual intercourse. In fact, commitment, not multiple partners, distinguishes "good girls" from "bad girls." Thus, there is considerable pressure on women to remain faithful. Tragically, women's greatest risk may be within committed relationships, where fear of losing the relationship interferes with introducing effective risk-reduction strategies. For instance, in a sample of single, pregnant, inner-city Black women, most reported having one partner in a "monogamous" relationship. However, in reality, their behavior could better be described as serial monogamy. These women felt protected from risk by virtue of having one partner at a time. Thus, fewer than 10 percent used condoms consistently and 35 percent had never discussed AIDS prevention with their partners (Lawrence et al., 1998; Schneider and Stoller, 1995).

In addition to self-labeling a relationship as monogamous and ignoring the risk of serial exposures, Black women may recognize the risk but find condom use undesirable for other reasons. Research suggests that some Black women appraise condoms negatively, viewing condoms as unromantic, interfering with spontaneity, and detracting from sexual pleasure. Perhaps most important is the meaning condoms had for these women's self-esteem and sense of morality. Many of these women felt that they did not want to use anything that was associated with prostitutes, casual relationships, lack of trust, and disease. As one teenage girl told the senior author, "I wouldn't want my boyfriend to use a condom because that would be like he thought I was dirty." Sadly, these women prefer to eschew condom use in order to maintain an idealized images of themselves, their partners, and the relationship (Lawrence et al., 1998; Moore and Burt, 1982; Schneider and Stoller, 1995).

Finally, in order to lower the risks of HIV, it is important to understand the major transmission routes. These routes are markedly different for Blacks and Whites. According to the Centers for Disease Control, until December 1992, male same-sex intercourse constituted 76 percent of White and only 35 percent of Black cases. Blacks acquire the disease through either injection drug use (40 percent) or a combination of drug use and intercourse between gay men (6 percent); only 15 percent of Whites reported the drug route. For all ethnic groups, the trend is a movement away from contracting HIV from sexual relationships among gay partners and more through intravenous drug use. Almost three-fourths of Black women's cases are linked to drug injection, either directly (56 percent) or indirectly through sex with intravenous drug users (20 percent). Furthermore, bisexuality transmission was more commonly reported by Black than White men (Lewis, 1995). In sum, although Black women have fewer partners than White women and are less likely to be exposed to risk through same-sex intercourse, they have far more windows of opportunity to be at risk. There are certainly more drug abusers than gays and lesbians, more Black men in prison than whites, and far more Blacks living in poverty conditions. Furthermore, the risk factor of both Black males and females, particularly those with few resources, may increase because of their perception of "relative risk." In the context of other social realities, poverty's own survival risks may outweigh the fear of AIDS and the pressing realities of life may diffuse sexual risk concerns.

The one sexual perversion that many Black women encounter is rape. Contrary to popular belief, most rapes committed by Black men are committed against Black women, not White women. Many of the sexual assaults of Black women by Black men go unreported. There is a significant number of date rapes that occur daily, especially in lower-class life. It often happens when a woman leads a man to believe that she will have sexual relations with him but protests when he reaches the point of vaginal penetration. Sometimes she is ambivalent about sexual relations. Other times it may be forcible intercourse. Most rapes do involve friends or acquaintances of the women involved (Staples, 1999; Anderson, 1989; Lloyd, 1991). Even some upwardly mobile males find reason to justify rape. During the sexual revolution era, more than a third of Black college males believed that if a woman is inappropriately dressed, it is her fault if she gets raped (Johnson, 1989a).

When it comes to the sex book industry, Blacks are virtually absent. Despite the many books written on White sexuality, many of them best-sellers, there is not yet one empirical book on Black sexual patterns. White authors have written several books on interracial sexual activity, but few, if any, have the intimate understanding of Black culture and values to provide meaningful insight into this difficult and controversial subject. There is probably more Black involvement in film pornography. Whereas 1970s films infrequently featured people of color, by the 1990s the gay male pornographic industry began featuring the Black body but largely maintained racial segregation. With the advent of the Internet, the visibility of Blacks in contemporary pornography increased (Thomas, 2002). Quite a few of the recent pornography films have featured Black female actresses, most of them in interracial sexual action. The same is true of pornographic books and magazines. The Report of the Commission on Obscenity and Pornography (President's Commission, 1971) reported that the typical patron of pornography films is a White, middle-aged, middle-class married male. The same commission theorized that there is nothing particularly harmful in viewing sexually arousing films. However, many of the regular patrons of these materials are sexually frustrated. One study found that its Black middle-income respondents were uniformly against pornography, and 82 percent believed it to be harmful to society (Timberlake and Carpenter, 1990).

Summary

When the sexual revolution began in American society in the 1960s, Blacks were slow to adapt to it and did not participate in any significant numbers in certain aspects of it. By the 1970s, premarital sexual activity had become the norm for the formerly conservative middle-class Black female. It is impossible to address any issue in Black male-female relationships without taking note of the shortage of eligible and "desirable" Black men. Not only are there about 1.5 million more Black females than Black males in general, but the sex ratio is extremely imbalanced among college graduates. For a long time, Black women have outnumbered Black men.

Consequently, sexually conservative college-educated Black women often meet the sexual demands of their male peers, fully realizing that if they do not, the men can always find other women who will. Once liberated, voluntarily or not, middle-class Black women have indulged in a full range of sexual expression. No longer confined to the outdated notions that "nice" women do not enjoy sex, sex outside marriage, or unconventional sexual practices, Blacks have abandoned traditional taboos. Oral sex, for instance, became something that a majority of Blacks engage in. But some of the excesses of the sexual revolution have never taken strong hold among Blacks. Few Black women have willingly engaged in one-night stands or changed sexual partners indiscriminately.

Some sexual practices, such as group sex, sadomasochism, and father-child incest, are rarely observed among Blacks. Black gay men are more open and tolerated, at least on the part of Black males, than in the White community, and lesbianism is now receiving a better reception than previously reported.

In the 1980s, the news media began to report the end of the sexual revolution, announcing that men and women were looking for commitment and marriage instead of casual sex. This new sexual conservatism coincided with the aging of baby boom women (those born between 1946 and 1960) and the election of Ronald Reagan, a conservative president who supported traditional sexual ideals. Because women were getting older and facing biological deadlines for bearing a child, they started looking for fathers instead of sexual partners.

Adding to the rising tide of conservatism has been the AIDS epidemic. AIDS was originally thought of as a White male's disease. However, during the 1990s the epidemic shifted steadily toward a growing proportion of AIDS cases in Blacks and Hispanics, who were already infected disproportionately more than Whites, while infection among same-sex partners decreased. According to the Centers for Disease Control, Blacks constituted 38 percent and Hispanics 18 percent of AIDS cases at the turn of the twenty-first century (Centers for Disease Control and Prevention, 2001).

Although just over one-third of Americans acquire AIDS through heterosexual sex, worldwide it is still a disease of heterosexuality. Its rapid spread among heterosexuals in the United States is evident in newly diagnosed HIV cases: slightly less than half are heterosexuals who had sex with each other or injected drugs. Young Black women appear to be at highest risk (Dotinga, 2004). For Americans age twenty-five to forty-four, AIDS was the leading cause of death for non-Hispanic Black men and the third leading cause for Black women (Centers for Disease Control and Prevention, 2001).

Among the confidential HIV reporting group, in 2001 Black women represented nearly 51 percent of all those diagnosed. Of all pediatric HIV cases, Black children under age thirteen represented almost two-thirds (Centers for Disease Control and Prevention,

2001). It is far easier for Black women to become infected because of the high use of intravenous drugs among males and the higher incidence of bisexual males. Even if fewer than one million Americans of all ethnic groups are living with HIV/AIDS, in the large world of Black singles, imbalanced gender ratio, and high sexual activities, Black women must be vigilant.

Fortunately, according to national health surveys Blacks are becoming more attentive in the wake of the AIDS epidemic. In comparison to other ethnic groups who have changed their behavior, Blacks, regardless of socioeconomic status, are most likely to state that they have changed: Blacks, 46 percent; Hispanics, 37 percent; and Whites 26 percent. Furthermore, the most significant decrease in teen pregnancy occurred among Black teens, which reflects their more effective use of contraceptives (Child Trend, 2003).

Any objective examination of Black sexual behavior would reveal that there are many variations in the type and frequency of sexual activity among this group; that the racial differences have their origin in cultural and class differences, not innate biological traits; and that changes over time have brought about a convergence in the sexual attitudes and behavior of the two racial groups. In the light of the stereotypical views of Black sexuality that existed in the past, it is all the more amazing to find that in some circumstances, Blacks have more conservative sexual values than European Americans. The motivation behind the previous labeling of Blacks as sexually immoral is quite clear, as we currently witness the redefinition of behavior that was once alleged to be peculiar to Blacks. More euphemistic terms are applied to the same behavior among European Americans. This society apparently restructures its attitudes and practices when the sexual "deviants" are members of the majority group. While we can agree that these events are a mark of human progress, it cannot be ignored that when the same behavior is found among the Black population, the result is the collective indictment of an entire racial group and a concomitant denial of its civil and human rights. As the pace of sexual change makes it difficult to make moral distinctions between racial groups, let us hope that cultural differences in sexual behavior will be recognized as no more than diversity in the spectrum of possible responses to sexual stimuli. Designations of racial groups as superior or inferior on the basis of their sexual values and behavior have no place in a rational and humanistic society.

5

Singlehood and Partner Selection

U nmarried people have become the largest minority group in the
United States. If we count individuals who have never married or are divorced, separated, or widowed, they account for 98 million Americans, or nearly half of America's population over the age
of fifteen, and their numbers have shown a steady growth (Crowder
and Tolnay, 2000; U.S. Census Bureau, 1992, 2002a). This has been
a neglected group in the literature because of their transient status; in
earlier years, most would eventually have entered the ranks of the
married population.

Increasingly, however, Americans are beginning to view singlehood as a way of life. Some choose it voluntarily, and others will be
forced into making the choice. Black Americans are more likely to
face the dilemma of singlehood or marriage. As a group, they are pro-
portionately more likely to be unmarried, divorced, separated, or widowed. Approximately 70 percent of the Black female population aged
fifteen to forty-four fall into the singles category (Cantave and Harrison, 2001; U.S. Census Bureau, 1992, 2002a). Moreover, singlehood
poses much more of a problem for them because of the shortage of
men, the different cultural traditions under which they were raised,
fewer institutional supports for coping with unmarried life, and the inevitable complications stemming from their status as a racial minority. Until recently, rarely has the family literature directly dealt with
this subject, despite the magnitude of the Black singles situation in

America. Sparked by the close connection between the growth in female-headed households and the related rise in poverty among children, social scientists have given greater attention to marital behavior (Crowder and Tolnay, 2000). And since Black children are disproportionately represented among the poor, Black singlehood cannot be ignored.

The data on Black women reflect some unhappiness with the institution of marriage or their difficulty in entering into a legal union. One of the largest surveys of Afro-Americans discovered that only 42 percent were married and another 42 percent were involved in a romantic relationship. Of the remaining subjects, who seem most disenchanted with relationships between the genders, a third preferred to be in a marriage or roommate relationship (Tucker and Taylor, 1989). In 1985, the Gallup poll reported that 56 percent of Black women considered the ideal lifestyle as marriage and a full-time job. A 1999 survey of 317 nonrandomly selected Black single and married women revealed distinct cohort differences. The group holding the most positive views of marriage were married, higher-status women and those entering adulthood in the 1940s and 1950s when there existed fewer career choices for women and two-parent households peaked. The most unfavorable views on marriage were held by those entering adulthood in the late 1970s, 1980s, and early 1990s—the post–sexual revolution era and the male shortage peak. Furthermore, while the overwhelming majority disagreed with the notion that a successful career should be more important than a successful marriage or that there are fewer advantages to marriage today than in the past, the less educated never-married women were less likely to endorse the importance of marriage over career (King, 1999). Even among the most occupationally successful Black women—corporate managers—those unmarried (the majority) reflect the reality of a limited available selection, not an alternative set of values that do not hold marriage in high esteem (Toliver, 1998). Consistent with the majority sentiment, among women aged fifteen to forty-five, 73.5 percent of Black women had married by the age of forty to forty-five, the age range by which most women who will ever marry have already done so (Cantave and Harrison, 2001; London, 1991).

Although the times are changing, it is hard to imagine a society in which large numbers of people reject the idea of marriage. America's forefathers obviously considered singlehood a threat when they imposed a special tax on men who insisted on remaining bachelors. As we look at contemporary America, we see how far we have come from the days when birth, marriage, and death were the three supreme experiences in life. Not only are there fewer marriages, but people are marrying at a later age. In the 1960s, the average American got married between the ages of twenty and twenty-four, and during that decade 92 percent of all women married by age thirty. By 1990, only 81 percent were married in their twenties. Moreover, between 1970 and 2000, the proportion of never-married thirty-year-olds more than tripled (Wright, 2002). It would be easy and comforting to assume that Americans are delaying marriage until a later age. But the proportion of singles has also increased for the age group thirty to thirty-four. While many will eventually marry, it is conceivable that a large proportion will remain single throughout their lives (Cantave and Harrison, 2001; U.S. Census Bureau, 1992; Wright, 2002).

With few exceptions, Black slaves, particularly in the last century of slavery, were not allowed to have a legal marriage. Marriage was, and is, essentially a contractual relationship, and the slaves were not permitted to enter into legal contracts for any purposes. However, there were relationships between male and female slaves that were socially, if not legally, recognized. After slavery ended, the freed slaves went to great lengths to have their relationships legalized. A legal marriage was a status symbol to a group deprived of such rights for two centuries. They married in record numbers, and by far the majority of Blacks were lodged in nuclear families by the beginning of the twentieth century (Gutman, 1976).

As further evidence of the Black emphasis on marriage, the census data for about 1900 indicate that more Blacks than Whites eventually entered into marital relationships (U.S. Census Bureau, 1972).

The questions that need to be answered are what has happened and why. It is easier to explain what has happened than the reasons behind it. While the upward trend in singlehood exists for the entire U.S. population, the trend toward singleness and away from marriage is more pronounced among Blacks. Ninety-five percent of all Black males and 92 percent of Black females are still unmarried by age twenty-four. More significant, 55 percent of Black males are still single by age thirty-four, and 49 percent of Black women have not married by the same age (U.S. Census Bureau, 1996b). As unexpected as those figures may be, they do not tell the entire story. Individuals who are separated, divorced, or widowed must be counted as single. When we include these Blacks with the never married, we find that at any given point in time, about 65 percent of all adult Blacks are not married and living with a spouse. Hence, this is not an unique group of people we are discussing. Perhaps as important as why it happened is how significant it is to the functioning of the Black community.

Before exploring the answers to those questions, we wish to make our own position clear. Some feminist scholars and others have posited singlehood as a viable alternative to marriage. That is not our perspective. Most Blacks do not see their singleness as a choice but as a condition forced on them by certain vicissitudes of life in America. This does not mean that Black singlehood is a pathological form or that all Black marriages are happy or functional. What it does signify is that being single and Black is problematic in many cases. It requires coping with certain problems that either do not occur in the conjugal state or happen with less frequency. Let us be clear at the outset that not all people are single in the same way. Some may be living with another person, and the relationship takes on all the qualities of a marriage; others have children who occupy their time and satisfy certain emotional needs; and a number of them may be wedded to a career. Some singles reside in intergenerational families that provide for some emotional and financial needs, making their marital status a lower priority. At the same time, there are those who are actively dating and ardently pursuing a spouse. Some scholars believe that the bottom line of all these different configurations is conflicts in the male-female relationship. Remaining unmarried, or dissolving a marriage, is the most fundamental expression of an inability or unwillingness to resolve that conflict (Franklin, 1984).

As to the significance of Black singlehood for the functioning of the Black community, there are certain ramifications that are felt collectively. In contrast to the ideology that singlehood is a viable alternative, it must be interpreted as a symbol of role failure in the normative sense. Perhaps we need some redefinition of roles. No person has yet come up with a known workable alternative. Alternative family substitutes such as open marriage, communal living, and heterosexual cohabitation have been tried and found wanting, and Blacks never embraced those family substitutes. Being single and living alone is not a role that relates to any other role. It is the ultimate expression of individuality in a society that is based on an organic togetherness. However, as we shall see, many Blacks find structural barriers to their desire to bond with members of the other gender. Concomitant with individual flaws that make men and women incompatible are social forces that are operative in Black life in a more pronounced manner than seen in mainstream society.

Characteristics of Black Singles

Over the past thirty years, the proportion of Blacks married and living with a spouse has undergone a steady decline. From the 1970s to the mid-1980s, a clear picture emerged of Blacks who had the highest marriage rate: middle-class Blacks ages twenty-five to forty-five. As the income level rose, so did the number of men who were married and living with their wife. Many were still married to their first wife, and many of those who divorced subsequently remarried. In contrast, Black women who graduated from college were the least likely to have married. Among those who did marry, especially those who had five or more years of college, their divorce rate was higher and their remarriage rate lower than for Black women with less education. Ironically, the Black men who were least likely to marry or remarry were those who had less than a high school education (U.S. Census Bureau, 1985). This suggests that marriage rates in the 1980s were a function of education (or status) for Black men and women, but in different directions.

By 2002, Black females' higher educational attainment did not appear to have much of an impact on reducing the probability of marrying. Among those females with master's, professional, and doctorate degrees, those with professional degrees (for example, lawyers, medical doctors) are least likely to marry. However, they are just as likely or more likely to marry than their less educated sisters. Black males, regardless of higher degree type, have higher rates of being married than do Black females. Furthermore, having any type of degree beyond high school increases their chances of being married as compared to those with lesser education.

The clearest picture that emerges is the link between income, marital status, and gender. Once earnings exceed $40,000, the gap between married males and married females widens. Eighty percent of Black males and 74 percent of Black females earning $40,000 to $74,999 are married. This gap is most pronounced for those earning more than $75,000 (most likely professionals): 86 percent of males and 69 percent of females are married. Moreover, at every income level above $15,000, females are at least twice as likely to be divorced (one exception is the $25,000—39,999 range). The most dramatic gender difference appears among those making $75,000 or more: females are three times more likely to divorce (7.1 versus 27.3).

Evidently, relatively affluent Black men not only are less likely to become divorced, but if they do, they are more likely to remarry soon. In contrast, relatively affluent divorced Black women may find that most of the desirable men have already married or remarried, leaving them a smaller and less desirable marriage pool. This gender differential points out a basic problem for Black women seeking to have marriage with a professional career or high earnings: the more they earn and the more demanding their occupation is, the less likely they are to get married or remain married. Having it all is primarily reserved for males.

Types of Singles

Singles are not a monolithic group. The categories that the Census Bureau uses are the never married, the widowed, the separated, and the divorced. Gays and lesbians will not be discussed here because of the lack of data available on this group. Among Blacks, for a long time, the largest number in the twenty-five to forty age group has been the separated. Lower-income Blacks have long used physical separation as a form of marital dissolution. The expense of a divorce generally deterred many of them from seeking legal recognition of a union torn asunder. Very few middle-class Black singles allowed a marital disruption to remain in a legal limbo. The time between physical separation and divorce proceedings for that class is typically brief, except in cases where ambivalence about the termination of a marriage exists. Among some men, it is often a ploy to ward off pressures for marriage from a future consort. Those who are only separated do not differ greatly from the divorced, except that they may have a reduced desire to remarry again or may have a lower income status. Since 1980, the lower-income group has married less often, thus reducing the numbers in the separated category (U.S. Census Bureau, 1992).

The divorced form the second-largest category in this age cohort and may be qualitatively different from the never married. Usually they are older, and many have children. Actually, the majority of Black singles ages fifteen to sixty-two were previously married. It is only in the age group below forty that most have never been married. We would expect to find some difference between the never married and formerly married with children. The divorced persons with children often form attenuated families and carry out most of the same functions as other nuclear families. The pull of marriage may not be as great as among childless singles.

Very few Black singles under age sixty are among the widowed. While the average Black widow has lost her husband at an early age, with the dramatic exception of females without any high school education (39 percent), very few (females less than 10 percent and males less than 3 percent) Black singles under age fifty-five have lost a spouse through death. However, by age sixty-four, 24 percent of Black women but a relatively low 6 percent of Black men have lost a spouse. The high rate of widowhood for women with low levels of education is disturbing. Those with less than a high school education are most likely to be among the poor, who are most likely to experience poor health, criminal activity, and imprisonment. Evidently, their mate loss is highly related to drug use, AIDS, homicide, and imprisonment. It is likely that the Census Bureau overstates the number of women who lose their spouses through death, since some women prefer to claim widowhood rather than report that their mate is in prison (Crowder and Tolnay, 2000; Glick, 1988; U.S. Census Bureau, 2002b).

Although we consider all individuals who are not married and living with a spouse as part of the singles category, not all of them are single in the same way. Stein (1976), for instance, developed a four-celled typology containing the features of voluntariness and permanence. His four types of singles are classified as (1) permanently and voluntarily single, (2) permanently but involuntarily single, (3) temporarily and voluntarily single, and (4) temporarily, involuntarily single. Although these categories might be useful as units of analysis, they imply certain value assumptions about singlehood that we do not share. Considering that the median age of Black singles is under forty, to posit their singlehood as a permanent status would seem premature. As for the voluntary nature of their single status, that is impossible to determine. Although a number of Black single women report receiving marriage proposals, the reason for their refusal appears to be the rejection of the particular male, not the institution of marriage (Tucker and Taylor, 1989). The self-concept of Black singles may instead reflect their need to avoid cognitive dissonance. That is, when there is an inconsistency between a status and a belief system, the individual may reduce the dissonance by altering her beliefs (Festinger, 1957). To ensure self-acceptance, many single women declare themselves happy and voluntary in their single status.

Any analysis of Black singlehood would be more valid if we used the concept of a singles career. This concept designates objective movements that one may make through the singles world. Within these movements are manifest changes in the self-concepts that accompany relocations in that milieu. The most common, and of greatest interest to us, is the free-floating single. This type of single is totally unattached to any other person and dates randomly with or without the purpose of seeking a committed relationship. Another type is the individual in an open-couple relationship. This person has a relatively steady partner, but the relationship is open enough to encompass other individuals in a sexual or romantic liaison. Sometimes it is an open-couple relationship in a unilateral sense, with one of the partners deceptively pursuing other parties. Occasionally it is merely the failure to define the relationship explicitly by either of the couples. A related type is that of the closed-couple relationship. In this case, the partners look exclusively to each other to have their needs for sex and affection met. By mutual agreement, fidelity is expected, and the partners are emotionally bound to each other (Staples, 1981).

We could call this next group the committed singles: individuals who are cohabiting in the same household and are engaged to be married or otherwise have an agreement to establish a permanent relationship. In many ways, they do not share the singles lifestyle. Rather, they often maintain the same existence as married couples but without the legal validation. Those committed to a permanent relationship are emotionally bound to each other; as long as the commitment lasts, they spend most of their leisure time together and encounter few of the problems that perplex other singles.

Another singles stage through which people may pass (or that they may stop at) is accommodation. There are two types of accommodation: temporary and permanent. Among the younger group of singles (under age forty-five), the accommodation to their single status will be temporary. They will lead a solitary existence except for friendships. In the case of women, it can mean refusing all dates, and for men, failing to pursue any heterosexual contacts. Certainly, they are asexual and cease all sexual activity. Some accommodationists may temporarily adopt an alternative lifestyle or sublimate through work, school, or religion. The permanent accommodationist is generally in an older age cohort. Many Black singles over the age of forty-five tend to be more permanently resigned to their single status. At this age many single women, particularly those with little education, are widows and do not plan to remarry. Others have been married, have children who are now adults, and devote themselves to the grandparent role (Tucker and Taylor, 1989; Staples, 1981).

The Influence of Sex Ratios

Another element that contributes to the large number of single people among Blacks is the sex ratio. In the age range of twenty-five to sixty-four, there are about 1.5 million more females than males, or 85 Black males for every 100 Black females. Between ages eighteen and thirty-four, the sex ratio is even lower: 83 to 100. The excess females increase the probability of unmarried females, and the scarcity of males reduces the number of possible husband-wife combinations. Historical patterns of racial discrimination affecting health patterns and resources have created a gap between the life expectancies of Blacks and Whites. Blacks can expect to live about ten years fewer than Whites, and the percentage of Black females who are aged sixty-five or over is greater than the percentage of Black males in that age group. Thus, the operation of the normal age-specific and gender-specific death rates reduces the number of males versus females in the population as age advances, modifying the gender ratio in the relevant portion of the population (U.S. Census Bureau, 2002a, 2002b; Stockard and Tucker, 2001; U.S. Department of Health and Human Services, 1985; Cremation Association of North America, 2004).

The abnormally high mortality rate for Black males of a marriageable age or younger is attributed to the effects of inner-city living. Death rates for young Black males are much higher than for any other sex-race group (Wright, 2002). This is due in part to the large number of deaths from homicides, AIDS, suicide, and drugs. The pressures of poor urban life, the inability to find work, the impact of society's surveillance of their behavior—such as police vigilance in minority neighborhoods—and the self-directed violence of America's Black males all combine to kill off the youth of the Black community at an alarming rate (Gibbs, 1988b; Ragsdale, 2000). One unfortunate effect of living in a racially stratified society is the development of a tendency of Blacks to kill Blacks. The highest rate of homicide involving Americans can be found among Black men. They are most likely to be defendants in homicides involving other Blacks: 94 percent Black-on-Black homicide since 1976 (U.S. Bureau of Justice Statistics, 2002). In 1988, one in one thousand young Black males died in a homicide. That rate was about six times greater than that for all people in that age group, and although slightly less true, as late as 2000 this rate remained (Balthazar and King, 2001; Mydans, 1990; U.S. Bureau of Justice Statistics, 2002). Blacks are far less likely than Whites to turn their anger on family members, and they show particularly low rates of eldercide (29.9 percent of Blacks versus 68.5 of Whites).

The homicidal acts of Black men are directly traceable to social pressures and racial influences. Black victims are overrepresented in homicides involving arguments or drugs and underrepresented in homicides involving sex-related, poison, and workplace killings. In general, the poorer a person is, the more likely he or she will be victimized (U.S. Bureau of Justice Statistics, 2002; Wright, 2002). The traumatic experience of being a Black man in a society that does not provide avenues for masculine expression—gainful employment and adequate income—apparently takes its toll. This is particularly true for Black males in the fifteen-to-twenty-five age range.

An additional factor contributing to an imbalance of the genders is the large number of Black prisoners in the nation's jails. Most of the Black prisoners are males, and most are poor. Their victims often come from families earning less than $7,500 a year. For White, Black, and other groups, the rate of incarceration is staggering. Inmates in federal, state, and local adult correctional institutions grew from 163,800 men and women during 1998 to reach a new high of 5.9 million by 2000. Of these, Blacks represented a disturbingly high proportion. In 1997, Black males in their twenties represented 8,630 per 100,000 residents compared to 2,703 among Hispanic males and 868 among White males. The rate among Black American males ages forty-five to fifty-four in the same year was larger than the highest rate among Hispanic males, ages twenty to twenty-nine, and three times larger than the highest rate among White males, ages thirty to thirty-four. Most are incarcerated for nonvictim offenses such as drugs. In fact, over the past two decades, imprisonment of drug offenders has grown at an even higher rate than the general explosive growth of incarceration in the United States during that same time. Although drug offenses are roughly equal among the White American and Black American populations, Blacks are imprisoned for drug offenses at fourteen times the rate of Whites (Balthazar and King, 2001; Currence and Johnson, 2003). Partially as a result of changing sentencing policies and mandatory minimum sentences for various crimes regardless of mitigating circumstances, U.S. imprisonment rates are the highest in the world. About one of every four Black men between the ages of twenty and thirty is in a state, federal, or local jail. Black offenders spend more time in prison and on parole than Whites convicted of the same offenses, except for kidnapping. For Black American men, women, children, and communities, the consequences are enormous (Robinson, 2002; Balthazar and King, 2001; Ostrow, 1991; U.S. Bureau of Justice Statistics, 1990).

When selecting a mate, Black women must consider the nature of the pool from which they will draw. In 98 percent of marriages with a Black bride, the groom will be a Black male. Hence, her pool consists of the unmarried Black males with a variety of attributes. The most crucial factor in the search for mates is the excess number of women over men during the marriageable years. According to the U.S. Census Bureau (1991a), there are almost 1.5 million more Black women than men over the age of fifteen. By the Census Bureau's own account, there is an undercount of about 925,000 Black males who exist but were not added to the Black population total. These uncounted males are likely to be transient, homeless, and unemployed (Freeman, 2001; Joe and Yu, 1991; Stockard and Tucker, 2001) and thus not viable husband candidates. Since there is an excess number of Black males at birth, the subsequent shortage of Black males over the age of fourteen must be attributed to their higher infant mortality rate and the considerably greater mortality rate of young Black males through homicide, accidents, suicide, drug overdoses, and war casualties (Gibbs, 1988b).

The biggest problem for Black women, however, is not the quantity in the available supply of potential mates but the quality. Whereas Black women may select a mate on the basis of a number of attributes, a minimum prerequisite is that he be gainfully and regularly employed. According to a study by Joe and Yu (1991), almost a majority of working-age Black males fail to meet those minimum prerequisites. After an analysis of the economic and census data, they concluded that 46 percent of the 8.8 million Black men of working age were not in the labor force. Based on 1982 statistics, they found 1.2 million Black men were unemployed, 1.8 million had dropped out of the labor force, 186,000 were in prison, and 925,000 were classified as "missing" because the Census Bureau says it could not locate them.

Their study, moreover, overstates the number of "desirable" and available Black males in the marriage pool. Even with the census undercount, there are still a half-million more Black women over the age of fifteen than Black men. Also, we must subtract from the marriage pool Black men with certain characteristics that substantially outnumber Black women. Among those characteristics are Blacks serving in the armed forces. Approximately 90 percent of them are male. According to the U.S. Department of Defense, in 2000 Blacks represented 20 percent of the 1.4 million active-duty personnel, and Black officers represented slightly less than 10 percent of all officers. Although a slight decline in total Black enlistment has occurred since that time, the number of Black officers has increased on all forces. At least half of all Black officers came from twenty-one historically black colleges and universities (HBCU). Hence, their desire or exposure to potential Black mates can be expected to be high. While officers provided a richer pool of eligibles for Black females, a large number of Black male enlistees had poor prospects for employment in the civilian labor force (Butler, 2002; Hisnanick, 2001; Stewart and Scott, 1978).

Recently, the salary and other benefits (including cost of living allowances) of military personnel have improved, a number of Black soldiers are currently married, and the rate of Black enlisted officers with higher salaries has increased. However, the military does take out of circulation a number of marriage-age Black males by stationing them in foreign posts and isolated military stations. Furthermore, once their period of enlistment ends, Black veterans experience a higher rate of unemployment even in relation to Black civilian males with no military service (Stewart and Scott, 1978). Hence, military service only postpones the entry of Black males into the ranks of the unemployed, one reason that Black males have a higher rate of reenlistment, particularly for the army, than their White counterparts (Butler, 2002).

Among the factors that reduce the number of desirable Black males in the marriage pool is the high rate of underemployed Black males. The Commission on Civil Rights (1982) reported that Black men are overeducated for their jobs and have greater difficulty translating education into suitable occupations. Twenty years later, this racial disparity pattern of low return on education continues (U.S. Census Bureau, 2002d). Even college-educated Black males have an unemployment rate two to four times greater than their White peers. Among Black males employed in the labor force, one out of three will suffer from unemployment in a given year (Swinton, 1992). In Hampton's study (1980), the respondents who reported the highest number of employment problems had a marital disruption rate three times higher than the overall rate for the sample. His study receives support from the various Census Bureau reports published at the turn of the twenty-first century.

Another group of Black males regarded as undesirable or unavailable are those confined to mental institutions or otherwise mentally unstable. The environmental problems facing Blacks are such that they are more likely than Whites to suffer from mental distress. Blacks also use community mental health centers at a rate almost twice their proportion in the general population. Although their exact number is unknown, Black males are more likely to be committed to mental institutions than are Black women. The rate of drug and alcohol abuse is much greater among the Black population, especially males, based on their overrepresentation among patients receiving treatment services (U.S. Department of Health and Human Services, 1985). It is estimated that as many as one-third of the young Black males in the inner city have a serious drug problem (Staples, 1991b). Many of the mentally unstable or drug and alcohol abusers will have been included in the figures on Black males who have dropped out of the labor force or are in prison. The magnitude of the problem reinforces the fact that Black women are seriously disadvantaged in choosing from the eligible and desirable males in the marriage pool (Goldman, Westoff, and Hammerslough, 1984; Tucker and Taylor, 1989).

Dating as a Process

Each unit of the family begins as a dyad—usually two members of the opposite sex who occupy a range of roles based on the stage of their relationship. The first stage in the process of forming a family has historically been dating and courtship. Changes in attitudes toward the family have brought about variations in the practice of dating and courtship. Among the most marked of these changes are the different characteristics of its participants, the changing purpose of dating, and variations in its form. Dating, for instance, now involves more than very young people. The increasing numbers of individuals who remain unmarried until fairly advanced ages mean that a dating partner could as easily be thirty-eight years old as eighteen. The spiraling divorce and low remarriage rates have created another large pool of dating partners. Dating has also become time contained, often existing only for the moment or sexual or recreational purposes, and is no longer automatically presumed to be a prelude to courtship or marriage. Now it is more appropriate to speak in terms of nonmarital sex rather than premarital sex. Even the concept of dating has been modified, as men and women get together without making formal arrangements for an evening out in a public setting. Much of the previous description is relevant to the White middle class, which has developed a new ideology about the nature and content of the dating system. When we discuss Black dating, there are limitations to the generalizations we can make due to the limited literature on the subject.

The practice of Black dating can vary by epoch, region, and social class. In the past, when Blacks formed a small, cohesive community in the rural and urban South, what might be called dating behavior was centered around the neighborhood, church, and school. In general, it was a casual process whereby men and women met, formed emotional attachments, and later married. Most of the participants were members of larger social units, whose members or reputation were generally known to the community. As Blacks moved into urban areas outside the South, dating patterns modified due to the anonymity of individuals in that setting. The school and house party became centers for fraternizing between the genders, particularly in the working class. In the middle-class group, dating habits took on the characteristics of mainstream culture, as they participated more in activities like movies, dances, and bowling (Dickinson, 1978; Porter, 1979).

Very little is known about dating and sexual behavior in the Black community. Dating patterns may vary from community to community, region to region, and within and between the social classes in either of those areas. As among Whites, dating behavior involves a great deal of image management on the part of both males and females. In general, it is acknowledged that the male attempts to maximize sexual involvement with and minimize commitment to his female date. The reverse is usually true of the female. Success in reaching one goal or the other is often based on the principle of least interest—that is, who is more committed to maintaining the relationship and more likely to give in to the demands of the other partner—for sexual involvement or commitment to a steady relationship or marriage (Burgest, 1991).

It is the process of dating that most markedly distinguishes single from married people. The difference is not absolute, since many married individuals (particularly the males) have a strong presence in the dating game, but their relationships are discreet liaisons rather than the structured ritual involved in the dating situation. Although it is widely recognized that nearly all marriages in American society are preceded by some type of courtship, one often hears that people "do not date anymore." However, there is some question as to what has taken its place (Staples, 1981; Wehman, 2001). As one woman reported to us: "I have friends who consider the word 'date' or the situation known as 'dating' passé. They haven't really come up with new words for activities they are involved in which are essentially identical to dating" (Staples, 1981, p. 45).

One thing is certain: the process whereby the sexes form relationships has substantially changed. Dating began as part of the courtship process in the 1920s, when the concept of romantic love became increasingly popular among middle-class Whites. Prior to that time, marriages were arranged as a result of negotiations between two families or groups. Once individuals were ostensibly given free choice in the selection of a mate, dating became the method whereby unmarried men and women mutually explored each other's strengths and weaknesses as a potential spouse. In most cases dating partners were young and met each other in their respective communities. As a result, most Americans married persons who lived within six miles of them (Whyte, 1990).

Now, dating, or whatever else we choose to call it, is an entirely different matter. For some singles, it is the most valuable aspect of their life and provides them with an active social life, new experiences, a variety of new and interesting people to meet, freedom to sexually experiment, and so on. To others, it ranks as the most undesirable element in singlehood. However one responds to the dating situation, the one predictable element in it is its unpredictability. Once it ceased to be part of a structured courtship system, it became literally a form of social anarchy. The people in today's dating game are not necessarily young people who grew up together and are searching for compatible mates. They form a diverse group in terms of age, values, background, motives, and experiences. As a result, dating has a different character and dynamics than some thirty years ago. Individuals caught up in the dating game must develop skills and resiliency to cope with its chameleon-like structure (Burgest and Goosby, 1985).

Even in urban areas and among the middle class, Black dating in public places was restricted due to racial segregation in the South and a lack of recreational outlets in Northern Black communities (Dickinson, 1978). Most Blacks met their future mates in school, in the neighborhood, or at house parties. With the increasing mobility of middle-class Blacks, those sources of potential mates are no longer as available. Moreover, they now meet members of the opposite sex as individuals, whereas in the past they were part of a larger social unit. This has certain implications for those who participate in the dating game. It means that people are more subject to image management techniques, since they have little independent verification of a dating partner's character in settings that are new to both. Also, the controls on negative or antisocial behavior in dating situations are lessened when the social sanctions that can be exercised by relatives or friends are absent.

Not everybody is in the dating game in the same way. At one time or another, an individual may have a serious involvement with one person that takes up most of his or her time and attention. With the short duration of many relationships, and the awareness by many that "nothing lasts forever," most people fit into what Farber (1964) calls the permanent availability model. According to this model, almost everyone is always available to a member of the opposite sex, including those who are currently married. Due to the lack of legal or kin control, individuals go in and out of relationships, including marriage, freely. Hence, being involved in a "serious" relationship and participating in the dating game simultaneously is qualitatively different from being an unattached individual. It affords one a greater selectivity in choosing dating partners, a more leisurely pace in developing the relationship, and the ability to negotiate for higher rewards. No matter how one chooses to participate in the dating game, it still requires the ability to cope with different situations and diverse personalities.

Mate Selection Standards

Most heterosexual Black women have some concept of the ideal man they would like to marry. But like other aspirations, these aspirations are tempered by the reality of their lives. Since it is working-class Black women who suffer the most from poverty, their standards for a husband are most modified by the availability of such men in their environment. Despite the dilution of their mate selection standards, most Black women prefer the state of matrimony to a life of solitude. Many working-class Black women expect a life of celibacy to be even more ungratifying. Even an imperfect marital relationship is often better than a life that lacks love and companionship. Moreover, most of the wives receive some satisfaction in their relationship with their husbands (Heiss, 1988).

Within the Black middle class, women have a greater opportunity to realize their ideal standard for a marital partner. In selecting a mate, the middle-class Black woman is more likely to follow middle-class norms. There is more emphasis on romantic love and less on economic security. However, romantic love is not the only basis for marriage among the Black middle class. It may be that middle-class Black women make an a priori assumption that their husband can provide for them and seek to maximize the emotional gratification they will receive from a potential husband (Staples, 1981).

Still, most Black women maintain an ideal concept of the man they would like to marry. These idealistic standards of mate selection, however, must often be subordinated to reality. A working-class woman frequently will settle for a man who will work when he is able to find employment; avoid excessive gambling, drinking, and extramarital affairs; provide for the children; and treat her with respect. But even these simple desires cannot be fulfilled by lower-class Black husbands who are unable to find work and retreat into psychologically destructive behavior such as alcoholism and physical abuse of their wife (Heiss, 1988).

Middle-class Black women have a slightly better chance of fulfilling their desires for a compatible mate. They are likely to require economic stability, emotional and sexual satisfaction, and male participation in child rearing. Their desire for emotional fulfillment is supported by a study of 191 mostly middle- and upper-middle-level female managers, of whom 74 percent were single (Toliver, 1998). Detailing the feelings of these well-educated, salaried, and employed women, a clear message emerges: without someone to come home to after a stressful day at work, the job is of questionable value. Women repeated their need for emotional support and companionship. As one interviewee said, "I want a man with whom I can share my ideas and interests. I'm open to dating different kinds of men but . . . when it comes to marriage I want someone who'll be an equal partner, who I can have a relationship with that fulfills all my needs. Otherwise, I'll stay on my own and keep looking, and if I find the right man, fine" (p. 79). These women lacked the family support offered by marriage and children that most of their male colleagues enjoyed and the complete family structure—nuclear and extended—lauded by the Black community. They felt something was seriously missing from their lives. This study clearly demonstrates that these women upheld traditional values that affirm the importance of marriage and family. Hence, their singlehood reflects the reality of a limited available selection pool, not an alternative set of values that holds marriage in low esteem.

One aspect of White marriages is conspicuously missing: Black women do not expect their husbands to support them. Both Black men and women are in agreement that women will work after marriage. Mixed results exist across studies, but it has been found that the wife's employment does not pose a threat to the Black male's self-image under certain circumstances (Harley, 1994; Orbuch and Custer, 1995; Porter and Bronzaft, 1995). Black males are more likely than White males to believe that the wife has a right to a career of her own. The dual employment of both spouses is often necessary to approach the living standards of White couples with only the husband working. In general, women's salaries significantly contribute to the economic well-being of families, increasing the median family income from $53,240 in 1980 to $63,370 in 1998 (White and Rogers, 2001). It also reflects the partnership of Black men and women that has existed for centuries (Taylor, Leashore, and Toliver, 1988), but even this partnership is undermined by the fact that Black and Hispanic couples were one-fourth as likely to be impoverished as similar couples in which the man was the sole earner (White and Rogers, 2001).

The basis for selecting male dating partners can vary according to the values and needs of the individual female. A male with money—a rarity in the Black community—is much desired by many Black females. The male's personality is important, but all things being equal, his physique is rapidly becoming the most attractive element for Black women. The process of ranking males by body build can be called the masculinization of female mate selection standards. For years, males have evaluated females in terms of breast size, shapely legs, protruding buttocks, and other physical features. Now females are also beginning to rank males in terms of their physical attributes (Cash and Duncan, 1984).

Black women demonstrate a stronger preference for a physically attractive man than do White women. In a *Jet Magazine* survey of

Black women in Chicago ("Ten Things Women Notice About Men," 1982), Black women ranked the ten things they notice about men in this order: (1) dress/grooming, (2) personality, (3) eyes, (4) mouth/smile, (5) money, (6) physique, (7) thoughtfulness/walk, (8) intelligence/handsomeness, (9) chest, and (10) buttocks. Only four of the desirable attributes are nonphysical ones. Yet this physical emphasis does not ring true for the "super bachelors and bachelorettes" displayed in the May and July 2003 *Ebony* magazine issues. Perhaps because of their high achievement or high profile (including sports and media personalities and authors), character, spirituality, and common interest rank first for the women, and men rank personality equal to or above physical attributes. None of these singles mentions skin color as a selection consideration. The uniqueness of this group and the social desirability factor when divulging their values in a national magazine should be kept in mind. These men and women have high visibility and thus a rich pool of eligibles, setting them apart from those surveyed in *Jet*. Among those with lower profiles, mate selection no doubt takes on different features. Unlike their male cohorts, women place comparatively little emphasis on skin color. When they express a preference, it is for darker-skinned men. Many Black women say they do not trust light-skinned men and find darker men more dependable, settled, and attractive (Azibo, 1983).

Socioeconomic status figures more prominently in a man's life chances than in a woman's. When women are selecting a man for a husband, they generally consider his level of education and income first; since a woman is not only choosing a companion but is determining her standard of living, his physical assets are less important (Tucker and Taylor, 1989). That does not mean a man's physical attributes are totally insignificant. Men over six feet tall are more likely to obtain high-level executive positions than shorter men. Bald men suffer in employment opportunities and other areas relative to their peers with all their hair. The media have a preference for employing handsome men in visible positions. Certain social forces may account for the Black female's greater interest in a male's physical appeal. Partly it may be a function of the shortage of Black men with any tangible wealth. Ironically, since income is tied to skin color, if a Black woman finds a high-earning Black mate, her choice of skin color has already been limited through the process of institutional discrimination. Even in the twenty-first century, there continues to be a significant relationship between lighter-toned skin and higher socioeconomic status. Dark skin incurs a learning and earnings penalty for Blacks and Latinos (Hunter, Allen, and Telles, 2001; Keith and Herring, 1991). Perhaps more important is that many Black women are not dependent on a man for economic support. As a result, their standards for an acceptable mate have become oriented more toward the body.

Unfortunately, Black women seem to be heading in the same direction as Black men: rating people by their physical features rather than by their character. When personal characteristics that are genetically influenced make such an important difference in a person's status, a genetic determinism emerges that is very similar to the operation of racial attitudes. Since the standards of physical attractiveness are set and dominated by European Americans, it could presage an increase in group self-hatred.

Apart from racially determined physical characteristics, standards of beauty have varied over time and by culture. France, for instance, has regarded feet as a sex symbol. The United States has long been obsessed with female mammary glands, an anatomical asset that would seem senseless in precolonial Africa, where women did not wear clothing above the waist. While America currently worships the thin woman, corpulent females were more highly regarded in African societies because this connoted high status and good health. Certain factors seem almost universal in determining physical attractiveness. One is the rarity of a physical trait in its most exacting form. The more abundant a trait is, the less it tends to be highly regarded. Another is whiteness. Even in predominantly white cultures, blonds are the preferred coloration. They are especially valued by Mediterranean Whites (Hatfield and Sprecher, 1986; Staples, 1989).

As far as Black men are concerned, lightness of skin color is a dominant criterion in determining beauty among women. The "Black is beautiful" rhetoric notwithstanding, that has been the yardstick of beauty for Black women for the past four hundred years. According to Villa (1981, p. 202), "For many decades the lighter skinned females of the Black race were most preferred by Black men, because their color was closer to that of the white race, and the Black American had been conditioned for centuries by White Americans to believe that anything or anyone who resembled the whites had to be better. Any Black man who had a light-complected female (known in slang as a 'high yellow') possessed a status symbol of sorts."

The evidence for this cultural attitude is not forthcoming from Blacks. In any survey of mate selection standards among Blacks, skin color is rarely mentioned. When Berkeley psychologist Juanita Papillon did a study of the effect of skin color on the emotional makeup of Blacks, she found the higher the self-esteem, the darker the color (Stewart, 1979). Given that many Black men prefer their women light or White, the supply of such women is limited for a number of reasons. What, then, do Black males consider in their search for a desirable mate? A survey informs us on this question. When *Jet Magazine* ("Ten Things Men Notice About Women," 1982) surveyed Black males in Chicago on the ten things they notice about women, they listed them in this order: (1) face, (2) legs, (3) bust, (4) eyes/hair, (5) personality, (6) dress/intelligence, (7) smile, (8) buttocks, (9) walk, (10) hands/feet/voice/conversation/sincerity.

It is obvious from that ranking that a woman's primary assets are physical traits. Other sterling qualities, such as personality and intelligence, rank fifth and sixth, respectively, and the ability to hold a conversation and sincerity come in dead last. Moreover, the first four physical traits are generally those most common to White women. The face should be light and keen in features, legs and bust should be big, eyes round, hair long and straight. It is ironic that physical traits originally designed for other functions, to allow a group to adapt effectively to its physical environment, have become a benchmark of beauty. Black women actually need a combination of beauty and brains to attract a high-status husband, but it is still their looks that are the decisive factor. A sociologist did an empirical test of whether a woman's physical attractiveness was a predictor of her husband's status. He reported that if a White woman does not go to college, her attractiveness has a strong bearing on whether she married a high-status husband. If that same White woman goes to college, her looks bear no relationship to the status of her husband. But for the Black woman, attractiveness is influential in getting a high-status husband whether or not she goes to college. It plays a stronger role if she goes to college than if she does not, though (Udry, 1977).

The relationship between beauty and intelligence is a complicated one. In White culture, an attractive woman has less need to cultivate her intellectual potential because she can obtain a high level of self-esteem and class mobility (through marriage) without it. The same is not entirely true of attractive Black women. Most Black families, for instance, socialize all their female children to get a good education and not depend on a man for satisfying their material wants. Furthermore, to obtain high-status husbands, most beautiful Black women have to attend a college where they can meet them. Unlike Whites, the wealthiest Blacks are generally those with the most education (even Black athletes generally attend college). Many of them will be medical doctors and dentists who attended either Howard University or Meharry Medical School. Since both Howard and Fisk University (the undergraduate school next door to Meharry) have historically had high academic standards, women of limited intellect would experience difficulty in matriculating at those schools.

Alternatives to Monogamous Marriage

Singlehood is a complex phenomenon. To understand its multiple dimensions, we need to distinguish the condition of being unmarried from singlehood as a way of life. The historical data tell us that the overwhelming majority of Americans marry at some point in their life. Only about 4 percent of Americans have never married, and of those who get married and divorced, 79 percent remarry (U.S. Census Bureau, 1992; Wright, 2002). Those figures, of course, are based on past patterns and do not reflect the attitudes of single men and women who are under the age of forty and have never married. Yet it is possible that, antimarriage attitudes notwithstanding, most Black singles will eventually marry. And they will eventually marry for a very simple reason: the social structure does not provide any viable alternative.

This assumption may be regarded as heresy by antimarriage proponents. Literally hundreds of articles and a number of books have been written that endorse alternatives to the traditional marital union. There are several journals, academic and popular, devoted to exploring and justifying these alternative lifestyles. Support for them comes primarily from Whites, women, and gays, for reasons unique to those groups. Black endorsement of alternative lifestyles has been noticeably absent. This may not last long.

There appears to be a generalized ambivalence or discontent with marriage among those who are married and an anticipation of unhappiness in the conjugal state among those who are not. The unhappily married tend to be concentrated in the lower stratum of the social classes. Still, middle-class Black women do not escape the disaffection with marriage, although for slightly different reasons. They are often unable to find husbands of comparable status and have to face keen competition, both before and after marriage, should they find one. The official divorce rate is higher among middle-class Black women, although marital breakup is greater among working-class women, who do not use the divorce courts as frequently. At any rate, there is considerable dissatisfaction with marriage as an institution. But this dissatisfaction will not be translated into large numbers of Black women who never marry. Among Black Americans born in 1954, 86 percent of the men and 70 percent of the women are expected to marry by the time they are forty-five years old (Rodgers and Thornton, 1985). Also, a number of surveys report that approximately three-quarters of Black

American women want to marry, albeit few (36 percent) believe that it is better to marry than stay single (King, 1999).

As for the men, antimarriage attitudes are frequently voiced among lower-class Black men. Studies show that they fear public and private fights between spouses; see marriage as creating problems of how to feed, clothe, and house a wife and child; and experience anxiety about being able to ward off attacks on the health and safety of their children (Cazenave, 1983). These men are the most likely of all Blacks to remain legally unmarried. Middle-class Black men are less inclined to voice antimarriage perspectives. While claiming to enjoy the single life, they will eventually settle down in a permanent union. Unlike the other groups, they see themselves as having much to gain from marriage. They have an abundance of women from which to select, of different races and educational levels. Because of the shortage of men in their category, they can make favorable matches from the variety of women in the eligible female pool. Since society, and their own values, allows them considerable flexibility in choosing the woman to marry, their pool is infinite—actually ten times larger than the middle-class Black woman's. Moreover, marriage for them provides an image of respectability, steady and free sexual relations, regular and better meals, and so on. Within marriage, they maintain a certain freedom to pursue their careers and other activities. Furthermore, for a third of the ever-married Black men, marriage does not preclude extramarital dating and sex. It is small wonder that they see marriage in a positive light. They are the group of Blacks most likely to marry, and when divorced, to remarry (Glick, 1988; Tucker and Taylor, 1989; Wiederman, 1997).

Given the shortfall of Black men of a similar educational and income level, it can be assumed that many Black women will have to settle for an alternative lifestyle. The question remains, Is it really an alternative, and how viable is it? For Blacks in general, many of the alternative lifestyles advocated are nothing new. Having a child out of wedlock has long been known to the Black community. The latest figures show that 60 percent of Black children born in 1988 and 62 percent of those born in 2000 were conceived out of wedlock (U.S. Census Bureau, 1991a, 2000). Most Black women hardly consider raising a child alone an alternative lifestyle. About 51 percent of all Black households are headed by women, and they have the lowest income and most problems of all Blacks (Bane and Jargowsky, 1988). Prominent Black family sociologist Harriette McAdoo, quoted in a *Newsweek* article, warned, "These types of families should not be romanticized out of context. They exist for sheer survival in the face of real and threatening problems and the problems may be becoming overwhelming" ("Blacks' Fresh Trials," 1978, p. 77).

In any examination of alternatives to the conventional monogamous marriages, few, if any, appear desirable or viable. Some cannot be regarded as legitimate alternatives for Blacks (Williams, 1990). Dedication to a career seems irrelevant to a group of Black women who have been in the labor force for more than a century. Raising a child alone has become a traditional and often undesirable lifestyle of too many Black women. Those who realize the burden it imposes on both the mother and child are hardly inclined to view single motherhood as something they want or happily choose. Other alternatives contain flaws because they do not address the basic cause of Black singlehood: the shortage of Black males and the conflict between the genders. Heterosexual cohabitation, for instance, does not increase the number of males available or alter the ability of men and women to live in a harmonious relationship. Ironically, two of the most commonly mentioned alternatives, homosexuality and interracial marriages, are used more often by men, especially the more educated, thus compounding the problem of Black women seeking a heterosexual mate within the race (Binson, Stall, Coates, Gagnon, and Catania, 1995; Bell and Weinberg, 1978; Ernst, Francis, Nevels, and Lemeh, 1991; Tucker and Mitchell-Kernan, 1990).

Black people have had to deal with the shortage of men for a number of years. Through a variety of coping mechanisms, they have been able to marry and raise children. Much of this has been accomplished through the pattern of serial polygamy—that is, a person marries more than one person in his or her lifetime. Whether this will continue depends on how many Black women choose to redefine their options and priorities. Rather than use the misleading term *alternative lifestyles* to describe the behavior of middle-class Blacks, it is more appropriate to call them family substitutes or, even better, coping styles.

The expression *alternative lifestyles* implies that individuals are free to choose within an array of available options. But middle-class Black singles, especially women, are choosing within the limits of the existing social structure. They are free to choose among alternatives, not what those alternatives should be. In looking at the family substitutes available, we will see that people are products of their culture and cannot free themselves of it for greater individual freedom unless they first understand the constraints that culture imposes. Monogamous marriage is the only sanctioned institution in which the needs of most adults are met in the United States. The family substitutes are, at best, inadequate ways of satisfying these human prerequisites. Many of these family substitutes have been tried and found to be of short-term duration. They often are a revolving door rather than a family.

Summary

Relationships between Black men and women have had a peculiar evolution. Unlike the White family, which is typically believed to be patriarchal and sustained by the economic dependence of women, the Black dyad has been characterized by more egalitarian roles and economic parity in North America. The system of slavery did not permit Black males to assume the superordinate role in the family constellation, since the female was not economically dependent on him. Hence, relationships between the genders were ordered along sociopsychological dimensions rather than reflecting an economic compulsion to marry and remain married. This fact in part explains the unique trajectory of Black male-female relationships.

The growing trend toward singlehood among American Blacks is reflected in the fact that a majority of Black women over the age of fifteen are no longer married and living with a spouse. While the institutional decimation of Black males is the primary factor in this unprecedented number of singles, other sociocultural forces have an impact on the relationships between Black men and women. Among them are the changes in Black institutions and values that create barriers for Blacks in finding and keeping a mate. The conflict between Black men and women also stems from incompatible role enactments by the two genders. The older societal prescription that women are to be passive and men dominant is counteracted by other forces. Black women resist Black men's dominance, and Black men who wish to be in charge cannot fulfill the economic provider role, which supports the dominance of men in American society (Franklin, 1984).

The situation of Black singles is much too fluid, and the research on them too sparse, to pontificate about the direction of their family lifestyles. Given the circumstances, it is difficult to hold out much hope that the majority of Black women will marry and stay with one man their entire lifetime. Alternative lifestyles are conceptually flawed, however, because they do not take into account the effects of social forces over which most individuals have minimal control. Not only does American society fail to provide structural supports for persons engaged in alternative lifestyles, but it can and does punish individuals who violate its norms. Furthermore, the greatest punishment is administered by the individuals themselves when there is any incongruity between their lifestyles and the values they have internalized. In the past, the Black community provided some support for the coping mechanisms of its members. Whether the reality of the Black community can be accommodated to this new situation remains an open question.

6

Gender Roles and Male Sexism

In recent years, gender identities and roles have received a great deal of attention. While the debate in mainstream society has centered on the issue of female subordination and male dominance and privilege, Blacks have very different problems and priorities. They first have to overcome certain disabilities based on racial membership, not gender affiliation. However, that does not mean that gender roles within the Black community fail to carry advantages and disadvantages. In many ways, they do. But Blacks must contend with the insistent problems of a high unemployment rate; the declining life expectancy rate of Black men; rises in drug abuse, suicide, and crime; and educational failures. These problems do not inspire much support for a movement to equalize the condition of men and women in the Black community (Staples, 1991a).

Gender and Historical Forces

From a historical perspective, the Black male's role has changed as he has moved from the African continent to the shores of North America. This span of time has introduced the forces of slavery, discrimination, and wage exploitation in the determination of his masculine identity and role. As we have seen, women had an important place in African society; they often exceeded their European counterparts in the authority they wielded and the contribution they made to their respective social units (Terborg-Penn, 1991). But most areas of Africa were patriarchal, and males had a variety of influential roles. This changed with slavery.

Under slavery, the role of the father was, in essence, institutionally obliterated. Not only was the slave father deprived of his sociological and economic functions in the family, but the very etiquette of plantation life deprived him of even the honorific attributes of fatherhood, since he was addressed as "boy" until the vigorous years of his prime were past, when he was permitted to assume the title "uncle." If he lived with a woman in a "married" relationship, he was known as her husband (for example, as "Sally's John"), which again denied him a position as head of the household (White, 1985).

The structural barriers to Black manhood were great. In a capitalistic society, being able to provide basic life satisfactions is inextricably interwoven with manhood. The opportunity to provide for his family, both individually and collectively, had been denied the Black man. After emancipation, the economic role of the Black woman was strengthened as Blacks left rural areas and migrated to cities, where it was difficult for Black men to obtain employment. Increasingly, the Black woman was thrust into the role of family provider. Although Black men had previously held jobs as skilled craftsmen, carpenters, and so on, they were forced out of these occupations by a coalition of White workers and capitalists. In some instances, they found employment only as strikebreakers (Giddings, 1984; Davis, 1989). The jobs that were available lacked the security and level of income necessary to maintain a household. In addition, certain jobs historically performed by Black men (for example, waiter, cook, dishwasher, teacher, and social worker) often carried a connotation in American society of being "women's work" (Davis, 1989).

After slavery officially ended, the kind of role flexibility that existed during slavery continued for Black families. Despite theories to the contrary, male-present households were the norm in poor Black communities between 1880 and 1925. Families headed by women were hardly, if at all, more common than among comparable Whites

(Gutman, 1976). These two-parent black households were often dual-worker families, since many wives often worked alongside their husbands to obtain land and an education for their children. In the harsh economic conditions of the late nineteenth century, a certain egalitarianism developed within Black families, and the sharp dichotomy between male and female gender roles so common to antebellum Southern White families failed to develop (King, 1990; Davis, 1989).

Socialization into Gender Roles

Central to the understanding of Black gender roles is an investigation of the process of socializing men into their gender identity. The literature is full of assumptions—but little proof—about how Black males are reared in their families. A dominant, though unproven, theory is that the nature of the male role is not adequately conveyed to them because of absent or weak father figures. Others have contended that Black mothers raise their sons to be docile because of the risks to life and limb that an aggressive Black male is exposed to. Another common assumption is that Black mothers have traditionally favored female children over male children. All of these hypotheses need to be carefully tested by an examination of the socialization processes in the Black family and how they shape gender-role identity (Hale, 1982; Peters, 1997).

Because many Black men have been absent from the family due to welfare regulations and an inability to obtain regular employment, the Black mother has played a strong role in the ongoing care of Black children. Many Blacks have vivid memories of their mothers scrubbing floors in White households to put food on the table or to send them through college. Research studies that have attempted to study the matter unanimously find that Black children have a closer relationship with their parents than White children do. While Black parents may use physical discipline, they rarely practice the technique of withdrawing love from the children. This eliminates some of the anxiety and resentment that often result from that child-rearing method (McAdoo, 1997; Peters, 1997). And it is generally the mother to whom both male and female children feel closest. In his study of Black families, Scanzoni (1978) found that both Black males and females were more likely to view their mothers than their fathers as being a help to them in getting an education. However, the fathers were more likely to provide tangible material assistance, while the mothers gave counseling and encouragement to stay in school.

Given this history, it is puzzling as to why the Black mother has come under such strident attack in the last two decades for having a negative influence on Black male children. Such prominent Blacks as columnist William Raspberry (1984) and writer Shahrazad Ali (1989) have criticized Black mothers for their role in creating a host of undependable and low-achieving Black males. Since a near majority of Black families are headed by only a female parent, it is crucial to determine how well male children are raised when the mother is the sole parent.

Certainly, classic psychoanalytic theory assumed the existence of a strong father figure in the development of a healthy male identity. Sigmund Freud (1938), the father of psychoanalysis, believed the male child's first love object is the mother. When the son becomes aware that he cannot compete with the father for the mother's love, he subsequently identifies with the father and acquires his masculine characteristics. If this resolution of what Freud termed the oedipal complex does not occur, the attachment to the mother persists and the male child develops ambivalence toward the father and the masculinity he represents. Freud's theory has been criticized for not considering the social and cultural context in which male personalities develop. This theory was based on his therapy with White middle-class women in Europe during the nineteenth century. Other observers of Black culture have noted that the Black male child can form an attachment to and identify with other male figures in his environment, such as his uncles and grandfathers, when the male parent is absent (Taylor, 1986). Moreover, Lewis (1975) has noted that in Black American culture, children are considered sexual beings. Thus, the Black child's sexual identity is more easily tied to his definition of himself as a sexual being than to behavior that has arbitrarily been defined as masculine. In Black society, she claims, traits such as independence, nurturing, and assertiveness do not distinguish between males and females. A boy understands he is male on the basis of his sexuality, and a girl realizes her femaleness on the basis of her sexuality and her ability to bear children.

Much of the controversy over the Black mother's role was ignited by the publication of the widely criticized Moynihan report (1965). In it, Moynihan attributed much of the blame for Black problems to the existence of the so-called matriarchy. It was, he said, the dominance and influence of Black mothers over their sons that was responsible for their lack of achievement, especially in relationship to Black daughters. In addition, Moynihan's premise of the matriarchy might be questioned, since Black women still earn less than Black men (Mishel et al., 1997; U.S. Census Bureau, 1998). For example, in 1996 among full-time workers, Black women earned $21,470 compared to the earnings of $26,400 by Black men (U.S. Census Bureau, 1998). Still, it is noticeable and verifiable that Black women exceed Black men at nearly all educational levels (National Center for Education Statistics, 1991a; U.S. Census Bureau, 2000).

Other social scientists have claimed that Black mothers cannot give their sons a positive role model, so that the female-headed family hinders them in the development of a masculine identity. Some have gone so far as to assert that a large proportion of the Black male population is latently gay, the result of being raised in father-absent or mother-dominant households (Allen, 1981; Peters, 1997). The evidence for this assertion is highly questionable. One widely quoted study found that Black males scored higher on the femininity index of the Minnesota Multiphasic Personality Inventory test. Their femininity score was higher than that of White men, because they were more likely to agree with statements such as "I would like to be a singer" and "I think I feel more intensely than most people do" (Hokanson and Calder, 1960). Such evidence reveals no understanding of Black culture—specifically, of the traits that define masculinity among Black people. There is, in fact, no validation of the theory of massive homosexuality among Black men, and certainly no evidence that being raised by Black mothers would cause it (Baldwin, 1987; Laumann, Gagnon, Michael, and Michaels, 1994).

The whole question of how Black males can acquire an appropriate masculine identity in a household headed by a woman is answered by other research. There is ample evidence that a mother can communicate to her son the way men act. He can be shown the way men cross their legs, how they carry books, the way they walk, and so on. Furthermore, there are few Black male children who do not observe men in their environment. The Black community is much less sex stratified and segregated than mainstream White society. Blacks have few all-male or all-female clubs, associations, or schools. Men and women mingle easily in all walks of life (Hale, 1982). Hence, the Black male child has a number of male role models to choose from. Even in two-parent homes, the father may not be the person he will choose to emulate. Whereas he may idolize the male parent in early childhood, his later role models can be glamorous personalities such as movie stars, athletes, or fictional characters. During his late adolescence, the most admired role models will often be attractive and visible men who demonstrate certain valued competences or skills and are generally admired in the community (Taylor, 1986).

We can better understand the problems of the Black mother-son relationship by reviewing Black history and culture. As Lewis (1975, p. 221) has observed, "Many of the behaviors which Whites see as appropriate to one sex or the other, Blacks view as equally appropriate to both sexes or equally inappropriate to both sexes. The sex differences that do exist are more in the nature of contrasts than of mutually exclusive traits." Unlike some of the ancient societies of Asia, and even of Europe, Africa did not have a strong gender preference among children or the need to sharply differentiate men from women (Binion, 1990). Female independence coexisted with the recognition of male authority in many African societies (Sudarkasa, 1981). However, there were unusual circumstances that caused Black mothers to raise their sons differently in the postslavery era of the Southern United States. And it is that male socialization practice that is the subject of much criticism of Black mothers today.

Where such differential socialization has existed, a more likely explanation is the Black mother's fear for the safety of her son. In the pre–civil rights era in the South, a Black man with too much temper and too much ambition would have had his life shortened if he acted too aggressively toward Whites (Dollard, 1957). As a result, the Black mother had to teach her son to be obedient and compliant (Allen, 1981; Peters, 1997). White society would tolerate the independence of Black women but not that of Black men. Where this socialization practice continues, the Black mother's overprotection of her son can foster dependency in him and hinder his ability to make important decisions as well as erode his sense of manliness and the ability to achieve and accomplish (Staples, 1984).

Young Black girls also have a close relationship with their mothers. At a fairly young age, they assume heavy household responsibilities such as cooking, cleaning, and child care. By the age of nine, many of them are given the charge of their younger siblings. The sharing of household responsibilities builds a positive relationship between mother and daughter. The close relationship Black mothers have with their daughters has led to the charge that Black mothers express a preference for female over male children. But such allegations are unsupported by any evidence (Bell-Scott, 1991).

Although Black mothers and fathers express some level of support for gender equality for both their daughters and sons, social class shapes their attitudes. Black families who are second generation and securely middle class promote egalitarian socialization of both their male and female children more strongly than do those who recently have become middle class (the "transitionalists"). It appears that

newly arrived middle-class parents who are in the process of dis-
tancing themselves from their lower-class origin, with its negative
racial images, are more likely to conform to White middle-class con-
ventions as a sign of their respectability. However, while transitional
or less educated parents believe in supporting traditional roles in the
home, they still remain committed to gender equality in the workplace. Furthermore, less educated Black fathers support their daughters' career aspirations, but remain ambivalent about very young sons'
cross-gender interest in cooking and housework, even if they themselves participate in such household tasks (Hill, 2002).

In addition, the seemingly inconsistent role expectations for
work and home are consistent with the double consciousness that
Black people experience living in a predominantly White society.
Black Americans may internalize European Americans' idea that
women's roles should be circumscribed by home and family. However, their commitment to familial values, the tradition of sharing
roles, the history of slavery (which subjugated women to the same
labor and hardships as men), and the contemporary necessity for
dual earners make conformity to White traditional norms undesirable or unrealistic.

It must be noted that empirical evidence on Black male and female children's gender role socialization is limited. The studies on gender role attitudes and behavior of Black adults are assumed to be
grounded in early socialization. In general, studies on Black adults find
a pattern of egalitarianism in that husbands and wives share work and
family roles (Hill, 1999, 2002; Taylor, 2000; Hunter and Sellers, 1998;
Taylor, Chatters, Tucker, and Lewis, 1990). Regardless of gender, more
than 88 percent of American Blacks agree that men and women
should share child care and household tasks (Hill, 1999). This egalitarianism within the home may be somewhat deceiving in that most
of the activities that males and females tend to perform in their marriages are typically gender specific. Females tend to do cooking, cleaning, and nurturing, and the males do gardening and handyman-type
work around the home (Haynes, 2000). Nevertheless, relative to

Whites, Black wives report greater participation from their husbands in female-typed tasks (Orbuch and Eyster, 1997).

With regard to females' work orientation, a higher percentage of Black women participate in the paid labor force and are less likely to see their participation and being a wife and mother as mutually exclusive (Strong, DeVault, and Sayed, 1998). In fact, one study of Black American women indicated that 37 percent identified as androgynous, 18 percent feminine, and 24 percent masculine (few identified undifferentiated). The large number of those with masculine identification is consistent with the demanding responsibilities and cultural expectations requiring instrumental and active traits of women. Similarly, Black males are more androgynous than White males. Often they are encouraged to be androgynous at home or in the Black community but masculine in the larger community (Hill, 2002; Franklin, 1984).

Interestingly, some believe that this mixture of male-female expectations (androgyny) is a hidden blessing. Flexibility and integration are important aspects of androgyny. Individuals who are rigidly masculine or feminine cannot easily adapt. Several studies reveal that androgynous individuals show greater resilience when faced with stress (Strong, DeVault, and Sayad, 1998). Given this research, it is not unexpected that androgynous Black American men have better mental health as measured by lower depressive symptoms than those who are feminine- or masculine-typed. In being androgynous and embracing both femininity and masculinity, they provide themselves with a broad and diverse repertoire of self-perceptions and coping styles useful in buffering economic, social, and racial discrimination as well as adjustment skills for shifting gender role expectations (Brown, McGregor, and Gary, 1998).

In short, gender socialization is complex (Burgess, 1994) and neither purely traditional nor egalitarian (Franklin, 1984; Hill, 2002). Although egalitarianism is a dominant force, it is shaped by social class and cultural attitudes. For example, belief in husbands as the entitled primary breadwinner is stronger for those who are older, less educated, more religious, more financially strained, and living in urban areas (McLoyd, Cauci, Takeuchi, and Wilson, 2001). As Black women continue to strengthen their position in educational attainment relative to their domestic partners and as their income closes in on that of males, gender role expectations for themselves and their children, and the gender roles of their partners, will become even more complicated.

Probably one of the most salient differences is in Black children's sexual education. Since some Black mothers realize that the avenue to sexual gratification will be an open one for their children, they instruct them early in matters of pregnancy and sexually transmitted diseases. It is alleged that Black girls are socialized to be more independent, disciplined, and cautious than Black boys. There is some evidence that there are fewer social conformists among Black females at a fairly early age (Peters, 1997). One reason for this differential socialization is the belief that Black men are basically worthless and irresponsible; consequently, less is expected of them. The other side of this theory is that Black women are morally and intellectually superior to Black men, and hence one can expect more from them (Franklin, 1986).

Historically, Black families (not mothers alone) were more likely to send their daughters to college because the sons were needed to help on the farm. Another compelling reason for sending the daughters to college was to help them avoid becoming domestic servants in White households. While household work can be, and is, a noble occupation, in the pre–civil rights movement era, it often entailed the risks of sexual harassment for many young Black women. During that period, only two occupations were generally available to Black women: domestic worker or schoolteacher. Thus, it was more important that they go to college and avoid those risks, since the sons had a greater variety of occupations, with less risk, available to them. Moreover, much of this gender difference can be traced to the higher dropout rate of Black men in secondary school. And the reason for the Black male's higher dropout rate is aptly noted by Hale (1982, p. 66). "Traditional classrooms," she says, "are generally oriented toward feminine values. Teachers are disproportionately female, and the behaviors tolerated and encouraged are those that are more natural for girls."

Black Male Sexism

Most men are conditioned through the socialization process to believe that they are endowed with qualities of leadership and that women should play a subordinate role in human affairs. Black men cannot help but be affected by the stereotyped roles of men and women. To some degree, they internalize the same values of male supremacy that White men do.

However, various social forces have prevented Black males from carrying out the oppression of Black women to the same degree that White males oppress White women. Black people have had little control over the enactment of their roles. Black males have not been as overbearing with their Black women partners because White society has more severely restrained the behavior of Black men than of Black women. This partly accounts for the very important role of Black women in American history (Collins, 1990; hooks, 1984). Yet historical records also reveal a number of Black male sexists during the postslavery period. After the Civil War, there were numerous cases of Black men demanding a superior position in the family. Even during slavery, the freed Black male became a patriarch because he had purchased his wife and children from their slave masters. But most Black men were enslaved and had no authority over any individual; in fact, they lacked control over their own lives (Giddings, 1984; King, 1990).

In reviewing the attitudes of Black male leaders, writers, and scholars toward Black women, one finds a mixture of affection, recognition of their contribution to the Black struggle for liberation, and a desire to protect them from the ravages of White racism. Different Black men have exhibited these feelings in diverse ways. One needs to understand how the times they have lived in have shaped their attitudes toward women. When we analyze the views of the Black nationalist leaders, we find a return to the traditional male position that women should occupy a subordinate role. Most of these nationalist groups have based their position on historical experiences. In particular, some advocate a return to the African patriarchal system, where men make most of the decisions. They also want a reinstatement of the system of polygamy, in which Black American men could have more than one wife (Williams, 1990).

The Nation of Islam (commonly known as the Black Muslims) also relates its position on the role of women to past experiences, when Black men could not support and protect women, thereby abdicating any role of leadership. Also, Muslims base their attitudes toward the role of women in the Islamic religion. In traditional Muslim society, it is believed that men have a natural right to act as overseers of women. Black Muslims teach that no marriage can succeed if the woman does not look up to the man with respect. A man must have something above and beyond the wife in order for her to be able to look to him for psychological security (Ali, 1989; White, 1991).

When Malcolm X was a member of the Black Muslims, he echoed the same views, but he had a very close relationship with his wife. In his autobiography (Haley, 1965), he states that he depended heavily on her for the strength to endure some of the crises he faced. Malcolm believed that Islam was the only religion that gives both husband and wife a true understanding of love. According to him, when a woman loses her physical beauty in Western society, she loses her attractiveness. But Islam teaches individuals to look for the spiritual qualities in each other (Haley, 1965).

Malcolm's views changed radically after he left the Nation of Islam. In his twelve years as a Muslim minister, he preached so strongly about moral issues that even Muslims charged him with being misogynist. In retrospect, he admitted that every aspect of his teaching and all of his personal beliefs derived from his devotion to the Nation of Islam's leader, Elijah Muhammad. After Malcolm broke from the Muslims in

1963, he steered away from morality and addressed himself to current events and politics. His position on Black women just before he was assassinated was very supportive of their equal rights (Cone, 1991).

Even revolutionary nationalist parties such as the Black Panther party had questionable views on gender roles. At one time, the official position of the party was that the attempt to repeal abortion laws was a genocidal plot. One of the former leaders of that party, Eldridge Cleaver (1968, p. 158), stated that "Black women take kindness for weakness. Leave them the least little opening and they will put you on the cross. . . . It would be like trying to pamper a cobra." At least this sentiment was offset by Cleaver's other tributes to Black women. The position of writer and cultural nationalist Imrnamu Baraka (Sisters for Black Community Development, 1971) was a clear-cut call for Black female subordination. His organization had a doctrine concerning the Black woman's role in it. Women should not smoke, drink, wear slacks, or have abortions. They should not be involved in men's discussions except to serve refreshments. While the men are busy making decisions, women should occupy themselves with ironing, sewing, and cooking. The rationale for this gender segregation of effort was the need to develop a unique Black culture with no White concepts.

Reviewing some of the books written by Black men, one finds a certain ambivalence in them about Black women. Although the concept of the Black matriarchy emerged from the writings of E. Franklin Frazier (1939), he held a generally favorable opinion of Black women. He saw the slave woman as the protector of the race. Although he believed the matrifocal family was undesirable, he was appreciative of the sacrifices Black women had made for their families over the years. His most negative criticism of Black women was reserved for women of the middle class, a group he felt did not measure up to the intellectual and cultural abilities of middle-class White women (Frazier, 1957). Literature on Black women in the late 1960s was very negative. One of the most virulent criticisms of Black women can be found in Grier and Cobbs's book *Black Rage* (1976). Their treatment of Black women led one Black female reviewer to label Grier and Cobbs ignorant and stupid. The book, she asserted, is "a clumsy but effective attempt to modernize old stereotypes to explain topics of current interest" (Saxe, 1970, p. 58). Grier and Cobbs's thesis is that the Black woman has been made to feel that she is not worth much and that she arrives at this conclusion through the teachings of her mother, who is also filled with self-hatred. The book also contains other questionable assertions, such as that "Black women lack self-confidence, they are more skin color conscious, preferring those of light-skin, than Black men, and they have abandoned any interest in their feminine appearance" (p. 39). The authors go on to say that the Black woman aspires to the cosmetic beauty of White America. Since she lacks the qualities of attractiveness and feeling loved, her self-confidence is impaired. Instead of directing her hatred toward the object of her oppression, she directs it inward.

Many Black male authors summarily dismiss the women's movement as being irrelevant to Black women. Some call it a part of America's contradictions, and any contradiction in America should be seen as a White-against-Black movement ("The Black Sexism Debate," 1979). A Black male psychologist labels the women's movement a diversion, an activist way to ignore racism, and charged that it is merely another self-hate and self-destruct mechanism imposed by the White middle class. Many of the women in this movement, he says, are trying to substitute the latest revolutionary identity for an unfulfilling personality (Hare and Hare, 1984).

Ironically, negative assessment of the Black woman's role in the family came from a Black woman. Shahrazad Ali's book *The Blackman's Guide to Understanding the Black Woman* (1989) generated strong anger among Black American women, who felt it attacked them and blamed them solely for problems in the community and in relationships with Black men. Probably the most provocative statement in the book is Ali's suggestion that Black women who question the Black male's authority should be soundly slapped in the mouth. This led the respected columnist Dorothy Gilliam (1990, p. D3) to write: "It's a sad commentary on the state of Black folks in white America when a book written by a Black Muslim woman that tells Black men to slap Black women is selling like hot cakes in some areas of Washington." Still, the appeal of the book to some Black men was cogent testimony to their belief that they had been victims, not beneficiaries, of the independence and strength of Black women.

The views of those leaders and authors represented a few Black male opinions out of millions. But they reached many people. A Black female author retorted that Black men were largely interested in liberation for themselves and were not sympathetic toward Black females. Indeed, she claimed that Black female subordination was one of their chief goals. Black women should not be lulled into believing that the liberation of Black men was their greatest priority (Wallace, 1990). In support of her position, some reference Black males' denigration of women in gangsta culture.

Another controversial topic surrounds the role of rap and hip-hop cultures in addressing the image of Black women. Rap music along with its companion hip-hop culture not only developed as a source of entertainment for poor and working-class Black and Latino youth in New York City, but served as a voice for calling attention to needed changes in their communities. Paradoxically, while this music often alerts the public to problems concerning Black Americans, the values and behaviors that it frequently promotes in its lyrics and hip-hop culture may actually exacerbate these issues (Bynoe, 2001). In fact, the National Coalition on Television Violence, Women Against Pornography, and church groups have railed against the violence in this culture. More specific to our discussion is the fury over the treatment of Black women. The National Political Congress of Black Women was so enraged by misogynistic lyrics and gangsta rap that it barricaded the door of a Washington, D.C., record store chain, Nobody Beats the Wiz. The board of the National Association for the Advancement of Colored People (NAACP) unanimously repudiated the pro-rap views of its executive director, Benjamin Chavis, by issuing a proclamation: "We condemn the words, lyrics and images that degrade, disrespect and denigrate African-American women with obscenities and vulgarities of the vilest nature . . . that are portrayed in the lyrics and video images of popular music" (Gan, Zillmann, and Mitrook, 1997, p. 382). Images include pelvic thrusting and gyrations, breast and crotch clasping, and sexually provocative female rappers with barechested men, along with lyrics like "He's got me open like 7–11." Even women who hold traditional gender roles as wives, mothers, caregivers, nurturers, and teachers have not escaped the denigration found in some videos. Most criticism has been directed at male black performers (Coolio, Dr. Dre, Mack 10, Naughty by Nature, Onyx, Shaggy, slick Rick, and others), although some female rappers echo similar themes (Gan, Zillmann, and Mitrook, 1997; Ransby and Matthews, 1995). C. Delores Tucker, community leader and president of the National Political Congress of Black Women, expressed similar condemnation, giving attention to its effect on children: "Children want to dress like them [the performers], walk like them, talk like them and use language that you wouldn't believe. This is the filth that children are buying" (Gan, Zillmann, and Mitrook, 1997, p. 382).

Others, however, glorify gangsta artists as liberators of Black women's newly found sexual freedom and assertiveness. Still others defend the music on its deliverance of important social messages. Stephens and Wright (2000) contend that rap music is worthy of empirical studies to enhance our understanding of the lived experiences of urban families. Rap music allows one to capture the real human condition as experienced by marginalized groups. It identifies needed policy changes that may dismantle structural oppression (income, educational, wealth, and health disparities). This culture identifies individual behaviors, such as fatalistic ideologies, that undermine growth in the Black community. Hip-hop and rap also call attention to how living in an area with high unemployment, coupled with poor education and job skills, poses insurmountable obstacles to positive development of Black individuals, families, and communities.

The Rise of Black Feminism

As an organized social movement, few Black women or men have embraced the organized White feminist movement's concepts or strategies. But White women have embraced the methods of the Black liberation movement. Many techniques used in forging the women's movement were borrowed from or paralleled those of the civil rights movement: all-Black organizations, creation of Black consciousness and identity, the changing of names that signified their unequal status, and so on. White women adopted some of these practices because they had been successfully used by Blacks. Women in the feminist movement have also asserted that their situation was very similar to that of Blacks (Giddings, 1984). It is to be expected that any group that defines itself as the object of oppression will share similar traits with other oppressed groups.

One of the most obvious similarities between women and Blacks is that both are discriminated against on the basis of their physical characteristics. Blacks suffer because of their skin color, and women encounter discrimination because of their gender. Both are said to be innately inferior, less intelligent, more emotional and dependent, and so on. Thus, they are discouraged from entering traditionally masculine jobs that command higher pay and are discouraged from training in these jobs. Both are consigned to low-paying, monotonous jobs where a high rate of absenteeism and turnover is typical. With both groups, their physical traits are said to create certain barriers to their social achievement and respect. Traditionally, women were frequently called "girl," and Black adult males were referred to as "boy." In both cases, the term implies that the individuals under discussion are not capable of full adulthood. This fact then becomes the explanation for their unequal status in society (Wolf, 1991).

Probably one of the most interesting similarities between women and Blacks is that membership in their group may transcend all other attributes they possess. Among Blacks, for example, their skin color is the one bond that ties them together. Even the wealthiest Black man faces some problems because of his blackness. For women, the double standard in society's attitudes toward age in men and women represents an obvious liability. Older women represent the lowest-prestige group in American society. Since the value of women is closely associated with their sex appeal and reproductive capacity, the aging process gradually diminishes their social and personal worth. One result is that middle age can be much more stressful for women than for men (Wolf, 1991).

Despite these commonalities, the nature of Black oppression is very different from that of women. As a group, Blacks generally live in separate quarters, where they suffer the worst of social ills. Women may be the only oppressed group in history that lives with their adversary. Yet because of their close ties to men, they do not share the economic deprivation of Blacks. The problems of substandard housing, poor nutrition, inadequate services, and lack of other essentials that affect Blacks do not affect White women to the same degree (Joseph and Lewis, 1981). Many of the conditions that middle-class White feminists have found oppressive are perceived as privileges by Black American women, particularly those with low incomes. The option not to work outside the home, for example, is a luxury historically unavailable to most Black women. According to King (1990), the desire to struggle for that option can, in such a context, represent a feminist position precisely because it represents greater liberty for certain women. More important, White feminists failed to address issues of class and race during the early years of the women's movement. They failed to see how class, race, religion, sexual orientation, able-bodiness, and other factors reduced the choices given to women who were not White and middle class (hooks, 1995).

Black Women and Feminism

Whether the women's movement is relevant to Black women is a subject of considerable controversy in the Black community. White women assert that Black and white women share a common op-pression and that Blacks cannot be free until women are free. Hooks (1981) questions whether certain women, particularly those self-identified feminists who are White and middle class, are truly op-pressed as opposed to discriminated against. Others have charged that the race-sex analogy is exploitative and racist (King, 1990).

In part, the oppression of Black women is a different brand of sex-ism from that faced by White women, such as in income inequality and wealth disparities (Hesse-Biber and Carter, 2000; Mishel, Bern-stein, and Schmitt, 1997; Oliver and Shapiro, 1995). There is less in-equality of income between Black women and men. In general, Black women earn 84 percent of the income of Black men (White women earn only 62 percent of White male income). College-educated Black women actually have a higher median income than college-educated White women and earn 85 percent of the median income of college-educated Black males (King, 1990). Also, Black women are better ed-ucated than Black men at most levels (Mishel, Bernstein, and Schmitt, 1997; National Center for Education Statistics, 1991b; U.S. Census Bureau, 1998). They hold more bachelor's and master's degrees and maintain a slight lead in doctorates. But Black men hold the lead in professional degrees ("Vital Signs," 1999). Despite having more edu-cation, Black women consistently earn less than Black men.

Furthermore, if color-blindness is viewed as the cure to ending racial discrimination, then it is not surprising that some individuals believe that women are already liberated. Black women, however, unlike White women, have fewer choices simply because of their multiple identities and locations in society. The *Journal of Blacks in Higher Education* ("Vital Signs," 1999) disclosed several findings that shed light on the complex marginalization of Black women. About 42 percent of Black women in corporate jobs believed that they had to play down their racial identity, and 54 percent of Black women reported being subjected to racial jokes in the workplace. White women do not play down their race and do not face racial jokes in the workplace. So for Black working women, the potential of sexual harassment is seasoned with racial harassment. It is reasonable to consider that Black lesbians would face discrimination based on their sexual orientation and might face discrimination based on their gender and race.

Black Feminism and Black Men

One group of Black women issued a manifesto that declared sexism to be a destructive and crippling force within the Black community (Combahee River Collective, 1982). Black feminism is not always a protest against male political and economic domination. Instead, it may reflect tension in interpersonal relationships. In referring to male joblessness and female-headed households, one woman writer has asserted that "these conditions are the result of economic transformations. They changed gender relations as they changed the marital, family, and labor arrangements of women and men" (Zinn, 1990, p. 262). This economic disenfranchisement, says C. W. Franklin (1987), is a gender phenomenon of such magnitude that it affects the meaning and definition of masculinity for Black men.

To address the multiple dimensions of Black family existence, that is, the way in which discrimination influences the psychological, economic, political, and legal dimensions of Black family life, requires a shared understanding between Black men and women, as well as Blacks and others in society. To this end, some Black men have embraced Black feminism, arguing that Black feminism may create unity in the Black community. Michael Awkward (1999) argues that Afrocentric feminism may provide men with an invaluable means of rewriting or re-vis(ion)ing themselves, their history, their literature, and their future. Black feminist thought offers Black men the opportunity to embark on critical discourse about the state of Blacks in the United States. In addition, it has the potential to broaden the critiques on oppressive practices used to maintain power and status or to redefine the meanings of gender for Black men and women, making it a valuable political tool for Blacks (Harris, 1995). In sum, feminism might provide a deliberate approach to identifying and challenging racism, sexism, classism, and any discriminatory treatment against Black women and men.

Despite the advantages, feminism can become a distracting and divisive mechanism of change. Black feminism could bring unity inside and outside Black communities, but it also may serve to create distrust among Blacks. Black feminism could distract attention from the dangers of racism, classism, and other discriminatory practices endured by Blacks (Bell, 1999). In short, instead of Blacks fighting institutionalized oppression, motivating youth to obtain the necessary education and skills to compete effectively in the economy, or addressing spending and investment planning needed to reduce wealth disparities, feminism may send the Black families on another path. Bell eloquently stated that the Black community must be watchful of divisive behaviors that distract it from the dangers lurking outside the community, dangers they know all too well and prefer to deny.

Summary

The Black male's response to the charge of sexism has been slow in coming. To a large extent, he believes, as do many White men, that women's demand for equal rights is a threat to whatever masculinity he has been allowed by the larger society. There is some resentment, particularly among middle-class Black males, about what is considered the preferential treatment of Black women in the workplace, since they may be used as a double minority in affirmative action hiring. But the impact of feminism is forcing some changes in Black male behavior, with some embracing feminism. One notes a discernible erosion of the sexual double standard, more men participating in child care, and the sharing of housework and decision making. One factor retarding these changes in male behavior is the excess number of women over men in the Black community. Because of the severe competition for the small pool of eligible Black males, many Black women are still forced to take marriage on male terms.

The machinations of American society have placed Black men in a position of relatively low employment and high underemployment; many are not keeping pace with the educational progress of other sex-race groups; and although their life expectancy has increased from 64.5 in 1990 to 68.9 in 2002 following a decline in life expectancy during the 1980s, they still lag behind Black females and White males and females (Child Trends Data Bank, 2004; Strong, DeVault, and Sayad, 1998; Staples, 1991a; C. W. Franklin, 1987). Thus, it is clear that for them, the problems caused by the legacy of racism will continue to take precedence over the need to address sexism. Although many middle-class Black males will increasingly adapt to the changing role of women, Black males of the working class will lean toward traditional roles as they continue to confront the challenge of economic survival (Landry, 2000). Many Black women, however, will refuse to permit men to define Black womanhood and will demand parity in the home and in all other aspects of life.

What will happen in the future is difficult to determine. Many Black men will continue to fall behind Black women in their educational and economic progress. Black women may begin to hold a larger proportion of higher-status jobs, although their pay reflects the values placed on societal constructions of jobs traditionally held by women. Some segments of American society will be pleased with this result, because they perceive Black women to be less threatening to their racial hegemony. At the same time, large numbers of Black women—and men—will continue to occupy the bottom rung of the socioeconomic ladder. Whether either is better off than the other is an academic question; the need is for both racial and gender equity. The issues of gender and race are too interwoven to separate at this time. Significant changes must await a serious effort by society to eliminate both racism and sexism from American life.

7

Marital Patterns and Interactions

The popular song of the 1950s declaring that "love and marriage go together like a horse and carriage" expresses the Western variety of love. Among Americans, love is almost exclusively celebrated as feelings of passion, excitement, and closeness. It is expected to precede marriage and thereafter to be the foundation for marriage. In its purest or ideal form, husband-wife love is monogamous and eternal and forsakes all other relationships (Blood and Wolfe, 1960; Crosby, 1991; Strong and DeVault, 1995). Black Americans' acceptance of this Western form of marriage is inconsistent with the customs of their African heritage. A historical understanding of Black marriage helps to illuminate the transformation that has taken place since preslavery days. Since Chapter One provides a broad historical account of Black families, we will only briefly review key aspects of this history that highlight the evolution of the love-marriage linkage, the primacy given to the husband-wife relationship, and monogamy.

History of Black Marriages

Traditional African societies gave low priority to expressions of love prior to marriage and higher priority to the economic and other functional interdependency between husbands and wives. If love and deep affection developed, they grew largely from living together and from the cooperation of husband and wife in the struggle for a livelihood.

Love as a prerequisite to marriage was considered potentially disruptive, for it involved individual choice, thus increasing the risk of bringing together individuals from different backgrounds. Marriage as a utilitarian device served to perpetuate family tradition and wealth along socially prescribed lines. Consequently, marriage and divorce in Africa were strictly regulated by the families of the bride and groom. They controlled it by arranging child marriages, isolating the genders premaritally, placing severe limits on the field of eligible mates, and matching the bride and groom. The elders made these arrangements without seeking approval from the state or religious bodies. In this sense, common law marriages in the United States that have the approval of the concerned families are directly in line with African custom (Herskovits, 1941).

African marriages were organized around two contrasting bases: consanguinity, which refers to blood kinship, and affinity, which refers to kinship created by law. In contrast to European custom, the consanguine group, not the conjugal pair, was paramount (Sudarkasa, 1988). As an example, the wife's tie to her own family was presumed to exist in perpetuity, whereas her tie to her husband could be dissolved. Despite the fact that the groom paid a bride-price in compensation for taking away a member of the family, the bride's family continued to maintain an active interest in her welfare. In matrilineal societies, the newlyweds lived in the compound of the bride's blood relatives, and the husband was considered an in-marrying spouse. In such societies, the wife's brother exercised so much authority, particularly over the children, that some anthropologists considered the husband a stranger in his own home (Stephens, 1963). Consistent with the importance placed on consanguinity, most brothers and sisters took sides with their siblings against their wives or husbands in a crisis. This is not to say that conjugality was totally discounted. The bride's husband was expected to guarantee good treatment, and wives were expected to reciprocate by working hard. However, the extended blood kin remained paramount.

Conjugality did not include the element of exclusivity found in European American marital dyads. In the context of polygamy, men and women frequently had sexual liaisons with more than one partner. These liaisons did not necessarily threaten marital stability. Children from such unions served to strengthen the lineage, particularly in patrilineage systems where men aspired to have as many children as possible.

This pattern of family organization meant that the stability of the family did not depend on the stability of the couple. When marriages dissolved, this did not have the ramifications of contemporary American divorce. Remarriages usually followed, and children remained with members of their lineage even if the in-marrying parent left the village (J. H. Franklin, 1987; Herskovits, 1941; Omari, 1965; Sudarkasa, 1988).

Slavery changed the African pattern of marriage formation and function. The greatest loss in this change was not the denial of legal marriage, because in Africa the state was not an active agent. Rather, it was the loss of strict kinship control over the marriage institution, which drastically changed the meaning and character of marriage. The slave master replaced consanguine authority. His ultimate interest was in economic profit from his slave investments; he had no regard for the slaves' African mores and kinship relationships.

Ironically, with regard to mate choice, slaves had greater individual freedom in colonial America than in Africa. Many slave masters allowed their slaves to pick their mate and required them only to ask permission to marry. On occasion, the master allowed them to pick a mate from another plantation or from the free Black population. After gaining their master's consent, the couple could live together without further formality. However, in most cases, the slaves conducted their own rituals. A typical account of this ritual is given by an ex-slave: "When you married, you had to jump over a broom three times. Dat was de license" (Meltzer, 1964, p. 46). "Jumping the broomstick" was usually done in front of other slaves or a slave minister, who included in his remarks the phrase "until death or distance do you part" (Simms-Brown, 1982). In some cases, a White clergyman would conduct a solemn ceremony.

While free slaves generally secured state licenses and had a religious ceremony, this was not always the case when they married a slave. Masters generally intervened in the process when slaves were slow in picking their own mate: "Marsa used to sometimes pick our wives fo' us. If he didn't have on his place enough women for the men, he would wait on de side of de road til a big wagon loaded with slaves come by. Den Marsa would stop de ole nigger-trader and buy you a woman" (Meltzer, 1964, p. 46).

Greater freedom existed in marital formation than in its dissolution. Although slave masters generally kept couples together for the sake of morale, the couple knew that the permanency of their marriage depended on the economic stability and interest of their master; in this, they had no control. Because masters separated families for economic profit, some slaves found themselves in polygamous arrangements. Slave women and men were first and foremost full-time workers and breeders for their master, and only incidentally a parent or spouse. Thus, whether slaves were in monogamous or polygamous marriages was of little concern to profit-hungry slave masters (Brouwer, 1975; J. H. Franklin, 1987; Stampp, 1956; Steckel, 1980).

Emancipation restored only a modified version of the African marriage formation. Families regained their control, but the state gained authority, polygamy eventually lost its appeal, and love as a precondition for marriage replaced the decision of the elders. The importance of the state became evident as thousands of former slaves who had "jumped the broomstick" in slavery formally renewed their vows. Acquiring a marriage license was tantamount to declaring one's freedom. However, not all ex-slaves embraced monogamy.

Retention of African polygamous practices was observed by nineteenth-century abolitionists working in the Sea Islands off the coast of South Carolina. They noticed that men who worked on more than one plantation often had wives and families in various locations on the islands. These polygamous arrangements were noted to be quite stable. Thinking that this "immoral" practice was rooted in their former slave life or their African culture, the abolitionists sent missionaries to convert these ex-slaves to monogamy and to the model of provider-dominant husband and domesticated-submissive wife. They appeared to be successful in bringing about the demise of polygamy. However, the need for cotton production during and after the war years as well as the continuing necessity for two incomes among Black families meant that the traditional submissive wife could be accepted only in principle, if at all.

Contemporary Custom

The dilution of the African tradition is also evident in the way contemporary Black Americans and African-educated young people differ in their definition of love or what they consider to be desirable traits in a mate. But before we consider this difference, we should note that no one study compares the marital expectations of modern African and Black American young adults. Our information is gathered from a few scattered studies that provide information on one or the other group. Although these studies are not directly comparable, taken together they provide a glimpse of the possible differences that exist.

Like American Black youth, modern educated African young adults have been influenced by the Western concept of love. Nevertheless, love has different meanings for these two groups. Unlike American Blacks, nonemotional factors outrank emotional and affectionate feelings for Africans. For both genders, affection is ranked ten on a fifteen-point scale for Africans, whereas for American young people, affection is not only a prerequisite for marriage, but among the majority of American Black females, it is considered a prerequisite for premarital sexual intimacy. Furthermore, for Africans, but not for Americans, obedience is explicitly stated as an important aspect of love. Based on their ranking of mate selection traits, both genders in Africa are identical in their desire to find a mate who will place love for their children before their love for their spouse. Children are seen as critical to the continuity of the lineage, and without children, a substantial number feel they would either leave their spouse or lose their love for them. Children are not even ranked as a component of love for Black Americans. Given the central place of children in traditional African society, it makes sense that what is generally considered to be "love" in the Western world is deemphasized in Africa in favor of the love that centers around children (Griffin, 1982; Johnson, 1978a; King and Griffin, 1983; Omari, 1965; Reiss, 1967). Moreover, in many African societies, virginity is expected of the bride. However, because of the importance of children and couples wanting to ensure that they are fertile, exceptions may be made for pregnant brides (African Wedding Traditions and Marriages, 2004).

Few Black Americans enter marriage without declaring their love for their mate. Yet marriages are not based solely on love. There are external forces or societal norms that dictate the relative characteristics of the couple. In general, males are expected to be superior in age and also in terms of social, economic, and educational status. However, there is a limit: a certain amount of homogamy or similarity is also expected. A male married to a female over four years his junior may be accused of "robbing the cradle," or if she is several years his senior, he may be accused of marrying for her money. *Meterogamy* refers to couples who have substantial differences in characteristics such as age and income. In addition, couples are expected to share the same marital history. For example, it is expected that divorced females will marry divorced males, and never-married females will marry never-married males.

Overall, society does not support substantial differences between couples, particularly racial or religious differences. Exogamous norms that forbid intermarrying on color and religious lines are often based on deeply grained prejudices. However, these norms also reflect society's belief about what is important for a successful marriage. Couple similarities in demographics are deemed important because they are believed to be an indication of shared values, interest, and mutual friendship networks, all of which support marital stability.

Societal norms for mate selection are not as easily met in the Black community. Since an imbalanced gender ratio exists, it is not surprising that relative to Whites, Black couples violate these norms more frequently. According to one national study, compared to White females, Black females are far more likely to marry someone at least four years older, and those females married once are more than twice as likely to wed formerly married men. Moreover, whereas 24 percent of White wives have higher educational status than their husbands, 36 percent of Black wives are higher. Among the college-educated husbands, the ideal in male educational superiority is most likely to be realized. Fifty-nine percent of husbands with some college had higher education than their wives, whereas only 11.6 percent of husbands with no college were higher. Half of the husbands with no college education had wives with the same amount of education (Spanier and Glick, 1980).

In the 1990s, 31 percent of Black and 19 percent of White middle-class wives had higher incomes than their husbands (Landry, 2000). Among all couples, only 21 percent of wives had more education than their partner. This educational disparity in favor of the wife is higher within Black marriages as implied from the higher percentage of Black women compared to Black men with at least a bachelor's degree (18 percent for women versus 16 percent for men). Among non-Hispanic Whites, a higher proportion of men than women had earned at least a college education (32 percent for men versus 27 percent for women) (U.S. Census Bureau, 2000).

Obviously, those with higher education have a larger field of marital partners. From their advantaged position, most choose to conform to societal norms by maintaining a superior educational position in their marriages. Black college men are relatively few and are in the best position to pick and choose.

And pick and choose they do. High preference is given to light-skinned women regardless of whether the men married before, during, or after the "black is beautiful" movement of the 1960s. The

Black nationalist movement may have changed Blacks' preoccupation with trying to become White through processing or straightening their hair, lightening their skin with commercial cosmetics, or tightening their lips to reduce their size, but it did not significantly change the preference for light-skinned women.

As far as the light-skinned women are concerned, dark-skinned men have become more desirable mates since the 1960s. Apparently, the Black pride of the 1960s coupled with the greater job and educational opportunities made dark-skinned men more ambitious than their lighter-skinned brothers. Darker-skinned men are more willing to sacrifice everything to get a better job, and in the height of the civil rights movement, they were more likely to achieve occupational mobility. Darker-skinned men prior to the 1960s may have had the same ambition, but there were few opportunities (Udry, Bauman, and Chase, 1971). Since women tend to select men on educational, occupational, or income attributes first, light-skinned women become color blind when offered a marriage proposal from an educated dark-skinned suitor.

Because many Black men still prefer light skin, dark-skinned women remain at a disadvantage in the marriage market. Despite Black males' light-tone preference, many still marry dark-skinned women for three reasons. First, dark-skinned women outnumber their lighter sisters. Second, since the 1960s, dark-skinned women have reduced some of the educational advantages light-skinned women had over them, thus increasing their desirability as suitable mates. Third, despite the darker males' earlier progress, one study reveals that lighter-toned males are disproportionately located in higher economic and occupational positions (Keith and Herring, 1991). Apparently the economic recessions and political conservatism that began in the 1970s continue to impede equal opportunity for all minorities, especially for dark-skinned men.

When light skin color is the dominant criterion for mate selection, Black women of all shades must deal with the competition from White women. With White women also available to Black males, they realize that Black males of higher status will no longer have to settle for light-skinned Black women. As Calvin Hernton (1965) puts it, now light-skinned women will have to stop "playing White" in the Black community and prove themselves as desirable females.

Interracial Couples

White women as competition is not a new phenomenon. Many believe that the gateway to the public display of affection between White women and Black men began with the 1966 *Loving* v. *Virginia* U.S. Supreme Court decision, which declared laws prohibiting interracial marriage unconstitutional. This is a logical turning point: between 1968 and 1985, the percentages of intermarriages outside the South showed a rapid increase from 3.9 to 10.0 for Black men and from 1.2 to 3.7 for Black women. Although beginning at a lower base level and not as dramatic, the South also showed increases in Black-White marriages during this period (Kalmijn, 1993). By 1998, the proportion of out-marriages had increased by over six times, with Black grooms and non-Black brides becoming increasingly common (Crowder and Tolnay, 2000).

Miscegenation laws are powerful, but throughout American history, there have been periods where they were ignored or did not exist. In the beginning, America made little social distinction on account of race (J. H. Franklin, 1987). Some scholars hypothesize that regardless of legal statutes, uneven sex ratios serve to encourage the formation of interracial unions. According to the sex ratio theory, people will marry more within their group if their own group has a relatively well-balanced distribution of the genders. Imbalances push the disadvantaged gender into scouting in the out-group's territory (Qian, 1999; Guttentag and Secord, 1983). Three points in history demonstrate this notion. As noted earlier, in the beginning of American slave history, there was a shortage of Black female slaves. Consequently, the number of sexual relations between Black slaves and indentured White women was fairly high. Black males were even encouraged to marry White women, since the children from such unions would also be enslaved, thereby increasing the property of the slave master (Staples, 1992).

A second period occurred during and after the Civil War, when the passage of antimiscegenation laws had already taken place. The shortage of White males created by the war resulted in an upsurge in White women who either married or cohabitated with Black men. The death and maiming of millions of White males meant that White women had to violate caste boundaries if they wanted a male mate (Blassingame, 1972). This was not a difficult mate choice for the many White women who had internalized the prevailing myths about the Black man's extraordinary strength and exhaustless sexual desire. Also, the social reforms during Reconstruction increased the Black man's social and economic status and heightened his appeal (Spickard, 1989).

Just as these sexual stereotypes may have stimulated White women, the Black male may have been attracted by the White woman's higher social standing as well as her forbidden-fruit status. The penalties for having sex with a White female were severe, and as far as some Black males were concerned, this created an aura of mystic enticement around all White women. Against this backdrop of taboos, lies, and stereotypes about Black sexuality and sacred White womanhood, the stage was set for mutual attraction. For the first time in American history, Black and White women openly competed for the attention of Black men, yet White men have always had the freedom to pursue any women, by force or mutual consent. Obviously, racial relations did not significantly change as a result of these few unions. They do, however, demonstrate how demographic changes, apart from the law, can alter mate selection choices.

Finally, during the late 1960s, Black men found themselves returning the White females' attention. Recruited for their athletic ability, they often found themselves on predominantly White campuses, where Black women were few or nonexistent. Given the more liberal atmosphere of college campuses, the civil rights movement, and White women's push for sexual and economic liberation, interracial dating and marriages took a sudden upswing. Black males and White females were meeting for the first time as equals with shared educational values and goals. White females found themselves emancipated from parental control and enmeshed in a network of friends that was more liberal than the one they left at home. Part of their new-found freedom was expressed through crossing the color line.

As the proportion of Black female students increased, they again found themselves competing for a scarce number of Black men. For them, a real crisis is created when Black college men cross the color line. College-educated Black women have a narrow field of eligibles. Not only do Black men become more scarce, but the qualities Black middle-class women look for become even harder to find (Crowder and Tolnay, 2000). Books such as Terry McMillan's *Waiting to Exhale* (1992) and featured articles in national magazines affirm the husband shortage in the Black community. There is a genuine fear among Black bourgeois women of the competition from White women for Black men that dates back to E. Franklin Frazier's observation some years ago. He noted that Black middle-class women attempt to justify their fear by stating that the Black man always has an inferior position in relation to the White woman or that he marries much below his social status. Frazier believes that such rationalizations by Black women conceal their deep-seated feelings of insecurity and inadequacy, since they have no objection to the marriage of a White man to a Black woman, especially if he is reputed to be wealthy (Frazier, 1957).

Studies show that while interracial marriages do not shield the Black partner from his lower position in society, Black men, like Black women, tend to marry in the expected socioeconomic direction: Black men down, Black women up. There is no evidence of hypergamy— that is, a situation where a White female gains more status in terms of education if she marries a Black man than if she marries within her own race (Heer, 1974; Tucker and Mitchell-Kernan, 1990).

On predominantly White campuses, the intensity of the competition between Black women and White women decreases as the size of the Black student population increases. This situation has caused some students of race relations to observe that the absolute size of the group also influences the rate of intermixing. On campuses where Blacks are found in small numbers, interracial mating increases; conversely, as the Black student body increases, the cross-racial mating decreases. On one large western state campus with a Black student population of one hundred males and far fewer females, over 90 percent of the Black males said they had dated interracially. This high percentage partially reflects the prestige many women students attach to dating an athlete (Sebald, 1974; Willie and Levy, 1972). Regardless of sports involvement, the evidence shows that a significant number of Black males have dated interracially (see Staples, 1981).

This pattern of group size and cross-racial mating appears so consistently that when it was first observed in the larger society, it was regarded as a sociological truism or a law of intermarrying. These theories based on sex ratios and group size do not explain, however, why so few Black women date and marry interracially when so few Black males are available. In many ways, Black women face a more complex situation. Black women suffer from a split image. In the eyes of Whites, she is a mixed bag—sexually alluring, romantically passionate, animalistic, motherly, and unattractive. Throughout history, White men believed that White women belonged on a pedestal and Black women in their bedrooms. Filling historical annals are numerous accounts of forced sex between White masters and female slaves, White bosses and Black workers, and rape by White men not acquainted with their Black victims. Few White men married Black women, for marriage assumed a degree of equality that White society would not accept.

This background of exploitation makes Black women suspicious of any advances from White men. When Black women accept dates from White males, they seldom give in to sex, particularly on the first date. According to one study, 70 percent of Black males and only 25 percent of White males reported having intercourse on at least one of their interracial dates. No White male reported having a one-night fling, whereas 50 percent of Black males had at least one (Sebald, 1974). Furthermore, many Black females are made to feel guilty by Black men when they jump the color line. This seems hypocritical: many of the males making the criticism date interracially themselves. This double standard works in the Black males' interest, since most of those who date White will only marry Black (Willie and Levy, 1972).

Another element holding back Black female–White male unions is the social expectation that the male will be the aggressor. White males are not generally motivated to date or marry Black women. Those who are interested feel that their motives may be misunderstood in the light of historical exploitation, while others fear social retribution, family disinheritance, or damage to their career. Furthermore, Hollywood has been a powerful force in promoting the European standard of beauty—long blond hair, blue eyes, thin noses—over negroid features. While women are more likely to select on the basis of earning power or ambition, men continue to be enticed by physical attractiveness as defined by White society (Tucker and Mitchell-Kernan, 1990; "The Black Male Shortage," 1986). Escaping this preferred European beauty may be the exotic appeal of nonnative-born Black women. Immigrant Black women who arrived in the United States during the 1980s were far more likely to marry White men than those who were native born (Qian, 1999). Although these forces have operated and do operate in some relationships, Black female–White male marriages have increased over the past thirty years (Crowder and Tolnay, 2000; U.S. Census Bureau, 1994).

Many Black women have altered their position on dating White males as they find it increasingly difficult to find a Black mate with status equal to or higher than their own (Staples, 1999; "The Black Male Shortage," 1986). Their attitude coincides with attitude changes in the general population. There is growing acceptance of interracial marriages. In a national survey, 20 percent of all Americans reported that they had dated interracially. Naturally, there were regional differences. The South had the lowest incidence of biracial dating (10 percent), while the West had the highest rate (one out of three) (Staples, 1992). College campuses recruit from a broad population base and consequently reflect more cosmopolitan attitudes. According to one study of 620 never-married undergraduates, half of the respondents felt open to involvement in an interracial relationship (Knox, Zusman, Buffington, and Hemphill, 2000).

Blacks of either gender are twice as likely as Whites to accept interracial relationships. Further, few college students allow their perception of their parents' objections to deter them from crossing the color line. By ethnicity, Black mothers and White fathers are usually the ones setting the norms of interracial relationships (Knox, Zusman, Buffington, and Hemphill, 2004; Goforth, 2003).

Organizational arrangements also foster egalitarian attitudes. Military services, for example, are generally desegregated, emphasize fair treatment, and create relatively homogeneous socioeconomic groups. White men who serve in the military are three times more likely to marry Black women than men who do not serve. Similarly, White women with military experience are seven times more likely to marry Black men than women without military service (Heaton and Jacobson, 2000). Blacks and Whites are meeting as equals not only on college campuses and in the military, but also in the workplace, in neighborhoods, and in the last bastion, the churches.

However, prejudice still exists. Some White parents still disown or isolate their children if they intermarry, and some Black families will accept a White in-law only if that person shows some appreciation or understanding of Black people. In addition to encountering the common discrimination against Blacks in general, such as in housing and the workplace, some interracial couples become estranged from their family and lifelong friends. Many interracial couples still claim that they are shut out of much of the social life in Black circles and do not fit perfectly within White social groups.

Contrary to popular wisdom of the early 1970s, children from such unions were found to be no worse off than Black children in general. They were considered Black by both communities and found themselves adjusting to Black problems and Black customs (Aldridge, 1978; "You Can't Join Their Clubs," 1991; Porterfield, 1973). However, as these children have reached young adulthood, some have begun to express discontent with their social status. There are those who claim that they are forced to choose between Black and White and wish for their own "beige" category. Many multiethnic Americans are forming support groups to help them deal with their unique issues (Atkins, 1991; Donloe, 1987; Porterfield, 1973).

Other popular accounts show biracial persons adjusting well to both their White and Black heritage ("You Can't Join Their Clubs," 1991). Without a large survey of biracial adult children, it is unclear whether interracial unions produce the "tragic mulattoes" or the "love children" who will be the catalyst for future racial harmony. More than homogeneous ones, interracial couples must undoubtedly rely on their own determination to continue the marriage when social support fails.

To optimize social congeniality, interracial couples generally search out communities that are more tolerant: the West as opposed to the South. The Tucker and Mitchell-Kernan (1990) study shows that a disproportionate number of mixed couples living in the West have migrated from the North, another country, or, though to a far lesser degree, the South. Their study also suggests that it is not sufficient for the host environment to be more tolerant. The likelihood of an interracial union is generally maximized if the individuals grew up in a racial environment where race relationships are somewhat more permissive, such as in urban areas or in the North or where they did not experience firsthand knowledge of racial tensions, such as in another country (Aldridge, 1978; Tucker and Mitchell-Kernan, 1990).

Whether moving to a more tolerant climate puts interracial couples on the same marital stability footing as Black-Black or White-White marriages is unclear. The few published studies are inconsistent (Tucker and Mitchell-Kernan, 1990; Heer, 1974; Monahan, 1970). Obviously the race difference is not in their favor. Not so obvious is the fact that many of these marriages violate other social norms—

homogamy in marital history and age. Compared to those in ho-
mogamous marriages, either or both women and men in interracial
marriages are more likely to be older, previously married, or significantly different in age from their partner (either older or much
younger than their partner). For example, White men married to
Black women in Los Angeles are on the average 6.7 years older than
their wives, whereas husbands in White marriages and Black marriages are only 1.5 and 1.0 years older on the average (Tucker and
Mitchell-Kernan, 1990; Bass, 1982).

All of these demographic differences are associated with a lower
chance of marital stability. Yet some argue that mixed marriages
begin with greater commitment, and so they can overcome these
odds. Others believe that interracial couples are doubly doomed because they violate societal norms on several fronts and marry for the
wrong reasons: rebellion against society or parents, sexual curiosity,
and status. A popular motive ascribed to Blacks is that they hate
being Black, and marrying White is a way of compensating for their
feelings of inferiority. The fact that many of those who remarry were
formerly married to members of their own race casts some doubt on
this motive. There is no question that a significant proportion of all
American marriages are formed on neurotic and irrational bases.
However, ascribing such judgments to all interracial couples does
serious injustice to the healthy individuals who have the courage
to ignore social norms and live out their love convictions. Furthermore, ascribing these negative motives feeds the racist concept that
Blacks and Whites are unable to live together in loving relationships. There is no scientific evidence that these motives differ by
racially homogeneous and heterogamous marriages. Most interracial couples if asked why they married will say they married for love
and common interest (Bass, 1982; Lewis, Yancey, and Bletzer, 1997).

About 22 percent (3.4 percent of all Black couples and 0.3 percent of all White couples) of interracial marriages are between Blacks
and Whites. Even when considering other possible racial mixtures,
interracial marriages represent only 2.4 percent of all marriages in the

United States (Crowder and Tolnay, 2000; Glick, 1988; Strong and DeVault, 1995). Thus, in the rest of this chapter, we focus on commonalities and variations among typical Black marriages: those in which the husband and wife share the same racial heritage.

Marital Sexuality

The literature on marital sex among Black couples is sparse. In the first decade of the twenty-first century, minimal information is available on those most likely to be married, the middle class. There are few longitudinal studies that focus on normative Black American sexual development, especially in marriages, and no studies of Black sexual development across the life span (Lewis and Kertzner, 2003). As noted earlier, the assumption is that Blacks have a relaxed attitude toward sex. This assumption is primarily based on limited data on working-class blacks as well as on extrapolations from data showing higher rates of liberal premarital sexual behavior and attitudes among Blacks than among Whites. It is true that Blacks, especially those in the lower class, have a more relaxed attitude toward premarital sex than Whites do. Attitude is not the same as experience, however, and active sexual behavior is not the same as satisfaction. According to one national study, Blacks and those in the lower class report higher levels of sexual dysfunction (Laumann, Gagnon, Michael, and Michaels, 1994). Furthermore, given the negative experiences many Black women have after their first premarital experience, there is no reason to totally romanticize Black marital sex (Johnson, 1978a; Oggins, Leber, and Veroff, 1993). Whether liberal attitudes and sexual behavior prior to marriage translate into affectionate and healthy sexual performance within marriage is also unclear. Few studies exist to help in separating fact from fiction.

There is no large-scale empirical study to test whether Frazier was correct in characterizing the middle class as having sexually starved women and glamorous sexually restless men who seek sexual promiscuity as compensation for their impotence in the White world. Undoubtedly, their dual-earner lifestyle results in battle fatigue that adversely affects the frequency and quality of their sex life. We suspect that like White dual-earner couples, the frequency of their sexual activities is lower than among couples who are not dual earners (Oggins, Leber, and Veroff, 1993).

The marriage chambers of Black couples are not devoid of the same complaints of insensitivity, sexual inhibitions, and unimaginativeness that echo through the bedrooms of Whites. According to one study, 10 percent of Black wives said that their husbands were never affectionate, and another 27 percent felt they were affectionate only once in a while. A quarter of these wives also indicated that their husbands perceive them as affectionate never or only once in a while (Addison, 1983; Wheeler, 1977). Although a quarter to a third represent a minority, it certainly does not add fuel to the various sexual stereotypes surrounding Black sexuality.

Of course, affection is not the same as sexual performance. However, for many, particularly females, it is an important precondition for heightening sexual pleasure. When marital tension exists, it tends to interfere with the affective or physiological responses that contribute to enjoyable sex. Among newlyweds, regardless of income level, Black wives who experience irritation or tension in their marriage are less likely to enjoy sex, particularly if they are parents (Oggins, Leber, and Veroff, 1993). As far as performance is concerned, therapists are reporting that Black American couples, primarily the nonpoor, are increasingly seeking therapy for a variety of sexual problems. This is due partly to the greater acceptance and availability of sex clinics, as well as to the increased ability to pay for such services through sliding-fee scales. Sex therapists are reporting that they are getting couples with performance anxiety and poor sexual communication because a significant number have internalized the myth of their own supersexuality.

Typifying such couples are Ann, a twenty-three-year-old shy and slightly overweight wife, and John, her tall and thin twenty-seven-year-old husband. Ann had been uninterested in sex during their six-year marriage. The problem intensified after the birth of their two children. John expected her to have sex every night during the two hours they were home together. Within these hours, family dinner also had to be served. John clearly felt he was "taking care of business," as was expected of a Black man. He even wore a badge sewn on his jeans that read "super-stud." Ann was filled with guilt because she did not live up physically or mentally to the image of the "sexy Black woman" (Wyatt, 1982). Clearly both partners attempted to emulate the stereotypes, despite the fact that their schedules and individual needs were not being met. Unfortunately, we do not know what proportion of Ann-and-John couples exist among all Black couples. But there may be as many as a quarter, and that is cause for concern.

Marital Conflict

Marriages are not without their conflicts. The amount of disagreement or hostility that may exist without breaking up a marriage varies. Some marriages thrive on constant bickering and violent behavior; in others, the marriage is threatened by the least bit of disagreement or hostility. The issues argued about range from the way the toothpaste is squeezed to decision making, from in-laws and music to political and religious issues. And as the emotional housekeepers of marriage, women see conflicts as being both more intense and more frequent than men do. We cannot possibly cover the myriad of conflict areas, so we will focus on those on which scientific information is available.

Conflict over decision-making style is the cause of much tension for working-class Black families. In those few cases when wives make unilateral decisions, the marriages tend to break up. Husbands who insist on using this style create a great deal of negative feelings between themselves and their wives, but their behavior is less likely to result in separation or divorce. Undoubtedly, their behavior is more tolerated because it fits into the culturally prescribed role of a male being in control of his family.

As important as decision making is to the Black working class, it is much more important in White families, where strict male and female roles are most often observed. Crossing over into the husband's domain does not have the same impact in the Black family, where role assignments are more flexible. Nevertheless, Black working-class families are sensitive about how conflicts are resolved. Wives who perceive that their husbands "give in" often during their arguments are more likely to stay in the relationship than wives who believe that their spouse never or seldom gives in. Furthermore, "giving in" has its greatest benefits in democratic marriages, as opposed to those that are nondemocratic (DeJarnett and Raven, 1981; Osmond, 1977; Scanzoni, 1978; Strong and DeVault, 1995).

When blow-ups occur, they are most likely to be about sex (Osmond, 1977). Sexual fights are not so much about the sexual performance of their mate, since many Black women are assumed to have relaxed and accepting attitudes toward sex. Rather, tension is most likely to be sparked by extramarital affairs, which are fairly common. When Robert Bell (1970) asked his Black working-class female subjects if a wife should expect running around, 56 percent of them answered yes. Over the years, this expectation has not changed.

Lower-class men, particularly those who have a marginal relationship to both jobs and community organizations, have difficulty developing intimacy. Although many factors undermine their efforts for marital harmony, it is their struggle with two competing sets of values that weighs heaviest. Most desire stable, long-term marriages, but they also want relationships with women outside marriage. Their first image is that of a good husband and father who works hard to provide for his family. The second self-image is that of a single young man who is attractive to many women and is perceived by them as a swinger and a good lover. Lower-class communities hold both images in high esteem, but the second image is seen as more heroic. When there are problems with work that leave these men feeling vulnerable and incapable of filling the provider role, they seek compensation in the image of the swinger and lover (Gooden, 1989).

Often, extramarital affairs involve using grocery money for drinking, gambling, new clothes, and entertaining the many available women in the Black community. Consequently, fights over money become a secondary issue in the marriage.

The fact that money is seldom the dominant issue may seem odd, since a nationwide survey showed that 54 percent of American families frequently argue over money (Strong and DeVault, 1995). Perhaps these lower-class couples seldom fight over it because there is little discretionary money available. Both partners clearly understand that their limited financial resources must go for survival: food, shelter, and clothing. When the money fails to reach home because of the vices of one or the other spouse, it becomes a source of serious conflict. Because many lower-class couples possess ineffective conflict resolution skills, many arguments degenerate into physical fights that are often interrupted by the police (Bell, 1971; Gooden, 1989; Rainwater, 1966).

Within the middle-class family, the conflicts are more likely to be centered around money. Reasons given for marital tension are preference in social activities and extramarital affairs. Unlike their lower-class brothers, their commitment to marriage and the companionship and attention marriage provides make them work harder at resolving conflicts in a constructive way. Furthermore, when marital conflict arises, middle-class couples are more likely than lower-class couples to be guided in effective conflict resolution by successful parental role models or the active intervention of maternal or paternal advisers.

This is not to say that extramarital affairs do not exist. In contrast to their lower-class counterparts, middle-class husbands do not make such affairs public if they can help it. But like lower-class husbands, they have experienced a double self-image. In college, many lived out the playboy image by having women friends on campus whom they considered marrying and others in town whom they dated just for fun. But once they got a job and established linkages with community organizations, they were able to live out their primary dream of husband-father who provides for his family and receives positive affirmation both at home and in the community. The difference between the lower-class and middle-class husbands primarily reflects their socialization and relationship to the outside world (Gooden, 1989).

Family Violence

In the past three decades, family violence has emerged as an urgent social problem in American society. Determining an accurate rate of violence is hampered by poor record keeping, especially by inconsistencies in the way violence is measured by courts, police, shelters, clinics, social service agencies, and researchers (Klein, Campbell, Soler, and Ghez, 1997; Gordon, 1988). Our best national data indicate that each year, one-third of American women experience at least one physically or sexually violent act, one in eight involves serious injury, and one in twenty-five marriages is plagued with perpetual violence. Estimates of the number of husbands or live-in partners who inflict physical violence on their current or former mate range from 960,000 to four million incidents (U.S. Department of Justice, 1998; Lockhart and White, 1989). For women ages fifteen through forty-four, domestic violence is the leading cause of injury (Williams, 2000). Verbal abuse is even more prevalent. Popular wisdom indicates that marital violence is endemic to Black families. In movies, books, plays, newspapers, and television documentaries, the fussin' and fightin' theme is constantly repeated. The Color Purple, an Academy Award–nominated movie, powerfully portrays male-female relationships around the early 1900s as turbulent, hostile, and bitter; major scenes involve incest and spouse abuse. At other times, the themes of committed love, tenderness, and androgyny have been interwoven into the complex scenes of Black family life. This early portrait of male-female tension has contemporary relevance.

Today, many Blacks believe that over the past fifty years, a growing distrust, even hatred, between Black men and Black women has emerged (Cazenave and Smith, 1990; Wallace, 1979). Their hatred is provocatively conveyed in Ali's *The Blackman's Guide to Understanding the Blackwoman* (1989). Ali, a Black Muslim, claims that Black women's unwillingness to submit to men of their race is the cause of Black men's poor condition and the Black family's destruction. Moreover, she does not limit her charges of insubordination to working-class women. All Black women are said to be guilty of complaining, whining, and disrespect. Ali's disdain for "uppity" Black women is forcefully made when she instructs the Black man to give his woman a solid, open-handed smack in the mouth when she is disrespectful. It is important to keep in mind that Ali's Muslim background biases her nonempirical and polemical thesis toward extolling the virtues of female submissiveness and male dominance.

Hip-hop music represents an additional promotion of violence against Black women. Specifically, the lyrics and imagery of gangsta rap carry strong abusive and violent messages demeaning women (Gan, Zillmann, and Mitrook, 1997). Descriptions of women as deserving of violence if they disobey their pimps and reducing women to sexual objects prompted two Black women—U.S. Senator Carol Moseley-Braum (D-Illinois) and C. Dolores Tucker, chair of the National Political Congress of Black Women—to lead the Senate Juvenile Justice Subcommittee in moving to censor this popular expression of misogyny. (We provide another brief discussion of hip-hop in Chapter Six.)

Despite these popular images, there is little reason to believe that Blacks are inherently more violent than Whites or that Black men and women have declared open warfare. First, a discrepancy exists between rhetoric and reality. While the majority of Blacks believe that Black male-female relationships have deteriorated over the years, few characterize their own personal relationship as essentially negative. Moreover, those with the most positive attitudes are married, whereas the most negative feelings are expressed by the nonmarried (Cazenave and Smith, 1990). If beliefs are not based on personal experience, then they must derive from popular myths.

Undoubtedly, these myths are internalized, rhetoric is repeated, and little thought is given to the incongruence between personal experiences and popular belief.

Furthermore, Black females recognize that Black males face occupational discrimination that makes them less responsible and trustworthy and generally not in control of their destiny. For this reason, they rate Black males relatively low on their ability to provide adequately. But this does not mean that Black men are rejected. Over forty years ago, Frazier (1957) noted that Black males compensate for not being able to play the "masculine role" by cultivating their "personalities." Black females respond positively to Black males' expressive qualities, ranking these qualities far higher than White women and men rank the expressive qualities of White men. Thus, despite the fact that Black females expect to be disappointed in the provider role, they continue to find Black men lively, gregarious, vigorous, and exciting partners (Frazier, 1957; Turner and Turner, 1983).

Any violence existing in Black families reflects to a considerable degree the particular social and economic predicament in which Blacks find themselves. The reality of Blacks' differential exposure to violence must be acknowledged. They are overrepresented among youth dying from nonbiological causes, or what is known as the "new morbidity": accidents, homicide, and suicide. In 1977, the number of young Black men dying from homicide (5,734) surpassed those killed from 1963 to 1972 in the Vietnam War (5,640) (Gibbs, 1988a). While it is true that since the 1970s the intimate homicide rate has fallen for Blacks in every gender and relationship category (in contrast to no change among Whites), Blacks' homicide rate remains higher than Whites' (U.S. Bureau of Justice Statistics, 2002). Black psychiatrists Pouissant, Grier, and Cobbs stress the intense frustration Black men face as a result of being shut out of the mainstream of American life. They suggest that the high incidence of Black-on-Black homicide reflects subliminal anger that is vented on convenient victims within their immediate environment (Grier and Cobbs, 1976; Pouissant,

1983). Their interpretation is echoed by Marsh (cited in Williams, 1999), who contends that Black American women are subjected to sexual assault and domestic violence because Black men are frustrated, feel powerless, experience economic instability, and vent their anger on defenseless spouses. It is certainly true that Black crime is more prevalent among the underclass (Star, Clark, Goetz, and O'Malia, 1979). Yet Blacks in general face constant assaults on their self-worth that may not be physical but that nevertheless produce scars that cripple psychologically and create subliminal rage. This has the potential of exploding within the family.

Whether Blacks are caught in a "culture of violence" that permeates their family life is debatable. Scientific knowledge is hampered by the tendency to exclude Blacks from the analysis, even in those cases where they are represented in the sample. The greatest flaw in the studies, particularly the early ones, is the failure to account for the effect of social class when comparing rates of violence among Black and White families. Blacks are overrepresented in official marital violence statistics not only as a result of racial bias but also because of their overall low socioeconomic status. Thus, social class is a key factor to consider.

High income and employment are the best shields against family violence. Conflicts around family decision making are strongly related to social class. Not only do working-class couples report more conflicts in this area than the upper and middle classes, but these conflicts are more likely to result in violence (Cazenave and Straus, 1979; Lockhart and White, 1989; Uzzell and Peebles-Wilkins, 1989). This is not surprising, since traditional gender roles appear more frequently within Black and White working-class marriages (Jackson, 1991). Many working-class husbands have few material resources that translate into power within the family. Thus, they may embrace society's prescription of male dominance in the home. Hampered by communication skills that are often vague and limited, they frequently resort to nonverbal messages and control (Foley, 1975; Uzzell and Peebles-Wilkins, 1989). Opposition from the "little woman" challenges their self-esteem, masculinity, and demand for authority. In the heat of an argument, they are most likely to sense a loss of their family power and to react violently.

This relationship between social class and violence breaks down when type of abuse is considered. Working-class families are more likely not to report abuse and to be victims of severe violence. A higher proportion of middle-class women compared with those in the lower and upper classes report being pushed, grabbed, or shoved by their husbands. Despite their higher rate of "mild violence," they are less likely than their upper-class counterparts to report their abuse to the police or professionals (Lockhart and White, 1989). It is important to note that mild violence is not only more typical than severe violence, but less likely to reach the attention of authorities. The high level of mild violence within the middle class may reflect their high work ethic and social marginality. They have been called "strivers and strainers" and "conspicuous consumptionists." Their emphasis on appearance, as demonstrated by excessive spending on clothing and cars, often reflects status panic and anxiety. Their newly achieved status is precarious. The lack of a solid economic base within the Black middle class was noted as early as 1957, when E. Franklin Frazier published his classic thesis, *The Black Bourgeoisie*. They are dependent on Whites for their salaries and wages and are just two or three paychecks removed from the working class. This situation heightens tension and the potential for violent behavior.

Financial insecurity is no doubt intensified in Black families living the middle-class lifestyle on one person's salary. This is certainly suggested by the higher degree of abuse reported by unemployed wives within the middle class as compared to their employed counterparts. The causal direction of the effect of employment is unclear. Perhaps the added income from dual earners enhances the economic security of the family in general and reduces the environmental stress that often results from financial deprivation. Or the effect may be more direct—that is, the mere fact of employment enhances a wife's family power position and independence, making her less vulnerable than the dependent unemployed wife (Uzzell and Peebles-Wilkins, 1989).

Adding to this lack of power is an isolation factor. A Black homemaker will most likely not find companionship with other Black wives, since most are working. If she lives in the suburbs, she is likely to be further removed from the Black community and must create bonds with White homemakers. These bonds, however, are too often superficial. If she is not active in a Black church or other Black organizations, she experiences social isolation. In the eyes of some in the Black community, she is an anomaly: too "uppity" or lazy to work. Consequently, relative to employed wives, unemployed wives may be minimally integrated into the community, lacking the friendship networks that could provide support and protection during extreme stress (Cazenave and Straus, 1979).

In addition to factors contributing to domestic violence, it is important to consider the victims' rationale for not reporting their abuse. Black women may underreport because they (1) may be afraid of contributing to the stigmatization and stereotyping of people of color being violent; (2) lack awareness of available services or perceive them as insensitive to the racial and cultural realities of their lives; (3) desire to live up to the resilient, strong women in the face of all odds; (4) believe that the police when called will arrest their partner merely because he is Black and then he will be a victim of police maltreatment; and (5) may believe that few options exist in terms of other relationships or economic survival. Data may corroborate this suggested reluctance. One study found in comparing White and Black women in domestic violence shelters that Black women experienced significantly more severe abuse in the six months prior to entering the shelter (Asbury, 1999). Similarly, other sources reveal that when attacked, Black wives are significantly more likely than White wives to retaliate and to kill their mate after repeated and long-term abuse (Uzzell and Peebles-Wilkins, 1989).

One should not assume, however, that this reflects higher family violence among Blacks: just the opposite is true. In a 1979 national probability study, Blacks as compared to Whites reported a lower rate of spousal slapping at every income level except those in the $6,000 to $11,999 bracket (Cazenave and Straus, 1979). If a culture-of-violence explanation has any merit, it may have more relevance for Whites than Blacks. Through the ages, the family has served as a haven from extrafamilial abuses that Blacks must endure. It is likely that this family function has not been severely weakened even in the context of escalated violence against Blacks in American society at large.

Marital Dissolution

Prior to 1974, "until death do us part" reflected the reality of most marriages. By 1974, a watershed in American family life was reached: more marriages ended by divorce than death. Today, if the trend continues, 49 percent of all individuals between the ages of twenty-nine and thirty-five will divorce by age seventy-five. A disproportionate number of these divorces will involve Black couples. Combined data from several national surveys indicate that between 1973 and 1980, 37.2 percent of Black males and 22.2 percent of White males who had ever married were divorced. Among females, 42.2 percent of Blacks and 23.5 percent of Whites were divorced (Strong and DeVault, 1995). Whereas three-quarters of all Black marriages were intact in the 1960s, barely half are so today. The proportion divorced is highest among Black females (Gallagher, 1996; U.S. Census Bureau, 1991a, 2002a; Glick, 1988).

The divorce trends are clear, but the underlying reasons for divorce are not as clearly understood. Economic factors rank high among the reasons given for divorce. (These are covered in greater detail in Chapter Three.) Briefly stated, it is well understood that divorce is highest among low-income couples. Obviously, however, not all working-class couples divorce, nor do all middle-class couples remain married.

Other demographic forces as well as personal factors come into play. Among the demographic factors related to divorce are length of courtship, age at time of marriage, presence of children, education, differences in husband and wife's background, parental marital history, geographical location, marital noncohabitation, and religion. These factors provide valuable information on groups; however, we gain little to no knowledge about the individuals involved. Unfortunately, even individuals do not always know their motives, and sometimes the intensity of their pain leads them to blame others or deceive themselves. In this chapter, we review noneconomic demographic forces as well as some of the individual reasons Black couples give for separation and divorce (Rindfuss and Stephen, 1990; Strong and DeVault, 1995).

Black marriages end in separation, divorce, or widowhood with far greater regularity than do the marriages of Whites or Spanish-origin couples. This pattern is true regardless of class. By 1996, 48 percent of ever-married Black women divorced compared to 40 percent of ever-married White non-Hispanic women and Hispanic women (U.S. Census Bureau, 1996). Consistent with their higher rates of divorce and lower rates of remarriage compared to Whites, Black Americans consistently evaluate their marriages less positively. Furthermore, compared to White couples, Black wives and husbands more often perceive that they would be happier if they were not married. As not to distort the racial differences, however, it should be noted that regardless of race and gender, the majority of marital partners perceive that their overall happiness outside marriage would be higher than it is currently within marriage (Goodwin, 2003; Rank and Davis, 1996).

Despite their perceived happiness outside marriage, most Blacks define marriage as being very important to them personally, and an overwhelming number plan to marry. A trouble sign for marriages is the significant number of Black youth who indicate that their desired age for childbearing is earlier than their desired age at marriage. Many begin their childbearing in their teen years. Ten percent of the births to Black teenagers in the mid-1980s were legitimized by marriage. Unfortunately, for two major reasons, these marriages are struggling against the odds. Given the decline in marriages among Black females, it is estimated that this 10 percent rate was lower at the turn of the twenty-first century. A pregnancy prior to marriage by itself does not significantly increase the likelihood of divorce. However, if the pregnant woman is an adolescent, drops out of high school, and is crippled by economic problems during marriage, the divorce rate increases dramatically. Having a birth prior to marriage increases the probability of divorce, but the negative effect is stronger for Whites than for Black Americans (U.S. Census Bureau, 2002b; Strong and DeVault, 1995; McMurray, 1990; Moore, Simms, and Betsey, 1986).

First, many teenagers who marry interrupt their schooling in order to work. Black and White individuals who do not complete a unit of education (that is, elementary school, high school, or college) increase their chances for marital dissolution. As an example, Blacks who have only one to three years of college are more likely to divorce than those who complete high school. This pattern has been observed so frequently that it is called the Glick effect, named after Paul Glick, who first observed it. Glick suggests that dropping out of both school and marriage has a common root: lack of persistence. Thus, those who do not persist in school are not as likely as those who graduate to persist in their marriage. Yet it could also be argued that the differences in dissolution rates between dropouts and graduates result from the teenagers' immaturity (Bauman, 1967; Glenn and Supancic, 1984; U.S. Census Bureau, 2002a).

For both Blacks and Whites, adolescent marriages are more likely to end in divorce than marriages that take place when people are in their twenties, particularly if they marry after age twenty-six (Glenn and Supancic, 1984). This is primarily because among the younger set, neither partner has the economic skills to maintain a stable family, the commitment to stay together while most of their friends are enjoying the freedom of singlehood, or the maturity it takes to resolve marital conflicts constructively.

To strengthen their economic position, some join the U.S. Army in order to earn a steady check needed for supporting their families as well as providing the foundation for their children to thrive. Children from military families have a strong tradition of college matriculation. The number of Blacks, particularly females, who select the military services as an escape valve from economic deprivation and lack of jobs is partially reflected in their increasing enlistment since the 1970s and highlighted by their disproportionate presence in the 1991 Persian Gulf War (Butler, 2002; Hisnanick, 2001; Pinderhughes, 1991).

As a result of this overrepresentation of Blacks in the Persian Gulf War, a debate is raging on television, the Internet, and news conferences over whether the demographics of the military represent a fair distribution of the burdens of military service. A 2002 Department of Defense study found that soldiers from wealthier families were not well represented among the new recruits. Those with minimum education fail the entrance exam, leaving middle and lower socioeconomic enlisted recruits. Others report that 38 percent of the military's 1.1 million enlistees (and 45 percent of the Army overall) are ethnic minorities, while they make up only 29 percent of the general population. Black American women comprise nearly half the Army's enlisted women. Furthermore, according to the National Center for Education Statistics, the percentage of enlisted minorities far exceeds the percentage of minorities in postsecondary education colleges and universities.

Joining the debate, Donald Rumsfeld states that people are in the armed services today because they want to be there. But others argue that the armed service is not the first choice for many minority recruits. Ronald Waters, a University of Maryland political science professor, and William E. Spriggs, executive director of the National Urban League's Institute for Opportunity and Equality, assert that because the playing field outside the military is not level for Blacks and poor Whites, defending your country is a way to get a fair chance at succeeding (Fears, 2004). Thus, as the doors of job opportunity are closed in the private sector, many turn to the military.

Ironically, this solution places those married in a catch-22 situation. Although the reasons are not entirely clear, Black soldiers are three times more likely than their White buddies to be separated from their spouses while serving in the U.S. military. Perhaps this situation is caused by the fact that Black military spouses find it more difficult than their White counterparts to find a job when their spouse is relocated overseas. In the military as in the civilian population, Black married couples are heavily dependent on a second income to make ends meet. Rather than give up a job in hand and risk unemployment abroad, some choose to live apart. Unfortunately, those Blacks not living with their spouses are twice as likely as cohabiting Black couples to experience marital disruption (Harrison and Minor, 1978; McCubbin, Patterson, and Lavee, 1984; Rindfuss and Stephen, 1990). Thus, these Black soldiers place not only their lives on the line, but their marriages as well.

Second, three is a crowd when a couple is first married. Time is needed for adjusting to life as a couple. For teenagers whose previous single life involved minimum responsibilities and high social interaction with peers, the time needed for adjustment is even more critical. When a demanding baby is an immediate addition, the husband-wife adjustment time is greatly reduced. Even in the best of stable marriages, children tend to lower marital satisfaction. Childbearing families and families with preschool children experience a rate of marital disruption way above the national average. Moreover, the pressure from children exceeds that from economic forces (Hampton, 1982).

It is understandable that about half of all premaritally pregnant marriages end in divorce within five years, about twice the rate for those in which the woman is not pregnant at the time of marriage. For teenage parents, if the mother marries the father, the father may find full-time fatherhood more stressful than being a part-time dad. If she marries a nonbiological father, stepchildren may resent his step-role status, thus causing tension (Wineberg, 1999; Strong and DeVault, 1995). The proportion of divorces is even greater for Blacks, who have higher rates of premarital pregnancies than Whites. Despite their poor chances at a long-term marriage, a small proportion of lower-class teenagers continue to venture into matrimony, thinking that they can improve their economic position.

A significant proportion of all race-sex groups marry in their twenties. Although they do not face the disadvantage of early marriage, other factors may work against their marital stability. Those who have known their mate the longest before marrying are most likely to have a successful marriage (Chavis and Lyles, 1975; Jewell, 1989). Also, although not a strong factor, there is a slight tendency for the rate of divorce to increase if the parents of either spouse have been divorced. However, it is unclear as to whether it is the parents' divorce that is the culprit or the fact that children of divorced parents tend to marry earlier.

Another aspect of parental characteristics that weighs on the stability of Black couples, particularly those in the working class, relates to the parents of the bride and groom. If the husband's father has a higher occupational status than his wife's father, the marriage has a better chance of remaining intact. Interestingly, the effect of this disparity seems to hold regardless of the husband's own mobility (Osmond, 1977). This pattern is evidence of the power of gender norms that prescribe that the wife be inferior in status to her husband.

Heterogamy is another type of disparity that increases divorce probability. It refers to the selection of a mate whose personal and group characteristics differ from one's own. Many Black women find themselves in heterogamous relationships because of the male shortage. In broadening their field of eligible males, they often include men significantly older or younger, with lower educational achievement, and a history of at least one divorce. Many individuals who have been married previously have not worked out the problems from the previous marriage when they enter subsequent marriages. Thus, second marriages tend to be high risk (Bumpass, Sweet, and Martin, 1990; Glenn and Supancic, 1984; Kitson, 1985; Spanier and Glick, 1980). Age, education, and marital history differences reflect divergent experiences that may result in marital conflict. If heterogamous couples do not have an appreciation for these differences or if these differences get in the way of reaching desired goals, the marriage is headed for rocky shores.

A major strength of Black family life has been its social support system. Many marriages have weathered the storm through the active participation of extended family members and community support. As Blacks have become more urbanized or as they have moved from tightly knit Black communities, some of that support has been weakened. This is one reason that we see regional differences in divorce rates. Black couples, particularly those over age thirty-five, are more likely to divorce if they live in the North or West than in the South. Southern living is characterized by a high degree of social integration, with extended families, ethnic neighborhoods, low levels of residential mobility, and numerous church congregations. Such forces are weaker in other regions, especially in the West.

Religious affiliation as a deterrent to divorce is difficult to determine, since 80 to 90 percent of Blacks are Protestants (U.S. Census Bureau, 1991a; Chavis and Lyles, 1975). However, two aspects of religious attachment work in favor of marital stability: conversion and social support. First, 60 percent of recently married Black women may be expected to separate from their first husband, and about 45 percent will reconcile. The likelihood of reconciling triples for marriages in which one of the spouses changed religion in order to share the religion of the partner (Wineberg, 1999). Second, the social support quality of religion becomes important in maintaining marital stability as well as reducing postdivorce distress (Lawson, 1999; Olson and DeFrain, 1997). Group membership and low social isolation have long been associated with healthy emotional and psychological outcomes (Durkheim, 1951; Strong and DeVault, 1995). This is particularly true for Black American couples, who are more likely than White couples to interpret their marital experiences in the context of their social worlds—their religious community and kinship network. Hence, not surprisingly, church attendance reduces the probability of divorce. For the small number of Blacks in conservative religions such as the Catholic church, the Seventh-Day Adventists, and Jehovah's Witnesses, the ecclesiastical pressures for marriages to remain intact are probably very strong. All of these forces interlock to create spiritual, emotional, and instrumental support, the key social controls that tend to keep marriages intact.

For some, only death separates them from their mate. For those widowed over age sixty-five, twice as many Black males (21.5 versus 12.5) have lost their wives. These women not only leave a void in the hearts of their surviving spouse and children, but often leave behind grandchildren for whom they were the primary or co-caretakers. Although more women survive their husbands, Black women find themselves widowed earlier and at a higher rate (U.S. Census Bureau, 1996). Health issues become a major issue for many of the elderly survivors. The majority of widowers and widows who were having difficulty with the most basic personal care—walking, dressing, eating, and going to the toilet—prior to the lost of their intimate partner are left in a crisis.

Summary

Divorce is a harsh reality, and many forces operate to pull marriages apart. In a 1966 *Atlantic Monthly* article, sociologist Mervyn Cadwallader called marriage a "wretched institution," unworthy of salvaging (1966, p. 6). Others claim it is outdated and unnecessary (Melville, 1977). Still, nearly half of those Blacks who divorce will remarry, particularly the males (Bumpass, Sweet, and Martin, 1990). While an increasing number of Blacks, especially women, in their twenties are remaining single, Blacks continue to desire marriage. When the marriage dissolves, a majority seek still another. Among those who were over age sixty-five in 1996, only 6.2 percent of Black women and 7.2 percent of Black men had never married, representing only a slight increase from 1991 (Crowder and Tolnay, 2000; U.S. Census Bureau, 1991a, 1996). Even among younger people, the desire to marry continues.

In sum, millions of Black people continue to seek intimacy and fulfillment within marriage despite the odds. Only one in ten persons agrees that society could survive just as well without the institution of marriage (Billingsley, 1990; Melville, 1977). Rather than abandon the institution, there is a need to understand it and defend it against the external and internal forces that cripple its ability to absorb the shock of a changing and—for a sizable minority—hostile society.

8

The Challenges of Parenting

Only Black families and other minorities socialize their children under conditions that are in stark contrast to the American creed of life, liberty, and the pursuit of happiness. Despite social and economic advancements, a Black child still lacks a fair opportunity to live, learn, prosper, and contribute in America. Tragically, the Black infant mortality rate in the 1980s was the same as the White infant mortality rate in the 1960s. Today, Blacks are twice as likely as Whites to die during the first year of life. Although both Black and White infant mortality rates have fallen, there is no indication that Blacks will ever reach the level of Whites (Children's Defense Fund, 2003; National Center for Health Statistics, 1996; Leffall, 1990; Edelman, 1988).

One reason for this continuing disparity is the continuing higher poverty rate among Black children under age eighteen, a rate that has hit a record high for children in extreme poverty. The relative economic deprivation of Black children is even more striking when one realizes that one-third of Black children are poor compared to one-tenth of White children (Child Trends DataBank, 2002; Song and Lu, 2002). About 70 percent of Black children live in families with incomes less than twice the poverty level, while nearly two-thirds of all White children live in families with incomes more than twice the poverty level. Simply stated, Black children are more likely to get sick or die because they are three and one-half times more likely than Whites to be poor (Edelman, 1988; Peters, 1985; Swinton, 1991; U.S. Census Bureau, 1991a).

Nevertheless, the economic and educational status of some Black children and families improved during the 1980s and 1990s. Although the proportion of Black families with incomes less than $5,000 has increased by 38 percent, those with incomes greater than $50,000 has increased by 38 percent. Since the 1960s, the Black-White racial gap has narrowed considerably for both high school graduates and those with one to three years of college (Swinton, 1991; Reed, 1988; U.S. Census Bureau, 1991a, 1991b, 1989). Between 1967 and 1997, Black Americans benefited from a 31 percent boost in their real median household income, a rise that contrasts with an 18 percent increase for Whites, albeit a significant racial gap remains (U.S. Census Bureau, 1998).

Despite the undesirable rates of Black dropouts, the 1980s ended with the largest and best academically prepared high school graduates of any other Black group in history. By 1997, a gap no longer existed in high school graduation rates between Black and White Americans. And in 1998, Black college enrollment increased 50 percent over the number enrolled a decade earlier (U.S. Surgeon General's Report, 2003). Furthermore, in the 1980s, the decline in minority enrollment in graduate schools halted for the first time. Since then there has been a 6 percent increase in Black enrollment in graduate studies, with Whites showing virtually no change in enrollment (Syverson, 2001; Wilson, 1989). Although a substantial gap remains between Blacks and Whites in higher education, a small but significant number of Black parents have acquired upward mobility at this level. For these parents, higher education has empowered them with more resources for mediating the impact of the wider society's attack on their children.

Regardless of their particular socioeconomic circumstances, varying degrees of subtle and overt prejudice and discrimination threaten to destroy the self-concept, self-esteem, and aspirations of Black children. This threat is certainly more ominous among those with fewer economic and social resources. Yet even the most affluent cannot totally escape the negative fallout of a racist-oriented society.

Since slavery, Black parents have been preparing their children to become "somebody" in a White world that continues to treat them in various ways as "nobody." As we will see, with few exceptions, Black parents continue to labor for their children's future, and they have never ceased dreaming of their children living out the American creed: the pursuit of knowledge and happiness.

Emancipated Parents

Perhaps the crudest aspect of slavery was the way in which it crushed the hopes parents had for each child they brought into the world. For dying slave parents, it had to be agonizing to know that they were leaving their children in bondage. It did not matter how hard parents worked; they could not change the lot of those dearest to them. However, with the end of the slave system, hope came alive. For emancipated mothers and fathers, freedom did not mean release from backbreaking slave labor. Rather, it meant they could use their labor to improve their family's spiritual and material welfare and thus chart the upward mobility of their children.

This autonomy did not come quickly or easily. To reassert their unquestionable authority under slavery, former slave owners appealed to apprenticeship laws that bound Black children to unpaid labor until they reached adulthood. These same slave owners, however, took no responsibility for the welfare of the elders whose lifelong labor had been spent to support their genteel lifestyle. For the freed slaves, children were essential to both their economic support and the welfare of their elders. With fierce determination, parents fought to reclaim their children. While denouncing former owners' ruthless disregard for their families, freed Blacks with few exceptions accepted without grudge the duty, however heavy, of caring for aged parents. When families were able to work as a unit, the father often asserted his authority as head to protect his family from the employer's unfair and dangerous assignments (Berlin and Rowland, 1997).

The discipline and values imparted to children reflected the parents' retention of African values, disdain for their past bondage, and the need for all members to labor for family survival. Although parents disciplined with the liberal use of the rod, they refused to whip their children on the directive of White folks. Such a chain of command reeked of slavery and was intolerable. Older children were responsible for younger ones while parents were working outside the home, a practice consistent with that of their African progenitors.

When preschool children were unable to be cared for by older children or extended family members or if housing and board were inadequate, parents were creative in balancing work and family responsibilities. Some hired out their children to White employers to lessen overcrowded conditions at home and increase family income. Others who worked in the homes of White families took their young children with them so that they would not only have supervision, but would get at least one good meal a day. Still others resorted to having their youngsters of five or six picking cotton with them so that they not only could be supervised but could add to the family income. When possible, mothers took in washing and worked at home, assisted by older children who if left to their own devices might get into mischief (Jones, 1985).

Of course, there were those who found it impossible to simultaneously supervise children and work for their survival. Both W.E.B. Du Bois (1908) and E. Franklin Frazier (1939) attributed Black juvenile delinquency and child neglect to the inability of parents to supervise their children while working outside the home.

The devastating results of poverty are evident in the demographic profile of Black families. In the period from 1880 to 1910, Black women's fertility declined about one-third due to disease and poor nutrition. A twenty-year-old woman could expect to see one out of three of her children die before age ten and to die herself by age fifty-four, before her youngest left home (Jones, 1985; Blassingame, 1972).

Despite their poverty, parents instilled in their children the importance of self-dignity. As an example, fresh in their memory of slave days was the humiliation of being handed plain, drab, heavy clothes (two pieces a year). Thus, poor but proud parents instructed their sons and daughters to go without before accepting immodest or ill-fitting clothing from White folks. As a sign of their freedom, some Black fathers spent an inordinate amount of their sharecropping proceeds on colorful and elaborate garments for their children and wives. Most sharecroppers earned barely enough to keep body and soul together, but when possible, clothes were made or purchased for expressive rather than practical wear (Jones, 1985; Escott, 1979).

Even today, Black parents with little material means sometimes sacrifice their own appearance so that their children can be well dressed. Sometimes the importance of clothing is carried to the extreme, as it was for one cleaning woman. Between paying tuition and dressing her daughter to be one of the ten best-dressed women students at a major university, she did not have enough money to attend her own daughter's graduation. In its immediate context, this mother's action seems inappropriate. Yet within the historical context of Black slavery, her behavior takes on a different meaning.

The importance of clothing did not exceed the freed mothers' and fathers' hunger for education for themselves, but particularly for their children. Most felt that regardless of their past slave experience, they could die happy knowing that their children would live the balance of their lives in freedom and in pursuit of knowledge. Given the limited resources of parents and their community, it was not easy acquiring an education. Some parents attempted to educate themselves so that they could pass their knowledge on to their children. Their determination is demonstrated by the laundry woman who tied her book to a fence while she scrubbed. Throughout the South, when public and philanthropic support was not forthcoming,

Black women and men built schoolhouses and hired teachers on shoestring budgets. Unfortunately, most communities of parents could afford these teachers for only a couple of months out of the year (Franklin, 1974; Jones, 1985).

As the Reconstruction government took shape, the few Black political officials found sufficient support to establish a public school system for Blacks. Through the work of philanthropists, religious organizations, and the Freedmen's Bureau, 4,329 schools were operating for Blacks by 1870. Education, however, was far from equal in caliber to White schools. Lower salaries were paid to Black teachers, and White teachers in Black schools faced social ostracism. Parents had to fight hostile school boards that provided their children with poor facilities and White teachers who were considered unfit to teach White children—and therefore deemed adequate for Black children.

The shortcomings in the education of Blacks, particularly in attendance, stemmed not from the lack of zeal on the part of teachers, parents, and students, but from misunderstanding the needs of Blacks. Black families were preoccupied with survival. Many had to make tough decisions as to which child could be released from field responsibility to attend school; given that during the late 1800s, the average number of children was six or seven per family, this was a major decision. Sometimes the daughter was chosen so that she would not have to work for White folks. Frequently, however, the daughter's education had to take the back seat to the family's economic welfare. Recorded in history are testimonies from sharecropper daughters who complained that they were uneducated because their fathers felt they were needed far more in the field than in the schoolhouse.

When possible, fathers and mothers took on extra work so that they could send all their children to school and avoid the painful choice of choosing which of their children to educate. In the worst scenario, parents worked and children were either locked in their homes or left to roam the streets with only occasional supervision from neighbors, who had their own youngsters to attend to. More commonly, children as young as eight years old went to work in the field and either did not attend school or did so only irregularly. In the eyes of freed working parents, the ideal Black family was one in which the father worked full time, the mother devoted most of her time to rearing children and keeping house, and all the children attended school (Jones, 1985; J. H. Franklin, 1987).

The Contemporary Parenting Dilemma

Today, Black parents continue to pass to their children values for effective living and a quest for formal education (Hill, 1999). However, Black and White parents often differ in the way they inspire their children toward higher achievement. Black parents have often been criticized for "saying one thing" and "doing another." Specifically, they have been accused of having low expectations of their children and providing weak support, while setting unrealistically high goals. There is certainly ample research evidence to show that Blacks' aspirations for their children do exceed their expectations, whereas among Whites, aspirations and expectations are closely matched. Such disjointedness is said to make it difficult for Black children to set realistic goals and achieve academic success. Yet this disjointedness is easy to understand.

For example, three-quarters of Blacks enrolled in college in 1970 came from homes in which family heads had no college education. The fact that in 1985 the family income of more than half of Black college students was under $20,000, compared to only 15 percent of White students, attests to the greater willingness of Black parents to sacrifice financially for their children's education. It also reveals the high level of motivation of Black students.

Several studies show that a large proportion of Black lower-income mothers and fathers not only hope that their children will attend college, but spend time discussing educational options with them. Sixty-four to 92 percent of them limit television watching on school days, have rules for doing homework, and insist on their children maintaining a certain grade-point average. However, they are less likely than the more affluent Blacks to help their children with their homework, no doubt reflecting their own limited education. But even here, nearly 60 percent report they help with homework. Despite their own lack of educational achievement, many of these parents have specific occupations they would like their children, particularly their daughters, to pursue. Furthermore, among low-income youth, Black students as compared to White students have higher educational attainment and aspirations. Of Black students in grades 6 through 12 who come from families earning under $20,000, 86 percent expect to complete college compared with 80 percent of Whites. Furthermore, poor whites are less likely than poor Blacks to graduate from high school (Clark, 1983; Jackson, 1975; Hill, 1999; National Center for Education Statistics, 1991a; Reed, 1988; Robinson, Bailey, and Smith, 1985).

In addition, such disjointedness accusations do not take into consideration the role of racism. Compared to White children, Black children's own desires for achievement are not as strongly determined by the occupation of their parents. Black children are keenly aware of the role that racism plays in limiting job mobility and opportunities for their mothers and fathers. They have had daily experiences of watching the capable adults in their lives struggle with gaining education and work. Thus, Black parental encouragement and behavior have as much or more impact on the upward mobility of Black children than what their parents actually do for a living or the amount of education their parents have personally attained (Carnegie Council, 1977; Reeder and Conger, 1984).

Through example as well as words, Black parents must transmit to their children the realities of living in a society that is hostile to Black aspirations. In Scanzoni's study (1978) of middle-class Black families, many parents who were aware of their own deprivation tried to prepare their children for disappointments while encouraging them to set high goals. In striving toward the American dream, these parents taught their children the value of hard work, the importance of holding on to a job, and ways of preparing for and bouncing back from life's disappointments. Today, Black parents continue to provide racial socialization for the protection of their children. Recent studies suggest that fewer than a third of Black parents fail to provide their children with racial socialization messages (Fatimilehin, 1999; Taylor, Chatters, Tucker, and Lewis, 1990). Sometimes these messages are implicit in their discipline techniques. For instance, whereas White parents focus on their children's psychological well-being and give less concern to instilling strict conformity, Black parents continue to stress obedience, conformity, and school performance in order to obtain a good job. This no doubt reflects White parents' security in their children's current status and future success and Black parents' anticipation of greater challenges to success as a result of racial barriers (Hill and Sprague, 1999). Similarly, interracial children also receive racial socialization from their parents. They learn cultural pride and protective messages that prepare them to meet societal oppression (Fatimilehin, 1999).

Partly because of the many sacrifices Black parents have had to make for their families in a hostile environment, Black children have closer relationships with their parents than do White children. Of course, not all children have positive relationships. About one-third of Black adult children claim they do not want to be like one or the other parent, and about half of these reject their parents' lack of ambition, inability to provide economic rewards, or dysfunctional personalities. Although negative modeling generally means that parents behaved in an undesirable manner (overbearing or lacking aspirations), sometimes such identification developed from caring and intentional acts on the parent's part. Statements such as, "Son, work hard and go to school so that you can do better than your old man," demonstrate how some Black parents use their disadvantaged position to motivate their children for upward mobility (Clark, 1983; Scanzoni, 1978).

Cross-Gender Parent-Child Relationships

The gender of the child and parent not only determines how discipline and encouragement are given and received but how parent-child bonding is developed. Unfortunately, the narrow definition given to fatherhood (as provider) and the emphasis placed on boys' need for a male role model for healthy personality development ignore the father's expressive contribution to character development and social achievement in their female children. Similarly, the narrow definition given to mothers (as nurturing) ignores the contribution they make to the occupational attainment of their children. Given that Black fathers and mothers deem it appropriate to interchange or share the provider and expressive roles, the father-daughter and mother-son relationships are just as important for understanding child development and aspirations as are the mother-daughter and father-son relationships.

Few studies address father-daughter relationships and their link to daughters' well-being or upward mobility. One study of adolescent Black American girls in high-poverty Chicago neighborhoods showed that they had an array of father figures. It appears that when the girls' biological fathers were unavailable, social fathers stepped in. When nonbiological fathers took on parenting, the girls reported higher-quality attachments with them than they did with their biological father. And as long as the social or biological father remained involved in their lives, these girls exhibited low depressive symptoms, school behavior problems, and delinquent behavior (Coley, 2003). Furthermore, when fathers actively participate in their daughters' lives, the probability of teenage pregnancy decreases and the likelihood of their daughters' having positive male-female relationships increases (Cochran, 1997) .

The limited information on daughters from non-poverty-stricken environments suggests that both Black and White fathers contribute to the social and psychological development of their daughters. White high-achieving daughters generally have fathers who make an important contribution to their development. A book about the life and career histories of twenty-five White women in top management revealed that these women were extremely close to their fathers. Their fathers gave of their time, provided encouragement, taught them athletic skills, and, most of all, gave them strength to reject the opinions of those who placed limits on their ability.

Much the same can be said about the closeness of Black father-daughter relationships. Black fathers are especially close to their daughters (Veneziano and Rohner, 1998). They, more so than White fathers, encourage their daughters' independence. Furthermore, their encouragement has a greater impact on their daughters' occupational and educational attainment than does the encouragement received from mothers. The more educated the father is, the more likely he is to invest in and support his daughters' upward mobility. In contrast, the encouragement sons get from their fathers or mothers makes virtually no difference in their educational outcome (Reeder and Conger, 1984; Willie, 1988; Scanzoni, 1978). Once again, economics and access to resources influence the academic achievement of Black sons (Battle and Scott, 2000; Biblarz and Raftery, 1999).

In the early years of socialization, Black fathers appear to be significantly different from their White peers. They tend to have an authoritarian approach to parenting, in that they expect a set standard of conduct, believe in forceful compliance when necessary, and have few give-and-take discussions. Furthermore, unlike White fathers of daughters who succeed, they do not encourage individuality, independence, or nonconformity in their preschool daughters.

By White social science standards, their style of parenting is undesirable. Surprisingly, relative to White preschool daughters, the Black father's behavior produces daughters with exceptional independence and competence. Apparently their authoritarian parenting style is not a reflection of authoritarian personality disorder. In contrast, the authoritarian parenting style of White fathers is more likely to reflect an authoritarian personality syndrome: dogmatism and inflexibility motivated by repressed anger, emotional coldness, and a sense of impotence. For Black fathers, it is possible that the harshness typical of authoritarian-style parenting is offset by their demonstration of warm interactions in other areas important to their daughters (Hill, 1995; McAdoo, 1985–1986).

Our focus on father-daughter relationships is not to suggest that mothers are inconsequential in influencing the occupational choice of their daughters. In fact, compared to White daughters, Black daughters' occupational aspirations are more likely to be inspired by working mothers. Using their mothers as role models, they are more likely to see gainful employment as a requirement of adulthood rather than an option. The mothers' contribution to sons' occupational success also cannot be ignored, although quantitative research in this area is sparse. Qualitative reports show numerous male statesmen, scholars, lawyers, and physicians who have distinguished themselves in various fields giving credit to their single or married mothers.

Ben Carson was raised in inner-city Detroit by a divorced mother with a third-grade education. He lacked motivation, had terrible grades, and had a temper that threatened to put him in jail. But his God-fearing mother relentlessly believed in his capabilities, pushed him toward excellence, and despite his grades, challenged the school system to treat him as if he had promise. Today Carson is world renowned for his role in successfully separating Siamese twins joined at the back of the head. He generously gives credit to his mother's guidance (Carson, 1990). Similar stories can be repeated about the divorced mother who raised psychologist Kenneth B. Clark, whose research influenced the 1954 *Brown* v. *Board of Education* decision; the married employed mother who raised historian John Hope Franklin, former president of the American Historical Association and the United Chapters of Phi Beta Kappa; the single mother who raised Ralph Bunche, winner of the 1950 Nobel Peace Prize for mediating the 1948–1949 Arab-Israeli war; and numerous sports stars who proudly call themselves "mama's boys."

In analyzing numerous case histories of mothers of successful sons, Charles Willie (1984) concluded that regardless of whether Black women were single, married, widowed, poor, or nonpoor, they gave their sons constant company, care, early learning opportunities, and partial or full economic support. They expected good academic performance and had ambitions for their sons' high achievement. He even suggests that the more education mothers have relative to fathers, the more education the sons will attain. In Scanzoni's study (1978) of working- and middle-class adult children, nearly a majority of the adult children said their mothers help them materially, and the majority mentioned that their mothers encouraged or goaded them to get ahead. In fact, although fathers are more likely to provide material assistance, it is the mothers who are most likely to be credited by both sons and daughters as inspiring them to get ahead in education. A more recent study (Battle and Scott, 2000) using a national data set of Black male students compared father-only with mother-only households. The unexpected findings showed Black American single mothers doing as well as or better than single-father heads in socializing their sons for academic achievement and success. Although fathers also engage in helping with homework and talking with teachers, these activities are commonly referred to as "women's work." Hence, men may not be as inclined or prepared to fulfill this role. Also, women may have more support networks to assist them with rearing their sons; men, adhering to traditional notions of masculinity, may be less inclined to seek help.

Single Mothers and Educational Achievement

The greatest challenge in parenting is faced by the mother who must raise her children virtually alone. Because substantial numbers of Black men have been absent or infrequently at home due to welfare regulations, imprisonment, inability to obtain regular employment, or holding down multiple jobs that require long hours away from home, many children find themselves raised by their mothers. This situation has created a special bond between mothers and sons. Black adolescent males do not take kindly to any derogatory comments about their mothers, particularly if the father is absent. In "playing the dozens," a game where manhood is determined by the number of derogatory comments one can calmly withstand, it is often a slur on the mother that causes the player to lose his emotional composure. If these sons become financially successful, they generally purchase a house or car for their mothers with their first big check. In presenting these gifts, most of the men comment on the hardships their mothers endured for their sake (Staples, 1984).

Given the mother's historical role in the Black family, it is perplexing as to why Black mothers have come under such harsh attack in the social science literature and in the popular media. A review of fifty years of published research in the social sciences found that most of the developmental difficulties in child development were attributed to weaknesses in the family structure. The brunt of the attack has been on Black mothers who are poor, teenagers, or unmarried. These mothers have been accused of raising children with limited language, cognitive, affective, and intellectual development; low academic achievement; and low self-esteem. Also, children from these families were said to have a proclivity for delinquency and violence (Adams, Milner, and Schrepf, 1984; Baratz and Baratz, 1970; D. Franklin, 1988; Harrison, 1988; Jensen, 1969; Rainwater, 1970). Collins (1999) attributes this denigration of Black motherhood to the failure of scholars to replace Eurocentric views of Black motherhood with Afrocentric ideology, such as flexible boundaries between biological and community mothers for raising children. This misapplied Euro perspective perpetuates the earlier negative role of Black American mothers. Moynihan (1965) felt that in the absence of a male head, the mother's influence was so detrimental to male children that he recommended that sons join the army in order to escape the irregular, unpredictable, and female-biased child-rearing practices of their mothers.

Moynihan, like many of his predecessors, assumed that Black children from single-parent households "fail and flounder." Their failure is primarily attributed to the children's exposure to female authority when society sanctions male leadership. Furthermore, absent fathers generally mean that children are living in poverty and environments conducive to social pathology. The Head Start programs of the 1960s were postulated on the assumption of ineffective child-rearing practices of Black mothers and deficient home environments.

Apart from skin color, the most salient feature of Black children's social status is their speech pattern. Social scientists of the 1960s assumed that children's linguistic competence is closely linked to their intellectual capacity. This assumption was based on another belief—that languages could be hierarchically ordered—and that German was the "best" language for conceptualization. In fact, even today many Americans believe that the way Blacks speak is a strong determinant of their intellectual competency in other areas (Yearwood, 2003; Oubré, 1997; Mitchell-Kernan, 1982; Yetman and Steele, 1975). Since the speech pattern of Black children, particularly those of the lower class, differed from those of Whites, a primary task of the Head Start programs of the 1960s was to bring Black children's speech skills in line with White children's.

Observing that in lower-class homes, speech sequences of mothers seem to be limited and poorly structured syntactically, efforts were made to place preschool children in day care centers where they could learn standard English and thus improve their cognitive skills. Many of these same scientists dismissed any possibility of retention of African habits of thought and speech, and most important, they did not believe that Black Americans had a culture worth protecting. Thus, in their eyes, intervening in Black children's lives presented little or no risk. When they found that their efforts did not alter cognitive thinking, they argued that the mother's influence was so great that Head Start programs must begin earlier in the child's life and should be extended from three months to one year.

Such intervention assumes that a difference is tantamount to a deficit. No one can argue that the language system of many Blacks is different and can become a handicap to the child who is attempting to negotiate with the standard English-speaking mainstream. It is nonetheless a highly structured system that is adequate for abstract thinking. Black mothers and their children are no less able to think abstractly because of their language pattern than are Japanese children who attempt to speak standard English (Baratz and Baratz, 1970).

In the light of insufficient scientific evidence of a link between speech and intelligence, Black mothers were then accused of indirectly hindering their children's cognitive development by not providing enough social and sensory stimulation. When research showed that poor inner-city children receive an abundance of sensory stimulation, it was argued that ghetto stimulation is excessive and thus causes children to tune it all out, thus creating a vacuum for themselves. When it was found that the stimulation did not appreciably differ by social class, ghetto mothers' stimulation was considered ineffective because it was not as "distinctive" as that found within middle-class environments.

Finally, the lower-class mothers' teaching styles came under attack. Since so many of these mothers dropped out of school because of pregnancy, it was assumed that they had failed to learn proper parenting skills. Black mothers, unlike White mothers, are more likely to value obedience, conformity, and respect for authority as child-rearing goals. As an example, they direct their children to learn because the teacher or the parent said so rather than because learning is intrinsically rewarding. An appeal by Black mothers to external rather than internal inducement is considered inadequate in a White world, which stresses self-direction and individuality. Despite the fact that the evidence does not demonstrate a weaker link between this type of Black parenting style and readiness to learn, the Black style is considered inferior. In sum, it is apparent that lower-class Black mothers are a priori defined as inadequate because they are not White or middle class (Baratz and Baratz, 1970; Peterson and Peters, 1985).

Despite the social science bias against Black mothers, there is sufficient evidence showing problems among single unwed mothers and their children, regardless of race. Only recently have social scientists provided less pejorative and more objective data. The more convincing studies have followed a cohort of teenage mothers and their children over several years. These studies demonstrate that child development and future outcome are not as dependent on early childhood experiences as once believed. Recent research makes it clear that while early childbearing increases the risk of ill effects for mother and child as well as prolonged deprivation, there is only minor support for the popular image of the adolescent mother as unemployed, uneducated, and living on welfare with three or more unkempt, poorly motivated, and poorly socialized children (Kesner and McKenry, 2001; D. Franklin, 1988; Furstenberg, Brooks-Gunn, and Morgan, 1987).

First, most women who begin bearing children five to ten years earlier than their peers conclude childbearing five to ten years earlier than those peers. Thus, in the long run, their fertility is similar to that of their peers who delayed childbearing. Early motherhood is unlikely to establish a pattern of rapid childbearing if adolescent mothers receive family planning assistance, avoid another birth in the first few years following their first pregnancy, and remain in school. It is this last requirement that many believe presents the greatest challenge to teen mothers and their children.

It is believed that the teen mothers are unable to transmit educational values effectively to their children because they themselves have dropped out of school. Yet while a substantial number of adolescent unwed mothers drop out of school following pregnancy, a decade later nearly 70 percent obtain a high school diploma, 30 percent take some postsecondary courses, and at least 5 percent graduate from college. These statistics may not be surprising in that Black teenagers are less likely to marry or to leave school than are Whites. However, in comparing these early childbearers with older ones, it is clear that if they had postponed childbearing, they would have attained a year more education on the average, as well as avoided the difficult struggle of raising a child while in their teens. Of course, many were poor students prior to their pregnancy; thus, childbearing was less predictive of their educational failure. But more important, those 25 to 30 percent of teen mothers who do not complete high school are the ones most likely to depend on welfare, live in poverty, and produce children who fail academically and socially (D. Franklin, 1988; Furstenberg, Brooks-Gunn, and Morgan, 1987; Moore, Simms, and Betsey, 1986).

For the majority of teen unwed mothers, welfare dependency is not a permanent feature of their lives. By the time teen mothers reach their early thirties, nearly three-quarters have steady full-time jobs. Of these, the majority are either the exclusive breadwinner or the principal source of family income. Unfortunately, a third earn annual incomes below poverty level for a family of four; if they had postponed childbearing, fewer would have been poor, and far fewer of their children would have been at risk of school failure. Nevertheless, some scholars believe that teen childbearing is a trivial side issue, since many teenage mothers are seriously disadvantaged before they ever had children. Thus, regardless of their fertility record, the odds are against their escaping poverty (Furstenberg, 1991).

It is the poverty that presents the greatest difficulty to parenting (Lichter and Eggebeen, 1994). The effect of income is translated into poorer-quality neighborhoods. Youth in such neighborhoods have daily experiences with unemployment, illicit employment, and few models of high educational achievers. This milieu encourages early sexual activities and low academic achievement and presents a challenge to parents who must supervise their children (Massey and Denton, 1993; Furstenberg, Brooks-Gunn, and Morgan, 1987; Moore, Simms, and Betsey, 1986; Adams, Milner, and Schrepf, 1984). The effect of poverty is even more intense in rural areas, where there are fewer employment opportunities, lower wages, inadequate child care resources, and few social services. Not surprising, these economically depressed areas tend to cripple parents' sense of child-rearing efficacy. Once parents feel ineffective, children's academic and psychosocial competences suffer (Brody, Flor, and Gibson, 1999). For young people living in deprived communities, having a supportive family is critical to positive life outcomes (Apfel and Seitz, 1991).

The situation of impoverished mothers is worsened if their husband or boyfriend is imprisoned. The typical father inmate provided financially for the family prior to his arrest. Imprisonment results in lost family income, making it difficult to make ends meet. The hidden victims in the correctional system are the 1.5 million children left to deal with shame, stigma, anger, and guilt. In contrast to children of incarcerated mothers, who exhibit "acting-in behaviors" such as crying or withdrawal, children of incarcerated fathers are more likely to display "acting-out behaviors" such as running away or truancy. Boys usually experience more difficulty than girls. Despite these feelings and behaviors, children express love for their father and want him released.

Although some children feel guilty because they believe that they could have prevented their father's imprisonment, nearly all children by their very existence hold a powerful key to the father's successful rehabilitation. Recidivism is lowest for fathers who stay linked to their children, and the best predictor of father-child relationship is the mother. Hence, for the sake of the family welfare, mothers must take on the added responsibility of telephone calls, letter writing, and the expense of visiting prisons that are often located in remote areas with poor or nonexisting access by public transportation (Clark, 2001; Browning, Miller and Spruance, 2001; Tripp, 2001).

For impoverished mothers, education provides hope for employment and inspiration for their children. However, to be employed is not enough. Between 1995 and 2001, poverty rates dropped significantly for all but those in extreme poverty. Yet a family of four making double the federal poverty level finds it difficult to provide their families with basic necessities: housing, food, and health care. And more than 85 percent of the 27 million American children in low-income families have at least one working parent (National Center for Children in Poverty, 2003). The challenge for the twenty-first century is to provide the type of economy and national policy that supports adequate supervision of children and provides jobs that allow single- and dual-job families to provide for the basic welfare of their families and the tools to thrive.

Lower-Income Fathers

Of course, not all lower-class children are without involved fathers. Slightly over half of the children of unwed teenage mothers never live with their biological fathers. However, the limited studies on teen fathers do not support the popular image of them as uncaring and uninvolved (Waller, 2002). Although they often are unrealistic about parenthood, they express affection and concern for the mother and children. Many plan to meet social, educational, and financial expectations for their offspring. Realizing the awesome responsibility of parenting, Black adolescent fathers are more likely than those in other non-Black groups to complete high school. To complete their education or earn money, some delay living with their children for one to two years.

For those few involved in court-ordered support, about three-quarters pay nearly 80 percent of the full amount. Black mothers are less likely than White mothers to be awarded any type of support, and when they are awarded, they are more likely to receive smaller payments. It is noteworthy that despite the fact that in American society few fathers have sole responsibility for raising their children, Black fathers are more likely to do so than are White fathers (Conner, 1988; Furstenberg, Brooks-Gunn, and Morgan, 1987; Hill, 1989; Johnson and Staples, 1990; Kesner and McKenry, 2001; Marsiglio, 1987; Watson, Rowe, and Jones, 1990). Throughout the 1990s, this racial differential remained. Furthermore, between 1980 and 1990, Black families headed by men rose twice as fast as those headed by females. While three-fourths are caring for their own offspring, the remaining fourth care for other related children, such as nieces, nephews, and grandchildren (Hill, 1999). According to the 1996 National Survey of Families and Households, these fathers are increasingly young, never married, and poor. Yet they take on this role partly because they desire to be a better parent then their own father, and they anticipate satisfaction with fatherhood (Coles, 2001). Their anticipated success as fathers depends on their security in their masculinity, the degree to which they identify positively with their family of origin, and their level of effective coping skills (Christman, 1990).

Furthermore, substantial numbers of lower-class Black fathers in intact families work every day to keep their families together and healthy. Several studies confirm their active involvement with their children (Adams and Nelson, 2001; Hill, 1999; Whitmore, 1999; McAdoo and McAdoo, 1994). One study of a small sample of poor urban fathers showed 83 percent wanted for their children what they missed most: a good education. They believed that education will provide the best opportunities for their children. In addition, an overwhelming number of these fathers are involved in the daily decision making and disciplinary responsibilities concerning their children.

In disciplining, lower-class fathers perceive that it is their duty to provide punishment to their children for violating externally imposed rules. Generally this punishment is physical rather than verbal and given in line with the transgression's consequence rather than the child's intent. Given the fact that their children will most likely be involved in subordinate relationships with Whites, child-raising strategies that involve obedience, conformity, and respect for authority provide realistic preparation for life circumstances for low-income children. Interestingly, although these fathers perceive themselves as actively involved with their children and mates, they do not believe that other fathers are as active. This disbelief reflects their buying into the popular myth of unresponsive Black fathers (Conner, 1988; Furstenberg, Brooks-Gunn, and Morgan, 1987; Peterson and Peters, 1985; Robinson, Bailey, and Smith, 1985).

Black fathers and fathers in other racial and ethnic groups value companionship with their children more than the provider role. Perhaps this results from the fact that they have been put in a double bind. If Black men accept the White male culture's definition of what it is to be a man—that is, the sole provider—but are denied full employment, then they may create other alternatives. The most popular alternative we hear about is drugs and crime. However, the majority of lower-class

Black fathers in intact families have merely broadened their definition of masculinity to include expressive parent-child relationships. They have modified the traditional definitions of masculinity and enacted the definition that makes sense for them (Harrison, 1988; Johnson, 1989a; McAdoo, 1985–1986; Robinson, Bailey, and Smith, 1985; Waller, 2002). This may not be limited to the lower class. Cazenave (1979) found in his study of Black letter carriers that the greater the economic security, the greater was the involvement of the father in child rearing. Similarly, a more recent study of well-educated Black fathers of high-achieving sons (Hrabowski, Maton, and Greif, 1998) showed high levels of involvement in expressive and instrumental activities. These fathers facilitated the success of their sons by monitoring homework and grades, talking with teachers, firmly requesting schools to place their child in challenging classes, building their children's self-esteem through active listening, communicating strong Black male identity, and helping their sons to become independent by identifying resources both within themselves and the community.

Regardless of the definition Black fathers give to their role, they cannot escape the dominant culture's message that a good father is a good financial provider. During the 1970s and 1980s, when the American economy struggled to reach full employment while controlling inflation, Black unemployment climbed to over 9 percent. Concomitantly, Black single fathers showed significant declines in their perception of their parenting effectiveness. Despite this decline, their level of life satisfaction remained constant over time and they grew more hopeful. In keeping hope alive, they communicated to their children that they can find life satisfaction by holding on to infinite hope in the face of finite disappointments (Anderson, 2002; Adams and Nelson, 2001).

Child Abuse and Discipline

Some parents are so involved with their own problems that they act with indifference or even hostility toward their children. For example, family violence is known to be more prevalent among parents with major socioeconomic problems—the lower class, unemployed, and uneducated. In some intellectual quarters, it is thought that because Blacks are most likely to reflect these characteristics, they have higher rates of child abuse than Whites. Their position gains support from both the bias in reporting Black abuse and sensational media portrayal.

Socioeconomic status and ethnicity play a major role in determining who gets labeled abused. When children enter hospitals with major injuries, Black children are far more likely to be classified as victims of child abuse than are White children. Furthermore, if Black and White children with identical major injuries are observed, Black children are one-third more likely to be reported to authorities. Five percent of one group of 157 physicians claimed that the race and ethnicity of the child's guardians are so important that they would file a child abuse report on the basis of these traits alone. Lower-class White children experience the same bias when evaluated against upper-class Whites, a bias that has influenced the racial disproportionality found in the foster care system (see Chapter Nine). More affluent families deal with practitioners on a fee-for-service basis, which favors the least offensive diagnosis on the circumstances of a child's injuries (Hampton, 1987; Daniel, Hampton, and Newberger, 1983).

The overemphasis on Black violence is facilitated by the popular media portrayal of Black family life. In the powerful Broadway play *For Colored Girls Who Have Considered Suicide When the Rainbow Is Enuf* (Shange, 1977), the frustrations of Black men are taken out on Black children. The play's most shocking portrayal of Black family violence occurs when a father, angry at his woman, intentionally drops their child out of a window in their high-rise, low-income apartment. Consistent with this scene, Black parents who abuse their children are frequently those who suffer from severe economic adversity and stressful relations with their kin and find that they have no one to turn to for help (Daniel, Hampton, and Newberger, 1983).

Yet despite the hardships of Black parents, it appears that there are cultural norms and structural conditions that protect Black children in a way that they are not protected in the White community. A major national study on child abuse and neglect found that Blacks are less likely to report the occurrence of child, sibling, or parent abuse. Parental abuse is so rare or unacceptable that less than 5 percent of Black parents in blue-collar occupations report it, and none of those in higher occupations report behaving violently toward their parents (Cazenave and Straus, 1979). Although the majority of both Black and White parents slap or spank their children, Blacks are least likely to do so. This is especially the case for Blacks in white-collar occupations.

It appears that a major deterrent to child abuse is the number of children in the family and the number of years lived in the neighborhood. Family violence is far less likely in families with five or more children than in those families with one or two. This is particularly true for Blacks. The more years in the same neighborhood, the lower the rate of child abuse. Both observations strongly suggest that isolation is associated with abuse. They also suggest that parents of larger families may not only value children more, but may receive more child care help from within the family. Among Blacks, the relatively high degree of family-kin network and social ties serves to buffer against the even higher rates of violence one would expect from their socioeconomic circumstances (Cazenave and Straus, 1979).

The proliferation of drug abuse in Black communities threatens to escalate violence against children seriously. Already the news media are giving regular accounts of children being abused or killed by drug-addicted family members. Combating drug abuse should be a high priority in every community because it threatens to destroy the most innocent of human beings: children.

In general, a preponderance of evidence supports the assertion that Black parents administer harsh discipline to their children. Blacks are more likely than Whites to use corporal punishment and to see it as part of responsible parenting (Bradley, 2000; Alvy, 1987). Generally, this conclusion derives from studies comparing Black parents' discipline style to that of Whites. Frequently this comparison concludes that Black parents' disciplinarian practices are inferior. However, a simple Black-White comparison distorts the true discipline patterns within Black American families.

Studies giving attention to the internal dynamics of Black families, especially two-parent families, reveal that physical punishment is the least likely method (Bradley, 2000; Hill and Sprague, 1999). When such punishment is used, it is on preschool children and rarely with a switch or belt. Preferred practices include orders, particularly for younger children; parent-child discussions, which increases with the child's age; warning looks used for all ages; and withdrawing privileges for adolescents or giving them extra work. It also appears that fathers are more likely than mothers to elicit the desired corrective behavior with a warning look.

For Black parents, disciplinary strategies differ by gender and are partially affected by social class. Regardless of class, they are more likely to withdraw privileges from sons. And although spanking is rare, upper-middle-class Black parents apply it to their daughters, perhaps because girls have fewer privileges to withdraw than do boys. Overall, Black parents exhibit age-specific discipline, use a variety of methods, and use physical punishment in the context of discussion (Bradley, 2000).

The importance of understanding child discipline from an intracultural and class perspective cannot be overemphasized. Discipline viewed as overly restrictive in a benign middle-class environment may prove to be optimum supervision in a dangerous and impoverished neighborhood. Similarly, the growing diversity of cultures within Black communities means special attention must be given to value clashes when social institutions interact with immigrant families.

For instance, differential cultural views on corporal punishment place West Indian Black parents in direct conflict with school systems within the United States. In many Caribbean societies, parents and teachers work together in administering corporal punishment in the form of flogging with a belt, strap, or cane. Thus, when children misbehave in American schools, newly arrived West Indian parents often give permission for teachers to hit their child or request that the teacher send a note home so that they can beat the child. It comes as a shock to them that such discipline is forbidden not only in the schools but in the privacy of their own homes.

Many Caribbean parents and their children remark that without corporal punishment, children lose respect for their parents and teachers. So committed are these parents to this type of discipline that some school principals caution teachers not to send negative notes home to parents because often the students will return bruised the next day (Payne, 1989; Waters, 1999).

U.S. laws and policies against corporal punishment have at least two possible consequences. First, it has the potential of undermining the authority of many West Indian parents, who are often not prepared to invoke alternative ways of controlling their children. This places immigrant parents at a disadvantage. In the process of competing with the host country for their children's allegiance, they lose an important institutional ally: the schools. More fundamentally, they are asked to substitute intergenerational cultural practices that they deem effective and morally correct for practices that they see producing unruly, undisciplined, and disrespectful American children who drop out of school and engage in criminal activities. They see this forced assimilation in parental discipline as endangering the upward mobility and morality of their children. Second, some children become uncontrollable at school, since they think they can get away with anything, while others take their new-found freedom as a license to disrespect their parents.

In the vast majority of cases, the issue is not child abuse but rather culture clashes. Illustrating this point is the example of a teenage Jamaican boy who was repeatedly misbehaving. His father threatened to beat him, and the boy in turn threatened to call Social Services to report his parents. The parents responded by putting him on a plane with a one-way ticket back to Jamaica. Many members of his extended family met him at the airport and publicly beat him there (Waters, 1999). A T-shirt worn by a Californian immigrant reflects their deep sentiment: "The Floggings Will Cease When Morals Increase."

When cultures clash, the host society has the upper hand. The United States has the right to impose its laws on immigrant parents. Yet while some leading family scholars, such as Murray Straus, argue that any amount of parental corporal punishment has serious negative consequences for children, others contend that the consequences must be placed within a cultural context. From their perspective, it is wrong to deny ethnic minority parents their preferences in something as private as the rearing of their children. Ignoring the cultural context appears particularly ill advised given the more than thirty years of controversy over which model of child rearing is most efficacious. Specifically, the controversy centers on whether to adopt "permissiveness" or the opposite extreme, which supports parent-centered "authoritarianism," or the authoritative model, which integrates the two extremes. This controversy continues.

Summarizing thirty years of research on child development, a leading expert in the field concluded that "the extent to which spanking or any other form of aversive discipline is part of a harsh parenting pattern or is conditioned by warmth and the use of reason determines its meaning to the child and its consequent beneficial or detrimental effects" (Baumrind, 1996, p. 413). A prudent use of punishment within the context of a responsive, supportive parent-child relationship is a necessary tool in disciplining young children. Merely knowing that a parent hit his or her child is not sufficient to determine child abuse. A balance must be struck between protecting children and unwarranted interference in the preferences and practices of immigrant parents (Waters, 1999; Baumrind, 1996).

Self-Esteem in Black or White

Black children must deal with two realities: the Black community and the larger society dominated by Whites. In their interaction with Whites, they are told in various ways that they are socially, educationally, physically, and culturally inferior. The mass media constantly bombard Black children with images that suggest to them that White is preferred. White models and heroes are predominant in television, movies, music videos, billboards, magazines, and children's stories. A clear message is sent: one ought to be White if one is to be powerful, beautiful, economically successful, and socially acceptable ("Why Skin Color Suddenly Is a Big Issue Again," 1992). The prevailing assumption in European American social science is that the image Black people receive of themselves from the White community is the major determinant of Black self-concept. This perspective, derived from C. H. Cooley's social-looking-glass theory (1922), assumes that one's self-concept is primarily determined by how one is seen by significant others. Thus, Black children are assumed to despise themselves and their race because the White community devalues them. Once social scientists rejected the Black community and Black parents as viable active agents in socializing Black children, it was easy to accept the thesis of Black self-hatred.

The most often cited support for Black self-hatred comes from Kenneth and Mamie Clark's experiments (1950, 1958). From 1939 to the early 1950s, they presented children with Black and White dolls and discovered that Black and White children showed a preference for White dolls and described Black dolls in negative terms. It was assumed that Black children were suffering from low self-esteem and indirectly demonstrating disdain for Black people in general. This study began a long tradition of reporting lower self-esteem among Black children as compared to White children. Regardless of whether researchers used fantasy-like projective measures involving dolls, pictures, or line drawings, their conclusion was the same: Black self-hatred.

These studies have come under attack. Criticism centers on the fact that most of the studies showed very little consistency. The responses of children varied from one day to the other, shifted depending on the race of the experimenter, and showed reverse results when a mulatto doll was introduced. Furthermore, prior to the late 1960s, Black dolls were a novel stimulus to most children. Unable to find Black dolls, some experimenters had to construct their own.

Even through the 1980s, the majority of parents did not buy Black dolls for their children. Thus, many children may have been reacting to an unfamiliar stimulus. Also, after children made negative statements about cross-racial groups or their own race, they could be observed moments later playing with both same-race and cross-racial friends (Ramsey, 1987; Hare, 1985; Harrison, 1985). This disparity shows that children may prefer lighter-colored dolls without rejecting others like themselves. More profoundly, the interpretive framework of these studies has been rejected.

It is argued that the social-looking-glass theory has been erroneously applied. The assumption that the significant other persons are White ignores the fact that the most salient and direct contacts for Black children are the Black adults in their Black community. It is these individuals who are the most significant others in the life of Black children. If Black children have healthy self-esteem, it is because they perceive that they are well regarded by parents, relatives, peers, and church members (see Chapter Nine) or are skilled at highly valued activities.

A study of the psychological well-being of 2,107 Black adults lends support to the importance of Black referents. Those who attended all-Black elementary or high schools had higher self-esteem than those attending more integrated schools (Brown, 2001). Consistent with this finding are the personal testimonies of the successful adults who graduated from Carver/Phoenix Union Colored High School in Arizona. They attributed their accomplishments and self-esteem to the caring adults in their high school. These Black adults included not only administrators and teachers but the janitorial and cafeteria personnel. Interestingly, many alumni felt that integration robbed them of the most gifted and caring teachers of their educational experience (Johnson, 1999).

Furthermore, ethnic identity is linked to positive self-esteem regardless of whether children are of monolithic or mixed parentage. While mixed heritage children on diverse campuses are less likely to call themselves White than those on predominantly White campuses, self-esteem remains high regardless of self-label (Fatimilehin, 1999). These findings go against popular notions, particularly during the 1960s, that the offspring of interracial marriages suffer from low self-esteem and confused identity. Again, it is the messages that all children receive from those they regard warmly that determines how they feel about themselves.

The traditional interpretation of the social looking glass assumes that Black people consider the evaluation of them by Whites as objective (Jackson, McCullough, and Gurin, 1988; Hare, 1985; Baldwin, 1979). In practice, Black parents begin quite early teaching their children, particularly their daughters, the importance of maintaining a love for self and pride in being Black in a racist society (Taylor, Chatters, Tucker, and Lewis, 1990). The testimony of two mothers in a study of racial socialization of Black children clearly makes this point: "I'd like them [the children] to have enough pride, because if you have enough pride or self-confidence in yourself, you'll let a lot of things roll off your back." The second mother explains that she is instilling pride in her children "so nobody can put them down" (Peters, 1985, p. 165).

This early socialization appears to have its effect. The bulk of recent scientific studies, based on more representative and larger samples with social class controls, have ranged from detecting no racial differences to showing that Blacks score higher on self-esteem measures. One study of three thousand children found the self-confidence of Black girls to be higher than that of White and Latino girls (Daley, 1991). Black children learn to prevent negative racial attitudes from influencing their self-evaluation. Black teenagers and young adults, for example, give more credence to negative feedback from Black evaluators than to the identical feedback from Whites. These findings clearly show that knowing children's racial identity or preference does not provide a good indication of how they feel about themselves.

This protection of their self-worth is also evident in other areas. In school, for example, Black children are able to maintain high self-esteem even when faced with low academic achievement. If Black boys are performing poorly in school, they transfer their concepts of self-worth to areas where they are doing well, such as in sports or school popularity. Although research on area-specific Black self-esteem by gender is in its infancy, it appears that Black girls and boys differ in the areas in which they show high self-esteem. Whether this is primarily the result of community or family gender socialization is unclear (Jackson, McCullough, and Gurin, 1988; Hare, 1985; Clark, 1982; Baldwin, 1979). As we await more definitive information, it is encouraging to know that despite the fact that Black children must interact in a White environment that devalues their worth, their Black parents and significant others in their community have provided them with the spiritual and cognitive power to feel good about themselves.

Summary

All parents are challenged to prepare children to become productive citizens. Regardless of economic status, parents must strive to instill in their children enough self-reliance and self-esteem to confront life's challenges. Impoverished families certainly face the greatest difficulties. However, despite its obvious disadvantages, poverty can provide benefits that may escape the more affluent. This is best illustrated by an Anglo-Saxon Protestant male, age twenty-seven, who was raised by two highly educated parents in an affluent American suburb. Recounting the hardships and tough times of his father's childhood, he asked his father, "How could you raise me in the lap of luxury and expect me to develop character? . . . Didn't it occur to you that by sparing me from the hardships, . . . sacrifices, . . . hard work, and . . . fights you were robbing me of the chance to become the kind of man you are? . . . You know you are tough. . . . You know you can make a way for yourself and that you deserve to be where you are" (Campolo and Campolo, 1989, pp. 7–8).

While at least a third of all Black families encounter the character-building hardships and sacrifices that this son missed, their opportunity structure will not necessarily provide them with the success realized by this man's father. Being Black and poor is double jeopardy. Black parents face not only the task of building strong character in their children, but the challenge of making them understand that character alone may be insufficient for overcoming discrimination, prejudice, and other negative life circumstances.

In her study, Marie Peters (1985) asked Black parents what the most important thing is that they give to their children. Material wealth was not mentioned. Love and security, however, were deemed essential for overcoming the harsh realities of being Black in America. Lifting each other as they climb, many impoverished families generate these ingredients. Numerous successful Blacks look back on their childhood and realize that at the time, they did not realize they were impoverished. They only understood the love and security that derived from laboring together. Black love continues to be Black wealth. Unfortunately, too often even this precious asset is insufficient for achieving upward mobility.

9

Kinship and Community Support

If it were not for strong kinship bonds, Black men and women could not have survived the physical and psychic atrocities of slavery as well as the hardships of the Reconstruction and Depression eras. The slave community dramatically demonstrated affection and reverence for its families. Only deep affection could motivate runaway slaves to repeatedly risk their lives by returning to slave territory in the hopes of rescuing blood and in-law relatives.

The devastation of the Civil War and upheavals during Reconstruction revealed the far-reaching boundaries and elasticity of the family circle. Despite their own meager resources throughout this period, young and elderly adults adopted kin and nonkin children who were left homeless and destitute. Active compassion was repeated during the Depression of the 1930s, when thousands of families doubled up with aunts, uncles, cousins, and other relatives to weather the economic storm (J. H. Franklin, 1988; Jones, 1985; Gutman, 1976). Many of those who experienced the dreadful events prior to the twentieth century are now buried beneath the circular flat rocks that typically mark their graves. Occasionally, these stones can be found weathered and eroded; most are lost forever (Haley, 1986). However, the memory of Black ancestors' upward struggle has left an indelible mark on contemporary society. Today, relative to Whites and even to some ethnic groups of color, the Black community shows a higher level of multigenerational households, fosterage of kin and nonkin children, care for dependent family members, respect for elders, religiosity, and sacrificial efforts for the upward mobility of its members.

How much of this sense of family obligation is African survival and how much developed in the New World has been debated by various scholars (D. Franklin, 1988). The most vocal of these scholars have been Herskovits, Frazier, and Du Bois. Herskovits (1941) argued for continuity between Black American traditions, Frazier (1939) insisted that the Black American link broke under slavery, and Du Bois (1898) had more confidence in the survival of African religious practices than family traditions. Uncertain of African family survivals, Du Bois called for further research to settle the debate. His call was masterfully answered by the historical revisionist Herbert Gutman.

Gutman's revolutionary study (1976) provides sufficient evidence that African slaves continued to view kinships and the obligations flowing from them as the normal expression of social relations. To understand what survived in the New World, it is necessary to understand the nature of African family organization. In traditional African society, families are seen as enveloped in a large circle. Within this circle are smaller circles representing the ancestors, elders, fathers, mothers, and children. Even gods are envisaged as a series of family groupings. The use of circles can be seen in the physical arrangements of family compounds and the round huts within many traditional African villages. In essence, circles served as a constant reminder of interdependence, unity, humility, and the absence of greed (Diallo and Hall, 1989). Typical features of African extended families include strong elders and age-grade groupings, shared residence, joint activities, and children reared by a large number of relatives and community members (Diallo and Hall, 1989; Kayongo-Male and Onyango, 1984; Herskovits, 1941).

It is clear that certain kinship patterns were not fully re-created on American soil because of the unique circumstances of bondage; some found new meaning. New kinship patterns were created, and the origin of others is unclear. Regardless of the specific features, kinship obligation has served as the pivotal point for social organization for Black people since preslavery days. In the following section, our description of precolonial Africa reflects many of the characteristics of contemporary African families. African colonialism was even less able than American slavery to destroy African traditional familial practices. Thus, much of what is written in the past tense could very well be stated in the present.

The Circle of African Elders

Perhaps the most striking feature of African families was the large number of individuals who were rearing children. In traditional African communities, any adult had the right to order children to do simple tasks and to discipline them. To assess their precision in following orders, elders tested children by asking them to perform detailed tasks, such as gathering and bringing certain medicinal herbs. If the children proved themselves responsible, the elders would reveal to them the secrets and knowledge of their ancestors.

Failure to follow orders in every detail could incite the elders' anger. In the light of the importance of oral tradition, this anger was well placed. Oral communication was the primary medium for transmitting medicinal, ceremonial, and cultural traditions. When children were instructed in ritual practices and herbal secrets, any deviation in carrying out instructions could result in future generations' being led into practicing false traditions; more seriously, lives could be endangered by passing on an incorrect medicinal prescription (Diallo and Hall, 1989; Kayongo-Male and Onyango, 1984).

Grandparents served as important agents of socialization. They introduced young people to the sensitive topics of husband-wife relationships and sexual behavior as well as the values and traditions of the larger society. For example, each girl was assigned one grandmother who was responsible for training her to become the nucleus and educator of her future family. The grandmother gave training in the strict rules of conduct during pregnancy and helped her to develop the inner strength necessary to make personal sacrifices for the protection and well-being of her children (Kayongo-Male and Onyango, 1984).

There were spiritual as well as practical reasons for pleasing the circle of elders. Apart from the supreme being, God (*Nyame* among the Ashanti; *Kle* among the Minianka), it was the ancestors who had the greatest power and commanded the greatest respect. Through rituals and divination, the elders communicated with the ancestors. Thus, elders were in the best position to inform children of behavior that brings the wrath or pleasure of ancestors (Diallo and Hall, 1989; Kayongo-Male and Onyango, 1984; Herskovits, 1941). Ancestors interacted indirectly (through elders) and directly (through reincarnation). The coming and going between the visible and invisible worlds is vividly illustrated in a contemporary African drummer's account of his own birth: "I was born in my paternal grandmother's house in Fienso. She was the midwife who assisted all the births in our village. . . . I was born so quickly there was no time . . . for the customary attendance of the older women. My grandmother looked at my newborn face and said, 'Oh no, not him!' She recognized me as an ancestor returned to earth. This does not disturb me. I accept this double role of being both myself and an ancestor at the same time" (Diallo and Hall, 1989, p. 15). Despite this duality of being, children considered to be the reincarnation of an ancestor were still treated as unique individuals.

The Circle of African Children

Furthermore expanding the family were same-gender/same-age peer groups. Although they had a weaker authority than the elders over socialization, they had powerful control over the behavior of youth. Their influence extended into adulthood for males and ended at marriage for women in patrilineal societies. Unlike males, the women would marry in their teens and move to the homes of their husbands, becoming integrated into the women's group of their husbands' community. Peer groups had no leader, and all decisions were made by consensus. Many practices facilitated the feeling that children were equal. They ate from the same plate and dressed in similar clothing. While it is true that the eldest had more authority, there was no exclusivity in possessions. Any child could take the eldest's possessions without permission. During meals, the eldest ate only after the younger ones had satisfied their hunger.

Unlike mainstream American peer groups, traditional African peer groups were "pro-parents," working in conjunction with parental and kin values and goals. Discipline primarily took the form of social ostracism. Also, unmerciful teasing was used to help children accept or change the reality of their condition (being overweight or timid). Age-peer groups stayed together through the best and worst of times, kept secrets, and swore to come to the aid of any member in trouble. Making oneself available for the needs of the group was one of the most valued lessons learned within peer groups. The elders watched these groups closely, since the future of the village belonged to them (Diallo and Hall, 1989; Kayongo-Male and Onyango, 1984).

Fostering Children in African Societies

Because all adults were considered teachers and parents, African cultures such as the Minianka had no word for *teacher* or *uncle* and *aunt*. All adult males were considered fathers, and all adult females were viewed as mothers. As such, they were responsible for the teaching of all children. It was not unusual for children to spend the greater part of their childhood being raised not by their parents but by their "uncles" or "aunts," particularly if such kin were childless. At times, adults would foster even nonrelatives' children.

In addition, fostering children took the form of children exchange and "sister/brother-in-law parenting." Among married brothers, each would take one or more children from the other. These children knew who their biological parents were, although they spent most of their time away from them. Both their parents and uncles or aunts were called "father" or "mother." The practice of levirate or "in-law" parenting protected children and the family line. According to this practice, when a married man died, his brother inherited both his widow and children. If there were no surviving children, the children born of the widow's second marriage were referred to as if they had been fathered by the deceased in a type of "ghost marriage." A parallel arrangement, sororate, occurred in the case of the death of a child's mother. Rather than being disruptive, such arrangements served as a reaffirmation of trust among the kin members involved and reemphasized the belief that each child is not only a child of the parent but also of the larger kin group. Children are so highly valued for their role in maintaining the family line and a sense of immortality that even today, an African marriage is seen as meaningless without them (Mbiti, 1973; Kayongo-Male and Onyango, 1984).

The African kinship ties provided self-identity by absorbing all children and adults into existing kin networks. These ties were so strong that banishment, not death, was considered the supreme punishment. In marriage and divorce, kin had obligations for maintaining family continuity. The concept of neolocality—a couple or an unmarried woman with or without children sets up an independent household—was not a typical structure within African culture. When couples married, they joined a family village or compound of either the bride or the groom, depending on whether the society was patrilineal or matrilineal. The couples' children became the children of the compound. When couples divorced, the out-marrying spouse returned to his or her blood kin, and the children remained with the compound. Thus, children continued their lives with their father in patrilineal societies and their mother in matrilineal societies. Such a system ensured that children and adults would always be part of a familiar family circle (Diallo and Hall, 1989; Sudarkasa, 1988; Stephens, 1963). In essence, the concept of being one step removed from belonging to a family, such as in the case of stepfamilies, had little meaning.

Slavery's Namesakes and Postslavery Adoptions

Enslavement shattered consanguineal ties for all but a few slaves. However, during the Middle Passage—the journey from the continent of Africa to the New World—slaves converted kin relationships into symbolic (or fictive) kin ties. African children called their parents' shipmates "aunt" and "uncle." On the slave plantation, slave children were taught to call all adult slaves (kin and nonkin) "aunt" and "uncle." Such names converted nonkin into quasi-kin networks of mutual obligations. During slavery, the strength of kinship relationships was revealed in three major ways: naming children, fostering children, and the community welfare system (Miller and Smith, 1988; Gutman, 1976). As a way of spiritually linking dead and living generations, slave children were often named for living and dead blood relatives—grandparents, parents, aunts, and uncles. Surprisingly, slave daughters seldom carried their mothers' names, while sons often had their fathers' names. This is particularly noteworthy since the mother-child relationship was most likely to be maintained in the event of family breakup, and slave owners rarely recorded the names of slave fathers in plantation birth registries. This distinct naming practice in effect protected the loss of lineage when slave fathers were sold away from their families and thus underscored the importance of family ties in the slave community (Gutman, 1976).

A vivid sense of the slaves' connection with the dead is revealed in the frequent naming of children after deceased siblings. Slaves suffered from extraordinary rates of infant mortality (twice that of Whites) prior to and just after birth. The low priority White masters gave to family well-being of slaves meant that new mothers with infants often had to walk long distances from field to nursery to feed and care for their infants. Poor nourishment and inattentiveness contributed to the rate of only two out of three Black children surviving to the age of ten during the 1850–1860 period. Mothers' emotional suffering was partially relieved by their faith in the West African tenet that held that if you remember the deceased, they will never die. Remembrance took the form of naming surviving children after their dead siblings. Others who had suffered the loss of an infant gave a subsequent surviving child the name of the deceased sibling, because he or she was believed—in line with West African tradition—to be the deceased person reincarnated (Diallo and Hall, 1989; Jones, 1985; Kayongo-Male and Onyango, 1984; Gutman, 1976).

Obligation toward nonslave kin was compassionately expressed during and immediately after the Civil War. Although the exact numbers are unknown, numerous children were orphaned by the sale, death, desertion, and wartime dislocation of their parents. Many were absorbed into extended kin groups, and others found homes with nonkin. These "motherless children" were adopted by ex-slaves who could barely care for their own families. With unwavering care, some families would feed and house as many as half a dozen nephews and nieces, as well as additional non–blood kin children. When family absorption was virtually impossible, church and community funds were raised to build orphanages (Gutman, 1976).

Contemporary Issues in Kinship Care

In contemporary Black culture, fostering and informally adopting children continues to be a striking feature of the Black kinship experience. One reason is the historical bias against Black families in the policies and practices of formal adoption agencies. The fact that child services began and developed in the North during the nineteenth century made it unlikely that poor Southern Black children were of serious concern. Furthermore, child welfare systems were governed by two major philosophical orientations: individual responsibility for poverty and the Darwinian doctrine of the survival of the fittest. These two perspectives, coupled with racism, did not provide an appreciation of the breadth, depth, and causes of poverty following emancipation (Billingsley and Giovannoni, 1972).

Furthermore, the current screening criteria used by most agencies are designed to ensure that adopted children have economic security and a middle-class lifestyle; thus, preference is given to families that have the potential income of two middle-class parents. Too frequently, stable Black families with low incomes are disqualified.

Fortunately, Black children have never had to depend solely on institutions in the broader society.

The old tribal view that everyone belongs to someone and that Black children are a gift from God is evident in the efforts of Black adopting families and in the numerous community help programs offered by Black churches. It is well documented that in contemporary U.S. society, Black children are more likely than White children to be adopted by relatives. Around 35 percent of the 1.7 million children being reared by grandparents are Black or Black Hispanics (Generations United, 2003). Current data on the population of people thirty years and older show just fewer than 52 percent of Black children live with their grandparents, as compared to around 35 percent of Hispanics and 42 percent of Whites (U.S. Census Bureau, 2003d). Although informal adoption is more prominent among Black families (Hill, 1999), Black families do adopt children from public welfare agencies at four and a half times the rate of Whites and Latinos (Jones, 1989; Hollingsworth, 1998). This practice is not recent. In the 1960s, Black families informally adopted children with a placement rate more than ten times that of formal adoption agencies and formally adopted at a higher rate than White families of similar means (Hill, 1972). In the early 1980s, Blacks were over twice as likely as Whites to adopt related children or noninfants (65 versus 24 percent), twice as likely to absorb the first premarital live births into the homes of relatives or friends, and seven times less likely to put out-of-wedlock children up for adoption (Bachrach, 1986). Today, even Black middle-class families actively participate in taking in kin and nonkin on the basis of need (Taylor, Chatters, and Celious, 2003).

In line with West African tradition, adopted Black American children are treated no differently from other children within the extended family network. Cousins living in the same house are taught to regard each other as brothers and sisters. Seldom is a child labeled illegitimate as a result of the conditions of his or her birth. In clothes, food, and shelter, parents strive to treat each child fairly. However, informally adopted children often make a distinction between their adoptive mother or age-dominant figure (usually their grandmother) and their biological mother. They may even call their grandmother "Big Mom" or "Momma" and the biological mother "Little Mom" or by her first name ("Momma Nellie"). Parallel names may be given to fathers and grandfathers. Even aunts and uncles may be called "Mom" or "Dad." This practice is also common among Blacks in the Caribbean, suggesting a common African source.

In their eight-year study of Black extended families, Martin and Martin (1978) describe families who gave their children up to kin who needed companionship after the death of a spouse. The sense that children belong to the community is evident in the authors' description of family members who, without permission, simply took children whom they felt were neglected by their parents. Some refused to give the children back even when the parents demanded that they do so.

Other families who needed financial relief sent their children to live with a favorite aunt or uncle. During the period of Martin and Martin's study, 20 percent of children under age eighteen lived with their aunts or uncles (Hill and Shackleford, 1986). Perhaps the best example of the African root of child fostering is its cross-cultural expression within Black immigrant families. These families regularly rely on extended care. The stereotype of immigrants arriving in America depicts two parents and their children with their suitcases in front of a train, boat, or plane. For West Indian families, this is rarely true. Among two-parent families, one parent usually goes ahead in order to get established and then sends for the other spouse; sometimes the children come much later. Similarly, sometimes single parents initially migrate without their children. This serial migration is made possible because of the tradition and prevalence of child fostering in the Caribbean.

Children may remain in the islands to complete primary school, which is often considered superior to school in the States. Others do not migrate until they are older, because their working parents have no one they trust to supervise them or their parents lack the necessary finances to place them in an adequate child day care facility. Moreover, there is a general belief that America is a bad place to raise young children but a wonderful place for older children to get an education. Hence, most reunions take place in adolescence, primarily because in the British West Indies, school ends for all but the gifted much earlier than in America. This late migration presents problems. As children are going through a difficult developmental stage, they must also adjust to new parent-child expectations and a new culture. Abroad parents who were the source of designer jeans and expensive gifts when the children were in the home country now must limit or cease such gifts as they struggle to stretch their resources even further. In addition, parents must now invoke their authority, which is often more restrictive than children experienced in the more open and safer environment of the West Indies.

Although children do not feel abandoned when their parents leave them behind, once they arrive in America they soon learn that Americans view their situation as abandonment. This differential value system sometimes confuses them. Furthermore, those who raised them (kin or nonkin) for four or sometimes as many as seven years are often honored in ways that may rival or surpass the honor given to their biological parents (Waters, 1999). Whether children are native born or immigrant, kin or fictive kin who step in on their behalf gain family and community respect and gratitude. On the death of an adopting parent, it is not unusual for fostered nonkin children and blood kin to appear on the list of surviving relatives. Furthermore, the deceased is heralded as an earthly saint for taking in needy children. The old Southern proverb "If you knock de nose, de eye cry" (one hurts; all hurt) illustrates the importance placed on the interdependence of the Black community. As in African societies, a high value is attached to those who can relieve human suffering.

Despite this impressive record of Black compassion and self-reliance, the number of children in out-of-home care increased in the 1980s. In California, for example, foster care for Blacks increased from 47,700 in 1985 to 78,900 in 1989 (Hinds, 1990). During the last half of the 1990s, Black children's representation in out-of-home care across the nation showed a slight decrease. Nevertheless, in comparison to their presence in the general population, Black children are overrepresented: they are 20 percent of all children in the United States and 40 percent of the foster care system, whereas White children are 64 percent of this population and 38 percent of all children in foster care (Smith, 2000). Historically and currently, the grandmother has been the fallback when natural parents give up primary guardianship. Nearly 53 percent of Black children are being cared for by grandparents compared to less than 42 percent of Whites, 35 percent of Latinos, and 56 percent of Native Americans. Not all children reside with their grandparents; some reside with aunts, cousins, and other relatives, reflecting the extensive kinship networks and informal adoption within the Black community (U.S. Census Bureau, 2003d). Other Black children do not have the benefit of residing with kin. (See Chapter Ten for further discussion.)

Although the statistics clearly show the plight of Black children, the reasons for their plight are reflected in both legislative and personal decisions. For example, the Adoption and Safe Families Act (Public Law 105-89) of 1997 marks the latest policy change having adverse effects on Black children. The government's goal in enacting this law was to reduce barriers that inhibit the termination of parental rights and to create a stable home for children (Roberts, 2000). This approach is a significant departure from the theme of family preservation in previous legislation and places Black children at a greater risk of family disruption. For example, Black families are twice as likely to be involved in substantiated cases of child abuse, even though they do not abuse their children any more than other families (Sedlak and Broadhurst, 1996). And once they are in the system, Black as compared to White children receive fewer services, remain in foster care longer, and have lower access to home services (U.S. Department of Health and Human Services, 2000).

Legislation tells only part of the story. Personal decisions shaped by socioeconomic forces are the primary reasons for this surge in out-of-home placements. Child maltreatment, parental immaturity, family economic stress, parental divorce, and death are strong contributors. However, more weight must be given to decisions to engage in substance abuse, drug addiction, and drug trafficking, which leads to incarceration and family separation. Although recent statistics show the willingness of many Black families to formally adopt, the number of drug-exposed children has outstripped the capacity of the Black community to absorb them (Hill, 1999; Jones, 1989).

This situation has provided an additional rationale for transracial adoption, further fanning the fiery controversy over the development of Black identity and social coping skills of Black children raised in White families (Bartholet, 1999; Johnson, Shireman, and Watson, 1987; Roberts, 2000, 2002). Such adoptions find support at the federal level. In 1994, Congress passed the Multiethnic Placement Act, which prohibits agencies from making placements according to race or even considering race. This prohibition is also present in Title V of the 1996 Personal Responsibility and Work Opportunity Reconciliation Act. Disregarding this prohibition results in withdrawal of federal funds (Roberts, 2000, 2002). According to Hill (1999), these laws are misguided since they will not rescue older, harder-to-adopt Black children and wrongly assume that Black families are unavailable for adoption.

Supporting Hill's assertion of available Black homes are several studies (Hill, 1999) and organizations, such as the National Association of Black Social Workers. They contend that potential Black adopting families are still available. Nontraditional criteria and innovative Black adoption programs have flourished and have had unprecedented success in recruiting and placing Black children in Black homes (Hill, 1999; Lincoln and Mamiya, 1990; Washington, 1987). Others have identified additional approaches to remedying the overrepresentation of Black children in the foster care system, including allowing biological and foster parents to coparent their child or placing children with relatives instead of terminating parental rights (Roberts, 2000, 2002).

The question remains as to whether these new approaches can out-pace the drug epidemic, which is sending a rising number of Black parents to prison. When fathers go to prison, any child-rearing re-sponsibilities they had are quickly assumed by the mothers of their children with the help of kin. Although most families are hurt by the arrest and detention of the father, some families and marital relation-ships appear strengthened. This usually occurs when the offending par-ent's drug and alcohol addiction has created havoc within the family. Imprisonment allows the family to regain a new sense of self-reliance and to reorganize and pursue desired goals (Davis, 1990). Imprison-ment also has negative consequences for Black fathers who desire to be involved in their children's lives. Prisons may prohibit children's visitation, the facilities may not be conducive to visits by children, or the distance may inhibit regular visitation (Currence and Johnson, 2003). Furthermore, imprisoned fathers may not have the resources to make long-distance calls or their families may not be able to afford the high costs of collect calls.

As tragic as fathers' incarceration can be, the imprisonment of Black mothers is even more crushing to children. Of the 89,044 sen-tenced prisoners in state and federal jurisdictions in 2002, 36,000 were Black women (40.4 percent) and 35,400 were White women (39.8 percent). Moreover, in 2002, females entered prison at a faster rate than males (4.9 versus 2.4 percent)(Harrison and Beck, 2003). This increase is partially due to the heavy police presence in Black neighborhoods and the public nature of Black women's drug trans-actions. Their imprisonment is even more tragic today than in the past, since many more are incarcerated because of felony drug charges rather than misdemeanors, which carry shorter jail sentences.

For married mothers with addictions, a prison term often means the termination of their marriage. According to one prison official, "You see that with the visits. You rarely see the boyfriends coming out here. With men, the women take care of them. But the men don't take care of the women. They abandon them. It's pitiful" (Bohlen, 1989, p. A-1). Some children are unable to visit their mothers when prisons are located in remote rural areas. Often public transportation ceases running on weekends and holidays, when children are most able to visit. These women lose not only their partners, but also predictable physical contact with their children. The children of women inmates are frequently cared for by grandmothers, aunts, and sisters, who have the job of protecting them from drug-infested neighborhoods. Social agencies estimate that as many as 70 percent of the children in crack-ruled neighborhoods are being reared by older relatives, usually the grandmother.

Grandparents' Role in Kinship Care

Black grandmothers take up the parenting slack at a real sacrifice. Because they are related to the children, grandparents may get only a third of the cash assistance given to licensed group homes or licensed foster care parents who are unrelated to the child. Furthermore, many grandparents do not even know how to access foster care resources (Cox, 2000; Scarcella, Ehrle, and Green, 2003). Unemployed or retired grandparents have reported spending their life savings or cashing in their life insurance policies to make ends meet (Brown and Mars, 2000; Fuller-Thomson and Minkler, 2000; Minkler and Roe, 1993, 1996). However, the great majority have no life insurance to cash in, because they are members of America's 19.1 million impoverished Black families (Generations United, 2003; U.S. Census Bureau, 2003d).

A number of these grandmothers are young, in their thirties and forties, reflecting their own early initiation into childbearing and the fact that their children are repeating the cycle. Many are psychologically unprepared, feeling they are too young to be associated with their grandchildren (Burton and Bengtson, 1985). Finally settled into steady full-time jobs, most have no desire to resign, either because of job contentment or the difficulty they perceive in finding another job (Furstenberg, Brooks-Gunn, and Morgan, 1987). They must integrate the demands of employment with transporting children to day care centers and doctors' appointments and attending parent-teacher meetings, school performances, and Little League games. In sum, they find themselves balancing their job with the full range of parenting responsibilities. If their family demands also include a husband and other dependent relatives, the burden can be overwhelming. The degree to which Black grandparental experiences are influenced by the race and culture remains a question to be tested in the research.

The mental and physical health of grandparents who are solely responsible for parenting their grandchildren suffer because of their commitment to family (Cox, 2000). These health issues are heightened by the fact that many were already helping their own child in rearing their grandchildren, but with the parental imprisonment, substance abuse, and other mental health issues, grandmothers face the task alone. The psychological trauma and personal sacrifices associated with starting over again after rearing their own children puts them out of phase with their peers (Burton, 1992; Minkler and Roe, 1993) who are free of childrearing responsibilities. In addition, some grandmothers find themselves under siege from the violent and erratic behavior of the child's mother. One woman's daughter left her son with her, stole her car, and threatened to kill her when confronted (White, 1989). When parents have to get restraining orders to prevent their drug-addicted adult children from visiting them or their children, the extended family network is rendered ineffective.

Reciprocity in Kinship Care Arrangements

As children pass middle age, they rely less on their parents, and the flow of support reverses as their parents' health and income begin to decline. The health and economic situations of elderly Blacks have generally been poorer than those of elderly Whites. Hypertension among Blacks sixty-five to seventy-four years old is higher than among Whites in this age group. Blacks are more likely to be sick and disabled and to see themselves as being in poor health than White elderly. More often than Whites, they are likely to depend on one or two sources of government income (social security or Supplemental Security Income, or both) or to have no income. In these leisure years, many White elderly are pretty much able to buy anything they need, and a large minority saves and invests. But the large majority of Blacks scrape by or find themselves in financial difficulties, which stems from a life course of limited employment opportunities, low-paying and sporadic employment, and working in service jobs, such as cooks, housekeepers, waiters, and barbers (Hooyman and Kiyak, 1999). These years of economic deprivation take their toll (Murray, Khatib, and Jackson, 1989).

If it were not for extended families, a larger number of elderly Blacks would be homeless. While both Black and White elderly identify about the same proportion of adult children whom they can depend on for all types of help, the extended kin play a larger role for Black families. Black elderly are more likely to live in an extended household and less likely to be in a nursing home (Taylor, Chatters, and Celious, 2003; Hooyman and Kiyak, 1999). Consequently, the decision-making power of physically or mentally impaired elderly adults is more likely to be usurped by an adult child, a competent spouse, church family, or informal network of friends than by formal community agencies (Smerglia, Deimling, and Barresi, 1988; Hofferth, 1984; Hunter and Taylor, 1998).

Numerous arrangements for the support and respect of the elderly can be found in Black communities, including kin taking care of childless elderly (Johnson, 1995, 2000). It is not uncommon for elderly Blacks to be heavily supported by their own children and their grandchildren. For example, five adult siblings who grew up in poverty and experienced periodic welfare placed their mother in a comfortable middle-class retirement home. Each child was assessed a monthly fee according to his or her means. Their mother's social security check could then be used to her liking. Grandchildren were also instructed to continue this self-help if needed. Sometimes elderly parents are given the master bedroom in their children's home. This gesture is one way of making the grandparents more comfortable in their later years, while symbolically honoring their position in the family (Hunter and Taylor, 1998).

While in their children's home, grandmothers are more likely than grandfathers to become heavily involved in their grandchildren's lives. Grandmothers who live with their single-parent daughters or daughters-in-law see themselves and are seen by their grandchildren as being more active in supporting, disciplining, and controlling their grandchildren than grandmothers who have separate households. This relatively active participation of grandmothers is also true in two-parent multigenerational households. Grandchildren seem to benefit from having a grandmother in the home. They are better adjusted, and the quality of the emotional support they receive from their mother is greatly improved. However, many young grandparents prefer their grandchildren to live near but not with them (Wilson, 1986; Jackson, 1986). When these grandparents become ill, it presents a big emotional crisis in terms of lost support and their contribution to the family well-being. Given the fact that the typical Black family has limited economic resources, it becomes necessary to arrange creative home care. Children are often assisted by other members within their kinship circle. The greatest community assistance they receive is from the Black church (discussed below), which is second only to families in its response to the needs of Black people.

Kinship and Upward Mobility

The greatest contribution of kin is their support in the upward mobility and self-esteem of family members. With substantially lower incomes and assets than Whites, Black families do not typically have wealth to pass on to succeeding generations, and the earnings of two parents are essential for maintaining their socioeconomic standing. For the large number of single mothers, upward mobility is exceedingly difficult to achieve, and for most, the passing of wealth is inconceivable. This situation is much the same for many working- and middle-class Blacks whose parents and grandparents escaped poverty. As noted in Chapter Three, technological advances, company downsizing, loss of manufacturing jobs, foreign trade policies, and deficits in the U.S. economy have threatened, halted, or reversed the upward mobility of working poor and nonpoor Black families.

Thus, each generation must depend on its own efforts and support from same-generation kin. Whether Black families are moving from poverty to the working class, moving from the working class to the middle class, or merely maintaining economic stability, it requires intensive efforts and perseverance by family members in order not to slip into a lower economic situation. As an example, typically only single teenage mothers who receive help from kin are more likely to complete high school or obtain college experience. The critical family support they receive in lodging, food, and child care frees them to acquire those skills necessary to secure and maintain a job and move out on their own (Furstenberg and Crawford, 1978; Furstenberg, Brooks-Gunn, and Morgan, 1987; McAdoo, 1988; Goldscheider and Goldscheider, 1991; Taylor, Chatters, and Celious, 2003).

Although Black children often receive financial help from parents, they are less likely than White children to receive educational assistance beyond high school. The younger the parent, the fewer family financial resources are available for investing in college education for children. Available resources within extended families generally go to married adult children who are struggling to raise their own children (Goldscheider and Goldscheider, 1991; Taylor, 1986; Hill, 1972).

While evidence exists showing that parents' financial contribution to their children's educational expenses raises their children's educational expectations, nonmonetary resources are also important. One study of the supportive roles of relatives and community members showed that among postgraduate-educated Blacks, nearly a fifth had received financial assistance from relatives other than their parents. However, over half claimed that their own achievement was inspired by the example and encouragement of relatives.

With few exceptions, parental encouragement comes from parents who have never set foot on a college campus prior to attending their child's baccalaureate graduation. In reaching for their diploma, many graduates see their grandmother or some other supportive relative lose control with a shout of, "Thank you, Jesus! Our prayers have been answered." This spiritual and emotional backing partially explains why so many of the Black students enrolled in elite Black colleges in the 1970s were unlikely candidates, in the sense that neither of their parents had graduated from college and nearly 80 percent needed government financial assistance to remain in school (Goldscheider and Goldscheider, 1991; Manns, 1988; Hill, 1972). Apparently for many, emotional support, affirmation from others, and role modeling are essential motivating factors when parental economic support is lacking.

The old adage that "God helps those who help themselves" seems to be the guiding principle for Black parents assisting their upwardly mobile children. Black parents and children are more likely than Whites or Hispanics to be contributors to their children's educational expenses. The more that Black children contribute to their own expenses, the more their parents help them. In fact, Black parents contribute more than comparable White parents when their children show extraordinary effort to work and save for their education. In contrast, for White and Hispanic students, the more the parents contribute, the less they pay toward their educational expenses. White and Hispanic students appear not to have the same urgency about working as do Black students. Blacks as a group cannot have a lax attitude toward work as a means to upward mobility. Black students can expect to receive 50 percent less parental financial assistance than Whites because they are more likely to come from lower-income families, mother-headed households, and mothers who started child-bearing early (Goldscheider and Goldscheider, 1991).

If Black students fail to get adequate financial assistance from parents and other relatives, they either seek government financial aid or drop out to work. The government's spending priority creates a problem. According to the Children's Defense Fund (2003), the United States is number one in defense spending and military technology among industrialized counties, but it spends less than 20 percent on social and educational programs. Moreover, during the 1990s, the United States decreased spending on education by $954 million and increased its spending on prisons by $926 million (Ambrosio and

Schiraldi, 1997). Adding to the problem of educational attainment, young Black men and women still find it difficult to secure a job, making it difficult for them to support themselves. Thus, many Black students have no other choice but to drop out or join the army for its GI benefits.

In mapping their life course, youth look to both the future and the past. Many of those who temporarily drop out of school to work not only are saving for school but are actively contributing to their parents' household expenses. For while older Blacks are more likely to give than receive, they are not forgotten by their children. The more children earn and the greater their parents' financial need, the more they contribute. Their sense of family obligation is not limited to their parents. These older children try to help out financially in meeting the needs of their younger siblings and other relatives who are in school or unemployed. Regardless of whether they come from one-parent or two-parent families, Blacks in general contribute substantially more to their parental family household than do Whites. Sons contribute slightly more than daughters, no doubt reflecting their higher wages and the male provider expectation (Goldscheider and Goldscheider, 1991; "The Black Male Shortage," 1986; Martin and Martin, 1978).

The Black Church

Most churches cannot avoid becoming intimately involved in fulfilling the needs of Black family networks, including serving as an extended family network, providing guidance on marriage, and parenting. Families constitute the building blocks for the church congregations. Some churches are dominated by generations of kinship groups, so that the concept of the family or kin church is more reality than ideology. Through preaching, teaching, cooperative benevolence, symbols, belief systems, morality, and rituals, the church welds community and unrelated families to each other. Within this context, the church is the modern tribe. Each member is referred to as "sister" or "brother," elders receive high respect, the minister is venerated as the earthly spiritual chief, and a host of unseen heavenly angels and a supreme Father are believed to be governing the living and the dead. With varying degrees of intensity, the church has historically served as the ordained leader of Black families.

After the Civil War, Black churches legitimized the informal marriages of many former slaves, demanded marital fidelity, designed programs to foster the leadership of men within families, encouraged honest hard work, affirmed individual self-worth, and urged the family to function as an extended church by conducting family worship within the home. Most of these efforts have not been seriously challenged, especially in the light of the fact that more Black women than men are actively involved in the church (Lincoln and Mamiya, 1990; Poole, 1990; Chatters and Taylor, 1998). Today, the church continues to provide leadership, spiritual sustenance, and material support to children, adults, and families.

Parents often bring their children to church, and sometimes older children are required to attend because their parents believe that only within the religious extended family can their children get moral education and develop positive group identity and personal self-worth (Lincoln and Mamiya, 1990; Poole, 1990). The church provides its members with a sense of identity and belonging (Billingsley, 1992). It has not only provided a refuge in times of severe trouble, but it continues to give members weekly reinforcement in dealing with personal and social stressors.

Yet there have been questions as to whether the church has provided the environment necessary to overcome the psychological stigma of living in a racist society. This concern was prevalent during the time that the Clark and Clark doll test experiments were popularized (see Chapter Eight). If children's preference for White dolls is indicative of self-hatred, this challenges the message of the Black church. Without self-acceptance, the Christian command to love your neighbor as yourself is problematic. Likewise, minimum credence could be given to the claim that salvation brings wholeness to human personalities if Black children detest themselves and their people (Lincoln and Mamiya, 1990; Baldwin, 1979).

Today, many scholars do not believe that Black children's rejection of Black dolls reflects their hatred for themselves and their race. However, preferences for White dolls may still imply that children perceive that it is preferable to be of another race. Black parents and churches must still struggle with the meaning of race, particularly when socializing children (Lincoln and Mamiya, 1990).

In this struggle, how much importance should be placed on Whites' evaluation of Blacks is of concern. It is doubtful whether the most significant others in Black people's lives are Whites. Recent research shows that negative feedback from Whites may not represent a salient source of influence on Black self-concept. This research suggests that because most Black people associate racism with White people, they tend to discredit Whites' negative evaluations of them (Baldwin, 1979). Thus, it is unlikely that the soul of Black folks is based primarily on the opinions of Whites.

As with Whites, the significant others in the early experiences of Black children are others of similar color. The limited use of television and the pervasive racial segregation from the 1930s to the early 1950s meant that this was even more true than in today's less segregated society. Lending support to this is the Clarks' finding (Clark and Clark, 1950) that children from segregated settings (the South) made more choices favoring brown dolls than did children in interracial nursery schools.

Martin Luther King Jr. once stated that the most segregated hour in America is Sunday morning. He was referring to the historical racial segregation of America's religious institutions, although this pattern of behavior is experiencing some changes. Apart from the negative implication of this fact, this situation has worked to the benefit of Black people, particularly children. For the majority of Blacks, the church has served as a buffer against the negative feedback of the White community. It is the only institution that has historically operated independent of the White power structure. As such, it has been in a position to chart its own missions (Harris, 1987; Baldwin, 1979).

One of the powerful missions of the Black church is affirming the worth of every human being. The doctrine that every human being is made in the image of God and the promise that God will punish the sinful violators of human dignity not only serves to discredit Whites' evaluation of Blacks but has prevented the complete dehumanization of Blacks through the ages. Furthermore, for some Blacks, the message that the meek will inherit the Kingdom of God subtly elevated the humanity of Blacks over Whites and provided additional strength during the difficult period of bondage (Baldwin, 1979; Fordham, 1975).

Serving as a surrogate parent, the church provides activities that reduce children and youth's participation in risk-taking behaviors (Chatters and Taylor, 1998). Within the church family, children as well as adults find their self-esteem affirmed in many ways. For many Black children, it is within the church that they first learn to read and speak publicly. Children who falter when giving an oral or musical presentation hear the pews and walls resonate with the encouraging "Amens" and "Go on, child; it's all right." Whether the presentation is perfect or imperfect, there are always adults waiting in the foyer to applaud a young child's efforts. Such responses allow children to be affirmed as they are and to continue practicing and performing without the fear of rejection. This message of affirmation is presented to children in still another way. One of the major strengths of the church has been its willingness to provide status that is not available in the White society. Children see the dignity of even the lowliest person confirmed. The head deacon can be a janitor, the head usher a domestic worker, and the young people's association leader a medical doctor. Regardless of their station in the larger society, all receive recognition and status in the church.

Perhaps one of the most important functions the church performs is creating a forum in which children can emulate adult role models. In Scanzoni's 1978 study of Black working- and middle-class families, ministers ranked second only to schoolteachers, and Sunday school teachers ranked third among the adult role models who showed an interest in the youth. In his book on the life of Martin Luther King Jr., Keith Miller (1991) gives credit to King's Sunday school teacher for helping to shape the thought and character of one of the most important Americans in the twentieth century. If affirmation and value setting were the only contribution of Black churches, this would be enough to applaud. Their contribution does not stop here. Serving as concert hall, art gallery, and public forum, the church has trained singers, artists, mayors, congressional representatives, and thousands of youth for public leadership.

Although church services are oriented toward adults, every major Black denomination in the United States offers a wide range of programs for the youth. There are special sabbaths such as Children's Day and Children's Church that allow children to take leadership. Youth are inspired by programs that honor members who have distinguished themselves in their chosen profession. Evening socials, banquets, picnics, sports teams, and church outings are designed for both youth and adult fellowship. For many children, the first trip out of their local community was made possible by a church-sponsored event. To support these off-campus activities, some churches buy buses, and at least one denomination has a travel agency and owns a bus company. Others own elementary schools and colleges. Most of these schools were originally founded in response to segregation in the public school system. Eighty-six percent of Black churches support these schools, believing that they continue to provide a nonracist environment in which a healthy Black self-identity can be realized (Lincoln and Mamiya, 1990).

The Black church continues its focus on children, especially the one-third who are mired in poverty. To attack the myriad problems these children face, some of the larger urban churches maintain day care centers for working parents, job training for the unemployed, food and clothing banks, shelters for the homeless, emergency funds, drug abuse centers, and tutorial programs for parents and children within the community and in prisons. In addition, apart from raising money for orphanages, church societies have organized adoption programs. A noted example is the successful Black adoption program inspired by the Black Catholic priest George Clements. Against strong opposition from his superiors, this priest adopted a child before beginning a nationwide campaign urging each Black church to adopt at least one Black child. In Illinois, the One Church, One Child program is cosponsored by the Interdenominational Coalition of Black Churches/Pastors and the Illinois Department of Social Services. With each pastor encouraging families to adopt at least one child, the number of Black children of all ages awaiting adoption has dropped from seven hundred to about sixty. In sum, these churches are providing the whole gamut of unattended needs associated with being poor in Black America (Lincoln and Mamiya, 1990; Harris, 1987; Frazier, 1964).

In addition to responding to the economically disadvantaged, churches are being challenged to address the institution of marriage. Apart from baptism, marriage is one of the most sacred unions sanctioned by the church. Yet although Blacks are frequent church attenders, their marriages are counted among the most at risk for joining the one in two marriages ending in divorce. Some believe that Black Protestant churches are reluctant to address marital relationships, particularly from the pulpit, because their members might perceive the pastor of moving from preaching to meddling. Whether this holds any truth or not, many churches are speaking publicly about the marital crisis. In addition to providing premarital counseling and marital enrichment seminars (for example, Catholic), some churches (for example, Seventh-Day Adventist) have developed departments of family ministries at their highest administrative level. Black churches are not only responding to troubled marriages but enriching marriages by professionally training their pastors and lay ministers to conduct marriage retreats and educational seminars and, through role modeling, honoring those couples who show lifelong marital commitment.

Whether people are old or young, the church is compelled to respond. Those fifty years and older are particularly important since they are the preservers of church tradition. They, especially the women, are more likely than the young to support the church with their tithes, offerings, attendance, and loyalty. They are also more likely to internalize the teachings of the church and to engage in church activities beyond weekend services (Taylor and Chatters, 1989). To encourage the prayers of and visitations to house-bound or infirm members, many Black churches publish weekly lists of those who are shut in because of illness or old-age impairments.

While it is to be expected that church members receive spiritual and moral support, one study showed that one out of five members also receive financial assistance, goods and services, or total support (Lincoln and Mamiya, 1990; Taylor and Chatters, 1989). At times, the collection plate is passed in order to turn the heat on in Sister Mills's home or to pay for Brother Monroe's operation. Sometimes minivans are purchased for providing church and shopping transportation for the elderly. Using grants from the U.S. Department of Housing and Urban Development or congregational funds, a few churches have purchased real estate to provide safe and convenient public housing for their elderly and disabled members. Some wealthy entrepreneurs and entertainers have challenged churches to match them in buying abandoned houses not only to house low-income members but to purge the community of crack houses.

There is general agreement that the church is a prominent institution in the Black community. Yet it has not been without its critics. The emphasis placed on family values and moral integrity after emancipation was motivated by political as much as scriptural concerns. It was hoped that conformity to White family norms of morality would advance the Black race into full acceptance into the White world. When Blacks migrated to urban areas, their hopes were shattered. They found low wages and the dehumanization of racism and other forms of oppression. Black troops sent to defend democracy in Europe were segregated from White troops and returned to encounter racism at home. The persistence of these conditions has led Blacks to question the significance of the Black churches' formula for uplifting the race. Disenchantment has given rise to Black sects, cults, storefront churches, and nationalist movements, such as the Nation of Islam and the Universal Negro Improvement Association of Marcus Garvey. The rapid growth of more secular organizations, such as the National Urban League and the NAACP, indicates that an increasing number no longer see the church as the only vehicle for advancing the race (Poole, 1990; Lincoln and Mamiya, 1990).

One area that continues to be an extremely sensitive and difficult issue for the church is HIV/AIDS. Unlike many cancers, hypertension, and cardiovascular diseases, the transmission of HIV/AIDS through sexual contact has led to the stigmatization of its victims. Moreover, religious conservatives and those with homophobia tend to treat those with AIDS like lepers, deserving of the consequences of their "sins." In addition, the stigma against drug abusers as immoral has also inhibited faith communities in the AIDS crises. However, public campaigns for support of those with AIDS, as well as the rapid spread of the disease among children in Africa and the United States, cloud issues of morality. Furthermore, as it is recognized that the fastest growth of HIV/AIDS is in the heterosexual community and not among gays, the urgency of the epidemic is becoming universally felt. Churches that once ignored this health issue have revisited their mission of outreach. Many are now playing a vital role in intervention and prevention. Moreover, some are collaborating with universities to provide effective services and resources (Martin, Younge, and Smith, 2003). In sum, churches have come out of their morality closet to do what they potentially can do best: compassionate service. Nevertheless, some continue to criticize Black churches for their slow response to critical social issues.

Despite this disenchantment, fewer than 15 percent of Blacks believe that Black churches are not a force that continues to integrate and support the physical, social, and spiritual needs of the Black community. Seventy-seven percent of the Black population claim church membership, and slightly less than three-quarters (71 percent) attend church monthly (Billingsley, 1992). Rather than give up on the church, the laity is doing what it has done in the past: adapting its theology to the times. The majority of Black laity still believe that part of the church's mission is to liberate individuals from economic, political, and physical suffering. They expect pastors to embrace the spirit of ministers such as Nat Turner, Denmark Vessey, and Martin Luther King, whose religious convictions moved Blacks toward greater freedom for themselves and their families. But some question whether churches or the existing family social support network can adapt in time to meet the needs of vast numbers of Black youth.

An entire generation of teenagers and young adults, particularly Black males, is slipping from the reach of their families and traditional help systems. For the first time in Black history, a generation of unchurched youth is emerging from Northern and Western urban areas and to a lesser extent Southern cities. The high unemployment (40 to 80 percent) among Black teenagers during the 1980s forced many onto the streets; this rate rested at just over 68 percent in 2003 (U.S. Bureau of Labor Statistics, 2003). In their need for survival and their search for meaning, a significant minority are finding formal and informal employment in gangs and illegal activities. For some, gangs have replaced their loyalty to their parents, siblings, and the church. In its worst manifestation, gang warfare has resulted in the massacre of entire families.

Imprisonment is a natural outcome of illicit street life. In some prisons, Black males constitute nearly the entire prison population (Harrison and Beck, 2003). A substantial number of women between the ages of twenty-five and thirty-four with felony records were high school dropouts. Even if they are released from prison, the job prospects for poorly educated Blacks with a criminal record are dismal. Ironically, the overall annual cost of supporting each inmate is higher than tuition, room, and board at an elite private college (Thomas, 1992; Morganthau, 1992). Few Black congregations are involved in prison ministries, and over half of prison inmates in many prisons do not receive visits from families or friends (Lincoln and Mamiya, 1990).

Of course, 75 percent of all Black male youth have selected legitimate survival strategies, and the vast majority of all Black families are law abiding. These families are challenged to address many pressing issues for the Black community that stem from those mired in poverty, the unskilled and skilled unemployed, and the millions of Black children born within a sociopolitical structure that makes it difficult for them to thrive.

Summary

It is unclear which specific features of the African family circles of ancestors, elders, and children are directly linked to Black American families today. There is no doubt, however, that Black American patterns of naming and fostering children reflect their high regard for kinship ties. Through these ties and the self-help gospel practiced by families and churches, Black Americans weathered the hardships of the transatlantic slave ship voyage, enslavement, emancipation, and the post-Reconstruction era. Furthermore, without the support of kin, upward socioeconomic mobility would be an elusive dream for many.

Despite the effectiveness of Black kinship ties and self-reliance, the unique conditions of postindustrial society demand concerted efforts on the part of all individuals and support groups within the Black community. Urban problems have become so severe that ordinary citizens are seeking grassroots solutions. In one city, Black middle-class professionals "adopted" thirty-six members of an eighth-grade class, providing counseling to the fatherless, academic tutoring, and college tuition money for the twenty women and thirteen men who made it through high school.

In the late 1970s, Edmond Burton, a dentist, armed with his Radio Shack Model One computer, began giving neighborhood kids job training after school and Saturdays. He taught them basic computer skills on twenty computers and trained them in the techniques of job interviewing—and they got hired. In Cleveland, Charles Ballard of the National Institute for Responsible Fatherhood and Family Development coaches unwed fathers to behave like responsible men. Soft Sheen Products Incorporated initiated a learning center in Chicago's worst housing project. Gregory Boyle, a Jesuit priest, heads the Jobs for the Future program that finds work for gang members in East Los Angeles. He offers crack-dealing youth five dollars an hour to go straight—and most do. The Crown Heights Youth Collective in New York has five thousand youth involved in a program that provides help with job development, counseling, and interview self-presentation. Seventy-five percent of the youth who complete this program are placed in entry-level positions. A central motto for all these groups is "Nothing works to build sound families like work" (Mathews, 1992).

More recently, Kevin Johnson, former all-star point guard with the Phoenix Suns, returned to his childhood community to make a difference. Before retiring from the NBA in 2000, he began reclaiming his former neighborhood, an ongoing project. Angry that his childhood neighborhood had been taken over by drugs and drug dealers and that Sacramento High School, which he, his parents, and his grandfather had attended, was crumbling academically, physically, and spiritually, he launched a plan to save his entire community. As a result of contentious but successful meetings with the Sacramento City Teachers Association and the Sacramento High School board and attracting $7 million in donations, he spruced up the ten-acre campus and split it into six separate schools, having a different academic focus. In 2003, he began the school year with 1,560 students and a waiting list of 100. Moreover, prior to leaving the Suns, he began renovating several blocks in his Oak Park neighborhood, driving out drug pushers, convincing the office of the Sacramento Symphony to move to the neighborhood, and re-creating through art and passion a familial community atmosphere. His community and the employees are held to a high ethical standard, which reflects Johnson's strong religious upbringing. Today he and his mother, affectionately called Mother Rose, live in the area and give hands-on attention to the community children and residents who benefit from the upscale barbershop, community theater, Starbucks, bookstore, bank, and elementary and high school campuses (personal interview, 2003; Tresiowski, 2003).

These efforts are praiseworthy. Yet they are insufficient for fighting job discrimination, political logjams over urban anticrime bills, and reforms in the health care and school systems. As the resources of these individuals and grassroots organizations thin in the face of severe urban problems, heavy pressure is being placed on the most powerful groups in the Black community, particularly Black churches. Church leaders in turn realize the need for an astute understanding of the political process. Along with social scientists, they have specific recommendations for political strategies.

Among many strategies, churches and faith-based organizations are urging public officials to provide financial incentives for preventive and intervention help systems already in place in the Black community. Using their influence, Black Protestant churches and the National Black Catholic Congress are pushing for reform in many directions: accurate treatment of Black family life in textbooks and the media, elimination of racial bias in the criminal justice system, employment for Black youth, full compensation for grandmothers supporting grandchildren left without their parents, changes in the child welfare systems (Roberts, 2000, 2002), extension of Medicaid to young parents living in extended households (Mullen, 2000), and adequate medical and nutrition services for those families without financial resources.

Black churches historically have had a liberation theology dictated by the deprived position of the Black population. They have traditionally provided programs designed for the social, political, physical, and spiritual needs of Black families and their communities. It is Black churches, with their circle of intersecting families and spiritual leaders, that are in the best position to foster the strong tradition of intergenerational kin support. They, more than any other organized group, are the trustees of future Black generations.

10

Social Change, Challenges, and Prospects

A s scholars and practitioners involved with families, we are all aware of and concerned about the alleged deterioration of the Black family. The rising tide of female-headed households and out-of-wedlock births has reached dramatic proportions and taken a deadly toll on the society in terms of high school dropouts, increased crime rates, and the increased number of welfare-reliant families. While the effects are known, the causes are generally reduced to those of promiscuous sex and Black family values—or the lack of such values as a strong work ethic, commitment to marriage and family, and a belief in the monogamous nuclear family (Gilder, 1981). Those who subscribe to these cultural generalities tend to ignore the fact that the statistics on Black family "pathology" reflect economics more than race-bound promiscuity and other values. Whereas the Black middle class has an above-average divorce rate and may be sexually active prior to marriage, they are not a cause for concern. Like Whites, they remarry or are self-supporting in the event of a divorce. If their nonmarital sexual activity culminates in a pregnancy, middle-class Black women follow the mainstream model and get an abortion or marry the father.

The State and Public Policy

According to Bell and Vogel (1968), the family contributes its loyalty to the government in exchange for leadership that will provide direct and indirect benefits for the nuclear family. While there is little doubt that Black families have been loyal to the political state in America, it appears that they have derived few benefits in return. Although the political system has the power to affect many of the conditions influencing Black family life, it has failed to intervene in the service of the Black population and, in fact, has been more of a negative force in shaping the conditions under which Black families must live. As Billingsley (1968, p. 177) has stated, "No subsystem has been more oppressive of the Negro people or holds greater promise for their development."

Historically, we find that state, local, and federal governmental bodies have been willing collaborators in the victimization of Black families. Under slavery, marriages between slaves were not legal since the slave could make no contract. The government did nothing to ensure stable marriages among the slave population or to prevent the arbitrary separation of slave couples by their owners. Moreover, the national government was committed to the institution of slavery, a practice that was most inimical to Black family life (J. H. Franklin, 1987).

For reasons that may be related to the sacrosanct nature of the family in America, this country has rarely had any clearly defined plans or policies concerning the family. The closest thing has been the welfare system, which has actually done more to disrupt families than to keep them together (Jewell, 1988). In the light of the continuing decline in the resources of Black extended families and the escalating socioeconomic problems they face, some sort of family support system seems necessary. While the Black family has an extended character to it, it is no longer as viable a support force as it once was. The central problems facing Black families require much greater attention than they have received so far. To improve Black family life also requires well-formulated public policies and appropriate programs that address these problems.

In general, the government's efforts have been sporadic, misguided, and ineffective. Certainly aspects of the welfare program Aid to Families With Dependent Children (AFDC), which required the male's absence from the family as a condition for assistance, did nothing to strengthen families. In response to six decades of poor results from federal poverty programs, such as AFDC, welfare reform became law on August 22, 1996, when President Clinton signed the Personal Responsibility and Work Opportunity Reconciliation Act. Since 1996, states no longer are required by federal law to give assistance to all poor families. This legislation gives states a block grant, with a fixed amount of money to use at their discretion in serving needy families. Most fundamentally, this act eliminated the open-ended federal entitlement programs by creating time limits and stringent work conditions for receiving cash benefits. Replacing dependency with work was the most applauded goal of the block grant entitled Temporary Assistance for Needy Families (TANF). Hence, parents with a child age one or over are required to participate in a work activity. Under TANF, a family of three (parent and two children under age eighteen) may qualify for TANF if their gross income is below $784 a month and assets are worth less than $1,000. Furthermore, there is a four-year lifetime limit on cash assistance, and no adult recipient can receive assistance more than twenty-four months within any five-year period.

Work is a major component of TANF. In fact, fiscal penalties are levied on states that fail to meet the designed work-participation rates by a given time: 50 percent or more for 2002 and beyond. These work activities help recipients gain the experience needed to find a job and become self-sufficient. States have wide discretion over the work requirements. They can deny benefits for a few weeks or a lifetime if a parent with a child age one or over does not participate in a work activity, does not find a job within the two-year time line, or violates the family cap by having another birth while on assistance. In addition, states can deny cash aid to teenage parents and require that unwed teen parents be in school and living at home with an adult (Safford, 2003; Hill, 1999). Arizona, one of the first to implement statewide changes to the welfare system, began with at least three important features of welfare reform: child care as incentive to work, educational incentives, and individual development accounts (IDA). IDAs are savings accounts for restricted high-return investments: postsecondary education and training, first-time home purchase, starting a business. They're designed to increase the savings of the working poor by matching their savings with public and private funds.

Since all adult recipients with a child over age one must participate in a work activity, an attempt is made to ease the difficulties of balancing work and parenting for those TANF recipients who find work through a Child Care and Development Block Grant. However, in order to qualify for child care, parents must meet strict guidelines. For example, under Arizona's welfare provision, Employing and Moving People Off Welfare and Encouraging Responsibility (EMPOWER), child care is provided for families with incomes 135 percent of the federal poverty level or 100 percent of the poverty level for families in special circumstances.

When a recipient meets these income requirements, child assistance is given to cover the time spent in work, education, or training activities if the participant is working at least twenty hours or working the minimum twenty hours and pursuing postsecondary education or training activities that are reasonably related to employment goals (such as a vocational degree or certification course). After leaving welfare, a family may qualify for up to twenty-four months of transitional child care if the family income does not exceed 135 percent of the federal poverty level. In essence, by providing the experience needed to find a job and become self-sufficient, child care subsidy programs are intended to encourage work. Ironically, many of those leaving welfare for work will become part of the working poor. And it is precisely this group who is least likely to have access to dependable and quality child care. Moreover, opponents of this requirement question the wisdom of mothers being forced into work when their child is under age two to go into training for jobs that promise to keep them among the working poor. Many analysts agree that reforms, coupled with tight labor markets, allowed many Black women to move into the job market. However, since there is a fixed cash amount, one major concern is the inability of assistance to respond to economic downturns. What will be the possible effect of recessions on those who moved from welfare to work during the booming 1990s? While all the evidence is not available, caseloads have risen, on average, by about 5 percent for each percentage point increase in unemployment (Anderson, 2002; Hill, 1999).

To increase the probability of lifetime learning and family employment, the EMPOWER program grants cash benefits only to unwed minor parents under age of eighteen who stay in school and reside in the home of a parent, legal guardian, or other adult relative, and all the recipients' children are required to attend school. Clearly, encouraging education is laudable. Yet forcing children to remain in a home that may already be taxed by economic deprivation, overcrowding, or intergenerational conflict may not be in the best interests of the child. Exempting parents who are at risk of neglect or physical or emotional harm may be an insufficient safeguard, given the case overload of the average caseworker and numerous cases escaping the protection of the courts. In addition, the resources for providing extended training and education are inadequate for providing long-term results (Hill, 1999; Johnson, 1997).

The IDA is a response to the need to raise the asset ceiling. Under the old welfare system, eligibility rules required that a family not have significant economic assets as a condition for receiving even the minimal subsistence level: savings had to be depleted or nearly so, the value of one's car could not exceed a prescribed limit, and stocks and bonds in the children's name had to be cashed in, even if they were gifts from grandparents. Consequently, recipients entered welfare on the economic edge, usually with $1,500 in assets, with home equity excluded (Johnson, 1997; Churchill, 1995; Oliver and Shapiro, 1995). Under EMPOWER, recipients can have $2,000 (including savings, bonds, stocks) in resources with exemptions of one home and one car regardless of their value. It also allows welfare recipients to set aside money to achieve education or training goals. Given the difficult time Black families have acquiring any assets and supporting educational pursuits, the IDA is particularly relevant (Johnson, 1997).

Although it is too early to reach conclusions, it is clear that while welfare block grants might succeed in reducing the welfare rolls, the employment that former TANF recipients will probably receive will be sporadic low-wage jobs without benefits (Hill, 1999). In fact, some early reports show that some recipients in employment training programs did not find stable employment, and their personal earnings at best were only slightly higher than public assistance. These studies conclude that the recipients' acquired skills were too low to move them toward economic self-sufficiency (Hamilton, 2002; Monroe and Tiller, 2001). Yet some believe that the sharp reduction in Black child poverty between 1996 and 2001 was due to welfare reform. They note that welfare rolls have plummeted, employment of single mothers has increased dramatically, and child hunger has declined substantially. Dissenters note that this improvement can easily be attributed to the economic upswing in the 1990s. Furthermore, they are quick to point out that the number of children in extreme poverty (family incomes below half the poverty line) hit record high rates after 1996. Unless polices and resources change, states' limited funds will not sustain child care and medical benefits beyond twenty-four months. Thus, TANF recipients will face challenges to remaining employed, potentially leading to increased homelessness among Black women and their children and an increase in the number of children in foster care.

Although this latest reform has attempted to respond to earlier deficiencies, for example, by providing opportunities to plan a more secure future through allowing personal education accounts and higher assets, other proposals for family stability and upward mobility have been suggested. They include a universal family allowance and programs for first-time home buyers to ensure that poor families and marginalized groups have better access to a college education and lifelong learning, elimination of gender discrimination in employment, creation of community-controlled day care centers and child development programs, expanded government employment programs, and incentives for private employers to hire disadvantaged youth (Mason, Skol-nick, and Sugarman, 1998; Wilson, 1998; and Oliver and Shapiro, 1997). Only through a combination of these measures will Blacks have choice in family arrangements (Dewart, 1991).

Supporting the need for such public policy are the findings of the Commission on Civil Rights (1991). The commission found poverty endemic among fully employed Black women. Their wages are so low in comparison to fully employed men that an employed status is not sufficient to remove them from poverty. This insufficiency continues to be evident in that more than 85 percent of the 27 million American children in poverty have at least one working parent (National Center for Children in Poverty, 2002, 2003). In fact, despite the economic booms of the 1990s, among 2.1 million poor children under age three, more are from working families than ever before. American society continues to pay women salaries that are often adequate only when they supplement a male breadwinner's income. Since a majority of Black families with children under the age of eighteen are headed by a woman, who is generally the sole wage earner, these families are consigned to poverty. Because the educational level of Black women is above that of Black men, the method of comparable worth is one mechanism for attaining income parity with their male counterparts.

Leashore (1991) documents that Black men have a different set of problems. Many of them are unable to secure full-time employment and have a variety of health and educational problems. While it may be futile to argue who is worse off, it must be noted that childless Black males are seldom eligible for any welfare benefits in many states. Other than a life of crime or enlisting in the military, most of them are left without any options for survival in this society. Leashore has called for a national effort to provide job training, full employment, health care, and so on. Such measures are particularly critical for noncustodial fathers who struggle with consistently paying child support (Hill, 2003).

It will be necessary to advance a public policy to reverse the trend toward an upward redistribution of wealth. Yet when asked whether the federal government should see to it that every citizen has a job and good standard of living, 65 percent of Blacks but only 24 percent of Whites thought so (Harris and Williams, 1986). Whites are less likely than Blacks to endorse affirmative action (89.2 versus 43.7) (Kinder and Winter, 2001) and more likely to give support to the idea of individuals "getting ahead on their own" versus government intervention (Harris and Williams, 1986). Again, there is an assumption by Whites that government programs encourage minorities to be indolent. In the more racially homogeneous countries of Europe, public policy has long been used to support an equalization of wealth. In contrast, the American body politic elected a political administration that has spent trillions of dollars on military buildup and far less on social programs (Ciarrocca and Hartung, 2002; Berry, Corbin, Hellman, Mason, Smith, Stohl, and Valasek, 2001–2002). The victims of that policy are largely families with children—one in five of whom live in poverty (Seccombe, 2001).

Finally, it would be instructive to note that the direction of change is the same for all families in the United States. Where Black families were in 1960, White families are in the new millennium. The trend toward out-of-wedlock births (Whites accelerating at a higher rate), female-headed households (Whites accelerating at a higher rate), divorce (racial gap rapidly closing), and other changes in family structure are largely an artifact of the changing economic base of family life (McLoyd, Cauce, Takeuchi, and Wilson, 2001; U.S. Department of Health and Human Services, 1995; Moynihan, 1987). Instead of relying on racial stereotypes as an explanation for a group's family structure, we need to understand that Black families are only farther down a road that all families are traveling.

The Economic Factor

Any discussion of the changes in the Black family over the past forty years has several common assumptions: Black family problems are a function of the decline of familial values and the triumph of hedonism over the discipline and perseverance necessary for marital stability. In some quarters, the old canard is that slavery and its concomitants destroyed the value of family life for many Black Americans. Any objective analysis of marital and family patterns in the United States would reveal the trends of unwed mothers, higher percentages of low-wealth and single-parent families, and the weakening of the patriarchal, monogamous, and nuclear family for all racial groups during the past third of a century (Strong, DeVault, and Sayad, 1998; Skolnick, 1992).

A combination of forces has contributed to the decline of the nuclear family, among them the weakening of the patriarchy by the increasing economic and psychological independence of women, the sexual revolution, greater mobility and urbanization patterns, and the liberalization of divorce laws. Many of those same causes have an impact on Black family structure; however, a more central source appears to be the declining participation of Black men in the labor force. While we have addressed how the shortage of Black men has led to the increase in single-parent households, marital dissolutions, and out-of-wedlock births earlier, we also need to understand the reasons behind the growing unemployment and underemployment rates of Black males.

One reason is that employment in government service, an important source of jobs for Blacks, declined when governments used tax monies to subcontract services to private businesses. This was particularly true of defense work, which was generally contracted out to private firms whose workforce was largely White and male. Besides these unemployment trends, other forces were at work. One of them was the shift of jobs from inner cities to White suburbs. Between 1976 and 1986, twenty of the nation's largest metropolitan areas had at least three-quarters of their labor force growth occur outside the central urban business districts (Center for the Study of Social Policy, 1999). Consequently, many jobs were moved away from poorly skilled and displaced racial minorities. Along with the shift of jobs from cities to suburbs has been the fact that the greatest increase in jobs has occurred in small businesses, another factor that works against Blacks. Small businesses often recruit workers through informal means and look for a "personality and cultural fit" in workers. This frequently means that currently entrenched European American workers bring in their friends and relatives to work for the same firm, a process that largely excludes Black Americans. The advantage of huge, bureaucratically organized, strongly led organizations for Blacks is that it is easier to change racial employment patterns in them than in small ones that hire friends and relatives or people of the same ethnic background and where the personal prejudices of the employer can be decisive in hiring decisions.

A critical factor in Black unemployment trends has been the decline of industrial manufacturing job opportunities (where Blacks gained steady employment during and after World War II) and the proliferative growth in jobs in the service and information processing spheres (U.S. Census Bureau, 2001b; Zeisset, 2000). Between 1980 and 2000, manufacturing jobs dropped from 28.4 to 19.5 million, while service jobs grew from 71.5 to 80.5 million (U.S. Census Bureau, 2001b). This new economy shifted middle-income salaried Black families into low-income service jobs, markedly undermining the ability of working-class parents to provide for their families (Hill, 1999).

These service jobs often require no specific skills beyond literacy and tend to be nonunionized, meaning that they lend themselves to subjective, and hence arbitrary, recruitment and employment practices. These jobs also have low salaries, few or no benefits, and fewer opportunities for advancement. In 1994, Black men were twice as likely to be working in service jobs as compared to White men (Collins, 1996; U.S. Census Bureau, 2000). Unlike the service industry, industrial manufacturing jobs have the distinction of being highly unionized, with retention being determined by seniority, not employer discretion. They rarely require standardized tests for entry-level jobs, and the demonstration of job proficiency is fairly precise. Overall, Black men hold jobs in the most vulnerable job sectors—those that have experienced the greatest amount of downsizing, restructuring, relocating, layoffs, and marginal wages.

Of course, it is alleged that large numbers of Black men lack the minimal literacy skills necessary for employment in the service and information processing industries. In the 1980s, a shocking 44 percent of Black males were estimated to be functional illiterates, a considerably higher number than thirty years earlier (Kozol, 1985). Seven years later, the results remained disturbing. Blacks, particularly males, on the average scored 49 to 63 points below Whites on three measures of literacy: prose, document, and quantitative. Without taking class or cultural biases into account, those Blacks scoring low were less likely to understand complex issues, to read and comprehend tables and figures, and to complete applications or forms or manage a checking account (National Center for Education Statistics, 2002). Certainly, some responsibility for these high rates lies with the public school system, which promote students without their having obtained reading and writing skills. It might be noted that the federal government decreased its funding of public education during the 1980s, although spending on education increased between 1990 and 2000 (Hoffman, 2002).

A constellation of interlocking factors, some of them already noted in this chapter, has pushed Black men and women out of the labor force and into the shadow economy of drug sales and petty theft, a fact that has increased their percentage in the American federal and state prisons population by 200 percent between 1980 and 1996 (Blumstein and Beck, 1999). Spending on corrections has increased faster than any other type of state-level funding, exceeding that spent on education. The privatization of prisons is considered America's newest growth industry. Lockhart Renaissance and Work Facility, a private prison owned by Lockhart Technologies Incorporated (LTI), employed 150 workers in Austin, Texas, to build air-conditioner parts and circuit boards. However, it laid these employees off and replaced them with workers behind bars, where the average wage is between $.23 and $1.15 per hour. A former president of LTI praised the utility of what he referred to as "a captive work force," declaring that "they're rarely ill . . . they're delightful to work with" and "they don't have family problems" (Ward, 1998, p. 50). On the contrary, their family problems are many, as we discussed in Chapter Six. Ironically, the jobs they could not get in their freedom are now available to them in their imprisonment.

Unfair criteria for sentencing contributes to the overrepresentation of Blacks in the criminal justice system. In 1995, Congress passed a cocaine disparity act, which is resulting in the incarceration of more Blacks than Whites. In spite of the fact that both crack and powder cocaine have equal effects, crack cocaine offenders (predominantly Black) receive more severe sentences than offenders who possess the same or larger amounts of powder cocaine (predominantly Whites) (Hill, 1999). It is an American tragedy that a combination of labor market dislocation, out-of-control drug trafficking, and racially biased penalties are exponentially increasing incarceration among urban youth.

For the majority of Blacks who choose legitimate employment, they must find their footing in the malfunctioning of America's free market economy, which created a million millionaires but forced several millions into a new kind of poverty. America's emphasis on competition, reflected in the loss of millions of jobs to other nations using cheap labor to provide inexpensive imports, has propelled many high school graduates to seek college degrees as an entry into white-collar work ("Income Inequality," 1998; Mishel, Bernstein, and Schmitt, 1997). Those Black males not enrolled in school or who fail to complete high school face a double dilemma in this evolving economy: they are not competitive with the White and Black women whose literacy and interpersonal skills are better, and the menial jobs that once were their monopoly must now be fought over with newly arrived immigrants and prison laborers. All of these groups are exploited by this situation (Ward, 1998; Stewart and Hyclak, 1986).

Despite the fact that early work experiences predict a more positive employment future, all youth, but especially Blacks, are particularly vulnerable to joblessness. Black youth encounter many difficulties in finding work. Across the nation, White male teenagers have a higher employment rate than Black male teenagers (71.1 percent versus 52.2 percent). Moreover, the White male teenager ultimately uses his kinship and friend-of-the-family networks more effectively to secure employment, while many Black male teenagers who lack such networks drop out or never join the workforce. Those living in areas with high levels of poverty or unemployment are less likely to find jobs, yet youth with employed parents are more likely to find jobs regardless of race (Gardecki, 2001; Wilson, 1998). The poor employment prospects for young Black males also are illustrated by the fact that some employers refuse to hire them for jobs that are totally subsidized by federal funds (Wilson, 1998). Furthermore, while employers in low-wage industries, such as fast food outlets, are complaining of an inability to fill job vacancies in affluent suburbs, there are still more young workers than jobs in the central cities. Even when fast food and other minimum wage jobs are available, many Black teenagers rightfully perceive them as dead-end positions that have no long-term payoff. Young White workers are often obtaining part-time and summer work at wages of $9.00 or $10.00 an hour, while Black high school graduates in Los Angeles found average entry-level jobs at $4.75 an hour in 1991 (Rutten, 1991). These trends did not change much in 1998, with teens earning about $5.15 per hour. However, White and Hispanic young men earned more than Blacks, and Hispanic females earned less than all of these groups (U.S. Department of Labor, 2000).

Other barriers to employment remain. A director of a youth employment program states that "minorities have a 30 percent chance of being hired when dispatched to an interview. But, when we send someone who is not a minority they get hired" ("Summer Vacation Travails," 1986). Sadly, these teenagers often find themselves competing with their older neighbors for these same jobs. This sharp distinction between summer job prospects in central cities and the suburbs belies the rosy projections for young workers in the 1990s ("Employers Prefer Whites, Study Says," 1991). Black youth have poorer employment opportunities even though more of them participate in cooperative education, technical preparation, internships, and apprenticeships than White youth (U.S. Department of Labor,

2000), which calls for continuous efforts to improve youth employment opportunities and academic attainment.

For adults who are able to find white-collar jobs, they find their salaries do not match the cost of living. Of the white-collar jobs added since 1980 and mostly occupied by women, a third are in retail, where the average annual salary in 1984 was $9,521 (Jaynes, 1990) just slightly above the $10,609 government's poverty level for a family of four. Currently, the median income for service jobs is $17,805 for women and $26,000 for men. Clearly, workers in these jobs must struggle. In confirming their plight, the National Center for Children in Poverty (2003) states that it is not until a family of four reaches twice the federal poverty level ($36,800) that parents can provide their children with basic necessities, like housing, food, and health care (U.S. Census Bureau, 2003c). Black family income will continue to be stifled as long as their primary earners are overrepresented in the two less promising job sectors.

Meanwhile, the electorate continues to elect political administrations widely perceived as representing the interests of the wealthy. The small benefits that have trickled down have gone largely to middle-class White males. Between 1980 and 1986, government expenditures on the military increased by 100 percent. Furthermore, after the terrorist attacks of September 11, 2001, military spending reached a rate not seen since World War II (National Radio Project, 2000; Brown, Wolf, Starke, and Jacobson, 1986). The $1 trillion that the United States has spent on its military buildup has diverted capital away from the improvement of basic industries in such vital areas as steel, automobiles, and machine tools, the very sector of the economy where most Black men are located. Moreover, funding for programs needed by the most disadvantaged received relatively little in the light of the need. For example, based on the 2002 budget authorized by Congress, the government allocated $343 billion for the military, $45 billion for education, and $20 billion for training, employment, and social services (Berry et al., 2001–2002). It is not surprising that the concentration of joblessness in the Black community has resulted in unemployment receiving a low priority among mainstream Americans. As Reeves (1986, p. 85) has observed, "One of the secrets of the acceptance of the doubled crisis level in Black unemployment is the fact that unemployment among adult white males is still in the old range, below 6 percent." Certainly, the captains of industry would not want full employment, which would create a situation where employers would have to bid for workers rather than the reverse.

Private Decisions and Public Trends

Almost forty years since the publication of the Moynihan report (1965), the figures Moynihan cited as evidence that the Black family was deteriorating have doubled, and almost tripled in some areas. How is it that a group that regards family life as its most important source of satisfaction finds a majority of its women unmarried? Why does a group with more traditional sexual values than its White peers have a majority of its children born out of wedlock? How is it that a group that places such emphasis on the traditional nuclear family finds a near majority of its members living in single-parent households? While theorists have offered a number of answers, we suggest the major explanation has to do with the structural conditions of the Black population.

The basis of a stable family rests on the willingness and ability of men and women to marry, have children, and fulfill socially prescribed familial roles. In the case of women, those roles have traditionally been defined as giving birth to children and socializing them; providing sexual gratification, companionship, and emotional support to their husbands; and carrying out domestic functions such as cooking and cleaning. There is abundant evidence that Black women are willing and able to fulfill those roles (Collins, 1986). Women maintain roles as homemakers, employees, or some combination of these roles. The roles of men in the family are more narrowly confined to economic provider and family leader. There are indications that close to a majority of young Black American males cannot implement those roles (Bowman, 1985). When it comes to a choice between remaining single or getting married, individuals often do a cost-benefit analysis. Marriage is frequently a quid pro quo arrangement. The desire to enter and maintain a conjugal relationship is contingent on people's perception of the benefits, as well as the anticipated costs, of such a relationship (Jewell, 1988).

As much as family and nonfamily male-female disruptions have a negative impact on the psychology of males and females, the reality is that even when the rationale for the behavior of the male is understood, it does not negate the fact that the female is still forced to view male-female relations in terms of the cost-reward dichotomy. This approach may signal that Black women, when confronted with eligible Black men who cannot give them financial security, willingly opt for a rational exchangist view that says that poverty in singlehood may be preferable to poverty in marriage, with all the accompanying stresses and tensions of marital discord. Even when the attraction of emotional attachment or sexual satisfaction is present, it loses its force eventually if financial security is not forthcoming. Hence, the economic exchange becomes the most potent and the most useful model of exchange relations.

There is no great mystery as to what has happened to the Black family in the past forty years: it has experienced an acceleration of trends set in motion during the 1960s. A highly sexualized culture has conveyed to American youth through the media, in clothing, and by example the notion that nonmarital sexual relations are not only acceptable but required for individual fulfillment. Furthermore, the consequences of teenage sexual behavior are counteracted somewhat by easier access to effective contraceptives and abortion. The number of pregnant teenagers has not actually increased—only the proportion of births to that group of women as a result of the rapid decline in births to older married women. While the nonmarital sexual activity rates of Black and White teenage women are converging, Black females are more likely to engage in unprotected intercourse and less likely to marry or have an abortion if they become pregnant (Jones and Battle, 1990; U.S. Department of Health and Human Services, 1995).

While it is reasonable to question the wisdom of young Black women attaining motherhood at such an early age, their decision to bear children and raise them alone reflects their traditional values and limited options. Among Black males under age twenty-one, the official unemployment rate in the 1980s was 27 percent, and as many as 60 percent of young Black men remain outside the workforce (Larson, 1988). The situation has not improved: 68.4 percent of Black men between the ages of sixteen and nineteen were without work in 2000 (U.S. Bureau of Labor Statistics, 2003). While employment may be easier for Black women to obtain, it often is in dead-end jobs that pay only half the wages that White males earn. Rather than remain childless and husbandless, these women choose to have children and raise them alone. A good explanation of these life choices is given by Hortense Canady (1984, p. 40), president of Delta Sigma Theta sorority, the largest Black Greek organization, serving over 190,000 college-educated women: "Having a child is probably the best thing that's ever going to happen to them in their whole lifetime and the only thing they can contribute—this is not true in most other countries in the world. . . . If you belong to a class or a group of people who have no educational opportunities stretching out before them, no other goals, that is probably the single best thing that's ever going to happen to you in your life."

Having limited educational and career options to set against bearing a child is not the only reason for the increase in female-headed households. For years, a welfare system that often required men to be absent from the home contributed to the problem. Hence, Black women realized that the meager welfare payments were more reliable than a class of men who may never know gainful employment in their lifetime (Rein, 1982). Since employment and income are the measure of a man's masculinity in this society, men who have neither do not tend to feel good about themselves or act positively toward their wives and children. In the Hampton study (1980), for example, husbands who were not satisfied with themselves had a fairly high level of marital disruption.

In the context of Blacks' unfavorable position in the American economy, Black females lack "desirable" men with whom to form monogamous marriages. According to Joe and Yu of the Center for the Study of Social Policy (1991), between 1976 and 1983, the number of Black families headed by women rose by 700,000, and the ranks of Black men out of the labor force or unemployed increased by the same number. During the last forty-five years, almost 75 percent of Black men were working in 1960, and Black families headed by women accounted for 21 percent of all Black families in the same year, but by 1982, only 54 percent of all Black men were in the labor force, and 42 percent of all Black families were headed by women. By the year 2002, 68 percent of Black men had jobs, and female-headed households represented 43 percent of all households—virtually unchanged from 1982 (U.S. Census Bureau, 1991a, 2002a, 2003b). That the improved employment status of men has had virtually no effect on single-headed household begs an explanation. When Moynihan observed a similar break in pattern during the 1960s, he concluded that Blacks had lost their value for marriage. Yet there is no compelling evidence that was true then or now.

What is clear is that unemployment rates alone cannot fully account for the decrease in marriage rates or a rise in female-headed households. Apart from births to unwed parents, households headed by women result from divorce, separation, and, to a far lesser rate, widowhood. For all families, divorce has been rising. Despite a slower divorce rate, Blacks continue to have higher rates of divorce than those in the general population (McLoyd, Cauce, Takeuchi, and Wilson, 2001). The growth in divorce was particularly marked among those who married in the late 1960s and early 1970s. For ever-married Black women who married in the 1940s, 18 percent eventually divorced, a rate only slightly higher than that for White women of that era. In contrast, 60 percent of those married in the late 1960s and early 1970s (a high unemployment era) had already become divorced by the 1980s (Gallagher, 1996). More recent data show 31 percent of Whites but 47 percent of Blacks divorcing within the first ten years of first marriage, when they are most likely to have birthed children (Bramlett and Mosher, 2002). The combination of increasingly high rates of never marrying, high rates of sexually active teenagers who ineffectively use contraceptives, high levels of teen pregnancy (peaking in the 1990s), higher divorce risk for teenagers who marry, lower rates and older ages of remarriage, and the unabated high divorce rates means that single-parent households have interpersonal factors that meld with economics to continue the acceleration of these rates.

Structural conditions interacting with the gender role expectations that males should be the clear economic provider lead some Black men and women to separate or divorce. As Hampton (1980) found, the pressures that push many Black males out of other social institutions within society also work to push them out of marital relationships. In Hampton's study, the highest percentage of disrupted marriages (27.4 percent) was observed among wives with incomes accounting for 40 percent or more of the family's income. Hampton's explanation was that when women have other means of support in the form of welfare or their own earnings, they may be less constrained to remain in a personally unsatisfying relationship. Alternatively, the wife may be satisfied with the husband's role, but her high income may threaten the husband's authority and status, undermining his self-concept.

American divorces are often driven by a premium placed on personal fulfillment and the belief that children are better off when a bad marriage ends. Yet in their 1997 book, *A Generation at Risk,* Amato and Booth make important distinctions in types of divorce outcomes. According to their research, the worst situations for children are high-conflict marriages that last and low-conflict marriages that end in divorce. Most divorces fall into the latter category. A striking 70 percent of divorces end low-conflict marriages. For those Blacks not fraught with severe conflict and abuse, a decision to stay and work through problems not only aids in reversing the broken home trend but, more important, provides much promise for their children's psychological well-being. Individuals have virtually no control over shifts in the economy. However, they do have control over their personal readiness. The economic status of the workforce is strongly influenced by educational attainment. As we have seen, this is truer today than at any previous time. The skill level and trainability of workers is a major factor in determining the self-confidence of job seekers as well as whether they will get a job, how much they will be paid, and how long they will retain the job. Those unable to adapt to the changing economy because of their lack of academic preparation become even more disadvantaged. It is on this group that William J. Wilson built his thesis in *The Declining Significance of Race* (1980). For the first time, the changing economy of the past several decades resulted in institutional forces' supplanting race as the dominant factor responsible for racial inequality. It is also this larger group rather than the fewer number of academically prepared group that has the greatest potential for having an impact on the rate of female-headed households (Anderson, 2002).

Women, both Black and White, are better prepared to deal with the educational qualifications of an economy based on high-technology and service industries. For example, Black women received two-thirds of all 1996 bachelor's degrees awarded to Blacks (Special Report, 1999). In 1996, 59.7 of all 1996 bachelor's degrees awarded in science and engineering went to Black women ("Vital Signs," 1999), highlighting the gender differential in education among Black men and women. Jobs in technologically based industries require good reading and writing skills at precisely the time when the ability of the public school system to produce students with the necessary attributes is declining. Black and Hispanic males have the highest rates of functional illiteracy among the 23 million Americans so classified (Kozol, 1985; National Center for Education Statistics, 2002). One explanation is that when a Black male perceives the opportunity structure as not allowing for his upward mobility through education, he is more likely to divert his energy into sports, music, or hustling. Messner (1995) notes that the poor quality of their education, the attitudes of teachers and coaches, and the antieducation sentiment held by peers has made it easier for Black men to focus on sports or their physical abilities as a way to establish power and status. Black females—with fewer opportunities—continue to progress in the same educational system (Vital Signs, 1999; Hale, 1982). One caveat is that although some ethnographic research reports that many Black youth are reputed to disparage high-achieving peers as "acting White," most national studies reveal that among students, the majority of Blacks as compared to Whites are just as supportive, or more so, of academic achievement by their peers. Peers do not appear to be the primary culprits. Unfortunately, too many teachers' expectations of students tend to be more determined by race and class than by the student's actual ability (Hill, 1999). Black students must draw deeply within themselves to overcome such attitudes.

This gender disparity in higher educational achievement must be put in the context of the sex ratio: there are fewer men available to achieve these diplomas of higher learning. While a significant number of Black men are educationally deficient, all are not. The men who are choosing not to pursue baccalaureates also have other legitimate options: military, career training programs such as computer technologies, information sciences, law-related careers, and medical technologies. Some estimates suggest that more than 70 percent of future new jobs will not require a college degree. According to the journal *Black Issues in Higher Education* (Proprietary Preference For-Profit Colleges, 2000), a California campus of the ITT Technical Institute of California was the top producer of baccalaureates for minorities in engineering-related technologies, followed by Strayer College and Devry Institute of Technology, both private institutions. Yet the value of a general bachelor of science degree is its flexibility, an important commodity in an often unpredictable economy (Stockard and Tucker, 2001).

Much debate surrounds differential racial values with regard to marriage. Some argue that a retreat from marriage by Black females is a value forced on them by economic forces. Others argue that, nevertheless, it is a value with natural consequences for singlehood and single-parent households. But is it a value? Is it a value that works independent of economic considerations? In a rare study of the effects of attitudes on marriage, Sassler and Schoen (1999) examined a national probability sample of Black and White never-married adults ages eighteen to thirty-four during two time periods: 1987–1988 and 1992–1994. A Black woman was most likely to marry if she had positive views of how her life would improve if she were to marry. In this sense she was no different from White women with similar altitudes. However, Sassler and Schoen's data show that regardless of race, positive attitudes about marriage were not by themselves enough to enter matrimony. In fact, despite a more positive view than Whites of how their lives would be improved with marriage, Black women were no more likely to wed than White women. What accounts for the large racial differences in marriage rates was not attitude toward marriage in general but the higher importance Black women placed on themselves and a prospective partner's being financially ready before settling down. Their data suggest that the experience of economic uncertainty among Black men, even those who have full-time employment, remains a significant factor in Black marital decision making.

Some researchers have demonstrated that unbalanced gender ratios have certain predictable consequences for relationships between men and women (McLoyd, Cauce, Takeuchi, and Wilson, 2001; Kiecolt and Fossett, 1997; 1995; Guttentag and Secord, 1983). Some demographers suggest that even a slight sex ratio drop below 100 can have dramatic social consequences, giving rise to interracial marriages, higher rates of singlehood, divorce, out-of-wedlock births, and female-headed households in different historical epochs and across different societies. For example, Crowder and Tolnay (2000) found that interracial marriages significantly reduced the marriage pool and the likelihood of marriage for Black women. Black educated women are most disadvantaged, since men who intermarry tend to have relatively high levels of education and occupation. Hence, given that the men most likely to have benefited from the 1990s economic boom and shift were the most skilled and academically prepared, the marriage market for Black educated women would not have shown much appreciation. Overall, with an excess of more than 1 million Black women than Black men, there would not be enough men to create monogamous unions even in the best of circumstances and mutual dyadic attractions.

Under positive conditions, there are good indications that the Black family is strong. Although challenged and wounded, Black families remain committed to hard work, role flexibility, family kinship, and strong spiritual orientation (Hill, 1999). A central question that remains is why Black family traditional ideology has not changed or adjusted to changing conditions. One answer is that it has changed among one stratum of the Black population: the middle class. Within that segment of the Black community, mainstream values, even changing ones, are stronger because they have a higher level of acculturation into those norms due to their greater participation in the majority group's institutions (Staples, 1981). Even among this group, however, traditional values are still strong and exert an influence on their ideological posture toward the family. In part, that is a function of their recent entry into the middle class and the retention of values from their class of origin. Another factor is that their participation in mainstream institutions and embrace of normative ideologies are still marginal, keeping traditional values attractive to many. For example, some Black couples value egalitarian family roles, but their actual family behaviors follow traditional gender roles of the husband as the provider and the wife as housekeeper who does the cleaning and cooking (Haynes, 2000). Gary, Beatty, and Price (1983) found that their middle-class Black subjects cited their family life as the source of most satisfaction, while the source of least satisfaction was their jobs. Hence, traditional family life remains the one viable option for

Black Americans of all socioeconomic strata because it is less subject to the vagaries of race than any other institution in American life.

Similarly, lower-income Blacks sustain traditional beliefs about marriage and the family because the many traumas experienced by this group have led to a stronger belief in the value of the family as a resource for their survival in a society not always hospitable to their aspirations. Other than the church, the family has been the only institution to serve as a vehicle for resisting racial discrimination and facilitating the movement toward social and economic equality. Another factor may be the continued physical and social isolation of Blacks, especially lower-income Blacks, from members of the majority group, who are in the forefront of social and cultural change. In any context of social change, there is a gap between the ideal statements of a culture and the reality in which people live out their lives—a time lag between the emergence of new cultural forms and their internalization by the individuals who must act on them. Thus, it would appear that Black family ideologies will change only as the social and economic isolation of Blacks diminishes.

In many ways, this situation is nothing new for the Black population. Social scientists continue to view the deterioration of the family as the problem, when in reality, the underpinnings of Black family structure are the structural conditions that prevent the fulfillment of Black family ideology. Given the political and economic trends, there is little reason to expect an abatement of these trends in the Black family. The problem of the Black family cannot be solved without resolving the economic predicament of Black men (Taylor, 2000). They are one and the same.

Best- and Worst-Case Scenarios

As we have seen at many points in this book, the future of the Black family is inextricably tied up with the current and future status of the Black male. If we look at Black male attitudes toward marriage, these findings may be a product of the employed Black man's reluctance to marry or the fact that college-educated men have greater access to prospective mates both within and outside the Black marriage market (Sassler and Schoen, 1999).

Unless unforeseen social forces reverse current trends, women are likely to achieve superiority over men in the vital areas of education, occupation, and income. Already, Black women are more educated than Black men at every level, including doctorates. The 1990 figures reveal that 20.7 percent of Black women are managers and professionals compared to 15.9 percent of Black men. In the year 2000, a slight increase occurred, with around 25 percent of employed Black American women over the age of sixteen holding managerial or professional jobs, such as engineers, dentists, teachers, and lawyers, compared to 18 percent of Black men (McKinnon, 2001). College-educated Black women earned approximately 85 percent of the income of college-educated Black men, up from 81 percent in 1995 and 75 percent in 1979 (Stockard and Tucker, 2001; Rowe and Jeffries, 1996). As Black women gradually gain ground, it is possible that a role reversal may take place. Since they will not need to marry a man to attain a decent standard of living, many of them may begin to select dating partners and husbands on the basis of sex appeal rather than the traditional criterion of socioeconomic status. Conversely, Black men may become the gender bartering their sexuality for a "good marriage" with a successful woman.

The shortage of Black men who are desirable and available for marriage will continue throughout the twenty-first century. Black women may adapt to their situation by a variety of means. Women bisexuals may increasingly turn to lesbianism as a viable option to meet their need for affection and companionship. Among the women who experience the greatest shortage of men, those over the age of sixty, a kind of gray lesbianism may emerge in response to the unavailability of men. In the college-educated segment of the Black female population, out-marriages to men of different races may become one of their adaptive responses to the male shortage. Some of them may seriously consider participating in polygamous relationships or liaisons with married men instead of remaining celibate and childless their entire lives (Scott, 1999).

For the vast majority of Black women, there will continue to be some involvement with Black men. Chances are that some will experience a monogamous marriage with or without children and that many will continue to be sexually active at an early age, to bear children out of wedlock, and to rear them with the assistance of a female-based kin network. These varying likely behaviors are reflected in the views of seventy Black single women enrolled in two urban universities (Porter and Bronzaft, 1995). Their future plans included Black men, but the potential personal trajectories varied. Only a few women were uncertain about their future plans relating to marriage, career, and family. Taking on the more traditional view, a small group desired to be full-time homemakers with children (2 percent). However, the majority wanted to be married, either in a dual-career marriage without children (10 percent) or with children (63 percent). Others made the purposeful decision to become a single mother (4 percent) or a single, career-oriented woman without children (11 percent). The common themes of domesticity or caregiving and working woman continue to be a part of the fabric of Black women's experiences (Harley, 1994). As seen in Porter and Bronzaft's study (1995), Black women will likely have varying periods of cohabitation with a man, and many will strive for legal marriage. However, given the uneven sex ratio and the socioeconomic state of Black Americans, marriage rates will continue to decline except in the case of Black men with a college education, the one subgroup in the Black community not plagued by low income, high rates of unemployment, and a shortage of compatible mates.

As for Black men, their employment chances will rise or fall with changes in the economy and other demographic changes in American society. If the economy continues its transformation from a goods-production to a service-dominated economy, Black men's participation rate in the labor force may decline, since the latter type of economy favors women. That will mean their continued dependence on the underground economy, cohabitation with a woman of some means, or living at home with their parents. One countervailing force could be the shortage of young workers that was predicted by the year 2010, when large numbers of the baby boom generation reach retirement age. Demographic projections were that by the year 2000, 40 percent of the school population graduating into the workforce would be Black (Ferleger and Mandle, 1991). If not Black, certainly minorities in general would be the source of increased numbers of minority high school graduates, a racial shift to be monitored for its actual impact on post–high school employment patterns. An indication of this shift is reflected in California, where the proportion of White public high school graduates decreased from 61 percent in 1985 to 47.2 percent in 1995 and is expected to drop to 39.4 percent by 2005 (California Postsecondary Education Commission, 1997).

Blacks must live with the reality that while a rising economic tide lifts all ships, their ship will come in last for the foreseeable future. Although Black workers made significant gains in the labor force in the previous four decades, their success has not closed the Black-White economic gap in America. They remain two to three times more disadvantaged in most economic areas. At best, Blacks kept pace with other workers during the rapid employment expansion (Anderson, 2002).

Without a doubt, Blacks will continue to find ways of rising to overcome the challenges of the marketplace. For example, Black college graduates who find poor job opportunities are flocking to graduate school to get a more competitive edge (enrollment nearly doubled since 1980). It appears that while Black college graduates no longer earn less than White high school graduates, at the postbaccalaureate level they have to be twice as credentialed to compete. This is evident by a higher percentage of White college students going directly into the workforce after receiving their college degree. A half-century ago, Black students were admonished by their elders that to make it in this world, they must finish high school. A generation ago, high school graduates were told that graduating from college would secure their future. Now the conventional wisdom is that in order to have the good life, they must earn a graduate or professional degree ("New Statistics on What Happens to Young Blacks," 1999). Black students can only hope that the outcome of this last pursuit does not shortchange their efforts.

A best-case scenario for Black families would be the election of an enlightened government that would provide the conditions for the strengthening of Black family life. First and foremost would be the implementation of a full employment policy. Hill (1999) suggests that tax credits that subsidize the exporting of American jobs abroad should be reversed so as to provide greater incentives for creating decent jobs at home. Others propose that full employment would require a substantial redistribution of income from the relatively affluent to the poor through a rigidly enforced system of progressive income taxation and the reduction of military expenditures to the bare minimum necessary to defend the country from an attack by foreign nations or terrorists. This would not mean the creation of a huge federal bureaucracy, since it would be necessary only to fund already existing projects and agencies such as highway construction, housing, education, the postal service, water conservation, public parks, child care, and the like. There is no reason to make it racially based, since Blacks would automatically share in the benefits of a full employment economy. Some government-financed training programs in community-based institutions would be necessary to develop and improve skills of some undereducated workers (Hill, 1999).

Another proposed governmental act would be the formulation of a family allowance or children's allowance plan, already in effect in most other Western nations (Hill, 1999; Kahn and Kamerman, 1983–1984). This family allowance should be set at the level most economists agree is a good standard of living, not the poverty level, which permits families to exist only at the lowest standard of misery. The allowance would be provided to all American families, reducing the stigma of current welfare programs, and the rigid system of progressive income tax rates would retrieve it from more affluent families. A family allowance plan would permit all families to have a decent income and to work out other difficulties in their relationships as best they can. While it will work to the advantage of most American families, it should benefit Black families most by lifting their ability to create and maintain a family from under the scourge of economic pressures.

Families will not be able to survive without proper health coverage. Although plans vary for comprehensive care, spending between $300 and $600 a month for a family of four appears normative. In comparison, $203 is the average monthly premium for a member of Congress with the Federal Employees Health Benefits health plan (U.S. Office of Personnel Management; Cypen, 2003; Thorpe, 2003)). Affordable and guaranteed health benefits are essential to reduce rates of infant mortality, low-birthweight babies, and poverty among the poor, working poor, and near-poor. If we are to have an effective response to the mental and physical health of Black families, we must target the areas in which they lag behind the general population. Hence, the treatment and research agenda of the National Institutes of Health and the Centers for Disease Control must give priority to addressing the etiological factors related to why, compared to Whites, the cancer rate for Blacks is 30 percent higher; infant mortality is three times higher among even highly educated mothers; and they are far less likely to receive advanced and intensive treatment, more likely to receive radical and severe treatments such as amputations, more likely to be misdiagnosed or diagnosed as having severe mental illnesses, three times more likely to have children hospitalized for asthma, and less likely to have children immunized for preventable childhood illnesses. Furthermore, cultural insensitivity often deters Black parents, elders, and children from seeking help. Thus, Black organizations need to partner with the health system to develop treatment protocols that integrate the development of cultural competence (Matthews, Menacker, and MacDorman, 2003; Neighbors, 1997;

Institute of Medicine, 2002). Also, additional government resources must be allocated for substance abuse and HIV/AIDS, which if unabated threatens to have escalating and devastating effects for not only the Black community, where it is seven times higher than in the general population, but the nation at large. To address these pervasive and complex problems, a targeted national program is needed. In January 2000, the Department of Health and Human Services launched Healthy People 2010, a comprehensive, nationwide health promotion and disease prevention agenda to improve the health of all people and to eliminate health disparities by the first decade in the twenty-first century.

The push by President Bush in 2002 to strengthen faith-based and community organizations by offering federal start-up funds for addressing drug abuse and compassion efforts at the grassroots level certainly fits within the natural self-help mechanisms already present in Black communities. There is a need for the government to coordinate its efforts with local organizations and for local organizations to coordinate their efforts with each other. Their joint efforts would be best served by giving priority to enhancing youth development in a way that is sensitive to cultural traditions and promotes positive racial identity (Hill, 1999). Furthermore, the efforts of successful entrepreneurs such as Kevin Johnson (former Suns NBA player) in restoring low-income depressed urban areas must be followed by others, a task that takes cooperation from multiple corners of our communities. Finally, the government alone cannot raise the disturbing trend of illiteracy, miseducation, and poor education. The case of the University of Michigan race-based admission policy controversy serves to highlight the need for grassroots vigilance of the color-blind policies that have both intended and unintended negative consequences for the education of our youth. While enhancing basic skills and academic achievement, guaranteeing universal health care, and family allowances may not drastically reduce the rate of female-headed households (as it is intricately linked to the uneven sex-ratio), they do promise to lift Black families and our country into a new era where the pursuit of health, happiness, and economic security is truly a matter of choice.

Summary

The challenges Black people face are essentially the same now as for the past century. Those problems are related not to family stability but to the socioeconomic conditions that tear families asunder. In general, the problems are poverty, income and wealth disparities, health, discrimination, and racism. While the past decade has produced a slight reduction in racial segregation and White stereotypes of Black inferiority, Blacks are still singled out for discriminatory treatment in every sphere of American life—in terms of home ownership, resources, and access and treatment in social welfare programs. Moreover, although Whites are in agreement about the racial discrimination Blacks are subjected to, any national effort to remedy these practices has a low priority among White Americans.

Low socioeconomic status continues to plague many Black families. Educational attainment does not result in equal outcomes: Blacks continue to have lower incomes than whites with similar educational backgrounds. Whereas some Blacks have achieved a higher standard of living as a result of the civil rights movement, large numbers of Blacks continue to live below the poverty level. A disproportionate number of these Blacks are female heads of families. They have more responsibilities and less income than any other group in American society. Yet no effective programs are being proposed to meet the needs of one-half of all Black families.

Making futuristic predictions about the nature of any group's family life is a risky endeavor. Few, for instance, could have projected what has happened to the American family as a whole in the past forty years. Of course, there were trends leading us in certain directions, but it was the acceleration of those trends that caught many by surprise. In the case of the Black family, the research literature is still so sparse and biased that we have practically no attempts to analyze Black families of the future or alternative family lifestyles. But certain barometers of the future can be seen in the light of the existing social conditions for Blacks as well as in terms of the trends in sexual behavior, fertility patterns, gender-role changes, and marital adjustments.

Some adaptations to alternative lifestyles will occur because large numbers of Blacks, especially the middle class, are taking on the values of the majority culture. However, Blacks as a group will continue to face certain problems that may not be unique to them except to the extent of their prevalence. The continuing high unemployment rate among Black men and women will still have serious ramifications for the kind of family life they will have. That will primarily be a problem of the lower-income group, but all classes will have to adapt to the increasingly critical problem of a male shortage and the consequences of it.

So far, the problem of the male shortage has been handled by a type of serial polygyny, where Black men have more than one wife in a lifetime but not at the same time. Some men remain married but are free floating in their relations with other women. Sharing of males may be necessary for a group with such an imbalanced sex ratio. However, it gives rise to many conflicts between men and women, who are strongly socialized into monogamous values. The instability of many Black marriages can be accounted for by this factor, as well as by the general range of forces that cause marital disruption. In the future, alternative family lifestyles should be well thought out and implemented in a way conducive to individual and group harmony.

It is difficult to project the future of Black families, because there are several parallel trends. Many Blacks are entering the middle class as a result of higher education and increased opportunities. At the same time, the future is dim for Blacks in the underclass. Automation is rendering obsolete the labor of unskilled Black men, who are in danger of becoming a permanent army of the unemployed. The status of Black women is in a state of flux: some welcome the liberation from male control, while others urge a regeneration of Black male leadership. Whatever the future of Black families, it is time to put to rest all the theories about Black family instability and give recognition to the crucial role of this institution in the Black struggle for survival.

Selected Readings

Berlin, I. (1998). *Many thousands gone: The first two centuries of slavery in North America*. Cambridge, MA: Harvard University Press.

Berlin, I. (2003). *Generations of captivity: A History of African-American slaves*. Cambridge, MA: Harvard University Press.

Berlin, I., & Rowland, L. (Eds.). (1997). *Families and freedom: A documentary history of African American kinship in the Civil War era*. New York: New Press.

Billingsley, A. (1999). *Mighty like a river: The Black church and social reform*. New York: Oxford University Press.

Cochran, D. L. (1997). African American fathers: A decade review of the literature. *Families in Society: The Journal of Contemporary Human Services, 78*(4), 340–350.

Dickerson, B. (Ed.). (1994). *African-American single mothers*. Thousand Oaks, CA: Sage.

Franklin, D. L. (1997). *Ensuring inequality: The structural transformation of the African-American family*. New York: Oxford University Press.

Gopaul-McNicol, S. A. (1993). *Working with West Indian families*. New York: Guilford Press.

Hampton, R. L. (Ed.). (1991). *Black family violence: Current research and theory*. San Francisco: New Lexington Press.

Hill, R. B. (1999). *The strengths of African American families: Twenty-five years later*. Lanham, MD: University Press of America.

Laumann, E. O., Michael, R. T., Gagnon, J. H., & Michaels, S. (1994). *The social organization of sexuality: Sexual practices in the USA*. Chicago: University of Chicago Press.

Lemelle, A. J. (1995). *Black male deviance*. Westport, CT: Praeger.

Malone, A. P. (1992). *Sweet chariot: Slave family and household structure in nineteenth century Louisiana*. Chapel Hill: University of North Carolina Press.

McAdoo, H. P. (1997). (Ed.). *Black families* (3rd ed.). Thousand Oaks, CA: Sage.

McCubbin, H., Thompson, E. A., Thompson, A. I., & Fromer, J. E. (1998). (Eds.). *Resiliency in African American families*. Thousand Oaks, CA: Sage.

McLoyd, V. C., Cauce, A. M., Takeuchi, D., & Wilson, L. (2001). Marital processes and parental socialization in families of color: A decade review of research. In R. M. Milardo, (Ed.), *Understanding families into the new millennium: A decade in review* (pp. 289–312). Minneapolis, MN: National Council on Family Relations.

Russell, K., Wilson, M., & Hall, (1992). *The color complex: The politics of skin color among African Americans*. New York: Doubleday Anchor.

Schwartz, J. M. (2000). *Born in bondage: Growing up enslaved in the antebellum South*. Cambridge, MA: Harvard University Press.

Staples, R. E. (Ed.). *Black families: essays and studies* (6th ed.). Belmont, CA: Wadsworth Press.

Stevenson, B. (1996). *Life in Black and White: Family and community in the slave South*. New York: Oxford University Press.

Taylor, R. J., Chatter, L. M., & Jackson, J. S. (Eds.). (1997). *Family life in Black America*. Thousand Oaks, CA: Sage.

Tucker, M. B., & Mitchelle-Kernan, C. (Eds.). *The decline in marriage among African-Americans: Causes, consequences and policy implications*. New York: Russell Sage Foundation.

Walters, M. C. (1999). *Black identities: West Indian immigrant dreams and American realities*. Cambridge, MA: Harvard University Press.

Willie, C. V., & Reddick, R. (2003). *A new look at Black families*. Walnut Creek, CA: AltaMira Press.

Wyatt, G. E. (1997). *Stolen women: Reclaiming our sexuality, taking back our lives*. New York: Wiley.

Young, G., & Dickerson, B. (Eds.). *Color, class and country: Experiences of gender* (pp. 112–127). London: Zed Books.

References

Absug, R. H. (1971). The Black family during reconstruction. In N. I. Huggins, M. Kilson, & D. M. Fox (Eds.), *Key issues in the Afro-American experience* (Vol. 2, pp. 26–41). Orlando, FL: Harcourt.

Adams, P. L., Milner, J. R., & Schrepf, N. A. (1984). *Fatherless children*. New York: Wiley.

Adams, V. H., & Nelson, J. (2001). Hope, happiness, and African American fathers: Changes between 1980 and 1992. *African American Research Perspectives, 7,* 148–156.

Addison, D. P. (1983). Black wives: Perspectives about their husbands and themselves. In C. E. Obudho (Ed.), *Black marriage and family therapy.* Westport, CT: Greenwood Press.

African wedding traditions and marriages. (2004, May 26). Umea, Sweden: Umea University. Available on-line: http://www.eng.umu.se/vw/Culture/African%20weddings.htm.

Aldous, J. (1969). Wives' employment status and lower-class men as husband-fathers: Support for the Moynihan thesis. *Journal of Marriage and the Family, 31,* 469–476.

Aldridge, D. (1978). Interracial marriages: Empirical and theoretical considerations. *Journal of Black Studies, 3,* 355–367.

Ali, S. (1989). *The Blackman's guide to understanding the Blackwoman.* Philadelphia: Civilized Publications.

Allen, W. R. (1978). The search for applicable theories of Black family life. *Journal of Marriage and the Family, 40,* 117–130.

Allen, W. R. (1981). Moms, dads, and boys: Race and sex differences in the socialization of male children. In L. E. Gary (Ed.), *Black men.* Thousand Oaks, CA: Sage.

Allen, W. R. (1995). African American family life in societal context: Crisis and hope. *Sociological Forum, 10,* 569–592.

Alvy, K. T. (1987). *Black parenting: Strategies for training.* New York: Irvington.

Amato, P., & Booth, A. (1997). *A generation at risk.* Cambridge, MA: Harvard University Press.

Ambrosio, T., & Schiraldi, V. (1997). *From the classrooms to cell blocks: A national perspective.* Washington, DC: Justice Policy Institute.

Anderson, B. E. (2002). The Black worker: Continuing quest for economic parity. In L. Daniels (Ed.), *The state of Black America 2002* (pp. 51–67). Washington, DC: National Urban League.

Anderson, E. (1989). Sex codes and family life among poor inner city youths. *Annals of the American Academy of Political and Social Science, 501,* 59–78.

Apfel, N. H., & Seitz, V. (1991). Four models of adolescent mother-grandmother relationships in Black inner-city families. *Family Relations, 40,* 421–429.

Asante, M. (1987). *The Afrocentric idea.* Philadelphia: Temple University Press.

Asbury, J. (1999). What do we know now about spouse abuse and child sexual abuse in families of color in the United States? In R. L. Hampton (Ed.), *Family violence: Prevention and treatment* (2nd ed., pp. 148–167). Thousand Oaks, CA: Sage.

Atkins, E. (1991, June 5). For many mixed-race Americans life isn't simply Black or White. *New York Times,* p. B8.

Awkward, M. (1999). A Black man's place in Black feminist criticism. In D. W. Carbados (Ed.), *Black men on race, gender, and sexuality: A critical reader* (pp. 362–382). New York: New York University Press.

Azibo, D.A.Y. (1983). Perceived attractiveness and the Black personality. *Western Journal of Black Studies, 7,* 229–238.

Bachrach, C. A. (1986). Adoption plans, adopted children, and adoptive mothers. *Journal of Marriage and the Family, 48,* 243–253.

Baldwin, J. A. (1979). Theory and research concerning the notion of Black self-hatred: A review and reinterpretation. *Journal of Black Psychology, 5,* 51–77.

Baldwin, R. O. (1987). Femininity-masculinity of Blacks and Whites over a fourteen-year period. *Psychological Reports, 60,* 455–458.

Ball, R. E., & Robbins, L. R. (1986). Marital status and life satisfaction among Black Americans. *Journal of Marriage and the Family, 48,* 389–394.

Balthazar, M. L., & King, L. (2001). The loss of the protective effects of relationships of incarcerated African American men: Implications for social work. *African American Men, 6,* 31–41.

Bane, M. J., & Jargowsky, P. (1988). The links between government policy and family structure: What matters and what doesn't. In A. Cheslin (Ed.), *The changing American family and public policy*. Washington, DC: Urban Institute.

Baratz, S. S., & Baratz, J. C. (1970). Early childhood intervention: The social science base of institutional racism. *Harvard Educational Review, 40*, 29–50.

Bartholet, E. (1999). *Nobody's children: Abuse and neglect, foster drift, and the adoption alternative*. Boston: Beacon Press.

Bass, B. A. (1982). Interracial dating and marital relationships: A lecture. In B. A. Bass, G. E. Wyatt, & G. J. Powell (Eds.), *The Afro-American family: Assessment, treatment, and research issues*. Philadelphia: Grune & Stratton.

Battle, J., & Scott, B. M. (2000). Mother-only versus father-only households: Educational outcomes for African American males. *Journal of African American Men, 5*, 93–116.

Bauman, C. D. (1967). Relationship between age at first marriage, school dropout, and marital instability: An analysis of the Glick effect. *Journal of Marriage and the Family, 29*, 672–680.

Baumrind, D. (1996). The discipline controversy revisited. *Family Relations, 45*, 405–414.

Beckett, J. O., & Smith, A. D. (1981). Work and family roles: Egalitarian marriage in Black and White families. *Social Service Review, 55*, 314–325.

Belcastro, P. A. (1985). Sexual behavior differences between Black and White students. *Journal of Sex Research, 21*, 56–67.

Bell, A. P. (1978). Black sexuality: Fact and fantasy. In R. Staples (Ed.), *The Black family: Essays and studies* (2nd ed.). Belmont, CA: Wadsworth.

Bell, A. P., & Weinberg, M. (1978). *Homosexualities*. New York: Simon & Schuster.

Bell, D. (1999). The sexual diversion: The Black man/Black woman debate in context. In D. W. Carbado (Ed.), *Black men on race, gender, and sexuality* (pp. 237–247). New York: New York University Press.

Bell, N., & Vogel, E. (1968). *A modern introduction to the family*. New York: Free Press.

Bell, R. (1970). Comparative attitudes about marital sex among Negro women in the U.S., Great Britain, and Trinidad. *Journal of Comparative Family Studies, 1*, 71–81.

Bell, R. (1971). The related importance of mother-wife roles among lower-class women. In R. Staples (Ed.), *The Black family: Essays and studies*. Belmont, CA: Wadsworth.

Bell-Scott, P. (Ed.). (1991). *Double stitch: Black women write about mothers and daughters*. Boston: Beacon Press.

Benjamin, L. (1983). The dog theory: Black male/female conflict. *Western Journal of Black Studies, 7,* 49–55.

Bennett, L. (1981). Roots of Black love. *Ebony, 36,* 31–36.

Bennett, L. Jr. (2002, October). Music: Has it gone too far? *Ebony* vol. LVII (12), 146–147, 150.

Berlin, I. (1998). *Many thousands gone: The first two centuries of slavery in North America.* Cambridge, MA: Harvard University Press.

Berlin, I. (2003). *Generations of captivity: A history of African-American slaves.* Cambridge, MA: Harvard University Press.

Berlin, I., & Rowland, L. (Eds.). (1997). *Families and freedom: A documentary history of African American kinship in the Civil War era.* New York: New Press.

Bernard, J. (1966). *Marriage and family among Negroes.* Upper Saddle River, NJ: Prentice-Hall.

Berry, M. F., & Blassingame, J. (1982). *Long memory: The Black experience in America.* New York: Oxford University Press.

Berry, N., Corbin, M., Hellman, C., Mason, C., Smith, D., Stohl, R., & Valasek, T. (2001–2002). *2001–2002 military almanac.* Available on-line: http://www.cdi.org/products/almanac0102.pdf.

Bibb, H. (1849). *Narrative of the life and adventures of Henry Bibb, an American slave.* Salem, NH: Ayer.

Biblarz, T. J., & Raftery, A. E. (1999). Family structure, educational attainment, and socioeconomic success: Rethinking the pathology of matriarchy. *American Journal of Sociology, 10,* 321–365.

Billingsley, A. (1968). *Black families in White America.* Upper Saddle River, NJ: Prentice-Hall.

Billingsley, A. (1990). Understanding African-American family diversity. In J. Dewart (Ed.), *The state of Black America 1990.* New York: National Urban League.

Billingsley, A. (1992). *Climbing Jacob's ladder: The enduring legacy of African American families.* New York: Simon & Schuster.

Billingsley, A., & Giovannoni, J. M. (1972). *Children of the storm: Black children and American child welfare.* Orlando, FL: Harcourt.

Billy, J.O.G., & Udry, J. R. (1985). The influence of male and female friends on adolescent sexual behavior. *Adolescence, 20,* 21–32.

Binion, V. J. (1990). Psychological androgyny: A Black female perspective. *Sex Roles, 22*(7/8), 487–507.

Binson, D., Stall, R., Coates, T. C., Gagnon, J. H., & Catania, J. A. (1995). Prevalence and social distribution of men who have sex with men: United States and its urban centers. *Journal of Sex Research, 32,* 245–254.

The Black male shortage. (1986). *Ebony* [special issue], pp. 22–25.

The Black sexism debate. (1979). *Black Scholar, 10*, 1–96.

Blacks' fresh trials. (1978, May 15). *Newsweek*, p. 77.

Blassingame, J. (1972). *The slave community.* New York: Oxford University Press.

Blau, P. (1964). *Exchange and power in social life.* New York: Wiley.

Blauner, R. (1972). *Racial oppression in America.* New York: HarperCollins.

Blood, R. O., & Wolfe, D. M. (1960). *Husbands and wives: The dynamics of married living.* New York: Free Press.

Blumstein, A., & Beck, A. J. (1999). Population growth in U.S. prisons, 1980–1996. In M. Tonry & J. Petersilia (Eds.), *Prisons, crime and justice.* Chicago: University of Chicago Press.

Bohlen, C. (1989, April 9). Number of women in jail surges with drug sales. *New York Times*, p. A1.

Booth, A. (Ed.). (1991). *Contemporary families: Looking forward, looking back.* Minneapolis, MN: National Council on Family Relations.

Bowman, P. (1991). Work life. In J. S. Jackson (Ed.), *Life in Black America* (pp. 124–155). Thousand Oaks, CA: Sage.

Bowman, P. J. (1985). Black fathers and the provider role: Role strain, informal coping resources, and life happiness. In W. Boykin (Ed.), *The Seventh Conference on Empirical Research on Black Psychology.* Rockville, MD: National Institute of Mental Health.

Bowman, P. J. (1989). Research perspectives on Black men: Role strain and adaptation across the adult life cycle. In R. L. Jones (Ed.), *Black Adult Development and Aging.* Berkeley, CA: Cobb and Henry.

Bradley, C. (2000). The disciplinary practices of African American fathers: A closer look. *Journal of African American Men, 5*, 43–55.

Bramlett, M. D., & Mosher, W. D. (2002). Cohabitation, marriage, divorce, and remarriage in the U.S. In *Vital and Health Statistics* (series 23, no. 22). Hyattsville, MD: National Center for Health Statistics.

Brien, M. J. (1997). Racial differences in marriage and the role of marriage markets. *Journal of Human Resources, 32*, 741–778.

Brock, R. (1991). Future of mom and pop businesses in the Black community. *Crisis, 98*(5), 10–12, 14.

Brody, G. H., Flor, D. L., & Gibson, N. M. (1999). Linking maternal efficacy beliefs, developmental goals, parenting practices, and child competence in rural single-parent African American families. *Child Development, 70*, 1197–1208.

Broman, C. L. (1988). Household work and family life satisfaction of Blacks. *Journal of Marriage and the Family, 50*, 743–748.

Broman, C. L. (1991). Gender, work-family roles, and psychological well-being of Blacks. *Journal of Marriage and the Family, 53,* 509–519.

Brouwer, M. G. (1975, July). Marriage and family life among Blacks in colonial Pennsylvania. *Pennsylvania Magazine of History and Biography,* pp. 368–372.

Brown, D. R., & Mars, J. (2000). Profile of contemporary grandparenting in African American families. In C. B. Cox (Ed.), *To grandmother's house we go and stay: Perspective on custodial grandparents* (pp. 203–217). New York: Springer.

Brown, D. R., McGregor, K. C., & Gary, L. E. (1998). Sex role identity and depressive symptoms among African American men. *African American Research Perspectives, 4,* 77–82.

Brown, I. C. (1949). *Race relations in a democracy.* New York: HarperCollins.

Brown, L., Wolf, F. C., Starke, L., & Jacobson, J. (1986). *State of the world 1986.* Washington, DC: Worldwatch Institute.

Brown, T. N. (2001). Exposure to all Black contexts and psychological well-being: The benefits of racial concentration. *African American Research Perspectives, 7,* 157–171.

Browning, S. L., Miller, R. R., & Spruance, L. M. (2001). Criminal incarceration dividing the ties that bind: Black men and their families. *African American Men, 6*(1), 87–102.

Bullock, A., & Stallybrass, O. (Eds.). (1977). *The Harper dictionary of modern thought.* New York: HarperCollins.

Bumpass, L. L., Sweet, J. L., & Martin, T. C. (1990). Changing patterns of remarriage. *Journal of Marriage and the Family, 52,* 747–756.

Burgess, N. J. (1994). Gender roles revisited: The development of the woman's place among African American women in the United States. *Journal of Black Studies, 24,* 391–401.

Burgest, D. R. (1991). Sexual games in Black male-female relationships. *Journal of Black Studies, 22,* 645–656.

Burgest, D. R., & Goosby, M. (1985). Games in Black male/female relationships. *Journal of Black Studies, 15,* 277–290.

Burton, L. (1992). Black grandparents rearing children of drug-addicted parents: Stressors, outcomes, and social service needs. *Gerontologist, 32,* 744–751.

Burton, L. M., & Bengtson, V. L. (1985). Black grandmothers: Issues of timing and continuity. In V. L. Bengtson & J. F. Robertson (Eds.), *Grandparenthood: Research and policy perspectives.* Thousand Oaks, CA: Sage.

Butler, J. S. (2002). Military organizations: Best practices and the status of Black Americans. In *The state of Black America 2002* (pp. 93–101). Washington, DC: National Urban League.

Bynoe, Y. (2001). The roots of rap music and hip hop culture: One perspective. In *The state of Black America 2001*. Washington, DC: National Urban League.

Cade, T. (1970). *The Black woman: An anthology*. New York: Signet.

Cadwallader, M. (1966, November). Marriage as a wretched institution. *Atlantic Monthly*. Available on-line: http://www.theatlantic.com/issues/66nov/cadwallader.htm.

California Postsecondary Education Commission. (1997, April). *California's changing demography: More faces, new faces*. Sacramento: State of California.

Campolo, T., & Campolo, B. (1989). *Things we wish we had said: Reflections of a father and his grown son*. Dallas: World.

Canady, H. (1984, March 19). Words of the week. *Jet Magazine*, p. 40.

Cantave, C., & Harrison, R. (2001, October). Marriage and African Americans. Joint Center Data Bank. Available on-line: http://www.jointcenter.org/DB/factsheet.

Carnegie Council. (1977). *All our children*. Orlando, FL: Harcourt.

Carson, B. (1990). *Gifted hands: The Ben Carson story*. Washington, DC: Review and Herald.

Cash, I. F., & Duncan, N. C. (1984). Physical attractiveness stereotyping among Black American college students. *Journal of Social Psychology, 122*, 71–77.

Cazenave, N. (1979). Middle income Black fathers: An analysis of the provider's role. *Family Coordinator, 28*, 583–593.

Cazenave, N. (1981). Black men in America: The quest for manhood. In H. P. McAdoo (Ed.), *Black families*. Thousand Oaks, CA: Sage.

Cazenave, N. (1983). Black male-female relationships: The perceptions of 155 middle-class Black men. *Family Relations, 32*, 341–350.

Cazenave, N., & Smith, R. (1990). Gender differences in the perception of Black male-female relationships and stereotypes. In H. E. Cheatham & J. B. Stewart (Eds.), *Black families: Interdisciplinary perspectives*. New Brunswick, NJ: Transaction.

Cazenave, N., & Straus, M. (1979). Race, class, network embeddedness, and family violence: A search for potent support systems. *Journal of Comparative Family Studies, 10*, 281–299.

Center for the Study of Social Policy. (1999). World without work: Causes and consequences of Black male joblessness. In R. Staples (Ed.), *The Black family: Essays and studies* (6th ed.) (pp. 291–311). Belmont, CA: Wadsworth.

Centers for Disease Control and Prevention. (1991). *HIV/AIDS surveillance report*. Atlanta, GA: Author.

Centers for Disease Control and Prevention. (2001). *HIV/AIDS surveillance report* vol.13(2). Atlanta: Author.

Charles, K. K., & Hurst, E. (2002). The transition to home ownership and the Black-White wealth gap. *Review of Economics and Statistics, 84*, 281–297.

Chatters, L. M., & Taylor, R. J. (1998). Religious involvement among African Americans. *African American Research Perspectives, 4*, 83–93.

Chavis, W. M., & Lyles, G. (1975). Divorce among educated Black women. *Journal of the National Medical Association, 67*, 128–134.

Child Trend. (2003, November). *Facts at a Glance*. Washington, DC: Author.

Child Trends DataBank. (2002). *Children in poverty*. Available on-line: http://www.childtrendsdatabank.org/indicators/4Poverty.cfm.

Child Trends DataBank. (2004). *Life expectancy*. Available on-line: http://www.childtrendsdatabank.org/indicators/ 78LifeExpectancy.cfm.

Children's Defense Fund. (2003). *Where America stands*. Washington, DC: Author.

Christensen, H. T., & Johnson, L. B. (1978). Premarital coitus and the Southern Black: A comparative view. *Journal of Marriage and the Family, 40*, 721–732.

Christman, K. (1990). Parental responsibility and self-image of African American fathers. *Families in Society: The Journal of Contemporary Human Services, 71*, 563–567.

Churchill, N. (1995). Ending welfare as we know it: A case study in urban anthropology and public policy. *Urban Anthropology and Studies in Cultural Systems and World Economic Development, 24*, 5–35.

Ciarrocca, M., & Hartung, W. D. (2002). Increases in military spending and security since 9/11. Available on-line: http://www.worldpolicy.org/ projects/arms/news/SpendingDOD911.html.

Clark, K. B., & Clark, M. P. (1950). Emotional factors in racial identification and preference in Negro children. *Journal of Negro Education, 19*, 341–350.

Clark, K. B., & Clark, M. P. (1958). Racial identification and preference in Negro children. In E. E. Maccoby, T. M. Newcomb, & E. L. Hartley (Eds.), *Readings in social psychology* (3rd ed.). Troy, MO: Holt.

Clark, M. L. (1982). Racial group concept and self-esteem in Black children. *Journal of Black Psychology, 3*, 75–88.

Clark, R. M. (1983). *Family life and school achievement: Why poor Black children succeed or fail*. Chicago: University of Chicago Press.

Clark, T. (2001). The relationship between inmate visitation and behavior: Implications for African American families. *Journal of African American Men, 6*, 43–58.

Cleaver, E. (1968). *Soul on ice*. New York: McGraw-Hill.

Cochran, D. L. (1997). African American fathers: A decade review of the literature. *Families in Society: The Journal of Contemporary Human Services, 78*, 340–350.

Cochran, S. D., & Mays, V. M. (1999). Sociocultural facets of the Black gay male experience. In R. Staples (Ed.), *The Black family: Essays and studies* (6th ed.) (pp. 349–355), Belmont, CA: Wadsworth.

Coleman, L. M., Antonucci, T. C., Adelmann, P. K., & Crohan, S. E. (1987). Social roles in the lives of middle-aged and older Black women. *Journal of Marriage and the Family, 49,* 761–771.

Coles, R. (2001). African American single full-time fathers: How are they doing? *Journal of African American Men, 6,* 63–82.

Coley, R. L. (2003). Daughter-father relationships and adolescent psychosocial functioning in low-income African American families. *Journal of Marriage and the Family, 65,* 867–875.

Collins, L. V. (1996, February 5). Facts from the Census Bureau for Black History Month. Available on-line: http://www.census.gov/Press-Release/blkhis1.html.

Collins, P. H. (1986). The Afro-American work/family nexus: An exploratory analysis. *Western Journal of Black Studies, 10,* 148–158.

Collins, P. H. (1990). *Black feminist thought: Knowledge, consciousness, and the politics of empowerment.* Boston: Unwin Hyman.

Collins, P. H. (1999). The meaning of motherhood in Black culture. In R. Staples, *The Black family: Essays and studies* (6th ed.). Belmont, CA: Wadsworth.

Combahee River Collective. (1982). A Black feminist statement. In G. T. Hull, P. B. Scott, & B. Smith (Eds.), *But some of us are brave: Black women's studies.* Old Westbury, NY: Feminist Press.

Commission on Civil Rights. (1982). *Unemployment and underemployment among Blacks, Hispanics, and women.* Washington, DC: U.S. Government Printing Office.

Commission on Civil Rights. (1991). Disadvantaged women and their children. In R. Staples (Ed.), *The Black family: Essays and studies* (4th ed.). Belmont, CA: Wadsworth.

Cone, J. H. (1991). *Martin and Malcolm in America.* New York: Orbis.

Conner, M. E. (1988). Teenage fatherhood: Issues confronting young Black males. In J. T. Gibbs (Ed.), *Young, Black, and male in America: An endangered species.* New York: Auburn House.

Cooley, C. H. (1922). *Human nature and the social order* (rev. ed.). New York: Scribner.

Cooper, M. H. (1998). Income inequality. *Congressional Quarterly Researcher, 8,* 337–360.

Coughlin, E. K. (1987, October 2). Scholars work to refine Africa-centered view of the life and history of Black Americans. *Chronicle of Higher Education,* p. A10.

Cox, C. B. (Ed.). (2000). *To grandmother's house we go and stay: Perspectives on custodial grandparents*. New York: Springer.

Cremation Association of North America. (2004). Expectation of life at birth and at specified ages. Available on-line: http://www.cremationassociation .org/docs/life_expectancy.pdf.

Crosby, J. F. (1991). *Illusion and disillusion: The self in love and marriage* (4th ed.). Belmont, CA: Wadsworth.

Crowder, K. D., & Tolnay, S. E. (2000). A new marriage squeeze for Black women: The role of racial intermarriage by Black men. *Journal of Marriage and the Family, 62,* 192–207.

Currence, P., & Johnson, W. E., Jr. (2003). The negative implications of incarceration on Black fathers. *African American Research Perspectives, 9,* 24–32.

Cypen, S. H. (Ed.). (2003, July 10). Cypen & Cypen newsletter: *What health benefits do members of Congress receive?* Available on-line: http://www.cypen .com/pubs/2003july10.htm.

Daley, S. (1991, January 9). Girls' self-esteem is lost on way to adolescence: New study finds. *New York Times,* p. B1.

Daniel, J. H., Hampton, R. L., & Newberger, M. D. (1983). Child abuse and accidents in Black families: A controlled comparative study. *American Journal of Orthopsychiatry, 53,* 649–653.

Darity, W. A., Jr., & Myers, S. L., Jr. (1984). Does welfare dependency cause female headship? The case of the Black family. *Journal of Marriage and the Family, 46,* 765–779.

Davis, A. (1971). Reflections on the Black woman's role in the community of slaves. *Black Scholar, 2,* 2–16

Davis, A. (1983). *Women, race, and class*. New York: Random House.

Davis, A. (1989). *Women, culture, and politics*. New York: Random House.

Davis, A., & Davis, F. (1986). The Black family and the crisis of capitalism. *Black Scholar, 17,* 33–40.

Davis, L. G. (1990). Trends in themes of African American family research 1939–1989: A synopsis. *Western Journal of Black Studies, 14*(4), 191–195.

DeJarnett, S., & Raven, B. H. (1981). The balance, bases, and modes of interpersonal power in Black couples: The role of sex and socioeconomic circumstances. *Journal of Black Psychology, 7,* 51–66.

D'Emilio, J., & Freedman, E. (1988). *Intimate matters: A history of sexuality in America*. New York: HarperCollins.

Demos, V. (1990). Black family studies in the *Journal of Marriage and the Family* and the issue of distortion: A trend analysis. *Journal of Marriage and the Family, 52,* 603–612.

Dewart, J. (Ed.). (1991). *The state of Black America 1991*. New York: National Urban League.

Diallo, Y. D., & Hall, M. (1989). *The healing drum: African wisdom teachings*. Rochester, VT: Destiny Books.

Dickinson, G. E. (1978). Dating behavior of Black and White adolescents before and after desegregation. In R. Staples (Ed.), *The Black family: Essays and studies* (2nd ed.). Belmont, CA: Wadsworth.

Dilworth-Anderson, P., Johnson, L. B., & Burton, L. M. (1992). Reframing theories for understanding race, ethnicity, and families. In P. Boss, W. J. Doherty, R. LaRossa, W. R. Schumm, & S. K. Steinmetz (Eds.), *Sourcebook of family theories and methods: A contextual approach*. New York: Plenum.

Diop, C. A. (1987). *Precolonial Black Africa: A comparative study of the political and social systems of Europe and Black Africa*. Trenton, NJ: Africa World.

Dolcini, M. M., Coates, T. J., Catania, J. A., Kegeles, S. M., & Hauck, W. W. (1995). Multiple sexual partners and their psychosocial correlates: The population-based AIDS in multiethnic neighborhoods. *Health Psychology, 14*, 22–31.

Dollard, J. (1957). *Caste and class in the southern town*. New York: Doubleday.

Donloe, D. C. (1987, January 22). Interracial center fills a need for racially mixed. *Los Angeles Sentinel*, p. A5.

Dotinga, R. (2004). *One third of new HIV cases are heterosexual, Feds report*. *ScoutNews*, February 19. Available on-line: http://www.keepmedia.com:/Register.do?oliID=225.

Douglass, K. B. (1999). *Sexuality and the Black church*. New York: Orbis Books.

Draughn, P. S. (1984). Perceptions of competence in work and marriage of middle-age men. *Journal of Marriage and the Family, 46*, 403–409.

Du Bois, W.E.B. (1898). *Some efforts of the American Negroes for their own betterment*. Atlanta: Atlanta University Press.

Du Bois, W.E.B. (1908). *The Negro American family*. Atlanta, GA: Atlanta University Press.

duCille, A. (1990). "Othered" matters: Reconceptualizing dominance and difference in the history of sexuality in America. *Journal of the History of Sexuality, 1*, 102–127.

Durkheim, E. (1951). *Suicide: A Study in Sociology* (A. Spaulding & G. Simpson, Trans.). New York: Free Press. (Original work published 1897).

Edelman, M. V. (1986, August). Save the children. *Ebony*, pp. 53–54, 58–59.

Edelman, M. W. (1988). An advocacy agenda for Black families and children. In H. P. McAdoo (Ed.), *Black families* (2nd ed.). Thousand Oaks, CA: Sage.

Elkins, S. (1968). *Slavery: A problem in American institutional and intellectual life.* Chicago: University of Chicago Press.

Employers prefer Whites, study says. (1991, May 15). *San Francisco Chronicle,* p. A2.

Engels, F. (1950). *Conditions of the working class in England in 1944.* New York: Oxford University Press.

Engram, E. (1982). *Science, myth, reality: The Black family in one-half century of research.* Westport, CT: Greenwood Press.

Ernst, F. A., Francis, R., Nevels, H., & Lemeh, C. A. (1991). Condemnation of homosexuality in the Black community: A gender-specific phenomenon? *Archives of Sexual Behavior, 20,* 579–585.

Escott, P. D. (1979). *Slavery remembered: A record of twentieth-century slave narratives.* Chapel Hill: University of North Carolina Press.

Farber, B. (1964). *Family organization and interaction.* San Francisco: Chandler.

Farley, R., & Allen, W. (1987). *The color line and the quality of life in America.* New York: Russell Sage Foundation.

Fatimilehin, I. A. (1999). Of jewel heritage: Racial socialization and racial identity attitudes amongst adolescents of mixed African-Caribbean/White parentage. *Journal of Adolescence, 22,* 303–318.

Fears, D. (2004, February 4). Draft bill stirs debate over the military, race and equality. *Washington Post,* p. A3.

Ferleger, L., & Mandle, J. R. (1991). African Americans and the future of the U.S. economy. *Trotter Institute Review, 5,* 3–7.

Festinger, L. (1957). *A theory of cognitive dissonance.* New York: HarperCollins.

Firebaugh, G., & Harley, B. (1995). Trends in job satisfaction in the United States by race, gender, and type of occupation. *Research in Sociology Work, 5,* 87–104.

Fogel, R. S., & Engerman, S. (1974). *Time on the cross: The economics of American Negro slavery.* New York: Little, Brown.

Foley, V. D. (1975). Family therapy with Black, disadvantaged families: Some observations on roles, communication, and technique. *Journal of Marriage and the Family, 37,* 29–38.

Fordham, M. (1975). *Major themes in northern Black religious thought, 1800–1860.* Hicksville, NY: Exposition Press.

Foster, H. (1983). African patterns in the Afro-American family. *Journal of Black Studies, 14,* 201–232.

Fox, G. L., & Inazu, J. K. (1980). Mother-daughter communication about sex. *Family Relations, 29*(3), 347–352.

Franklin, C. W. (1984). Black male–Black female conflict: Individually caused and culturally nurtured. *Journal of Black Studies, 15,* 139–154.

Franklin, C. W. (1986). Conceptual and logical issues in theory and research related to Black masculinity. *Western Journal of Black Studies, 10,* 161–166.

Franklin, C. W. (1987). Surviving the institutional decimation of Black males: Causes, consequences, and intervention. In H. Brod (Ed.), *The making of masculinities*. London: Allen & Unwin.

Franklin, D. (1988). The impact of early childbearing on developmental outcomes: The case of Black adolescent parenting. *Family Relations, 37,* 268–274.

Franklin, J. H. (1974). *From slavery to freedom: The history of Negro Americans* (4th ed.). New York: Knopf.

Franklin, J. H. (1987). *From slavery to freedom: The history of Negro Americans* (6th ed.). New York: Knopf.

Franklin, J. H. (1988). A historical note on Black families. In H. P. McAdoo (Ed.), *Black families* (2nd ed.). Thousand Oaks, CA: Sage.

Frazier, E. F. (1932a). *The free Negro family*. Nashville, TN: Fisk University Press.

Frazier, E. F. (1932b). *The Negro family in Chicago*. Chicago: University of Chicago Press.

Frazier, E. F. (1939). *The Negro family in the United States*. Chicago: University of Chicago Press.

Frazier, E. F. (1949). The Negro family in America. In R. Ashen (Ed.), *The family: Its function and destiny*. New York: HarperCollins.

Frazier, E. F. (1957). *The Black bourgeoisie*. New York: Free Press.

Frazier, E. F. (1961). Sex life of the African American Negro. In A. Ellis & A. Abarbanel (Eds.), *The encyclopedia of sexual behavior*. New York: Hawthorn Books.

Frazier, E. F. (1964). *The Negro church in America*. New York: Schocken Books.

Frederickson, G. M. (1976, September 30). The Gutman report. *New York Review of Books*, pp. 18–22, 27.

Freeman, E. M. (2001). Homelessness among African American families. In S. Logan (Ed.) *The Black family: Strengths, self-help, and positive change* (pp. 67–82). Boulder, CO: Westview Press.

Freud, S. (1938). *The basic writings of Sigmund Freud* (A. A. Brill, Trans.). New York: Modern Library.

Fuller-Thomson, E., & Minkler, M. (2000). America's grandparent caregivers: Who are they? In B. Hayslip Jr. & R. Goldberg-Glen (Eds.), *Grandparents raising grandchildren: Theoretical, empirical, and clinical perspectives* (pp. 3–21). New York: Springer.

Furstenberg, F. F. (1991). As the pendulum swings: Teenage childbearing and social concern. *Family Relations, 40,* 127–138.

Furstenberg, F. F., Brooks-Gunn, J., & Morgan, S. P. (1987). Adolescent mothers and their children in later life. *Family Planning Perspectives, 19,* 142–151.

Furstenberg, F. F., & Crawford, A. G. (1978). Family support: Helping teenage mothers to cope. *Family Planning Perspectives, 10,* 322–333.

Furstenberg, R., Hershberg, T., & Modell, J. (1975). The origins of the female headed Black family: The impact of the urban experience. *Journal of Interdisciplinary History, 6,* 211–233.

Gallagher, M. (1996). *The abolition of marriage.* Washington, DC: Regnery Publishing.

Gallup, G., Jr. (1985, May 13). Women want babies and jobs. *San Francisco Chronicle,* p. 2.

Gan, S., Zillmann, D., & Mitrook, M. (1997). Stereotyping effect of Black women's sexual rap on White audiences. *Basic and Applied Social Psychology, 19,* 381–399.

Gardecki, R. M. (2001). *Racial differences in youth employment.* Available on-line: http://stats.bls.gov/opub/mlr/2001/08/art6full.pdf.

Garvey, M. (1967). *Philosophy and opinions of Marcus Garvey.* London: Cass.

Gary, L. E., Beatty, L. A., & Price, M. (1983). *Stable Black families: Final report.* Washington, DC: Institute for Urban Affairs and Research.

Generations United. (2003). *Fact sheet—Grandparents and other relatives raising children: Challenges of caring for the second family.* Washington, DC: Author.

Genovese, E. D. (1974). *Roll, Jordan, roll.* New York: Pantheon.

Gibbs, J. T. (1988a). The new morbidity: Homicide, suicide, accidents, and life-threatening behaviors. In J. T. Gibbs (Ed.), *Young, Black, and male in America: An endangered species.* New York: Auburn House.

Gibbs, J. T. (1988b). Young Black males in America: Endangered, embittered, and embattled. In J. T Gibbs (Ed.), *Young, Black, and male in America: An endangered species.* New York: Auburn House.

Gibbs, J. T. (1990). Developing intervention models for Black families: Linking theory and research. In H. E. Cheatham & J. B. Stewart (Eds.), *Black families: Interdisciplinary Perspectives.* New Brunswick, NJ: Transaction.

Giddings, P. (1984). *When and where I enter: The impact of Black women on race and sex in America.* New York: Morrow.

Gilder, G. (1981). *Wealth and poverty.* New York: Basic Books.

Gilliam, D. (1990, October 11). Sick distorted thinking. *Washington Post,* p. D3.

Gilmore, S., DeLamater, J., & Wagstaff, D. (1996). Sexual decision making by inner city Black adolescent males: A focus group study. *Journal of Sex Research, 33,* 363–371.

Glenn, N., & Supancic, M. (1984). Social and demographic correlates of divorce and separation in the United States: An update and reconsideration. *Journal of Marriage and the Family, 46,* 563–576.

Glick, P. (1988). Demographic pictures of Black families. In H. P. McAdoo (Ed.), *Black families* (2nd ed.). Thousand Oaks, CA: Sage.

Goforth, N. R. (2003). Attitudes and behaviors of college students toward interracial dating. Loyola University. Available on-line: http://clearinghouse.mwsc.edu/manuscripts/390.asp.

Goldin, C. D. (1983). Female labor force participation: The origin of Black and White differences, 1870–1880. *Journal of Economic History, 43,* 16–48.

Goldman, N., Westoff, C. E, & Hammerslough, C. (1984). Demography of the marriage market in the United States. *Population Index, 50,* 5–26.

Goldscheider, F. K., & Goldscheider, C. (1991). The intergenerational flow of income: Family structure and the status of Black Americans. *Journal of Marriage and the Family, 53,* 499–508.

Goode, W. (1960). A theory of role strain. *American Sociological Review, 25,* 483–496.

Goode, W. J. (1959). The sociology of the family. In R. K. Merton (Ed.), *Sociology today.* New York: Basic Books.

Gooden, W. E. (1989). Development of Black men in early adulthood. In R. L. Jones (Ed.), *Black adult development and aging.* Berkeley, CA: Cobb & Henry.

Goodwin, P. Y. (2003). African American and European American women's marital well-being. *Journal of Marriage and the Family, 65,* 550–560.

Gordon, E. T., Gordon, E. W., & Nembhard, J. G. (1994). Social science literature concerning African American men. *Journal of Negro Education, 63,* 508–531.

Gordon, L. (1988). The politics and history of family violence. In A. S. Skolnick & J. H. Skolnick (Eds.), *Family in transition* (6th ed.). Glenview, IL: Scott, Foresman.

Graves, J. L. (2001). *The emperor's new clothes.* New Brunswick, NJ: Rutgers University Press.

Grier, W. H., & Cobbs, P. M. (1976). *Black rage.* New York: Bantam Books.

Griffin, J. T. (1982). West African and Black American working women: Historical and contemporary comparisons. *Journal of Black Psychology, 8,* 55–73.

Gutman, H. (1976). *The Black family in slavery and freedom, 1750–1925.* New York: Pantheon.

Guttentag, M., & Secord, P. (1983). *Too many women: The sex ratio question.* Thousand Oaks, CA: Sage.

Hale, J. E. (1982). *Black children: Their roots, culture, and learning styles.* Provo, UT: Brigham Young University Press.

Haley, A. (1965). *The autobiography of Malcolm X.* New York: Grove Press.

Haley, A. (1986). We must honor our ancestors who helped us survive. *Ebony, 41*, 134, 138–140.

Hall, G. M. (1970). The myth of the benevolent Spanish slave law. *Negro Digest, 19*, 31–38.

Halle, H. T. (2002). *Charting parenthood: Statistical portrait of fathers and mothers in America.* Washington D.C.: Child Trend.

Hamilton, G. (2002). *Moving people from welfare to work: Lessons from the National Evaluation of Welfare-to-Work Strategies.* New York: Manpower Demonstration Research Corporation.

Hamlet, J. D. (2004). The reason why we sing. In A. Gonzalez, M. Houston, & V. Chen (Eds.), *Our voices* (4th ed., pp. 113–115). Los Angeles: Roxbury.

Hampton, R. L. (1980). Institutional decimation, marital exchange, and disruption in Black families. *Western Journal of Black Studies, 4*, 132–139.

Hampton, R. L. (1982). Family life cycle, economic well being, and marital disruption in Black families. *California Sociologist, 5*, 16–32.

Hampton, R. L. (1987). Race, class, and child maltreatment. *Journal of Comparative Family Studies, 18*, 113–126.

Hare, B. R. (1985). Re-examining the achievement central tendency: Sex differences within race and race differences within sex. In H. P. McAdoo & J. L. McAdoo (Eds.), *Black children: Social, educational, and parental environments.* Thousand Oaks, CA: Sage.

Hare, N., & Hare, J. (1984). *The endangered Black family: Coping with the unisexualization and coming extinction of the Black race.* San Francisco: Black Think Tank.

Harley, S. (1994). Reclaiming public voice and the study of Black women's work. In D. L. Sollie & L. A. Leslie (Eds.), *Gender, families, and close relationships: Feminist Research Journals* (pp. 189–209). Thousand Oaks, CA: Sage.

Harris, F., & Williams, L. (1986). JCPS/Gallup poll reflects changing views on political issues. *Focus, 14*, 4.

Harris, J. H. (1987). *Black ministers and laity in the urban church: An analysis of political and social expectations.* New York: University Presses of America.

Harris, L. C. (1995). The challenge and possibility for Black males to embrace feminism. In D. W. Carbado (Ed.), *Black men on race, gender, and sexuality: A critical reader* (pp. 383–386). New York: New York University Press.

Harris, W. (1976). Work and the family in Black Atlanta. *Journal of Social History, 9*, 1319–1330.

Harrison, A. O. (1985). The Black family's socializing environment: Self-esteem and ethnic attitude among Black children. In H. P. McAdoo & J. L. McAdoo (Eds.), *Black children: Social, educational, and parental environments.* Thousand Oaks, CA: Sage.

Harrison, A. O. (1988). Attitudes toward procreation among Black adults. In H. P. McAdoo (Ed.), *Black families* (2nd ed.). Thousand Oaks, CA: Sage.

Harrison, A. O. (1989). Black working women: Introduction to a life span perspective. In R. L. Jones (Ed.), *Black adult development and aging*. Berkeley, CA: Cobb & Henry.

Harrison, A. O., & Minor, J. H. (1978). Interrole conflict, coping strategies, and satisfaction among Black working wives. *Journal of Marriage and the Family, 40,* 799–805.

Harrison, P. M., & Beck, A. J. (2003). *Prisoners in 2002.* Washington, DC: U.S. Bureau of Justice Statistics.

Harvey, A. (Ed.). (1985). *The Black family: An Afro-centric perspective.* Washington, DC: Commission for Racial Justice, United Church of Christ.

Harwood, E., & Hodge, C. C. (1971). Jobs and the Negro family: A reappraisal. *Public Interest, 23,* 125–131.

Hatfield, E., & Sprecher, S. (1986). *Mirror, mirror: The importance of looks in everyday life.* Albany: State University of New York Press.

Hatfield, E., & Walster, G. W. (1981). *A new look at love.* Reading, MA: Addison-Wesley.

Haynes, F. E. (2000). Gender and family ideals: An exploratory study of Black middle-class Americans. *Journal of Family Issues, 21,* 811–837.

Heaton, T. B., & Jacobson, C. K. (2000, Winter). Intergroup marriage: An examination of opportunity structures. *Sociological Inquiry, 70,* 30–41.

Heer, D. M. (1974). The prevalence of Black-White marriage in the United States, 1960 and 1970. *Journal of Marriage and the Family, 36,* 246–258.

Heiss, J. (1975). *The case of the Black family: A sociological inquiry.* New York: Columbia University Press.

Heiss, J. (1988). Women's values regarding marriage and the family. In H. P. McAdoo (Ed.), *Black families* (2nd ed., pp. 201–214). Thousand Oaks, CA: Sage.

Hendricks, L. E. (1982). Unmarried Black adolescent fathers' attitudes toward abortion, contraception, and sexuality: A preliminary report. *Journal of Adolescent Health Care, 2,* 199–203.

Herek, G. M., & Capitanio, J. P. (1995). Black heterosexuals' attitudes toward lesbians and gay men in the United States. *Journal of Sex Research, 32,* 95–105.

Hernton, C. (1965). *Sex and racism in America.* New York: Doubleday.

Herskovits, M. (1941). *The myth of the Negro past.* Boston: Beacon Press.

Hesse-Biber, S., & Carter, G. L. (2000). *Working women in America: Split dreams.* New York: Oxford University Press.

Hill, N. (1995). The relationship between family environment and parenting style: A preliminary study of African American families. *Journal of Black Psychology, 21*, 408–423.

Hill, R. (1966). Contemporary developments in family theory. *Journal of Marriage and the Family, 28*, 10–26.

Hill, R. (1983). *Comparative socio-economic profiles of Caribbean and Non-Caribbean Blacks in the United States.* Unpublished manuscript.

Hill, R. B. (1972). *The strengths of Black families.* New York: Emerson Hall.

Hill, R. B. (1989). Critical issues for Black families by the year 2000. In J. Dewart (Ed.), *The state of Black America 1989.* New York: National Urban League.

Hill, R. B. (1990). Economic forces, structural discrimination, and Black family instability. In H. E. Cheatam (Ed.), *Black families: Interdisciplinary perspectives* (pp. 87–105). Brunswick, NJ: Transaction.

Hill, R. B. (1999). *The strengths of African American families: Twenty-five years later.* Lanham, MD: University Press of America.

Hill, R. B. (2003). The strengths of Black families revisited. In L. A. Daniels (Ed.), *The state of Black America 2003* (pp. 107–149). Washington, DC: National Urban League.

Hill, R. B., & Hansen, D. A. (1960). The identification of conceptual frameworks utilized in family study. *Marriage and Family Living, 22*, 299–311.

Hill, R. B., & Shackleford, L. (1986). The Black extended family revisited. In R. Staples (Ed.), *The Black family: Essays and studies* (3rd ed.). Belmont, CA: Wadsworth.

Hill, S. A. (2002). Teaching and doing gender in African American families. *Sex Roles, 47*, 493–506.

Hill, S. A., & Sprague, J. (1999). Parenting in Black and White families: The interaction of gender with race and class. *Gender and Society, 13*, 480–502.

Hinds, M. D. (1990, March 17). Addiction to crack can kill parental instinct. *New York Times*, p. A1.

Hine, C., Hine, W. C., & Harrold, S. (2004). *African Americans: A concise history.* Upper Saddle River, NJ: Prentice-Hall.

Hisnanick, J. J. (2001). Military service as a factor in the economic progress of African American men: A post–draft era analysis. *Journal of African American Men, 5*(4), 66–79.

Hite, S. (1976). *The Hite report.* New York: Macmillan.

Hofferth, S. L. (1984). Kin network, race, and family structure. *Journal of Marriage and the Family 46*, 791–805.

Hoffman, C. (2002). *Federal support for education, NCES 2002–006.* Washington, DC: U.S. Department of Education, National Center for Education Statistics.

Hokanson, J. E., & Calder, G. (1960). Negro-White differences on the MMPI. *Journal of Clinical Psychology, 16*, 32–33.

Hollingsworth, L. D. (1998). Promoting the same race adoptions for children of color. *Social Work, 43*, 104–117.

Homans, G. (1961). *Behavior: Its elementary forms*. Orlando, FL: Harcourt.

hooks, b. (1981). *Ain't I a woman: Black women and feminism*. Boston: South End Press.

hooks, b. (1984). *Feminist theory: From margin to center*. Boston: South End Press.

hooks, b. (1988). Homophobia in Black communities. *Zeta Magazine, 1*, 35–38.

hooks, b. (1995). Black women: Shaping feminist theory. In B. Guy-Sheftall (Ed.), *Words of fire: An anthology of African-American feminist thought* (pp. 270–282). New York: New Press.

Hooyman, N., & Kiyak, H. A. (1999). *Social gerontology: A multidisciplinary perspective*. Needham Heights, MA: Allyn & Bacon.

Howard, D. (1988). A structural approach to sexual attitudes: Interracial patterns in adolescents' judgments about sexual intimacy. *Sociological Perspectives, 31*, 88–121.

Hrabowski, F. A., Maton, K. I., & Greif, G. L. (1998). *Beating the odds: Raising academically successful African American males*. New York: Oxford University Press.

Hughes, Z. (2003, August). The truth about one-night stands. *Ebony* vol. LVIII (10), 84, 86–88.

Hull, G. T., Scott, P. B., & Smith, B. (Eds.). (1982). *But some of us are brave: Black women's studies*. Old Westbury, NY: Feminist Press.

Hunter, A. G., & Sellers, S. L. (1998). Feminist attitudes among African American women and men. *Gender and Society, 12*, 81–99.

Hunter, A. G., & Taylor, R. J. (1998). Grandparenthood in African American families. In M. E. Szinovacz (Ed.), *Handbook of grandparenthood* (pp. 70–86). Westport, CT: Greenwood Press.

Hunter, M., Allen, W. R., and Telles, E. T. (2001). The significance of skin color among African Americans and Mexican Americans. *African American Research Perspectives, 7*(1), 173–184.

Income inequality. (1998). *CQ Researcher, 8*, 339–355.

Ingoldsby, B. B., Smith, S. R., and Miller, J. E. (2003) *Exploring family theories*. Los Angeles: Roxbury.

Institute of Medicine. (2002). *Unequal treatment: Confronting racial and ethnic disparities in health care*. Washington, DC: National Academy of Sciences.

Jackson, J. J. (1986). Black grandparents: Who needs them? In R. Staples (Ed.), *The Black family: Essays and studies* (3rd ed.). Belmont, CA: Wadsworth.

Jackson, J. J. (1991). Ordinary husbands: The truly hidden men. In R. Staples (Ed.), *The Black family: Essays and studies* (4th ed.). Belmont, CA: Wadsworth.

Jackson, J. S., McCullough, W. R., & Gurin, G. (1988). Family, socialization, environment, and identity development in Black Americans. In H. P. McAdoo (Ed.), *Black families* (2nd ed.). Thousand Oaks, CA: Sage.

Jackson, R. H. (1975). Some aspirations of lower class Black mothers. *Journal of Comparative Family Studies, 6*, 172–181.

Jaynes, G. D. (1990). The labor market status of Black Americans: 1939–1985. *Journal of Economic Perspectives, 4*, 34–42.

Jeffries, J., & Brock, R. E. (1991). African-Americans in a changing economy: A look at the 21st century. *Crisis, 98*(6), 22–32.

Jensen, A. R. (1969). How much can we boost IQ and scholastic achievement? *Harvard Educational Review, 39*, 11–23.

Jewell, K. S. (1988). *Survival of the Black family: The institutional impact of U.S. social policy*. New York: Praeger.

Jewell, L. N. (1989). *Psychology and effective behavior*. St. Paul, MN: West.

Joe, T., & Yu, P. (1991). The flip side of Black families headed by women: The economic status of Black men. In R. Staples (Ed.), *The Black family: Essays and studies* (4th ed.). Belmont, CA: Wadsworth.

John, D., Shelton, B., & Luschen, K. (1995). Race, ethnicity, gender, and perceptions of fairness. *Journal of Family Issues, 16*, 357–379.

Johnson, C. L. (1995). Childlessness and kinship organizations: Comparisons of very old Whites and Blacks. *Journal of Cross-Cultural Gerontology, 10*, 289–306.

Johnson, C. L. (2000). Perspectives on American kinship in the later 1990s. *Journal of Marriage and the Family, 62*, 623–639.

Johnson, C. S. (1934). *Shadow of the plantation*. Chicago: University of Chicago Press.

Johnson, L. B. (1978a). Sexual behavior of southern Blacks. In R. Staples (Ed.), *The Black family: Essays and studies* (2nd ed., pp. 80–93). Belmont, CA: Wadsworth.

Johnson, L. B. (1978b). The search for values in Black family research. In R. Staples (Ed.), *The Black Family: Essays and Studies* (6th ed.) (pp. 26–34). Belmont, CA: Wadsworth.

Johnson, L. B. (1980). *Marital and parental roles: A Black youth perspective*. Unpublished manuscript, Florida State University.

Johnson, L. B. (1988). Perspectives on Black family empirical research, 1965–1978. In H. P. McAdoo (Ed.), *Black families* (2nd ed.). Thousand Oaks, CA: Sage.

Johnson, L. B. (1989a). Sexual attitudes on SDA campuses circa 1978: A comparative perspective. *Spectrum, 19*(3), 27–34.

Johnson, L. B. (1989b). The employed Black: The dynamics of work-family tension. *Review of Black Political Economy, 17*(3), 69–85.

Johnson, L. B. (1997). Arizona empower programs: Parental responsibility and welfare of children. In K. Kyle and A. Schneider (Eds.), *The roles and responsibilities of parents from a Black perspective* (pp. 123–124). Temple: Arizona State University.

Johnson, L. B. (1999). *Project director's evaluation: Carver/PUCH oral history project.* Phoenix: Arizona Humanities Council.

Johnson, L. B., & Staples, R. (1990). Family planning and the young minority male: A pilot project. In D. J. Jones & S. F. Battle (Eds.), *Teenage pregnancy: Developing strategies for change in the twenty-first century.* Somerset, NJ: Transaction.

Johnson, P. R., Shireman, J. E, & Watson, K. W. (1987). Transracial adoption and the development of Black identity at age eight. *Child Welfare, 1*, 45–55.

Jones, C. (1989, May 21). Drugs add to a glut of adoptable Black children. *Los Angeles Times*, p. Al.

Jones, D., & Battle, S. (1990). *Teenage pregnancy: Developing strategies for change in the twenty-first century.* New Brunswick, NJ: Transaction.

Jones, J. (1982). "My mother was much of a woman": Black women, work, and the family under slavery. *Feminist Studies, 8*, 235–269.

Jones, J. (1985). *Labor of love, labor of sorrow: Black women, work, and the family from slavery to the present.* New York: Basic Books.

Joseph, G. I., & Lewis, J. (1981). *Common differences: Conflicts in Black and White feminist perspectives.* Boston: South End Press.

Kahn, A. J., & Kamerman, S. B. (1983–1984). Social assistance: An eight county overview. *Institute for Socio-economic Studies, 8*, 93–112.

Kalmijn, M. (1993). Trends in Black/White intermarriage. *Social Forces, 72*, 119–141.

Karger, H. J., & Stoesz, D. (2002). *American social welfare policy: A pluralist approach.* Reading, MA: Allyn & Bacon.

Kayongo-Male, D., & Onyango, P. (1984). *The sociology of the African family.* London: Longman.

Keith, V. M., & Herring, C. (1991). Skin tone and stratification in the Black community. *American Journal of Sociology, 97*, 760–778.

Keith, V. M., & Riley, A. (2001). Work conditions and psychological distress among African American women. *African American Research Perspectives, 7*, 104–116.

Kesner, J. E., & McKenry, P. C. (2001). Single parenthood and social competence in children of color. *Families in Society: The Journal of Contemporary Human Services, 82*, 136–144.

Kiecolt, K. J., & Fossett, M. A. (1995). Mate availability and marriage among African Americans: Aggregate and individual level analysis. In M. B. Tucker & C. Mitchell-Kernan (Eds.), *The decline in marriage among African Americans: Causes, consequences, and policy implications* (pp. 121–135). New York: Russell Sage Foundation.

Kiecolt, K. J., & Fossett, M. A. (1997). The effects of mate availability on marriage among Black Americans: A contextual analysis. In R. J. Taylor, J. S. Jackson, & L. M. Chatters (Eds.), *Family life in Black America* (pp. 63–78). Thousand Oaks, CA: Sage.

Kinder, D. R., & Winter, N. (2001). Exploring the racial divide: Blacks, Whites, and opinions on national policy. *American Journal of Political Science, 45,* 439–456.

King, A.E.O. (1999). African American females' attitudes toward marriage: An exploratory study. *Journal of Black Studies, 29,* 416–437.

King, D. H. (1990). Multiple jeopardy, multiple consciousness: The context of Black feminist ideology. In M. R. Malson, E. Mudimbe-Boyi, J. F. O'Barr, & M. Wyer (Eds.), *Black women in America: Social science perspectives.* Chicago: University of Chicago Press.

King, M. (1973). The politics of sexual stereotypes. *Black Scholar, 4,* 12–23.

King, R.E.G., & Griffin, J. T. (1983). The loving relationship: Impetus for Black marriage. In C. E. Obudho (Ed.), *Black marriage and family therapy.* Westport, CT: Greenwood Press.

Kinsey, A. C., Pomeroy, W. B., & Martin, C. E. (1948). *Sexual behavior in the human male.* Philadelphia: Saunders.

Kinsey, A. C., Pomeroy, W. B., Martin, C. E., & Gebhard, P. H. (1953). *Sexual behavior in the human female.* Philadelphia: Saunders.

Kitson, G. C. (1985). Marital discord and marital separation: A county survey. *Journal of Marriage and the Family, 47,* 693–700.

Klein, E., Campbell, J., Soler, E., & Ghez, M. (1997). *Ending domestic violence: Changing public perceptions/Halting the epidemic.* Thousand Oaks, CA: Sage.

Knox, D., Zusman, M. E., Buffington, C., & Hemphill, G. (2000). Interracial dating attitudes among college students. *College Student Journal, 34,* 193–200.

Komarovsky, M. (1988). The new feminist scholarship: Some precursors and polemics. *Journal of Marriage and the Family, 50,* 585–594.

Kozol, J. (1985). *Illiteracy in America.* New York: Morrow.

Krech, S. (1982). Black family organization in the nineteenth century: An ethnological perspective. *Journal of Interdisciplinary History, 12,* 429–452.

Ladner, J. (1971). *Tomorrow's tomorrow: The Black woman.* New York: Doubleday.

Landry, B. (1987). *The new Black middle class.* Berkeley: University of California Press.

Landry, B. (2000). *Black working wives: Pioneers of the American family revolution*. Berkeley: University of California Press.

Larson, T. E. (1988). Employment and unemployment of young Black males. In J. T. Gibbs (Ed.), *Young, Black, and male in America: An endangered species*. New York: Auburn House.

Laumann, E. O., Gagnon, J. H., Michael, R., & Michaels, S. (1994). *The social organization of sexuality: Sexual practices in the United States*. Chicago: University of Chicago Press.

Lawrence, J. S., Eldridge, G. D., Reitman, D., Little, C. E., Shelby, M. C., & Brasfiled, T. L. (1998). Factors influencing condom use among African American women: Implications for risk reduction interventions. *American Journal of Community Psychology, 26*, 7–28.

Lawson, E. J. (1999). Black men after divorce: How do they cope? In R. Staples (Ed.), *The Black family: Essays and studies* (pp. 112–127). Belmont, CA: Wadsworth.

Leashore, B. (1991). Social policies, Black males, and Black families. In R. Staples (Ed.), *The Black family: Essays and studies* (4th ed.). Belmont, CA: Wadsworth.

Leffall, D. L. (1990). Health status of Black Americans. In J. Dewart (Ed.), *The state of Black America 1990*. New York: National Urban League.

Lemann, N. (1991). *The promised land: The great Black migration and how it changed America*. New York: Knopf.

Leslie, L. A., & Grady, K. (1985). Changes in mothers' social networks and social support following divorce. *Journal of Marriage and the Family, 47*, 663–673.

Lewis, D. K. (1975). The Black family: Socialization and sex roles. *Phylon, 36*, 221–237.

Lewis, D. K. (1995). African-American women at risk: Notes on the sociocultural context of HIV infection. In B. E. Schneider & N. E. Stoller (Eds.), *Women resisting AIDS: Feminist strategies of empowerment* (pp. 57–73). Philadelphia: Temple University Press.

Lewis, G. (1990, April 28). Bennett idea on children draws jeers. *San Francisco Examiner*, p. A1.

Lewis, L. J., & Kertzner, R. M. (2003). Toward improved interpretation and theory building of African American male sexualities. *Journal of Sex Research, 40*(4), 383–395.

Lewis, R., Yancey, G., & Bletzer, S. S. (1997). Racial and nonracial factors that influence spouse choice in Black/White marriages. *Journal of Black Studies, 28*, 60–78.

Lichter, D. T., & Eggebeen, D. J. (1994). The effect of parental employment on child poverty. *Journal of Marriage and the Family, 56*, 633–645.

Liebow, E. (1966). *Tally's corner*. Boston: Little, Brown.

Lincoln, E. C., & Mamiya, L. H. (1990). *The Black church in the African American experience*. Durham, NC: Duke University Press.

Linville, P. W. (1987). Self-complexity as a cognitive buffer against stress-related illness and depression. *Journal of Personality and Social Psychology, 52,* 663–676.

Litwack, L. (1979). *Been in the storm so long: The aftermath of slavery*. New York: Knopf.

Lloyd, S. A. (1991). The dark side of courtship: Violence and sexual exploitation. *Family Relations, 40,* 14–20.

Lockhart, L., & White, B. W. (1989). Understanding marital violence in the Black community. *Journal of Interpersonal Violence, 4,* 421–436.

Lockley, T. J. (2001). *Lines in the sand: Race and class in Low County Georgia, 1750–1860*. Athens: University of Georgia Press.

London, K. A. (1991). *Cohabitation, marriage dissolution, and remarriage: United States*. Washington, DC: National Center for Health Statistics.

Lugalia, T. A. (1998, March). *Current population* (Report No. P20–514). Washington, DC: U.S. Census Bureau.

Malone, A. P. (1992). *Sweet chariot: Slave family and household structure in nineteenth century Louisiana*. Chapel Hill: University of North Carolina Press.

Malson, M. R. (1983). Black women's sex roles: The social context for a new ideology. *Journal of Social Issues, 39,* 101–113.

Malveaux, J. (1988). The economic statuses of Black families. In H. P. McAdoo (Ed.), *Black families* (2nd ed.). Thousand Oaks, CA: Sage.

Mannheim, K. (1936). *Ideology and utopia*. Orlando, FL: Harcourt.

Manns, M. (1988). Supportive roles of significant others in Black families. In H. P. McAdoo (Ed.), *Black families* (2nd ed.). Thousand Oaks, CA: Sage.

Marsh, C. E. (1993). Sexual assault and domestic violence in the African American community. *Western Journal of Black Studies, 17,* 149–153.

Marsiglio, W. (1987). Adolescent fathers in the United States: Their initial living arrangements, marital experience, and educational outcomes. *Family Planning Perspectives, 19,* 240–251.

Martin, E. P., & Martin, J. M. (1978). *The Black extended family*. Chicago: University of Chicago Press.

Martin, P. P., Younge, S., & Smith, A. (2003). Searching for a Balm at Gilead: The HIV/AIDS epidemic and the African American church. *African American Research Perspectives, 9,* 70–78.

Marx, K. (1936). *Capital*. New York: Modern Library.

Mason, M. A., Skolnick, A., & Sugarman, S. D. (1998). *All our families: New policies for a new century*. New York: Oxford University Press.

Massey, D. S., & Denton, N. A. (1993). *American apartheid: Segregation and the making of the underclass.* Cambridge, MA: Harvard University Press.

Mathews, T. (1992, May 18). Help begins in the 'hood. *Newsweek,* pp. 34–35.

Matthews, T. J., Menacker, F., & MacDorman, M. (2003). Infant mortality statistics from the 2001 period linked birth/infant death data set. *National Vital Statistics Reports, 52.* Hyattsville, MD: National Center for Health Statistics.

Mays, V., & Cochran, S. (1991). The Black women's relationship project: A national survey of Black lesbians. In R. Staples (Ed.), *The Black family: Essays and studies* (4th ed.). Belmont, CA: Wadsworth.

Mbiti, J. S. (1973). *Love and marriage in Africa.* London: Longman.

McAdoo, H. P. (1988). Transgenerational patterns of upward mobility in African-American families. In H. P. McAdoo (Ed.), *Black families* (2nd ed.). Thousand Oaks, CA: Sage.

McAdoo, J. L. (1997). The role of African American fathers in the socialization of their children. In H. P. McAdoo (Ed.), *Black families* (3rd ed.). Thousand Oaks, CA: Sage.

McAdoo, J. L. (1985–1986). A Black perspective on the father's role in child development. *Marriage and Family Review, 9,* 117–133.

McAdoo, J. L., & McAdoo, J. B. (1994). The African American father's role with the family. In R. G. Majors and J. U. Gordon (Eds.), *The American Black male: His present status and his future.* Chicago: Nelson-Hall.

McAdoo, J. L., & McAdoo, J. B. (1995). The African American father's roles within families. In M. S. Kimmel & M. A. Messner (Eds.), *Men's lives* (pp. 485–494). Needham Heights, MA: Allyn & Bacon.

McCubbin, H. I., Patterson, J. M., & Lavee, Y. (1984, October). *Black military family adaptation to crises: Critical strengths.* Paper presented at the 46th annual meeting of the National Council on Family Relations, Ethnic Minorities Section, San Francisco.

McKinnon, J. (2001, February 22). Census Bureau releases update on country's African American population. Available on-line: http://www.census.gov/Press-Release/www/2001/cb01–34.htm.

McLoyd, V. C., Cauce, A. M., Takeuchi, D., & Wilson, L. (2001). Marital processes and parental socialization in families of color: A decade review of research. In R. M. Milardo (Ed.), *Understanding families into the new millennium: A decade in review* (pp. 289–312). Minneapolis, MN: National Council on Family Relations.

McMillan, T. (1992). *Waiting to exhale.* New York: Viking/Penguin.

McMurray, G. L. (1990). Those of broader vision: An African-American perspective on teenage pregnancy and parenting. In J. Dewart (Ed.), *The state of Black America 1990.* New York: National Urban League.

Meltzer, M. (1964). *In their own words: A history of the American Negro, 1619–1865.* New York: Crowell.

Melville, K. (1977). *Marriage and family today.* New York: Random House.

Merton, R. K. (1972). Insiders and outsiders: A chapter in the sociology of knowledge. *American Journal of Sociology, 78,* 9–48.

Messner, M. (1995). Masculinities and athletic careers. In M. L. Anderson & P. H. Collins (Eds.), *Race, class, and gender: An anthology* (pp. 165–181). Belmont, CA: Wadsworth.

Miller, K. D. (1991, January 14). Scholar Keith Miller gives credit to King's Sunday school teacher. *ASU Insight,* p. 8.

Miller, R. M., & Smith, J. D. (1988). *Dictionary of Afro-American slavery.* Westport, CT: Greenwood Press.

Millette, R. E. (1990). West Indian families in the United States. In H. E. Cheatham & J. B. Stewart (Eds.), *Black families: Interdisciplinary perspectives.* New Brunswick, NJ: Transaction.

Minkler, M., & Roe, K. M. (1993). *Grandparents as caregivers: Raising children of the crack cocaine epidemic.* Thousand Oaks, CA: Sage.

Minkler, M., & Roe, K. M. (1996). Grandparents as surrogate parents. *Generations, 20,* 34–38.

Mishel, L., Bernstein, J., & Schmitt, J. (1997). *The state of working America: 1996–1997.* Armonk, NY: M. E. Sharpe.

Mitchell-Kernan, C. (1982). Linguistic diversity in the service delivery setting: The case of Black English. In B. A. Bass, G. E. Wyatt, & G. J. Powell (Eds.), *The Afro-American family: Assessment, treatment, and research issues.* Philadelphia: Grune & Stratton.

Monahan, T. P. (1970). Are interracial marriages less stable? *Social Forces, 48,* 461–473.

Monroe, P. A., & Tiller, V. V. (2001). Commitment to work among welfare-reliant women. *Journal of Marriage and the Family, 63,* 816–828.

Moore, K. A., & Burt, M. R. (1982). The consequences of early childbearing. In K. A. Moore and M. R. Burt (Eds.), *Private crisis, public cost: Policy perspectives on teenage childbearing.* Washington, DC: Urban Institute Press.

Moore, K. A., Simms, M. C., & Betsey, C. L. (1986). *Choice and circumstance: Racial differences in adolescent sexuality and fertility.* New Brunswick, NJ: Transaction.

Morgan, P. D. (2001). *Carolina rice: African origins, new world crop.* Cambridge, MA: Harvard University Press.

Morganthau, T. (1992, May 11). The price of neglect. *Newsweek,* p. 55.

Moynihan, D. P. (1965). *The Negro family: The case for national action.* Washington, DC: Office of Policy Planning and Research, Department of Labor.

Moynihan, D. P. (1987). *Family and nation*. Orlando, FL: Harcourt.

Mullen, F. (2000). Grandparents and welfare reform. In C. B. Cox (Ed.),
To grandmother's house we go and stay: Perspectives on custodial grandparents
(pp. 113–131). New York: Springer.

Murray, C. B., Khatib, S., & Jackson, M. (1989). Social indices and the Black
elderly: A comparative life cycle approach to the study of double jeopardy.
In R. L. Jones (Ed.), *Black adult development and aging*. Berkeley, CA:
Cobb & Henry.

Murstein, B. I., Merighi, J., & Malloy, T. E. (1989). Physical attractiveness and
the exchange theory in interracial dating. *Journal of Social Psychology*,
129, 325–333.

Mydans, S. (1990, December 7). Homicide rate for young Blacks rose by two
thirds in five years. *New York Times*, p. A1.

Myers, B. C. (1990). Hypertension as a manifestation of the stress experienced
by Black families. In H. E. Cheatham & J. B. Stewart (Eds.), *Black families: Interdisciplinary perspectives*. New Brunswick, NJ: Transaction.

Nathanson, C. A., & Becker, M. H. (1986). Family and peer influence on
obtaining a method of contraception. *Journal of Marriage and the Family*,
48, 513–525.

National Campaign to Prevent Teen Pregnancy. (2002/2003). *With one voice:
America's adults and teens sound off about teen pregnancy: An annual national
survey*. Washington, DC: Author.

National Center for Children in Poverty. (2002). *Research forum*. New York:
Columbia University Mailman School of Public Health.

National Center for Children in Poverty. (2003). *Research forum*. New York:
Columbia University Mailman School of Public Health.

National Center for Education Statistics. (1991a). *Digest of education statistics
1990*. Washington, DC: U.S. Government Printing Office.

National Center for Education Statistics. (1991b). *Race/ethnicity trends in degrees
conferred by institutions of higher education: 1978–79 through 1988–89*.
Washington, DC: U.S. Government Printing Office.

National Center for Education Statistics. (2002, April). *Adult literacy in America*.
Washington, DC: U.S. Department of Education.

National Center for Health Statistics. (1996). *Vital statistics of the United States,
1992*. Washington, DC: U.S. Government Printing Office.

National Radio Project. (2000, October 18). *Beyond the Sky's Limit: U.S. Military
Spending*. Oakland, CA: National Radio Project. Available on-line:
http://www.radioproject.org.

Neighbors, H. W. (1997). The (mis)diagnosis of mental disorder in African
Americans. *African American Perspectives*, *3*, 1–11.

New statistics on what happens to young Blacks after they graduate. (1999). *Journal of Blacks in Higher Education, 25,* 80–81.

New study of teenage sex. (1991, January 2). *San Francisco Chronicle,* p. A3.

Noble, J. (1978). *Beautiful, also, are the souls of my Black sisters: A history of the Black woman in America.* Upper Saddle River, NJ: Prentice-Hall.

Nobles, W. W. (1988). African-American family life: An instrument of culture. In P. McAdoo (Ed.), *Black families* (2nd ed.) Thousand Oaks, CA: Sage.

Nobles, W. W., & Goddard, L. L. (1986). *Understanding the Black family: A guide for scholarship and research.* Oakland, CA: Institute for the Advanced Study of Black Family Life and Culture.

Norment, L. (1992). Black men, Black women, and sexual harassment. *Ebony, 47*(3), 120–122.

Nye, I., & Berardo, F. (Eds.). (1981). *Emerging conceptual frameworks in family analysis.* New York: Praeger.

Oggins, J., Leber, D., & Veroff, J. (1993). Race and gender differences in Black and White newlyweds' perceptions of sexual and marital relations. *Journal of Sex Research, 30,* 152–160.

Oliver, M. L., & Shapiro, T. M. (1995). *Black wealth/White wealth: New perspectives on racial inequality.* New York: Routledge.

Olson, D. H., & DeFrain, J. (1997). *Marriage and the family: Diversity and strengths* (2nd ed.). Mountain View, CA: Mayfield Publishing.

Omari, T. P. (1965). Role expectations in the courtship situation in Ghana. In P. L. Van Berghe (Ed.), *Africa: Social problems of change and conflict.* San Francisco: Chandler.

Orbuch, T. L., & Custer, L. (1995). The social context of married women's work and its impact on Black husbands and White husbands. *Journal of Marriage and the Family, 57,* 333–345.

Orbuch, T. L., & Eyster, S. L. (1997). Division of household labor among Black couples and White couples. *Social Forces, 76,* 301–332.

Osmond, M. W. (1977). Marital organization in low income families: A cross-race comparison. *International Journal of Sociology of the Family, 7,* 143–156.

Ostine, R. (1998). Caribbean immigrants and the sociology of race and ethnicity: Limits of the assimilation perspective. *African American Research Perspectives, 4,* 68–76.

Ostrow, R. J. (1991, January 5). U.S. imprisons Black men at four times S. Africa's rate. *Los Angeles Times,* p. A1.

Oubré, A. (1997). Black English vernacular (Ebonics) and educability: A cross-cultural perspective on language, cognition, and schooling. African American Web Connection. Available on-line: http://www.aawc.com/ebonicsarticle.html.

Patterson, O. (1982). *Slavery and social death: A comparative study.* Cambridge, MA: Harvard University Press.

Payne, M. A. (1989). Use and abuse of corporal punishment: A Caribbean view. *Child Abuse and Neglect, 13,* 389–401.

Peters, M. F. (Ed.). (1978). Black families [Special issue]. *Journal of Marriage and the Family, 40,* 655–862.

Peters, M. F. (1985). Racial socialization of young Black children. In H. P. McAdoo, & J. L. McAdoo (Eds.), *Black children: Social, educational, and parental environments.* Thousand Oaks, CA: Sage.

Peters, M. F. (1997). Parenting in Black families with young children: A historical perspective. In H. P. McAdoo (Ed.), *Black families* (3rd ed.). Thousand Oaks, CA: Sage.

Peterson, G. W., & Peters, D. F. (1985). The socialization values of low-income Appalachian White and rural Black mothers: A comparative study. *Journal of Comparative Family Studies, 16,* 75–91.

Pietropinto, A., & Simenauer, J. (1977). *Beyond the male myth.* New York: Quadrangle.

Pinderhughes, D. M. (1991). The case of African Americans in the Persian Gulf: The intersection of American foreign and military policy with domestic employment policy in the United States. In J. Dewart (Ed.), *The state of Black America 1991.* New York: National Urban League.

Platt, T. (1987). E. Franklin Frazier and Daniel P. Moynihan: Setting the record straight. *Contemporary Crises, 11,* 42–51.

Pleck, J. H. (1989). Correlates of Black adolescent males' condom use. *Journal of Adolescent Research, 4,* 247–253.

Poole, T. (1990). Black families and the Black church: A sociohistorical perspective. In H. E. Cheatham & J. B. Stewart (Eds.), *Black families: Interdisciplinary perspectives.* New Brunswick, NJ: Transaction.

Porter, J. R. (1979). *Dating habits of young Black Americans: And almost everybody else's too.* Dubuque, IA: Kendall/Hunt.

Porter, M. M., & Bronzaft, A. L. (1995). Do the future plans of educated Black women include Black mates? *Journal of Negro Education, 64,* 162–170.

Porterfield, E. (1973, January). Black-American intermarriage in the United States. *Psychology Today,* pp. 71–78.

Pouissant, A. (1983). Black-on-Black homicide: A psychological political perspective. *Victimology, 8,* 161–169.

President's Commission. (1971). *Report of the Commission on Obscenity and Pornography.* New York: Random House.

Proprietary preference for-profit colleges gain momentum in producing graduates of color. (2000, July 9). *Black Issues in Higher Education*. Available on-line: http://www.phdproject.org/phd13.html.

Qian, Z. (1999). Who intermarries? Education, nativity, region, and interracial marriage, 1980 and 1990. *Journal of Comparative Family Studies, 30,* 580–597.

Quadagno, D., Sly, D. F., Harrison, D. F., Eberstein, I. W., & Soler, H. R. (1998). Ethnic differences in sexual decisions and sexual behavior. *Archives of Sexual Behavior, 27,* 57–75.

Ragsdale, B. L. (2000). Surveillance of African American men and its possible effect on social, emotional and psychological functioning. *Journal of African American Men, 5,* 33–13.

Rainwater, L. (1966). The crucible of identity: The lower class Negro family. *Daedalus, 95,* 258–264.

Rainwater, L. (1970). *Behind ghetto walls: Black families in a federal slum.* Hawthorne, NY: Aldine.

Rainwater, L., & Yancey, W. (1967). *The Moynihan report and the politics of controversy.* Cambridge, MA: MIT Press.

Ramsey, P. G. (1987). Young children's thinking about ethnic differences. In J. S. Phinney & M. J. Rotheram (Eds.), *Children's ethnic socialization.* Thousand Oaks, CA: Sage.

Rank, M. R. (1987). The formation and dissolution of marriages in the welfare population. *Journal of Marriage and the Family, 49,* 15–20.

Rank, M. R., & Davis, L. E. (1996). Perceived happiness outside marriage among Black and White spouses. *Family Relations, 45,* 435–448.

Ransby, B., & Matthews, T. (1995). Black popular culture and the transcendence of patriarchal illusions. In B. Guy-Sheftall (Ed.), *Words of fire: An anthology of African American feminist thought* (pp. 526–535). New York: New Press.

Raspberry, W. (1984). New interest in an old problem. *Chicago Tribune,* p. 11.

Reed, R. J. (1988). Education and achievement of young Black males. In J. T. Gibbs (Ed.), *Young, Black, and male in America: An endangered species.* New York: Auburn House.

Reeder, A. L., & Conger, R. D. (1984). Differential mother and father influences on the educational attainment of Black and White women. *Sociological Quarterly, 25,* 239–250.

Reeves, R. (1986, June 13). A look at unemployment. *San Francisco Chronicle,* p. B5.

Reid, I. (1939). *The Negro immigrant: His background characteristics and social adjustment, 1899–1937.* New York: Columbia University Press.

Rein, M. (1982). Work in welfare: Past failures and future strategies. *Social Service Review, 56,* 211–229.

Reiss, I. L. (1967). *The social context of premarital sexual permissiveness.* New York: Holt.

Riley, A. (2000). The quality of work life, self-evaluation, and life satisfaction among African Americans. *African American Research Perspectives, 6,* 22–29.

Rindfuss, R., & Stephen, E. H. (1990). Marital noncohabitation: Separation does not make the heart grow fonder. *Journal of Marriage and the Family, 52,* 259–270.

Roberts, D. E. (2000). *Is there justice in children's rights? The critique of federal family preservation policy.* Available on-line: http://www.law.upenn.edu/conlaw/vol2/num1/roberts_ct.html.

Roberts, D. E. (2002). *Shattered bonds: The color of child welfare.* New York: Basic Books.

Robinson, C. J. (1983). *Black Marxism: The making of the Black radical tradition.* London: Zed Press.

Robinson, I. F., Bailey, W. C., & Smith, J. M. (1985). Self-perception of the husband/father in the intact lower class Black family. *Phylon, 46,* 136–147.

Robinson, J. (2002, October 24). *Blacks in prison.* Available on-line: http://www.suite101.com/article.cfm/16619/95824.

Rodgers, W. L., & Thornton, A. (1985). Changing patterns of first marriage in the United States. *Demography, 22,* 265–279.

Rodgers-Rose, L. F. (1980). *The Black woman.* Thousand Oaks, CA: Sage.

Rodriguez, C. (2003, February 17). Study shows U.S. Blacks trailing immigrants from Africa, Caribbean found to fare better. *Boston Globe,* National/Foreign section, p. A3.

Rowe, A., & Jeffries, J. M. (1996). Changes in the economy and labor market status of Black Americans. In A. Rowe and J. M. Jeffries, *The state of Black America 1996* (pp. 13–77). Washington, DC: The National Urban League.

Rutten, T. (1991, August 2). Inner cities in need of a living wage. *Los Angeles Times,* p. E1.

Ryan, S., Manlove, J., & Franzetta, K. (2003). The first time: Characteristics of teens' first sexual relationships. *Child Trends Research Brief.* Washington D.C.: Child Trends.

Safford, W. (2003). Race, gender, and welfare reforms: The need for targeted support. In L. Daniels (Ed.), *The state of Black America* (pp. 41–92). Washington, DC: National Urban League.

Sassler, S., & Schoen, R. (1999). The effect of attitudes and economic activity on marriage. *Journal of Marriage and the Family, 6,* 147–159.

Saxe, J. (1970). Review of *Black rage. Black Scholar, 1,* 58.

Scanzoni, J. (1978). *The Black family in modern society.* Chicago: University of Chicago Press.

Scarcella, C. A., Ehrle, J., & Green, R. (2003). *Identifying and addressing the needs of children in grandparent care.* Washington, DC: Urban Institute.

Schneider, B. E., & Stoller, N. E. (1995). *Women resisting AIDS: Feminist strategies of empowerment.* Philadelphia: Temple University Press.

Schulz, D. A. (1991). The role of the boyfriend in lower-class Negro life. In R. Staples (Ed.), *The Black family: Essays and studies* (3rd ed.). Belmont, CA: Wadsworth.

Schwartz, J. M. (2000). *Born in bondage: Growing up enslaved in the antebellum South.* Cambridge, MA: Harvard University Press.

Scott, J. W. (1999). From teenage parenthood to polygamy: Case studies in Black polygamous family formation. In R. Staples (Ed.), *The black family.* Belmont, CA: Wadsworth.

Sebald, H. (1974). Patterns of interracial dating and sexual liaison of Black and White college men. *International Journal of Sociology of the Family, 4,* 23–26.

Seccombe, K. (2001). Families in poverty in the 1990s: Trends, causes, consequence, and lessons learned. In R. M. Milardo (Ed.), *Understanding families into the new millennium: A decade in review* (pp. 313–332). Minneapolis, MN: National Council on Family Relations.

Sedlak, A. J., & Broadhurst, D. D. (1996). *The national incidence study of child abuse and neglect.* Washington, DC: Administration for Children and Families.

Selik, R. M., Castro, K. G., & Pappaioanou, M. (1988). Distribution of AIDS cases by racial ethnic group and exposure category. *MMWR, 37,* 1–10.

Shah, F., & Zelnick, M. (1981). Parent and peer influence on sexual behavior, contraceptive use, and pregnancy of young women. *Journal of Marriage and the Family, 43*(2), 339–348.

Shange, N. (1977). *For colored girls who have considered suicide when the rainbow is enuf: A choreopoem.* New York: Macmillan.

Silver, H., & Goldschneider, F. (1994). Flexible work and housework: Work and family constraints on women's domestic labor. *Social Forces, 72,* 1103–1119.

Simenauer, J., & Carroll, D. (1982). *Singles: The new Americans.* New York: Simon & Schuster.

Simms-Brown, R. J. (1982). The female in the Black family: Dominant mate or helpmate? *Journal of Black Psychology, 9,* 45–55.

Simpson, R. (1983). The Afro-American female: The historical context of the construction of sexual identity. In A. Snitow, C. Stansell, & S. Thompson (Eds.), *Powers of desire: The politics of sexuality.* New York: Monthly Review Press.

Sisters for Black Community Development. (1971). *Black women's role in the revolution*. Newark, NJ: Author.

Skolnick, A. (1992). *Embattled paradise: The American family in an age of uncertainty*. New York: Basic Books.

Smerglia, V. L., Deimling, G. T., & Barresi, C. M. (1988). Black/White family comparisons in helping and decision-making networks of impaired elderly. *Family Relations, 37*, 305–309.

Smith, E. A., & Udry, J. R. (1985). Coital and non-coital sexual behaviors of White and Black adolescents. *American Journal of Public Health, 75*, 1200–1203.

Smith, E.M.J. (1985). Ethnic minorities: Life stress, social support, and mental health issues. *Counseling Psychologist, 13*, 537–579.

Smith, J. M. (2000). Race, kinship care, and African American children. *African American Research Perspectives, 6*(3), 54–64.

Snowden, F. M., Jr. (1970). *Blacks in antiquity*. Cambridge, MA: Harvard University Press.

Song, Y., & Lu, H. (2002, March). *Early childhood poverty: A statistical profile*. New York: National Center for Children in Poverty.

Sowell, T. (1978). *Three Black histories: Essay and data on American ethnic groups*. Washington, DC: Urban Institute.

Spanier, G., & Glick, P. (1980). Mate selection differentials between Whites and Blacks in the United States. *Social Forces, 58*, 707–725.

Special report: College degree awards: The ominous gender gap in African American higher education. (1999). *Journal of Blacks in Higher Education, 23*, 6–9.

Spickard, P. R. (1989). *Mixed blood: Intermarriage and ethnic identity in twentieth-century America*. Madison: University of Wisconsin Press.

Stampp, R. (1956). *The peculiar institution: Slavery in the ante-bellum South*. New York: Knopf.

Staples, R. (1973). *The Black woman in America: Sex, marriage, and the family*. Chicago: Nelson-Hall.

Staples, R. (1978). Race, liberalism, conservatism, and premarital sexual permissiveness: A biracial comparison. *Journal of Marriage and the Family, 40*, 78–92.

Staples, R. (1981). *The world of Black singles: Changing patterns of male-female relations*. Westport, CT: Greenwood Press.

Staples, R. (1982). *Black masculinity: The Black male's role in American society*. San Francisco: Black Scholar Press.

Staples, R. (1984). An explosive controversy: The mother-son relationship in the Black family. *Ebony, 39*, 74–78.

Staples, R. (1985). Changes in Black family structure: The conflict between family ideology and structural conditions. *Journal of Marriage and the Family, 47*, 1005–1114.

Staples, R. (1987). *The urban plantation: Racism and colonialism in the post civil rights era.* San Francisco: Black Scholar Press.

Staples, R. (1989). Beauty and the beast: The importance of physical attractiveness in the Black community. In N. Hare & J. Hare (Eds.), *Crisis in Black sexual politics.* San Francisco: Black Think Tank.

Staples, R. (1991a). Black male genocide: The final solution. In B. Bowser (Ed.), *Black male adolescents: Parenting and education.* Lanham, MD: University Presses of America.

Staples, R. (1991b). Substance abuse and the Black family crisis: An overview. In R. Staples (Ed.), *The Black family: Essays and studies* (4th ed.). Belmont, CA: Wadsworth.

Staples, R. (1992). Intermarriage. In *Encyclopedia of sociology* (pp. 968–974). New York: Macmillan.

Staples, R. (1999). Interracial relationships: A convergence of desire and opportunity. In R. Staples (Ed.), *The Black family: Essays and Studies.* Belmont, CA: Wadsworth.

Staples, R., & Mirande, A. (1980). Racial and cultural variations among American families: A decennial review of the family literature. *Journal of Marriage and the Family, 42*, 887–904.

Star, B., Clark, C. G., Goetz, K. M., & O'Malia, L. (1979). Psychosocial aspects of wife battering. *Social casework: The Journal of Contemporary Social Work, 60*, 479–486.

Steady, C. (1981). *The Black woman cross-culturally.* Rochester, VT: Schenkman.

Steckel, R. H. (1980). Slave marriage and the family. *Journal of Family History, 5*, 406–421.

Stein, P. (1976). *Single.* Upper Saddle River, NJ: Prentice-Hall.

Stember, C. (1976). *Sexual racism.* New York: Elsevier.

Stephens, J. H. (1984). Black grandmothers' and Black adolescent mothers' knowledge about parenting. *Developmental Psychology, 20*, 1017–1025.

Stephens, R. J., & Wright II, E. (2000). Beyond bitches, niggers, and ho's: Some suggestions for including rap music as a qualitative data source. *Race and Society, 3*, 23–40.

Stephens, W. N. (1963). *The family in cross-cultural perspective.* Troy, MO: Holt, Rinehart & Winston.

Stevenson, B. (1996). *Life in Black and White: Family and community in the slave South.* New York: Oxford University Press.

Stewart, J., & Hyclak, T. J. (1986). The effects of immigrants, women, and teenagers on the relative earnings of Black males. *Review of Black Political Economy, 15*, 93–101.

Stewart, J., & Scott, J. (1978). The institutional decimation of Black males. *Western Journal of Black Studies, 2*, 82–92.

Stewart, P. (1979, May 13). Shades of Black. *Oakland Tribune*, p. 18.

Stockard, R. L., Jr., & Tucker, M. B. (2001). Young African-American men and women: Separate paths? In *The state of Black America 2001* (pp. 143–159). Washington, DC: National Urban League.

Strong, B., & DeVault, C. (1995). *The marriage and family experience* (6th ed.). New York: West.

Strong, B., DeVault, C., & Sayad, B. W. (1998). *The marriage and family experience: Intimate relationships in a changing society* (7th ed.). Belmont, CA: Wadsworth.

Sudarkasa, N. (1981). Female employment and family organization in West Africa. In F. C. Steady (Ed.), *The Black woman cross-culturally*. Rochester, VT: Schenkman.

Sudarkasa, N. (1988). Interpreting the African heritage in Afro-American family organization. In H. P. McAdoo (Ed.), *Black families* (2nd ed.). Thousand Oaks, CA: Sage.

Summer vacation travails. (1986, June 8). *San Francisco Examiner*, p. D1.

Swinton, D. H. (1991). The economic status of African Americans: Permanent poverty and inequality. In J. Dewart (Ed.), *The state of Black America 1991*. New York: National Urban League.

Swinton, D. H. (1992). The economic status of African-Americans: Limited ownership and persistent inequality. In J. Dewart (Ed.), *The state of Black America 1992*. New York: National Urban League.

Syverson, P. D. (2001). *Enrollment rises for second year, according to early returns from the 2001 CGS/GRE survey of graduate enrollment*. Available at: http://www.cgsnet.org/Virtual>CenterREsearch/2001 Survey.htm.

Taylor, R. J. (1986). Receipt of support from family among Black Americans: Demographic and familial differences. *Journal of Marriage and the Family, 48*, 67–77.

Taylor, R. J., & Chatters, L. M. (1989). Family, friend, and church support networks of Black Americans. In R. L. Jones (Ed.), *Black adult development*. Berkeley, CA: Cobb & Henry.

Taylor, R. J., Chatters, L. M., & Celious, A. (2003). Extended family households among Black Americans. *African American Research Perspectives, 9*, 133–151.

Taylor, R. J., Chatters, L. M., Tucker, N. B., & Lewis, E. (1990). Developments in research on Black families: A decade review. *Journal of Marriage and the Family, 52,* 993–1014.

Taylor, R. J., Leashore, B., & Toliver, S. (1988). An assessment of the provider role as perceived by Black males. *Family Relations, 37,* 426–431.

Taylor, R. L. (2000). Diversity within African American families. In D. H. Demo, K. R. Allen, & M. A. Fine (Eds.), *Handbook of family diversity* (pp. 232–251). New York: Oxford University Press.

Ten things men notice about women. (1982, June 7). *Jet Magazine,* pp. 38–39.

Ten things women notice about men. (1982, May 3). *Jet Magazine,* pp. 52–53.

Terborg-Penn, R. (1991). Women and slavery in the African Diaspora: A cross-cultural approach to historical analysis. In R. Staples (Ed.), *The Black family: Essays and studies* (4th ed.). Belmont, CA: Wadsworth.

Thibaut, J. W., & Kelley, H. W. (1959). *The social psychology of groups.* New York: Wiley.

Thoits, P. A. (1983). Multiple identities and psychological well-being: A reformulation and test of the social isolation hypothesis. *American Sociological Review, 48,* 174–187.

Thomas, Evan. (1992, May 18). Crime: A conspiracy of silence. *Newsweek,* p. 37.

Thomas, J. A. (2002). *Pornographic film and video: Gay male.* Chicago: glbtq, Inc. Available on-line: http://www.glbtq.com/arts/porn_gay,2.html.

Thorne, B., & Yalom, M. (Eds.). (1982). *Rethinking the family: Some feminist questions.* White Plains, NY: Longman.

Thorpe, K. (2003). *Gephardt, Dean, Kerry and Edwards: How their health care plans compare.* Atlanta: Emory University Press.

Timberlake, C. A., & Carpenter, W. D. (1990). Sexuality attitudes of Black adults. *Family Relations, 39,* 87–91.

Toliver, S. D. (1998). *Black families in corporate America.* Thousand Oaks, CA: Sage.

Toure, Y. (1991, March 3). Elder statesmen: An era is passing for five authors known for reclaiming the role of Blacks in history. *Los Angeles Times,* p. E1.

Tresiowski, A. (2003, December 15). Rebound artist. *People,* pp. 97–98.

Tripp, B. (2001). Incarcerated African American fathers: Exploring changes in family relationships and the father identity. *Journal of African American Men, 6*(1), 13–29.

Tucker, M. B., & Mitchell-Kernan, C. (1990). New trends in Black American interracial marriage: The social structure context. *Journal of Marriage and the Family, 52,* 209–218.

Tucker, M. B., & Taylor, R. J. (1989). Demographic correlates of relationship status among Black Americans. *Journal of Marriage and the Family, 51*, 655–665.

Turner, C. B., & Turner, B. F. (1983). Black families, social evaluations, and future marital relationships. In C. E. Obudho (Ed.), *Black marriage and family therapy*. Westport, CT: Greenwood Press.

Udry, J. R. (1977). The importance of being beautiful: A re-examination and racial comparison. *American Journal of Sociology, 83*, 154–160.

Udry, J. R., Bauman, K. E., & Chase, C. (1971). Skin color, status, and mate selection. *American Journal of Sociology, 76*(4), 722–733.

Ulbrich, P. M. (1988). The determinants of depression in two-income marriages. *Journal of Marriage and the Family, 50*, 121–131.

U.S. Bureau of Justice Statistics. (1990). *Department of Justice National Corrections Reporting Program, 1985*. Washington, DC: U.S. Government Printing Office. Available on-line: www.ojp.usdoj.gov/bjs/.

U.S. Bureau of Justice Statistics. (2000). *Homicide trends in the U.S. by race*. Washington, DC: U.S. Government Printing Office. Available on-line: www.ojp.usdoj.gov/bjs/homicide/race.htm.

U.S. Bureau of Justice Statistics. (2002). *Homicide trends in the U.S.: Trends by race*. Washington, DC: U.S. Government Printing Office. Available on-line: www.ojp.usdoj.gov/bjs/.

U.S. Bureau of Labor Statistics. (2003). Employment status of the civilian non-institutional population by sex, age, race, Hispanic origin, 2001. Washington, DC: U.S. Government Printing Office. Available on-line: http://www.bls.gov/lau/table12full01.pdf .

U.S. Census Bureau. (1972). *Social and economic status of the Black population in the United States: 1971* (Current Population Reports, Series P-23, No. 42). Washington, DC: U.S. Government Printing Office.

U.S. Census Bureau. (1983). *America's Black population, 1970–1982: A statistical view* (Current Population Reports, Series P-20, No. 442). Washington, DC: U.S. Government Printing Office.

U.S. Census Bureau. (1985). *Marital characteristics*. Washington, DC: U.S. Government Printing Office.

U.S. Census Bureau. (1989). *The Black population in the United States: March 1988* (Current Population Reports, Series P-20, No. 422). Washington, DC: U.S. Government Printing Office.

U.S. Census Bureau. (1990). *Statistical abstract of the United States, 1990*. Washington, DC: U.S. Government Printing Office.

U.S. Census Bureau. (1991a). *The Black population in the United States: March 1990 and 1989* (Current Population Reports, Series P-20, No. 448). Washington, DC: U.S. Government Printing Office.

U.S. Census Bureau. (1991b). *Educational attainment in the United States: March 1989 and 1988* (Current Population Reports, Series P-20, No. 451). Washington, DC: U.S. Government Printing Office.

U.S. Census Bureau. (1992). *Marital status and living arrangements: March 1991.* Washington, DC: U.S. Government Printing Office.

U.S. Census Bureau. (1994). *Marital status and living arrangements: March 1994* (Current Population Report No. P20-484, Table A-4). Washington, DC: U.S. Government Printing Office.

U.S. Census Bureau. (1996, March). *Marital status of persons 15 years old and over by age, sex, region, and race.* Washington, DC: U.S. Government Printing Office.

U.S. Census Bureau. (1998, June). *The Black population in the United States, March 1997 (Update)* (Document No. P20-508). Washington, DC: U.S. Government Printing Office.

U.S. Census Bureau. (1999). *Selected social characteristics of the population by region and race.* Washington, DC: U.S. Government Printing Office.

U.S. Census Bureau. (2000, September). *The Black population in the United States.* Washington, DC: U.S. Government Printing Office.

U.S. Census Bureau. (2001a, February 22). *Census Bureau releases update on country's African American population.* Washington, DC: U.S. Government Printing Office.

U.S. Census Bureau. (2001b). *Unemployed and unemployment: Rates by educational attainment, sex, race, and Hispanic origin: 1992–2000.* Washington, DC: U.S. Government Printing Office.

U.S. Census Bureau. (2002a, February). *Number, timing, and duration of marriages and divorces: 1996* (Report Number P70-80). Washington, DC: U.S. Government Printing Office.

U.S. Census Bureau. (2002b, March). *The Black population in the United States.* Washington, DC: U.S. Government Printing Office.

U.S. Census Bureau. (2002c, March). *Educational attainment people 18 years old and over. Current population survey* (PINC-04). Washington, DC: U.S. Government Printing Office.

U.S. Census Bureau. (2002d, July). *The big payoff: Educational attainment and synthetic estimates of work-life earnings.* Washington, DC: U.S. Government Printing Office. Available on-line: http://www.census.gov/prod/2002pubs/p23-210.pdf.

U.S. Census Bureau. (2002e). *Moving to Homeownership: 1994 to 2002* (Document No. CB03-156). Washington, DC: U.S. Government Printing Office. Available on-line: http://www.census.gov/hhes/www/housing/movingto america2002/tab7.html.

U.S. Census Bureau. (2003a). *Age 16–19 percent jobless and percent employed in June, 1948–2003.* Washington, DC: U.S. Government Printing Office.

U.S. Census Bureau. (2003b). *American fact finder: Income distribution in 1999 of households and families: 2000 data set.* Washington, DC: U.S. Government Printing Office.

U.S. Census Bureau. (2003c, April). *The Black population in the United States: March 2002* (Document No. P20-541). Washington, DC: U.S. Government Printing Office.

U.S. Census Bureau. (2003d, August). *Occupations: 2000, Census 2000 brief* (Document No. C2KBR-25). Washington, DC: U.S. Government Printing Office.

U.S. Census Bureau. (2003e, October). *Grandparents living with grandchildren: 2000* (Report Number C2KBR-31). Washington, DC: U.S. Government Printing Office.

U.S. Department of Health and Human Services. (1985). *Report of the Secretary's Task Force on Black and Minority Health.* Washington, DC: U.S. Government Printing Office.

U.S. Department of Health and Human Services. (1995). *Report to Congress on out-of-wedlock childbearing.* Rockville, MD: U. S. Department of Health and Human Services, Public Health Service, Centers for Disease Control and Prevention, National Center for Health Statistics [DHHS Pub. No. (PHS) 95-1257]. Hyattsville, MD: U.S. Government Printing Office.

U.S. Department of Health and Human Services. (2000). *Safety permanency well-being—Child welfare outcomes 1999: Annual report.* Washington, DC: U.S. Government Printing Office.

U.S. Department of Justice. (1998, March). Available on-line: http://www.ndvh .org.

U.S. Department of Labor. (1990). *Employment and earnings, May 1990.* Washington, DC: U.S. Government Printing Office.

U.S. Department of Labor. (2000, June). *Report on the youth labor force.* Washington, DC: U.S. Government Printing Office.

U.S. Office of Personnel Management. (2003). *2003 FEHB premiums.* Washington, DC: U.S. Government Printing Office.

U.S. Surgeon General's Report. (2003). *Mental health: Culture, race, ethnicity.* Washington, DC: U.S. Government Printing Office. Available on-line: http://www.mentalhealth.org/cre/ch3_current_status.asp.

Uzzell, O., & Peebles-Wilkins, W. (1989). Black spouse abuse: A focus on relational factors and intervention strategies. *Western Journal of Black Studies*, *13*, 131–138.

Valentine, C. A. (1968). *Culture and poverty: Critique and counterproposals*. Chicago: University of Chicago Press.

Veneziano, R. A., & Rohner, R. P. (1998). Perceived paternal acceptance, paternal involvement, and youths' psychological adjustment in a rural, biracial southern community. *Journal of Marriage and the Family*, *60*, 335–343.

Villa, L. (1981). *The sexuality of a Black American*. Oakland, CA: Ashford Press.

Vital signs: The statistics that describe the present and suggest the future of African Americans in higher education. (1999). *Journal of Blacks in Higher Education*, *25*, 85–93.

Vontress, C. (1971). The Black male personality. *Black Scholar*, *2*, 10–17.

Wallace, M. (1979). *Black macho and the myth of the superwoman*. New York: Dial Press.

Wallace, M. (1990). *Invisibility blues*. New York: Verso.

Waller, M. R. (2002). *My baby's father: Unmarried parents and paternal responsibility*. Ithaca, NY: Cornell University Press.

Walters, R. (1975). *The new Negro on campus*. Princeton, NJ: Princeton University Press.

Ward, G. K. (1998). On prison: America's increasingly peculiar institution. *African American Research Perspectives*, *4(1)*, 47–60.

Washington, V. (1987). Community involvement in recruiting adoptive homes for Black children. *Child Welfare League of America*, *56*, 57–67.

Washington, V. (1989, November). *Child care policy, African Americans, and moral dilemmas*. Paper presented at the meeting of the conference titled *One third of a nation: African American perspectives*, Harvard University, Cambridge, MA.

Waters, M. C. (1999). *Black identities: West Indian immigrant dreams and American realities*. Cambridge, MA: Harvard University Press.

Watson, B. J., Rowe, C. L., & Jones, D. J. (1990). Dispelling myths about teenage pregnancy and male responsibility: A research agenda. In D. J. Jones & S. E. Battle (Eds.), *Teenage pregnancy: Developing strategies for change in the twenty-first century*. New Brunswick, NJ: Transaction.

Wehman, J. (2001, July 27). Study: College dating obsolete. *Cincinnati Post*. Available on-line: http://www.cincypost.com/2001/jul/date072701.html.

Westney, O. E., Jenkins, R. R., Butts, J. D., & Williams, I. (1991). Sexual development and behavior in Black pre-adolescents. In R. Staples (Ed.), *The Black family: Essays and studies* (4th ed.). Belmont, CA: Wadsworth.

Wheeler, W. H. (1977). *Socio-sexual communication between Black men and Black women*. Unpublished manuscript, Florida State University.

White, D. C. (1985). *Ain't I a woman? Female slaves in the plantation South.* New York: Norton.

White, E. C. (1989, May 22). Grandmothers bear a burden sired by drugs. *San Francisco Chronicle*, p. A2.

White, E. C. (1991, November 3). Black women find an oasis of respect: More and more turn to Islam for its stability and love of family. *San Francisco Chronicle, This World* sec., pp. 9–11.

White, J. E. (1992, May 11). The limits of Black power. *Time*, pp. 38–40.

White, L., & Rogers, S. J. (2001). Economic circumstances and family outcomes: A review of the 1990s. In R. M. Milardo (Ed.), *Understanding families into the new millennium: A decade in review* (pp. 254–270). Minneapolis, MN: National Council on Family Relations.

Whitmore, G. (1999). African American father figures and children's achievement. *African American Men, 4,* 34.

Why skin color suddenly is a big issue again. (1992). *Ebony, 47*(5), 120–122.

Whyte, M. K. (1990). *Dating, mating, and marriage.* New York: Aldine de Gruyter.

Wiederman, M. W. (1997). Extramarital sex: Prevalence and correlates in a national survey. *Journal of Sex Research, 34,* 167–174.

Williams, M. (1990). Polygamy and the declining male to female ratio in Black communities: A social inquiry. In H. E. Cheatham & J. B. Stewart (Eds.), *Black families: Interdisciplinary perspectives.* New Brunswick, NJ: Transaction.

Williams, O. J. (1999). African American men who batter: Treatment considerations and community response. In R. Staples (Ed.), *The Black family: Essays and studies.* (6th ed.) (pp. 265–279) Belmont, CA: Wadsworth.

Williams, S. E. (2000). Domestic violence and African American women in rural communities. *African American Research Perspectives, 6,* 79–85.

Willie, C. V. (1970). *The family life of Black people.* Columbus, OH: Merrill.

Willie, C. V. (1984). The role of mothers in the lives of outstanding scholars. *Journal of Family Issues, 5,* 291–306.

Willie, C. V. (1988). *A new look at Black families* (3rd ed.). Dix Hill, NY: General Hall.

Willie, C. V., & Levy, J. D. (1972, March). On White campuses, Black students retreat into separatism. *Psychology Today*, pp. 50–52, 76, 78, 80.

Wilson, M. (1986). Perceived parental activity of mothers, fathers, and grandmothers in three-generational Black families. *Journal of Black Psychology, 12*(2), 43–59.

Wilson, M., Tolson, T.F.J., Hinton, I. D., & Kiernan, M. (1990). Flexibility and sharing of child care duties in Black families. *Sex Roles, 22,* 409–425.

Wilson, R. (1989). The state of Black higher education: Crisis and promise. In J. Dewart (Ed.), *The state of Black America 1989*. New York: National Urban League.

Wilson, W. J. (1980). *The declining significance of race: Blacks and changing American institutions*. Chicago: University of Chicago Press.

Wilson, W. J. (1987). *The truly disadvantaged: The inner city, the underclass, and public policy*. Chicago: University of Chicago Press.

Wilson, W. J. (1998). Jobless ghettos: The impact of the disappearance of work in segregated neighborhoods. In L. A. Daniels (Ed.), *The state of Black America 1998* (pp. 89–107). Washington, DC: The National Urban League.

Wineberg, H. (1999). Separated Black women: Do they reconcile with their husbands? In R. Staples (Ed.), *The Black families: Essays and studies* (pp. 103–111). Belmont, CA: Wadsworth.

Wolf, N. (1991) *The beauty myth: How images of beauty are used against women*. New York: Morrow.

Wolters, R. *The new Negro on campus*. (1975). Princeton, NJ: Princeton University Press.

Wright, J. W. (Ed.). (2002). *The New York Times 2003 almanac*. New York: Penguin Putnam Group.

Wright, J. W. (Ed.). (2003). *The New York Times 2004 almanac*. New York: Penguin Putnam Group.

Wyatt, G. E. (1982). Identifying stereotypes of Afro-American sexuality and their impact upon sexual behavior. In B. A. Bass, G. E. Wyatt, & G. J. Powell (Eds.), *The Afro-American family: Assessment, treatment, and research issues*. Philadelphia: Grune & Stratton.

Wyatt, G. E. (1985). The sexual abuse of Afro-American and White-American women in childhood. *Child Abuse and Neglect, 9*, 507–519.

Wyatt, G. E., & Lyons-Rowe, S. (1990). African American women's sexual satisfaction as a dimension of their sex roles. *Sex Roles, 22*, 509–523.

Wyatt, G. E., Peters, S. D., & Guthrie, D. (1988). Kinsey revisited, Part II: Comparisons of the sexual socialization and sexual behavior of Black women over 33 years. *Archives of Sexual Behavior, 17*, 289–332.

Wyatt, G., Myers, H., Ashing-Giwa, K., & Durvasula, R. (1999). Sociocultural factors affecting sexual risk taking in Black men and women: Results from two empirical studies. In R. Staples (Ed.), *The Black family: Essays and studies* (6th ed.) (pp. 45–58). Belmont, CA: Wadsworth.

Yao, G. (1999). Racial inequality, welfare reform, and Black families: The 1996 Personal Responsibility and Work Reconciliation Act. In R. Staples (Ed.), *The Black family: Essays and studies* (pp. 357–366). Belmont, CA: Wadsworth.

Yearwood, S. (2003, August 14). Lack of cultural awareness nixes quality education. *Voices That Must Be Heard, 78*. Available on-line: http://www. indypressny.org/article.php3?ArticleID=1016.

Yetman, N. R., & Steele, C. H. (1975). *Majority and minority: The dynamics of racial and ethnic relations*. Needham Heights, MA: Allyn & Bacon.

"You can't join their clubs": Six mixed couples get together to talk about love, marriage, and prejudice. (1991, June 10). *Newsweek*, pp. 48–49.

Zeisset, P. (2000, June 29). Service industries—New economy's biggest generator of jobs: Mississippi leads states, census bureau reports. Available on-line: http://www.census.gov/Press-Release/www/2000/cb00–102.html.

Zetterberg, H. (1965). *Theory and verification in sociology*. New York: Bedminster Press.

Zinn, M. B. (1990). Family, race, and poverty in the eighties. In M. R. Malson, E. Mudimbe-Boyi, J. F. O'Barr, & M. Wyer (Eds.), *Black women in America: Social science perspectives*. Chicago: University of Chicago Press.

Zollar, A. C. (1986). Ideological perspectives on Black families: Related typologies. *Free Inquiry in Creative Sociology, 14*, 169–172.

Zollar, A. C., & Williams, J. S. (1987). The contribution of marriage to the life satisfaction of Black adults. *Journal of Marriage and the Family, 49*, 87–92.

About the Authors

Leanor Boulin Johnson is professor of family studies and African American studies at Arizona State University. She received her B.S. degree in social services from East Tennessee State University and M.S. and Ph.D. degrees in sociology from Purdue University. At Arizona State, she is the founding director of African and African American studies and currently teaches courses on family relations with emphasis on ethnicity. Boulin Johnson's main research activities have been in Black family studies, cross-cultural sexuality, and work-family stress. She has received several federal, private, and university grants to study work-family stress among Black and White police officers. In addition, she has been associate editor of the *Journal of Family Relations*, consulting editor for the *Journal of Sex Research*, and reviewer for several journals, and she has published numerous journal articles and book chapters. Her 1991 testimony before Congress on work-family issues provided an empirical base for a law enforcement family support act amendment to the 1991 congressional crime bill.

Boulin Johnson's consulting experience includes evaluating federal grant proposals for the National Institute of Mental Health from 1978 to 1981 and developing and conducting a sexual harassment study of more than twenty thousand federal workers for the Merit Systems Protection Board (1983). Other assignments include chairing the review panel for the National Research Council's Ford Foundation Postdoctoral and Dissertation Fellowships for Minorities (1991), consultant to national and local media, and expert consultant for the Federal Bureau of Investigation Academy Advisory Board for stress issues (1998–2000). She served on the board for the National Council on Family Relations from 1983 to 1985 and 1995 to 1998 and currently serves on the board of trustees for Pacific Union College. In 1991, the National Council on Family Relations awarded her the Marie Peters Award for excellence in the area of ethnic minority families, and in 1997 she received an Arizona Governor's Proclamation for her policy-relevant scholarship, leadership, and service.

Robert Staples is an emeritus faculty member of the University of California, San Francisco, and visiting fellow in the Centre for Australian Indigenous Studies at Monash University, Melbourne, Australia. He received his B.A. and M.A. degrees in sociology from California State University, Northridge, and San Jose State University, respectively, and his Ph.D. degree from the University of Minnesota. He has been an invited fellow at the Australian Institute of Family Studies on four different occasions and a visiting fellow at the University of Warwick in Coventry, England, in 1989–1990. His current research focuses on families of color in White settler nations.

Among the awards Staples has received for distinguished achievement have been commendations from the National Council on Family Relations, Howard University, the University of Zulia in Maracaibo, Venezuela, and the Association of Black Sociologists. He has written on many aspects of the Black family and has published fourteen books and more than two hundred articles on race relations and the sociology of the Black family. His books have been adopted as texts in more than five hundred universities in the United States, Africa, West Indies, and England. His professional service has included membership on the editorial boards of the *Journal of Marriage and the Family*, *Western Journal of Black Studies*, *Black Scholar*, and the *Journal of African American Studies*.

Name Index

Subject Index

252; and Black family disorganization, 55–56; and Black workers' benefits, 65; block grant program in, 279, 283; child care provisions in, 280; and decline of two-parent families, 55–56, 293–294; marriage and, 68; and work conditions, 279, 281

West Indian Blacks, labor force participation of, 70–75
Women's movement: and civil rights movement, 171; and race-sex analogy, 171–172; relevance for Black women, 168, 172–174